The Face of the Nation

Series Editors

Fiona Mackay, University of Edinburgh
Louise Chappell, University of New South Wales
Meryl Kenny, University of Edinburgh
Elin Bjarnegård, Uppsala University

The Face of the Nation: Gendered Institutions in International Affairs
Elise Stephenson

The Face of the Nation

Gendered Institutions in International Affairs

Elise Stephenson

OXFORD
UNIVERSITY PRESS

Oxford University Press is a department of the University of Oxford. It furthers
the University's objective of excellence in research, scholarship, and education
by publishing worldwide. Oxford is a registered trade mark of Oxford University
Press in the UK and certain other countries.

Published in the United States of America by Oxford University Press
198 Madison Avenue, New York, NY 10016, United States of America.

© Oxford University Press 2024

All rights reserved. No part of this publication may be reproduced, stored in
a retrieval system, or transmitted, in any form or by any means, without the
prior permission in writing of Oxford University Press, or as expressly permitted
by law, by license, or under terms agreed with the appropriate reproduction
rights organization. Inquiries concerning reproduction outside the scope of the
above should be sent to the Rights Department, Oxford University Press, at the
address above.

You must not circulate this work in any other form
and you must impose this same condition on any acquirer.

Library of Congress Cataloging-in-Publication Data
Names: Stephenson, Elise, author.
Title: The face of the nation : gendered institutions in international affairs / Elise Stephenson.
Description: New York : Oxford University Press, 2024. | Series: Studies in feminist institutionalism |
Includes bibliographical references and index.
Identifiers: LCCN 2023033402 (print) | LCCN 2023033403 (ebook) | ISBN 9780197632727 (hardcover) |
ISBN 9780197632741 (epub) | ISBN 9780197632758
Subjects: LCSH: International relations—Social aspects. | Diplomacy—Social aspects. |
Women diplomats. | Women ambassadors. | Women international relations specialists. |
Australia—Foreign relations administration. | Women diplomats—Australia. |
Women ambassadors—Australia. | Women international relations specialists—Australia. |
Feminist theory.
Classification: LCC JZ1253.2 .S75 2024 (print) | LCC JZ1253.2 (ebook) |
DDC 327.2082—dc23/eng/20230829
LC record available at https://lccn.loc.gov/2023033402
LC ebook record available at https://lccn.loc.gov/2023033403

DOI: 10.1093/oso/9780197632727.001.0001

Printed by Integrated Books International, United States of America

This book is dedicated to the women interviewed and the many more who dedicate their lives to representing the state on the world stage. Without you, these findings do not exist. With you, we record history. This book is dedicated to your resilience, strength, sincerity, and success.

This book is also dedicated to my wife, Mikhara; supervisors Sue, Anne, and Liz; sister Lara; parents Lauren and James; and to my Gran—the most powerful woman in my international affairs—and Granddad for your love.

Contents

Foreword   *xi*

1. **Where Are the Women?**   **1**
   Who Gets to Represent the Nation Internationally?   3
   Why Gender and International Affairs Matters Now: The Critical Juncture   6
   Australia's Evolving International Representation   12
   What Can We Learn from the Australian Case?   15
   Book Structure   17

2. **Exploring Theories on Gender and International Affairs**   **23**
   Understanding Feminist Institutionalist Theory   24
   Situating Intersectional Feminist Institutional within the Field of IR   33
   Gendered Nature of Diplomacy, National Security, and International Affairs   35
   Locating Gender in Australian International Affairs Agencies   40
   The Theoretical Frameworks   46
       Intersectional Feminist Institutionalism (IFI)   46
       A Framework for Studying International Institutions   47
       An Approach to Studying Institutional Change and Inequality   48

3. **Who I Researched and How I Did It**   **50**
   Being a Critical Feminist Friend   50
   Intersectional Feminist Institutional (IFI) Research Design   52
   Data Collection: On-Ground, In-Person, and International   56
       Qualitative Interviews   56
       Quantitative Trend Data   62
   Data Analysis: Themes, Narratives, and Trends   63
   Accessing Elites and Delving Into the Diplomatic Bubble   64
       Ethical Clearance   68

4. **Historical Developments in International Affairs and Deep Insights Into the Case Agencies**   **69**
   The Australian Cases: Institutional History and Cultural Relics   70
       Setting the Context   71
   Eliteness Eroded in the Department of Foreign Affairs and Trade (DFAT)   76
       Historical Forces   77
       Structure and Leadership   84
   More than a Golden Handshake: Defence   88
       Historical Forces   88
       Structure and Leadership   98

The Dark Side: Home Affairs	104
Historical Forces	104
Structure and Leadership	112
Police-Led Diplomacy: AFP	114
Historical Forces	115
Structure and Leadership	119
Overarching Trends	123

5. Which Women Lead International Affairs? 125

Where Are the Women of Colour?	126
Queering International Representation	132
A Class of Its Own?	137
Family and Baggage to Follow	139
Geographic Reach and Patterns of Deployment	140
Straight, White, and . . . Female?	142

6. Where Are the Women in International Affairs Leadership? 144

Tracing Women's Representation in Australian International Affairs	145
DFAT	154
Defence	156
Home Affairs	158
AFP	159
Divided by Gender, Status, and International Appointments	161
Overarching Themes and Trends	165

7. How Did You Get There? Career Paths and Leadership 168

Pathways to Posting	169
Strategising Around Difficulties on the Path to Progression	170
Politicised, Instable, and Obscured: Navigating How to Get an International Posting	173
Gendered Factors Determine Which Posts to Apply for and Accept	175
Experiences Once on Posting	181
Gendered Rules Define Deployment	181
Externalised (Gendered) Costs Underpin Experiences on Post	184
Returning from Posting	195
What Happens, and Why, Women Leave	197
Succeeding in Leadership Takes More Than Skills and Experience	200
Making It to the Global Stage	203

8. Why Do Women Remain Underrepresented (and Unequal) in International Affairs? 206

Novel Findings Transforming Our Understanding of Gender and International Affairs	208
More Militaristic Agencies More Proportionally Represent Women	209
Genteel Toxic Masculinities Dominate in More Traditionally Diplomatic Agencies	210
The Diplomatic Glass Cliff: Women's Representation and Diplomacy's Decline	212

    Women with Wives Fit the Heteronormative Diplomatic Institution   213
    Domestic Gendered Challenges Trump Those of International
        Representation   214
    Women's Experiences of International Affairs Are Consistent
        Across Agencies   216
    Implications of These Findings   217
  The Historical Gendered Legacies of Institutions   217
  Layering and Duplication of Gendered Institutions   221
    Leila's Story: Working in DFAT   223
    Danielle's Story: Working in Defence   224
    Talia's Story: Working in Home Affairs   225
    Meaghan's Story: Working in the AFP   226
    Implications   227
  Compounding Effect of Gendered Institutions   228
  Evolving Inequalities   229

Conclusion: How Inequality Evolves in International Institutions   231
  The Big Lessons Learned   232
  Implications for Global Affairs   238
  Where to From Here?   239
  Final Thoughts   240

Notes   243
Index   279

Foreword

The publication of this book could not be more timely. For one, it follows a period of rapid demographic changes in international affairs—the share of women has increased significantly in the 2000s, finally breaking up the previous male near-monopolies. To be sure, globally, women are still in the minority in international affairs. Men still make up roughly 80 per cent of bilateral ambassadors around the world, for instance, even if there are much larger shares of women at lower diplomatic levels. However, in some states, such as Australia, women now make up a majority or near majority of international affairs officials. And the situation is changing rapidly, with an increasing number of policy initiatives and recruitment efforts intended to raise the number of women in international affairs and to diversify diplomacy. Many are thus wondering what has happened to international affairs institutions with the recent increase in women.

The book is also timely in terms of its intervention in academic scholarship on gender and international affairs. In particular, in the past decade, a new and exciting body of studies on gender in Ministries of Foreign Affairs (MFAs) has developed, with case studies spanning the Americas, Asia, and Europe. This scholarship has shown that gender is integral to what MFAs are and how they operate. Historically, MFAs were masculinised in ways that ensured that diplomats were male elites backed by women in a range of support functions—as wives, secretaries, typists, and more. Along with rising numbers of women as diplomatic officials, new gender patterns have developed within MFAs. For instance, a number of studies have shown that men tend to be overrepresented in positions of higher diplomatic rank and that many MFAs exhibit functional differentiation, with men overrepresented in 'hard' units dealing with trade and security and women clustering in international development, human resources, and other putatively 'soft' policy areas. Elise Stephenson's book appears at a time when a lot of scholars are asking questions about the gender of diplomacy, not least the gender of MFAs. These scholars will be well served—and thrilled—to read this thorough examination of a topic that has primarily been explored in a series of more limited studies.

In a rich and compelling intervention full of fascinating insights, Stephenson takes a closer look at the ways in which gender inequalities in international affairs institutions may persist despite large recent increases in the number of women. She does so through a focus on Australia, a country where women are near parity in the Department of Foreign Affairs and Trade (DFAT) and where women occupy political leadership positions to a greater degree than most other countries in the world. And she does so through an innovative comparison of DFAT with three other institutions engaged in Australian foreign affairs: the Australian Federal Police (AFP), Defense (including both the civilian Department of Defense (DoD) and military Australian Defense Force (ADF)), and the Department of Home Affairs (Home Affairs). In refusing to focus on *either* military institutions *or* diplomacy, as most international relations scholars do, Stephenson's approach thus resembles McGlen and Sarkees's pioneering *Women in Foreign Policy: The Insiders* (1990), which compared the US State Department and Department of Defense some 30 years ago. Stephenson not only updates their analysis, but she moves it to a different case (Australia), adds additional institutions (federal police and Home Affairs), and deploys an intersectional approach that primarily highlights gender and sexuality but also race and class.

The payoffs of these moves are significant and manifold, indeed too many for me to recount here. So let me simply mention a few major takeaway points. Through her comparisons of Australian international affairs institutions, Stephenson confirms the finding that there are much larger numbers of women in diplomacy than in institutions tasked with security. However, she also shows that on other counts, women fare better in security institutions than in diplomacy. For instance, the share of women in leadership positions is equivalent to the overall share of women in Australian security institutions whereas there is a much smaller share of women in diplomatic leadership than in DFAT overall. Stephenson suggests that the presence of more formalised rules and clearer institutional structures and hierarchies serve women's career advancement well in security institutions, in contrast with diplomacy, which relies more on informal rules, norms and networks than security.

Through its intersectional approach, the book furthermore shows that although queer women are underrepresented in international affairs compared with their share of the general population, queer women tend to do better as diplomats than heterosexual women. They do so thanks to the support of their female partners, who—in contrast with most male partners—are willing to take on the role and tasks of the 'diplomatic wife'. Indeed, relying on a wealth of quantitative and qualitative data, which she analyses through an intersectional lens, Stephenson examines the placement, careers, roles, and experiences of women in Australian institutions in ways that bring forth and underscore the complexities of the positions of women in international affairs.

The book also raises the crucial question of whether the status of diplomacy is eroding along with the entry of large shares of women. Stephenson contends that this is the case in Australia, where DFAT has seen cuts in funding, policy influence, and prestige just as women are reaching parity in the institution, in contrast with the security institutions (where women remain in minority). Whether this holds for diplomatic institutions more generally is a question that Stephenson leaves for other scholars to explore. For instance, in the Swedish MFA, where women reached overall parity in the 1990s and near-parity in senior positions in the 2000s, there is little indication that diplomacy is losing status. Like most of the thought-provoking questions Stephenson raises, the question of the relation between institutional status and shares of men and women is very complex, demanding careful and contextual analyses. One of the many strengths of this impressive book is that it delivers its complex analyses in an accessible format. As a highly engaging read, the book is indeed an excellent resource not only for students in military and diplomatic academies but also for public officials and policymakers.

By Ann E. Towns

1
Where Are the Women?

> Women have a particular set of skills and perspectives to offer international relations that have been missing for too many years now. There is no excuse for it anymore.
> —Grace, Department of Foreign Affairs and Trade, 5 October 2018[1]

I was 23 when I walked into my first diplomatic household. It was an imposing home on the steep, jungled hillside of Hong Kong, with a large patio overlooking the ocean and a stream of international ships coming and going. It housed striking Indigenous artwork and pieces of typical Australiana designed to capture the hearts and minds of those who walked through the door. Tiny clip-on koalas and white crockery with the Australian emblem embossed in gold. A host of staff ducking in and out of rooms. This house was not really a house at all. When overseas, this was the home of the nation. Whoever lived in this home was more than the sum of their parts—they were also the face of that nation.

I was not a diplomat at the time and remain far from being a diplomat now. I was merely a poor student on a scholarship, playing at being the diplomat, caught up in the shiny lights and champagne glasses of international affairs. Yet surveying what was around me, it was my first distinct chance to look at the world through the eyes of those who get to represent it. I saw Angela Merkel on the stage to my north, Hillary Clinton vying for power in the US, and Julie Bishop locked in a battle for recognition and resources at home. These three cases of powerful women at the helm served to reinforce how the stories of women in international politics, diplomacy and defence were few and far between. Indeed, for the most part, I found international affairs was littered with stories of women overlooked and underrepresented, whose potential often went unmatched by opportunity.

The statistics were equally dismaying. I noticed the fact that women had only ever represented 6 per cent of mediators in international peace deals since 1992[2]—the so-called age of equality, when I was born. I noticed that 85 per cent of ambassadorships remained held by men.[3] I noticed that in my own country, it took over 100 years since federation and over 200 years since colonisation for Australia to appoint the first Indigenous female ambassador.[4] In fact, it was only in 2018 that this historic moment was met. The international institutions dedicated to representing their state had failed at their most basic duty: to represent their people.

Like most citizens around the world, though, we do care about whom represents us. We would not have the big family arguments at holidays or daily vitriolic media coverage of politics and politicians if we did not care about who speaks for us. The utilitarian in us might care about representation because it is better for nations. To start with, it leads to more durable, comprehensive, and collaborative decision-making, and a lower propensity for war. Representation equals better social and economic outcomes.[5] Yet more than just being what is good for us, we also care about representation because it is what is 'right'.[6] Indeed, in many countries we care about whom represents us because it fits with our values—whether those be explicit values around democracy and equality, or simply ideas that those living, of all stripes, deserve representation. And whether fulfilled or not, many of these values are integral to the core institutions that guide our political life.

This is why we have a gender problem in international affairs. As of September 2022, there are only 30 women serving as their country's head of state or head of government. Only 14 countries have achieved 50 per cent or more women in cabinets, and progress for women in ministerial appointments is made in mere 0.5 per cent increments.[7] In 2020, only 13 per cent of defence ministers globally were women,[8] and diplomatic and national security workforces are recognised as lagging well behind almost every other field of government.[9] This is not equality.

Further, even though women's representation in leadership is increasing, it does not seem to be changing fundamental issues of inequality in international institutions. More women alone do not make institutional gender equality—a core problem this book aims to explore. Indeed, despite many countries globally now increasing or verging on parity in representation in diplomacy, this book indicates that this has not lessened the gender inequalities that remain. In fact, in cases, the gender gap is increasing.

Australia presents a persuasive case study to explore this. Australia leads globally in terms of appointments of women to senior ambassadorial positions and demonstrates a surprising ability to proportionally represent women in national security leadership, relative to their overall employment. Yet Australia also demonstrates how deeply gendered, racialised, and heteronormative international institutions remain. Sure, we are no worse than most of the globe. But for a nation with some of the most robust anti-discrimination and equal opportunity laws, policies, and cultures, we are certainly not much better. If gender equality was achievable by policy alone, we would have already achieved it. Instead, Australian international affairs is plagued with gender discrimination, harassment and an entrenched sexism that has left women frequently overlooked, underpowered, and unrepresented. Worse, the stories, lives and experiences of those women who have walked along the frontline have barely been adequately recorded. This is a loss not just for the women themselves and their agencies, but for the public and international research community too.

It was the almost complete absence of women in power on the world stage that made me start this research. It was the statistics I found when I dug deeper that pushed me to trawl across more than ten countries and 65,000 kilometres to learn the stories behind the numbers. Yet it was the people that I met along the way that drove me to write this book. This book is the culmination of decades of lives lived offshore and mostly out of sight. It records and reflects the narratives of our most important women leaders on the world stage. It looks at institutional history and change through the eyes of women. It reflects on progress made and the change direly needed next. And it provides a glimpse into how gendered institutions apply in international affairs, in some cases inverting what we thought we knew about gender and the world stage.

Who Gets to Represent the Nation Internationally?

My interview with Jenny (not her real name) occurred before sunrise one warm February morning, as my phone rang out halfway across the world. We had been arranging to talk for several months. Jenny was originally reluctant to be interviewed. It was not because she did not want to share her story, but rather because she had already endured decades of gendered treatment that had seen her knocked back from promotions more than a dozen times. Now nearing retirement, we were both emotional as she told me her story. But it was the words of her colleagues that struck me most: 'You can't apply for this, you've got a fucking vagina'.[10]

In all my research, I am still yet to hear the official reasoning behind why genitalia might be so important to leading a nation in an official capacity in international affairs. This campaign of vitriol was more than just about Jenny's biological sex characteristics, however; it was a campaign against her gender— a social construct that shifts and is determined by people, not bodies.[11] It is against Jenny's gender that decades of discrimination, sexism and harassment continue to occur. Regardless of her colleagues' beliefs and workplace's at-times-archaic practices, Jenny's ability to apply for (and do) jobs in international affairs has nothing to do with what is between her legs.

Yet what became clear throughout this research was that *who* can represent the nation internationally is an exercise of authority and control that is often deeply gendered. Further, gendered challenges remain pervasive globally—not just siloed in one area of diplomacy or the military, but across the board in international affairs. And whilst virtually all existing scholarship on gender and international affairs focuses on either the military or on diplomacy (with a few exceptions, such as Cynthia Enloe[12] and McGlen and Sarkees's[13] work), comparing agencies and experiences across international affairs adds breadth and depth to what's known in a way that has seldom been done before. The stories and lives of those in the mainstream *and* margins of international affairs matter.

To be clear, things are improving in some arenas—and this book will explore those areas too. The highly structured nature of militaries, for instance, may offer women unique advantages when it comes to navigating otherwise opaque career trajectories in international affairs. Queer women may experience advantages in balancing the intensive 'double burden' facing many diplomatic households. Additionally, the layered international standards and domestic policy reforms are creating ever more favourable policy contexts for junior women starting their careers.

However, these snippets of progress remain troublingly outweighed by pervasive challenges—and this creates difficulties not just for those women who work in international affairs, but also for those researching international affairs. Even despite how common the challenges are, few are comfortable shining a light on the full depth and nature of challenges that women and those who do not fit the mould experience. For individuals, exploring the challenges can be painful, going through decades of microaggressions and major incidences that do not always abate with time and 'progress'. Institutions are often risk-averse and fear reputational damage, meaning there can be real reluctance to understand what is *not working* about the way things are done in organisations—and who is and is not left out. Whether through blissful ignorance or applying a purposeful blind-eye, individuals and institutions alike can often reject assertions of continued gendered, racialised, and other challenges—at least, until the evidence is presented directly in front of them. And from there, what they do with the information is often obscured, or if public, may provoke further delays as drawn-out review processes are committed and recommendations issued. Can our knowledge of a sector and its gender relations change the nature of the sector and gender relations going forward?

As a critical feminist friend this is what I hope will be achieved through publishing this book. For individuals and institutions, I hope this book presents evidence about the status quo of the international affairs institutions in which you operate, as well as insights and directions from which to deliver on transformative change. For other researchers, I hope this book enables further research and understanding around how gendered institutions stymy or promote change, as well as a framework for understanding and researching the multiply layered gendered international worlds in which almost every field of work now operates. For the casual reader or student, I hope that this book sheds insight, prompts reflection, and does justice to the stories told and untold of the many incredible and diverse women leading around the world in our international affairs. The insights generated from this book are therefore myriad in scope and in potential application, from outlining rich empirical evidence to developing replicable theoretical and methodological frameworks for further research.

The process however has not been easy. You can perhaps imagine the discomfort of studying gender relations in various male-dominated industries, from the media to the military, construction and beyond. There are two ways in which this research adds complexity to the usual challenges of the task. Firstly, seeking to understand the gendered institutions of international affairs institutions has specific challenges, from attempting to understand the inherently secretive and often publicly sexist institutions (as is the case for many national security agencies), to peeling back the layers on institutions that are adept at presenting a diplomatically honed, glossy image of the way things are (as is the case with many ministries of foreign affairs (MFAs) and diplomatic corps). Coupled with the nature of the duties involved, which are often high-profile, high-impact, and high-stakes, international affairs presents specific challenges for the gender researcher that amplify the importance of 'insider' accounts and analysis such as is covered in this book.

Secondly, all the institutions studied in this book are ones undergoing major changes. To a degree this book is a study of the progress of women in declining institutions, particularly as the role of traditional diplomacy changes with globalisation internationalising many previously domestic agencies and diminishing the central role, prestige, and power once held exclusively by MFAs. Equally, it is a study of the ways in which women remain barred from sectors experiencing a rapid increase or boom in resourcing or status. In many countries, 'hard' international affairs institutions like militaries dominate state resourcing over 'soft' diplomatic agencies,[14] and since 9/11, have had their share of revenue increase with women's opportunities seemingly not commensurately increasing with it.

This book therefore adds to our knowledge in very specific ways: (1) uncovering the state of gendered institutions in international affairs, and (2) uncovering the state of gendered challenges as institutions evolve. But why study this now, and why use a case study of Australia? Because of the critical juncture.

Why Gender and International Affairs Matters Now: The Critical Juncture

Two decades into the twenty-first century has revealed a gender leadership crisis like no other. Off the back of the #MeToo movement revealing systemic rape and sexual assault across global industries without exception, #BlackLivesMatter propelling the issue of structural racism out of the United States into all corners of the world including informing #IndigenousLivesMatter movements, and even Australia's 2021 #EnoughIsEnough stand against sexual harassment and misogyny in our highest offices of parliament, it is clear that the world is buckling under the weight of deeply discriminatory institutions.

With inequalities arguably embedded in human institutions since the dawn of time, what makes this moment different for gender and leadership as opposed to any other time in international affairs is simple. For the *first time* on a global experimental and observable level, some nations are reaching or close to reaching parity in representation and leadership across myriad different fields—including international affairs. This is both necessitating and provoking changes within institutions, from things as 'trivial' as the introduction of toilets for women in national parliaments (seemingly an unnecessary thing up until recent decades) to those as major as the United Nations Security Council Resolution 1325 in 2000, recognising for the first time the link between women, peace, and security on a global level. But it is also unclear to what degree this progress around women's representation is changing the embodied nature of inequality—the day-to-day or practical experiences and realities for women and diverse individuals on the global stage.

In the case of international institutions, what is crucial is that while we have seen some progress and gendered challenges may have changed in shape and degree, inequalities still exist. As we edge closer to equal representation in some states, cultural, institutionalised patriarchy (and racism, heterosexism, and classism) still seem to remain. This research therefore casts doubt on whether the progress made has really changed fundamental systems of inequality. Rather, I argue that inequalities in international affairs institutions merely adapt and evolve—systems of oppression may change but are hard to shake entirely. If supported more widely, this finding is deeply concerning.

This is why the Australian case is so important to understand. Australia is a clear leader in terms of women's representation in diplomatic leadership positions, more than doubling global averages. Women represent a majority of Australia's public service, and even a majority of many international affairs institutions, despite these agencies being known as the 'worst performing' in government for representation in leadership.[15] International affairs agencies have dedicated focus and resourcing for women's leadership, gender equality, cultural and ethnic diversity, and sexuality diversity policies, practices, secretariats, and networks. Australian law provides extensive equality and anti-discrimination provisions. Australia is even noted as the world's most multiculturally diverse nation.[16] Australia is in many ways the model subject for analysing policies, commitments, and evidence to date around gender—and other forms of—equality in international affairs. Indeed, whilst women represented between 6 to 35 per cent of women in senior diplomatic appointments globally in 2017–2018,[17] women represented over 40 per cent in Australia in the same period.[18] Further, in comparison with other militaries (NATO member and partner nations) Australia's military was ranked in the top three militaries for women's participation (ahead of New Zealand, and behind Hungary and Moldova).[19]

Given this, when I first undertook this research project, I hypothesised that the combination of progressive gender equality measures within government combined with an international context driving gender equality should make actors working within this sphere more gender equal, with better outcomes for women leaders, and agencies as a whole. In cases, progress is clearly being made. Yet the data uncovered demonstrates that despite all the progressive steps forward and women's representation verging on parity in some sectors, women continue to have specifically gendered experiences of international affairs. Women have *never* been equally represented in senior Australian international affairs. And despite the verging on parity, it was naïve to think that numbers alone instigate institutional overhaul.

Feminist institutionalist (FI) theory provides the base from which we can understand this complex nest of progress and resistance, of increased representation without necessarily equality. Despite recent shifts in Australia's formal foreign policy apparatus, informal gendered rules and norms continue to impact on women's underrepresentation in leadership and different experiences within government—because institutions are 'sticky', durable, and once made, often difficult to change.[20] Prominent theorists highlight that institutions are not so stable and durable that they are immune to *all* change however, with 'constructive' gaps between formalised rules and informal norms providing points of ambiguity and malleability.[21] Indeed, Cornut[22] argues that diplomacy is fluid and institutions, liquid,[23] indicating a degree of fragility, temporariness, vulnerability, and an inclination to constant change.[24]These seemingly oppositional concepts form the basis of this book: institutional durability *and* changeability help to explain why Australian international affairs remain marked by gendered differences in leadership despite the significant gains made. In short, inequalities evolve as institutions change.

It is this concept that I argue has great merit when considering other states' international affairs or even other fields in which women are gaining representation. Despite the observable gains, gendered institutions endure through adaptation. Through this book, I build this argument by interrogating institutional history across a range of international affairs agencies, unpacking over 30 years of statistics on gender representation, plus studying the demographics and stories of over 50 women currently in leadership for their experiences of international affairs. It becomes clear that while gendered challenges may have changed in shape and degree, they have not necessarily changed in overall nature. I argue that there are three key reasons explaining this entrenched gender inequality and why women remain underrepresented (or unequal) in international affairs:

- firstly, institutional histories tightly bound in selective and exclusionary practices have made gendered differences in treatment a normal, accepted mode of conduct;
- secondly, the duplication of gendered challenges across spheres not only domestic (like family, society and individual workplaces), but also international (with its own norms, rules and behaviours to match) have resulted in deeply layered local and international gendered challenges; and
- thirdly, the compounding effect of gendered challenges in these different domestic and international spheres, together with challenges at different stages of internationalised work (such as pathways to international posting, international representation, and return), careers (early, mid, late) and participants' lives make international affairs a fraught context for career progress.

This cumulative effect produces a workplace environment teeming with gendered rules. Additionally, progress made in terms of simple representation does not guarantee equality. Six core novel findings are additionally explored through this book, including:

1. Women are most proportionally represented in leadership and international representation in more militaristic and paramilitaristic agencies, and least proportionally represented in leadership and international representation in more traditionally diplomatic agencies.
2. More traditionally diplomatic agencies demonstrate 'genteel' toxic masculinities that are just as pervasive as military toxic masculinities, only in some cases more difficult to identify and therefore confront.
3. Women are becoming highest represented in institutions that are shrinking or stagnating in power, funding, and status, leading to a diplomatic glass cliff where women's functional power in leadership positions is constrained by the state of the institutions they occupy.
4. Queer women (with wives) fare better than their straight female colleagues (with husbands) in terms of meeting the diplomatic double burden required of envoys and their spouses.
5. Women reported experiencing more, and worse, challenges domestically within their agencies, rather than host countries when on international postings.
6. Most of the challenges experienced by women posted internationally were relatively homogenous across agencies, despite the wide variances in roles and portfolios.

Looking at both pockets of progress and the evolution of inequalities helps us to understand these internationalised institutions as they undergo change.

Throughout the course of this book, an Australian case study of four core international affairs institutions is used to gain both deep insight into a singular context and prompt reflection on the international implications of the findings. Spanning 'soft' to 'hard' international affairs, the case agencies include those involved in diplomatic, military, national security, intelligence, border protection and policing portfolios. The case agencies include the Department of Foreign Affairs and Trade (DFAT), Defence (inclusive of the civilian Department of Defence (DoD) and military Australian Defence Force (ADF)), the Department of Home Affairs (Home Affairs), and the Australian Federal Police (AFP). All are federal agencies and were chosen as the core agencies responsible for maintaining sovereignty and national interest through their respective portfolios. All cases have sufficient shared goals and international footprints, yet also have differences in terms of levels of women in leadership, policies supporting gender equality, and overall organisational culture and structure. All agencies have high profiles publicly and operate within contentious and fluctuating environments requiring planned foresight for maintaining national interests and the ability to adapt quickly to changing international priorities and circumstances. As the front 'face' of Australia's international affairs, agencies were chosen based on:

- size, representing the largest Australian Public Service (APS) and international-facing agencies;
- whether international engagement was part of their core activities; and
- whether senior executive leaders were part of international deployment or representation.

Whilst it is somewhat unusual to analyse the spread of agencies included, by analysing international-facing police, intelligence, and border protection institutions—ones that scholars do not normally treat as international affairs institutions—we can learn many new things about gender and international affairs. This is increasingly important, as globalisation has transformed state institutions into international institutions—with many seemingly 'domestic' agencies maintaining extensive international divisions, their own envoys, and missions overseas, and increased autonomy from the main arm of the MFA. The 'distinctive way of life' that characterises these agencies and their international deployments cements the participants and their case agencies as part of organised, enduring groups charged with representing Australian international affairs.[25] As diplomats and pseudo-diplomats, these diverse international affairs workers embody many traits and skills of traditional diplomacy whilst simultaneously re-defining the work of the state on the global stage.

Indeed, Aggestam and Towns understand diplomacy as a 'set of assumptions, institutions and processes for managing international relations peacefully'—a definition that does not exclude a wider set of international affairs institutions beyond the MFA.[26] Rossetti[27] characterises the traditional role of diplomats—'to provide information about their host country and report timely and reliable information about developments in their host countries'—as changing, expanding with new actors and new forms of public and informal diplomacy.

Given this scope, there are several things that become apparent from this analysis across international affairs institutions. To start with, women's representation varies in at least four respects: (1) the overall ratio of women in the agencies; (2) the ratio of women among officials deployed abroad; (3) the ratio of women in leadership positions; and (4) whether that ratio is proportionate to the overall ratio of women in the agencies. As for consistencies across all agencies, there (a) remains little diversity in employment beyond an increase in gender diversity, and (b) even despite some agencies ranking highly in terms of equal gender representation, women's experiences of inequalities are all largely consistent. Women are bound by many of the same challenges (and opportunities) across varying international affairs agencies, highlighting a more universal experience of international affairs than prior siloed research on gender and diplomacy or militaries might indicate.

Therefore, while the overarching question of this book seeks to get to the heart of *why women remain underrepresented in international affairs*, exploring the many nuances of gender inequality as it does so, additional research questions drawn on are more descriptive and detailed. Among them, they include:

- Why are women underrepresented across the four agencies? What accounts for the variation in their underrepresentation among the agencies?
- Why are women underrepresented in international deployment? What accounts for the variation in their deployment among agencies?
- What explains the ratio of women in leadership positions in each agency? Why is leadership proportionate in some of the agencies but not in others?
- Why do women still experience gendered (and racialised, heteronormative, and so on) challenges despite international affairs seismic changes over recent decades (from globalisation and increased internationalisation of domestic departments, to the rise in gender equality mandates, norms, commitments, and leadership rebalancing)? Why are the challenges so homogenous across the agencies?

Embedded throughout these questions are answers deeply multidimensional, experiences that coalesce at the intersection of race and ethnicity, sexual orientation, disability, rural or urban upbringing, class, education status, and more. Therefore, whilst this book seeks to centre gender at the pinnacle of analysis, it also seeks to contextually embed the research within a wider understanding of women's diversity and the intersectionality of layered inequalities.

The questions indicate an ambitious research agenda that will reveal findings previously obscured by the limitations of the current literature. What is gained by comparison is a richness in findings that transforms our understanding of international affairs. By doing so, we find that the agencies that appear to be doing the best in terms of gender representation and equal opportunity policies, are doing the worst at proportionally representing women. The reverse is true too: those that appear to be doing the worst and have some of the most blatant and public forms of sexism and misogyny, are indeed best at proportionally representing women. What is unravelled over the course of the book is a narrative that highlights the significance of agency history, identity, and visibility of gendered (and other) challenges, which explain variations in representation and some of the more novel findings.

Whilst we can celebrate the successes of leading politicians who have cracked the glass ceiling (and survived), we cannot forget that gendered, racialised, heteronormative, ableist, classist (and more) power structures continue to impact on who gets to represent their state internationally. As public servants, political appointees, and ministers in important international-facing roles, infrequently do they have the platform nor ability to share their experiences and challenges. Nor do we often celebrate their successes. And yet it is these international affairs leaders that make or break a nation's future in an increasingly globalised world. Leaders in international affairs 'articulate the meaning within which others from around the world work and live'.[28] They shape social and governance norms, frame what is important and marginalised, and play powerful and influential roles shaping laws and policies, negotiating on war, peace, and security, and representing states in international fora. In essence, who leads matters.

Australia's Evolving International Representation

The argument for 'why Australia' has been made; however, it is useful to start off by situating the reader as to the 'what' and 'how' of Australia's evolving gender representation. Women's exclusion from key agencies in Australian international affairs was marked by legal exclusion under the Commonwealth Marriage Bar until its abolition in 1966, and since then, social exclusion by way of an enduring legacy of discrimination and differential treatment.[29] In 1985, for the first time more women than men were enrolled in university, and as recruits in our premiere agency for foreign affairs—DFAT.[30] At that time, there were only two women heads of mission. More than three decades later, in 2017 when this research commenced women in DFAT represented only 26.8 per cent of senior ambassadorial positions in diplomacy and 25.7 per cent of SES appointments.[31] Women's pipeline to leadership was more than just leaky. This reasoning, in part, influenced the decision to launch DFAT's first *Women in Leadership Strategy* in 2015. Yet DFAT was also one of the last federal government agencies to address women's leadership in Australia. The path to women's contemporary representation in Australian international affairs has neither been linear nor guaranteed.

Australia is now making rapid progress towards being a world leader in gender equality in international affairs. In 2015, DFAT's then- Departmental Secretary Peter Varghese launched the *Women in Leadership Strategy*, the first such strategy to look into the reasons why women's career progression within the department was not equal to men's. The next year, Australia's first female Foreign Minister, Julie Bishop, launched Australia's first *Gender Equality and Women's Empowerment Strategy* across foreign policy, economic diplomacy, and development programs—one of only a few such foreign ministries to do so in the world. Around the same time, other agencies within the Australian federal government's international affairs apparatus were experiencing their own landmark events relating to gender. The Australian Human Rights Commission had recently handed down two damning reviews and a further two audit reports[32] on gender harassment and discrimination within Defence, contributing to the establishment of the *Defence Australian Public Service Gender Equality Strategy Action Plan 2016–2019*—further notable in that it has since lapsed, with no replacement or extension as at time of publication. The AFP created its first International Deployment Group's *Gender Strategy*, now in its second iteration. Plus, the Australian Border Force (ABF), which has since become an integral portfolio in Home Affairs, reported it had been established with a gender-equal senior leadership team, making it one of the first such portfolios (if not the first) to be established within government.[33]

Shortly after these developments, the 2017 *Foreign Policy White Paper* was handed down. In many ways, it was in stark opposition to earlier foreign policies, such as the 2003 Howard government-era White Paper, which contained no references to women or women's rights. In contrast, the 2017 *Foreign Policy White Paper* states: 'Gender inequality undermines global prosperity, stability and security. It contributes to and often exacerbates a range of challenges, including poverty, weak governance and conflict and violent extremism. Australia's foreign policy pursues the empowerment of women as a top priority'.[34] While the 2017 *White Paper* was far from a feminist manifesto, the connection between women's empowerment, gender equality and global governance was significant. The audience to which the *White Paper* was handed down to also spoke volumes in the history of Australian foreign policy. It included Australia's first female Defence Minister since federation, Marise Payne, Australia's first gay female *and* first Asian-born federal minister, Shadow Foreign Minister Penny Wong, and Australia's first female Departmental Secretary of DFAT, Frances Adamson. Matching the significance of the time, the *White Paper* was handed down in a particular moment in APS history that demonstrates there is currently a more feminist turn in Australian foreign policy. Such a turn is conceptualised as an increasingly feminist orientation, without the overtness and strict labelling of 'feminist foreign policy', as seen in other states (such as Sweden, for instance).

Across all APS departments, 50:50 gender parity in leadership targets by 2020 were set (and close to being achieved, if not already done).[35] Most agencies have embraced gender equality strategies, inclusive of targets and quotas that have begun to change the face of government. Australia now has its third female foreign minister and third female secretary of DFAT, with a new female minister for Home Affairs added in 2022 too. The combined effect of these changes suggests a more women- and feminist-informed era of Australian IR—what Lee-Koo sees as the emergence of pro-gender norms in Australian foreign policy 'by stealth', in which Lee-Koo notes that 'there is a genuine embrace of pro-gender norms, but the masculinist cultures of Australia's politics limit the capacity for it to be publicly debated and celebrated'.[36] From being chronically and severely underrepresented, with gender diversity in Australian international affairs agencies lagging significantly behind the APS and the corporate sector,[37] institutions in the field are amid rapid and seemingly dramatic gendered change.

Since DFAT's strategy was implemented in 2015, women's representation in international leadership increased by 14.6 percentage points in one year. Was formal institutional change all that was needed to help boost women's representation? If so, it suggests significant informal rules and norms were at play prior to the *Women in Leadership Strategy* that influenced 'who' could be chosen to represent Australia in leadership. It also highlights the need for further investigation.

In 2018–2019, women represented just over 47.2 per cent of all international A-based leadership positions within Home Affairs, which is notably higher than the other agencies. Even the agencies studied with the lowest representation of women in leadership, Defence and the AFP, are doing better than global averages.[38] Of Defence Attachés, 17.2 per cent of those deployed internationally were women, and in the AFP, 28.7 per cent of those deployed internationally were women.

These initial statistics indicate we have much to celebrate compared to global averages. Yet beyond the cause for optimism, caution remains. Since 1977 onwards, Australia enacted comprehensive anti-discrimination legislation at state, federal and international levels, with equal employment opportunity policy now specifically prescribed across public and private sectors. Women now outnumber men in the APS, representing 60.4 per cent of the workforce.[39] Women are equally represented across global politics and international affairs at secondary and tertiary levels,[40] with Conley Tyler, Blizzard, and Crane[41] further debunking theories that women are less motivated or lack interest in 'hard' international affairs. However, women have remained an almost complete minority of overall executive level (EL) and senior executive service (SES) appointments for as long as we have data.[42] Women's prospects for top appointments are worse than for men with comparable qualifications and experience, and their overall treatment as leaders indicates continued sexism, gender segregation and covert discrimination.[43] If formal gender equality policies were all that were needed to achieve gender equality within Australian international affairs, it should have already been achieved.

What Can We Learn from the Australian Case?

There are reasons to believe that international affairs institutions elsewhere are gendered in the same ways as in Australia. Australia shares a democratic system of governance, like half the world,[44] and shares the Westminster system of government with nations as broad as Britain, Canada, New Zealand, and many parts of the Pacific, Asia, and Africa.[45] Australia has an increasingly feminist foreign policy orientation, shared by nations like Sweden, France, New Zealand, Canada, Mexico, the United States, and the European Union.[46] Whilst Australia leads in the region, there is a growing proportion of women in international representation across Asia[47] and major international forces including the US and UK, plus Scandinavian countries, have foregrounded gender equality strategies in foreign affairs like Australia, in ways that are also increasing women's representation. In other words, as a leading case study, there is a lot to learn from Australia internationally on the representation of women and the substantive (or not) changes to gender equality as institutions shift.

The implications are worrying considering some of the core findings in this book. Indeed, rather than witnessing a decrease in gendered nature of international affairs institutions as women's representation increases, it becomes clear that gendered inequalities evolve. Women's experiences are marked by slower career trajectories and systemic exclusion from power. Bureaucratic diplomatic cultures are found to be marked, on occasion, by covert forms of toxic masculinity as much as militaries remain marked, on occasion, by overt toxic masculinities. International posting and promotions remain far from gender neutral and professionalised, despite rhetoric to the contrary. Posts remain structured around heteronormative, nuclear family models that assume copious lengths of unpaid labour and support (frequently borne by women), to function. Women who seek deeply international careers often do not progress at the same rate as their domestic-bound colleagues. International representation and leadership takes more than a combination of skills and experiences, but also mental attitude and support systems that enable women's success. In fact, without considerable other supports, the progress of women into leadership would not be possible based on skills and 'merit' alone. The opportunity that international roles might provide women was a consideration subsidiary to whether the opportunity was even possible, logistically, in the first place.

Women's experiences highlight substantial and systematic ways of being overlooked, underrecognised, and devalued. Women are overlooked during introductions and in groups are assumed to be junior or the note-taker. Women are barred access to certain military and security facilities internationally because of their gender. They are often not invited to informal events or gatherings important for informal and political knowledge on the status of negotiations or personal opportunities for career progression. Women are not socially permitted to engage in the same range of activities as their male counterparts when on posting and are more likely to be scrutinised or watched. Despite their status and position, women leaders are still subjected to sexual harassment and discrimination.

In other words, leadership is often no protection for women in international affairs, particularly for women of colour and queer women, as challenges multiply at the intersection of gender, race, and sexuality. If women miss advancing to a certain rank by a certain age, they may be assumed to be deficient in some manner, further holding back their careers with women blamed in a Catch-22 situation for their lack of advancement at similar rates to men. Often, women could either choose between going on international posting or progressing their career—a choice that at times punished women either way.

How well the challenges were navigable was directly correlated to their visibility. More militaristic international affairs institutions (the military, policing, and so on) were more overtly gendered yet provided women could endure the challenges of these agencies, their progression to leadership and deployment follows at a rate roughly comparable to their male colleagues. The same is not true for more traditional diplomatic international affairs agencies, for whom the challenges were more covert and genteel forms of toxic masculinities were evident. An enduring gap remained for these women—they had the lowest opportunity for leadership and international representation (proportional to opportunity), despite in some cases representing a majority of their agency. In these cases, women represent an enduringly arginalized majority teetering at the edge of a diplomatic glass cliff—where women are attaining equal or near-equal representation in leadership whilst the institution they represent is shrinking in funding, footprint, and status.

The segregation goes beyond vertical segregation by rank and leadership, to horizontal segregation across portfolios and posts. Women tended to be higher represented in 'soft' portfolios, human resources, and corporate governance, as well as in lower prestige and lower status countries. The most important negotiations with *allies*—that involve strategic partnerships, threat detection and important joint security operations—were roles dominated by men. In balancing relationships with countries emerging as *threats*—requiring a certain amount of management of relationships, balancing political power and military capability, and soft negotiation—roles were dominated by women. Glass cliff patterns of women's representation were evidenced—with women often given roles during periods of crisis or precarity, where the chance of failure was highest.

Significantly, the nominal participation of women has not equalled substantive changes in their roles—findings that through the course of this book we can now extend beyond diplomacy to other areas of international affairs. The gendered history of institutions matter to international affairs—and many international institutions remain path dependent. While it might be assumed that the gendered experiences of police officers, Defence Attachés, ambassadors, immigration counsellors, border protection officers, and surveillance and intelligence envoys would vary, the picture is far more homogenous in reality. Gender and other axes of inequalities evolve as institutions change and adapt. And there are myriad reasons why these trends should be more widely felt—in other states' international affairs, as well as other fields of internationalising work.

Book Structure

Given this context, this book draws on feminist institutionalist (FI) theory to explore women's narratives and institutional history—with the aim of understanding how international affairs is 'gendered'. Doing so helps us to explain both women's underrepresentation and their persistent marginalisation in the field. Based on the assertion that institutions matter, 'institutions' refer not solely to agencies, but also to the underlying system of rules that constitute daily life and human interaction. The gendered nature of both formal and informal institutions has a significant effect on whether, when and in what circumstances women can represent the state internationally. This has specific implications for the four Australian case agencies in which women's leadership and experiences are analysed.

A mixed method approach informed analysis of the agencies, comprising in-depth qualitative interviews with women leaders, quantitative data analysis on gender over the last 34 years, observation, and document analysis. The literature, critical feminist friend approach, research questions, and the quest to discover detailed, substantive understandings of women's leadership in Australian international affairs guided the choice of methodology. Such a rigorous methodology provided many opportunities for theoretical and empirical insights into the gendered nature of institutions in diplomacy and security, as well as important opportunities to triangulate the data. The mixed methods research approach chosen reinforces a feminist tendency towards 'face-to-face, qualitative and interactive methods', yet also recognises the benefits of quantitative data, particularly in uncovering trends and findings that would have remained obscured without holistic analysis.[48]

The primary data for this book comprised in-depth interviews with 57 women in executive level (EL) and senior executive service (SES) level positions, as well as named interviews with Australia's first female Prime Minister, Julia Gillard, and first female Foreign Minister, Julie Bishop. I focused on interviewing those who are or have represented Australia internationally in the last 10 years at the highest levels, and I have spent extensive time in the field learning from women both in their domestic and international postings across more than 10 countries and three regions, allowing observation to complement the interviews undertaken. The research also involved a further 27 informal discussions with former heads of departments (men and women), politicians, human resources managers, and other related individuals within the agencies to establish context, test ideas, and guide the research direction.

Analysing quantitative data from annual reports and the APS Employee Database (APSED) *Yearbook Statistics* since 1984 provided important trend data on the last 30 + years, breaking down gender, rank, and international deployment across the agencies. Textual and document analysis of surrounding policy informed an understanding of the formal rules, their implementation, successes, and gaps. Additionally, undertaking a comparative case study research design ensured a rigorous approach to understanding a complex field, in which many different individuals, agencies and stakeholders are involved in the same core duties of maintaining national interest and state sovereignty. Comparative research of gender and political institutions, gender, and diplomacy, and informal versus formal institutions are needed to address scholarly gaps, test findings across international institutions, and ultimately draw significant learnings around what is working in some institutions, and not in others.[49]

Therefore, there are significant learnings to be gained from this research. Firstly, the research presents the most comprehensive, rich qualitative and quantitative dataset on gender in Australian diplomacy and security to date, and one of the most significant novel case studies globally on the topic. Through doing so, it presents a rigorous baseline study into who is chosen to represent the state internationally, as well as how they got there and what their experiences have been, addressing important gaps within both the literature and international affairs institutions. It helps to raise the profile of pioneering women in the field, whilst simultaneously problematising why and how women have been systemically underrepresented. In a time of unprecedented technological, environmental, and social change, where women are noted as 'the most relevant emerging power this century', the analysis of these women's experiences has important ramifications not just within Australia, but more broadly. Specifically, if the country with the leading representation around women *still* evidences entrenched and rapidly evolving inequalities, a dire warning is issued for those following behind. Not only is the continued underrepresentation of women undermining the values of representative democracies, but there are also important ramifications for states' abilities to formulate global security, maintain state sovereignty and the determine of national interest.[50] As former Prime Minister Julia Gillard notes:

> I think there are challenges for DFAT and others that would also be true in big organisations everywhere. It's the overlay of a set of challenges that come when you're asking people to go overseas for large sections of their life. How do you reconcile that with work and family life? How do you reconcile the careers of spouses? The historic model of being an ambassador or high commissioner has been that a man does it with a non-working spouse . . . and we're finding it hard to move from that model. It's not a uniquely Australian challenge.[51]

Secondly, this research develops several new frameworks informed by FI theory to understand gendered institutions in international affairs. The argument for an intersectional feminist institutional (IFI) approach is made with the hopes of better understanding how not just one narrowly defined archetype of women—but women in all their diversity—experience foreign affairs and diplomacy. Additionally, the transferability of the framework for studying international institutions has great application across other agencies within government, as well as intergovernmental organisations and diplomatic missions globally, and indeed any more globalised workforce for whom gendered norms and behaviours are not just influenced by the domestic anymore.

This extends the relevance and significance of the book's theoretical contributions across multiple cross-cultural contexts. The international affairs context—where institutional gendered practices of agencies meet international politics and their specific hierarchies and gender practices—is a rich site for exploring how institutions act to constrain or enable leadership depending on gender *and* ethnicity, sexuality, and so on. These contexts are not simply domestic or international, but 'intermestic'—'where domestic and international policy issues and implications blend'.[52] Applying FI theory to develop the intersectional and international institutional framework contributes significant original findings to IR, particularly around gendered *and* racialised, heteronormative, and so on institutions that affect women's representation in international affairs.

Thirdly, the book offers original empirical findings, adding to core IR concepts from perspectives previously marginalised and excluded, uncovering substantial new knowledge in international affairs.[53] Comparison has broadened the research's impact and implications, leading to some of the most significant and counter-intuitive findings, demonstrating benefits of militaristic agencies in promoting more proportional leadership, plus providing key insights on the true cost of international affairs for those at the coalface—a burden disproportionately borne by women. Extending research beyond traditional conceptions of diplomacy to other forms across international affairs, such as defence diplomacy and police-led diplomacy, reflects important changes globally yet to be fully explored in research. Nontraditional portfolios which are becoming increasingly internationalised are important cases for analysis, as elements of traditional diplomacy erode or shrink and are reformed by new technological, political, and social realities that redefine and magnify disparate actors' roles determining national interest and securing state sovereignty.[54] Many of these empirical findings establish exciting foundations for future research.

Fourthly, this book contributes to FI methodologies, particularly in aiming to understand 'hidden' informal institutions and their intersection with formal institutions across contexts deeply layered and complex. The mixed methods research design, informed by the critical feminist friend approach, involved an extensive pilot and background phase of research, in-depth interviews, observation, and analysis of trend data over a period of decades that has revealed findings that would have been obscured by a temporal or one-sided approach to analysing women's underrepresentation. The ability to undertake research domestically and internationally was a further critical addition to the research, allowing the day-to-day realities of women's experiences to be observed and better understood.

Ultimately, this book addresses calls for research on how to best equip government leaders to meet the 'demands of the future' and bridge the gap in senior representation across international affairs.[55] The research serves a practical purpose by giving public administrators across foreign affairs, defence, immigration, intelligence and policing a way to think more effectively about the (often invisible) processes which produce equity outcomes. While evidence and rational analysis form only part of policy development in practice, evidence-based comparative research of this kind can play a decisive role in informing policymakers' judgments.[56] It also informs the conditions of the policy environment within which those judgments are made.[57] 'Whole of government' approaches to gender equality—particularly in foreign affairs—must be met with research that reflects this.

This book is designed with chapters able to be read standalone or in sequence. It is laid out as follows.

Chapter 2 explores the research to date and develops the theoretical and conceptual framework of the book. Extending feminist institutionalist (FI) theory to the spheres of diplomatic and security decision-making, I argue that multiply layered formal and informal gendered challenges, rules, norms, and practices impact on women's pathways to, and experiences of, international leadership. I situate the research in the field of IR and explore the gendered nature of diplomacy and national security, from both historical and conceptual perspectives. I examine how gender and institutions have previously been conceptualised with reference to Australian international institutions, before detailing the theoretical frameworks that explain women's underrepresentation and exploring their use in other internationalised contexts.

Following the literature review, Chapter 3 presents the methodology used to explore the women's experiences of international affairs leadership. This chapter details the on-ground, in-person, and international approach to data collection, as well as access to 'elites' and the diplomatic bubble, and ethical considerations.

Chapters 4, 5, 6, and 7 analyse the primary data collected during fieldwork in Australia and internationally. Chapter 4 provides a brief historical analysis of international affairs and each of the four case agencies, dissecting the policy and organisational environments and process-tracing the current more women-informed and feminist turn in foreign policy. This chapter is particularly important in grappling with the different organisational histories of the agencies and how they have evolved over time with regards to opening opportunities for women.

Chapter 5 characterises what the Australian women leaders 'looked like' by exploring the participant demographics and what we know about the representation of different ethnic backgrounds, sexualities, and classes. It seeks to give colour and a 'whole life' approach to whom represents the state, also exploring topics such as family and children and the geographic reach and patterns of deployment.

Chapter 6 presents some of the first surprising conclusions around militaristic versus diplomatic structures when it comes to international gender representation. It breaks down the data, demonstrating a broad pattern whereby women remain segregated by status, prestige and strategic importance of posts and positions gained.

Chapter 7 analyses women's pathways to senior leadership in the case agencies. This chapter concentrates on mapping women's career paths and the factors considered at each step of the journey to international representation and leadership. It presents key insights around the most likely time when women leave the 'pipeline', and the core considerations for doing so. It becomes clear that both formal and informal institutions impact on women's career trajectories, highlighting not just the time-lapse between institutional change and the desired result, but how some institutions resist change.

Chapter 8 collates the findings of the previous chapters on history, demographics, statist vics, and experiences. Applying the IFI theory to these deeply international contexts, three core trends explaining women's underrepresentation are found, including the legacy of history on the contemporary agencies, the complexity and duplication of gendered challenges, and the compounding effect of rules at different stages of women's careers and posting cycles. Additionally, six of the most novel findings from the research are explored. It becomes clear that complex institutions continue to exist in the face of the feminist turn in foreign policy, resulting in an environment teeming with gendered rules and norms of behaviour.

Finally, the conclusion summarises the big lessons learned and implications from the research for other contexts. I reflect on where we go from here and final thoughts in terms of what—and how best—we can learn from women's experience of international affairs to date.

2
Exploring Theories on Gender and International Affairs

> Whether it's in Afghanistan or any other country, you must have women involved in governing, nation building, and making decisions. It's at every level, from leaders in government and business, through to the grassroots level that women need to be included.
>
> —Julie Bishop, 3 April 2019[1]

Like many areas of life, international affairs has often been assumed to be a gender-neutral slate for deciding the fate and future of nations. Whilst most actors in official, state-sanctioned roles have historically been men, this is seen as nothing other than business as usual. Ann Tickner argues that international relations (IR) 'bases its assumptions and explanations almost entirely on the activities and experiences of men'.[2] Further, due to the primacy of realist orthodox approaches, the field of IR has privileged states as primary actors and 'hard' military power as central to how states negotiate war and peace.[3] Until recently, women have remained largely invisible in the field of international relations and excluded from leadership and participation in these key vehicles of international decision-making between states.[4]

The research to date on gender and international affairs is therefore revealing not only in what it says, but in what it does not say. Four core areas of the literature are covered in this chapter, including an exploration of (1) feminist institutionalist (FI) scholarship and three key gaps in the theory this book seeks to address; (2) an exploration of where international relations and FI research intersect; (3) the gendered nature of diplomacy, national security, and international organisations; and (4) the gendered nature of Australian international affairs. This chapter ends on the theoretical frameworks developed for (a) *intersectional* feminist institutionalism, (b) studying women's representation and experiences in *layered* institutions, and (c) understanding how gender inequalities *evolve* as institutions undergo change.

Through this chapter, key gaps are revealed, making space for three main academic contributions. Firstly, this book extends analyses that are typically made of one foreign affairs institution (diplomacy or the military, for instance) to encompass four (across portfolios as diverse as diplomacy and defence and policing and intelligence and home affairs). Secondly, this book aims to be more comprehensively intersectional in its analysis of gender and international affairs, bringing in sexuality and to a lesser degree race alongside gender in analysis. Thirdly, this book provides a wealth of new data on gender in international affairs institutions in Australia.

Understanding Feminist Institutionalist Theory

Much feminist political science has centred on seeking out 'real world puzzles', which have often been linked to institutional change and development.[5] The study of institutions is premised in the belief that institutions matter and can provide insight into why, how, when, where and what choices get made in our political reality.[6] Drawing from rational choice, discursive, sociological, and historical institutionalism, feminist institutionalism (FI) is a strand of new institutionalism (NI) that considers how institutional norms, practices and rules shape behaviour, politics, and power. Unlike the institutionalisms before it, FI is explicit in its focus on understanding the *gendered* nature of institutions, which can reveal important distinctions in political action taken, and its effects.

To understand FI deeply, an understanding of its predecessors is warranted. Rational choice institutionalism (RCI) concentrates on utilising the micro-level (actors—who are viewed as 'rational') to understand the macro-level (actors' effect on institutions). Rational choice institutionalists view institutions not only as structures of coordination but as structures of coercion, power, and domination.[7] Discursive institutionalism (DI) focuses on micro- to macro- levels of analysis, foregrounding the influence of ideas and discourse in shaping actors and institutions.[8] Institutions are viewed as both constraining and enabling factors in the construction of meaning. Discourse is one of the primary methods through which meaning is communicated, and so is the focus of analysis.

Sociological institutionalism (SI) makes many contributions drawn on in this research. It focuses on both micro- and macro- levels of analysis and reinforces the co-constitutive effect of institutions and actors.[9] SI frames institutions as reflecting actors' and societies' understandings of 'the way the world works'.[10] It analyses not only formal rules and processes, but symbols, cognitive scripts, and moral guides that provide 'frames of meaning' that influence human behaviour.[11] Actors within institutions are seen to follow a 'logic of appropriateness', prescribing acceptable forms of behaviour and well-worn paths of action.[12]

Historical institutionalism (HI) has also contributed much to FI and this research, particularly to the meso-level of understanding. HI focuses on 'real world' questions surrounding politics and history, viewing institutions as historical legacies of past struggles, and formal and informal rules. HI tends to see institutions as path dependent—once made, there are limited options for how institutions may change, evolve, and adapt.[13] Given the overwhelmingly gendered nature of institutional history, HI perspectives are enormously valuable in FI research.

Lastly, NI provides many salient contributions to the FI theoretical framework, presenting a more contemporaneous, 'new' institutional lens for research. However, a core contribution of FI is the explicit and specific focus on viewing and seeking to understand institutions as gendered. This was a major gap of past theory, which saw rational actors as genderless (or male), and institutions as blank, gender-neutral slates with equal effect on woman as on men. FI and its theorists therefore push further than prior gender-neutral or gender-blind analyses, to consider how institutions are gendered, which has effects on all the salient themes they seek to analyse: including, of course, power.[14]

As Mackay, Kenny, and Chappell note, 'to say that an institution is gendered means that constructions of masculinity and femininity are intertwined in the daily life or logic' of its actions.[15] The term 'institution' does not refer solely to an organisation, agency, or department, but also to the underlying system of rules that constitute daily life and human interaction. Institutions are stable, recurring operating systems that both prescribe and proscribe actions and sanctions—determining what behaviours are accepted, and what are not. Not only do these rules guide human behaviour, but humans have a co-constitutive effect on them. Thus, Chappell[16] recognises that both agents and structures are relevant to the study of power and politics, unlike previous studies that may have preferenced the importance of agents over structures, or vice versa. Rarely are gendered structures the result solely of top-down movements of power. Rather, gendered structures represent a complicated dance between actors and institutions that requires holistic and methodical explanation.

In defining institutions, Leach and Lowndes remind us that 'actors do not always follow rules, but they do know when they have broken them'.[17] Lowndes advocates for mapping patterns of behaviour to understand formal and informal 'rules of the game'.[18] She notes that they have five commonalities, being: specific to particular political or governmental settings; recognised by actors, even if not adhered to; collective in their effect; subject to some kind of third-party enforcement, even if this enforcement is informal; and are able to be described or explained to the researcher. From this understanding, institutions operate to constrain or enable certain actions, following a 'logic of appropriateness' that not only guides behaviour, but also whose behaviour is deemed appropriate.[19] There is an obvious association of rules with the formal—such as policies prescribing behaviour or laws with enforceable sanctions when breached. Yet rules are also associated with the informal—beliefs, norms, and practices, which may not be found in a rulebook or policy paper, but are still enforceable, and still have a marked effect on behaviour.[20] Andrew[21] notes that the formal is often founded on informal norms-based practices. While informal or hidden rules (often causing covert forms of discrimination and bias) have regularly been overlooked in the measurement and attainment of gender equality,[22] they do nonetheless have a considerable impact on women's underrepresentation and wider experiences of inequality.

FI offers insights into how institutions might encourage greater levels of women's representation,[23] how actors might devise their own strategies and tactics to make change,[24] and how positive cultural and gender changes within organisations might be resisted or obstructed.[25] Kenny[26] demonstrates that formal institutional reforms have proved powerful in increasing women's participation in politics. Yet formal rules do not always translate consistently to an informal level, which has resulted in the erosion and drift of policy implementation, particularly given that candidate selection in Kenny's research was 'largely guided by informal practices'.[27] Kenny notes that in Scottish political institutions, gendered change was often 'nested' within pre-existing, 'old' structures. Kenny's work is important for this research on gender in international affairs, as much focus within international institutions remains on what formal policies have changed, rather than what informal gendered rules remain within the old norms of behaviour. The growing focus on informal institutions in the literature is significant to this research, as international representation remains largely assessed accordingly to operational needs and 'who you owe favours to, rather than your skills', as one observer noted.[28]

Waylen[29] identifies how actors can either adjust collective expectations to new frameworks (such as gendered culture change) or stymie and distort the intended impact of that reform. She highlights four core ways in which institutions can change: displacement, drift, layering, and conversion. While displacement involves the wholesale replacement of old rules with new, this is an uncommon gender change strategy, usually because it relies on the absence of a strong veto, and rarely do those seeking to make change have the requisite power to instil change fully. Drift is generally not a chosen strategy that actors employ to enact change because it relies on slow-moving changes in an external environment that give institutions new meaning. Waylen notes that 'drift might be used where changes in wider societal norms and practices, combined with gaps in existing rules, facilitate the nonenforcement (turning a "blind eye") of some rules ... rather than their replacement'.[30]

On the other hand, layering and conversion are often witnessed in institutional change. Layering refers to the layering of new institutions on top of already existing ones. While layering is an important part of institutional change, Waylen notes that often actors do not wield sufficient power to enact the gendered change sought, which results in conversion—whereby actors exploit ambiguities in rules to get the outcomes they desire. Conversion can prove beneficial in influencing gendered change particularly where one group (women) may be systematically underpowered. Yet conversion also highlights inherent risks in attempting gendered change without having the formal power needed. All four methods of gendered change highlight the fact that institutional change is complex. Further, in the most successful cases, it is dependent on the power, endurance and will of critical actors.

Critical actors are those who have the requisite power and ability to influence change. However, critical actors have dual roles, not just championing gendered change, but also challenging or rejecting it. Thomson[31] highlights how critical actors may stymy the introduction of progressive gender legislation or resist gendered change. She notes that key individuals worked to preserve the status quo when it came to restrictive abortion laws in Northern Ireland, explicitly pushing back against any proposed change in legislation. These individuals came from across ethnic and ideological groups, demonstrating that sites of resistance are often multisituational and driven by different motivations, even though united in resistance. Thomson notes that these critical actors were typically more conservative in their approach. This finding has consistencies for actors in international affairs, particularly given that diplomatic and national security agencies are generally risk-averse, noted for their culture of conservativism.[32] Thomson's findings highlight that while critical actors can be important to ensuring that change happens, they can also be crucial for ensuring that change *does not* happen—often with the latter occurring over the former.

Analysis of formal policies delineate the institutional contexts within which women work, as well as how these institutions change or resist change. This is canvassed through the literature review and history and background sections of this book. Yet because Chappell argues that there is a gendered logic of appropriateness, whereby 'the masculine ideal usually dominates political and legal settings', studying the informal institutions is also key to analysis.[33] Narratives and observation, as sought through the in-depth interviews conducted in this research, provide an important source of insight into informal institutions. Narrative allows us to focus not only on what is said, but unsaid—'inaction, silences, and lacunae'.[34] The attention to both actors and institutions, and both formal and informal rules, then enables us to understand how 'even the most well-designed formal gender equality rules, such as efforts to increase the number of women in the public sector, often fail to produce their intended effects'.[35]

Examining the *unintended effects* of institutional change is therefore a task often left underanalysed. Even so, some literature does advocate for understanding whether instead of 'new' pro-gender equality policies are having a positive or neutral effect, they are having a negative effect for women leaders. Hudson and Leidl found that in the US State Department and USAID, 'gender programming requirements had become a thoughtless box-checking exercise that did not, in the end, help women'.[36] This is a key concern of some scholars— that governance feminism (the installation of feminists and feminist ideas into legal-institutional power) overlooks the background conditions, distributional effects, and unintended consequences of legal and policy reforms regarding women's violence and oppression.[37] Some have repeatedly argued that we cannot just add women or other minority groups to see a change in foreign policy.[38] Indeed, the data to date would suggest that this simplistic equation fails to produce a simplistic result.

Further, True notes that there is an assumption that changing gendered norms and rules are 'good things', stating that 'gender balance in state decision-making and women's presence as UN peacekeepers are emerging regulatory norms . . . that are expected to promote more democratic, transparent, and less corrupt government and to civilise international peacekeeping thus bringing about greater peace and security'.[39] Halley et al.[40] argue that our understanding of policy and institutional change must be distributional. True[41] presses feminist IR scholars to question whether new gender norms and rules (even those aimed at gender equality) should be promoted, given that it is exactly the presence of *old* norms and practices that have been known to harm women. This is a sentiment echoed by Keohane, who notes, 'we should not assume that the consequences in international relations of more egalitarian practices within some societies will necessarily be benign'.[42] An end goal of FI and this research may be emancipatory and seek to positively change conditions for women *and* the field, yet such aspirations should also be undertaken with care. As True[43] notes, having observed the harmful effects and difficulty in fighting against hegemonic masculinity and femininity, feminists have been, and should be, cautious about recommending the normalisation of any gender-specific behaviour.

Summarising some of the above FI theory to date highlights that (a) institutions can be seen as 'gendered' and (b) FI theory can be used to understand how institutions change or reject change in gender relations. It also highlights cautions and limitations of FI research, and the need to pay close attention to what is researched, found, and even advocated for. Research to date has covered contexts ranging from representation in politics, to women's experiences in international organisations, and the acceptance or rejection of gender-inclusive or feminist policy in government. It has looked at both formal institutions (policies, rules, laws) as well as a growing field around informal institutions (processes, norms, behaviours, and 'unwritten rules') that combine to create regimes of (in)equality in organisations, politics, and society. The literature highlights FI's many uses and provides templates and examples of ways the theory can be applied, which set this book up to provide its core contributions.

In particular, this book draws borrows from FI theory to unpack key policies, processes, norms, and behaviours, and leans on existing research in international contexts. Yet the book also contributes to three key gaps in FI theory as I see it to date. This includes more thoroughly incorporating intersectionality into FI theory, pioneering an intersectional feminist institutional (IFI) approach that is currently missed by sole or siloed focus on gender to the exclusion of all else, or a focus on other aspects of identity to the exclusion of gender.

A second core gap remains around understanding the layering of gendered institutions. In previous research, studies have often focused on the layering of pro-gender institutions (rules, norms, etc.) on top of each other to create more favourable operating environments for women. This is a valid and important aspect of research; however, layering also applies in the reverse: how sexist and gendered institutions may be layered to create less favourable environments for women, as well as how such regressive institutions may be layered and duplicated across multiple contexts, with previous research often focused on one limited country or social and political context. This leaves open a gap: understanding how gendered institutions operate when women's workplaces are multilayered and multidimensional, as is the case for international affairs agencies that operate headquarters in one context, and diplomatic missions and postings in another.

Thirdly, there is potential to expand FI theory to better understand how inequalities evolve during institutional change. Given the state of many political and social institutions globally, which are undergoing complex changes induced by technology, the COVID-19 pandemic, impending climate changes, and de- and re-democratisation, among other challenges, being able to account for how gendered institutions change, evolve, and adapt is a core growing need in research. These three core gaps in FI research as I see it are explored next and are key contributions of this book.

Over time, much theory across IR and FI has remained largely blind to the intersections of race, sexuality, class, disability (and so on) as they combine with gender. In response, intersectionality was first coined and problematised by Kimberlé Crenshaw[44] to denote how gender, race, class, and other systems of oppression combine to shape experiences and privilege. Some research has attempted to study the intersectional ways in which institutions operate. For instance, Kantola and Lombardo[45] found that feminist theorising of gender and politics reproduces its own hegemonies and marginalisations, whilst Hawkesworth[46] argued that US congress is both raced and gendered and Verloo et al.[47] examine the intersectional approaches in Belgium and the Netherland to find that compartmentalised thinking about inequalities still reigns in practice. However, few studies have analysed intersectionality under a united institutional framework, and most have relied on one element of intersectionality over another, often to the exclusion of understanding the layered nature of institutions.

Emerging researchers are attempting to fix this gap in applying intersectional analyses to institutionalist or feminist institutionalist approaches, such as Krook and Nugent, who conducted research on women and ethnic minorities in the British Labor Party. They argued that combining intersectionality with the insights of feminist institutionalism enables understanding of formal and informal rules, practices, and norms that 'are both gendered and raced'.[48] In doing so, they forge an 'intersectional institutional' lens to understand multiple axes of discrimination.[49] They argue for this approach to address the single axis thinking that predominates in gender or race research.

However, intersectionality as a field of research mainly arose from the narrowness and failings of feminism to consider more than just white women's experiences, developing out of critical race studies to unpack the interconnection of gender and race and other systems that oppress or allow privilege. In other words, intersectionality is inextricably tied to feminism—and remains so. Therefore, without interlinking intersectionality and feminism, (1) intersectionality on its own reduces individuals to specific demographic factors, which (2) may lead to an inability to identify common causes of oppression.[50] To divorce intersectionality from feminism fails to do justice to either analysis: you cannot have feminism without intersectionality, and to seek to understand intersectionality without feminism ignores some of the most basic and common underlying causes of oppression.

What may fit better therefore is an intersectional feminist institutionalist (IFI) framework—a framework crafted through this book that draws on Krook and Nugent's first approaches to mesh the two theories. Yet it goes beyond their dualistic approach to explicitly centre gender, whilst being sympathetic to and inclusive of other factors like race and so on. This better allows us to concentrate on gender as a category of analysis without being blind to other axes of inequality, enabling researchers to understand how institutions are not only gendered, but heteronormative, ableist, classed, raced and so on, with institutions having a compounding effect on women from diverse backgrounds.[51]

This also fits with Krizsan et al.'s book *Institutionalising Intersectionality*, which found that whilst 'there is scope for the implementation of new intersectional practices . . . this will require a more embedded intersectional thinking . . . than is apparent to date'.[52] Intersectional *feminism* must remain central to analysis, to produce the most robust analysis and findings. This addresses anxieties that a 'multiple equalities' agenda may undermine rather than facilitate gender justice, whilst also lending the strength that gender equality movements are gaining to other forms of equality and justice.[53]

Why the IFI approach matters to international affairs is then simple. Women from culturally and linguistically diverse (CALD) and sexually diverse backgrounds often experience higher rates of marginalisation, silencing, and discrimination,[54] and the diplomatic field is one with specific scripts around class, inclusion, and exclusion.[55] It is widely acknowledged that the gender pay gap when combined with the racial pay gap results in a specific experience for women of colour.[56] Ableism combines with gender inequalities to increase the prevalence of violence and sexual harassment against women with disabilities.[57] Queer women work at the intersection of both gendered and heteronormative and at times heterosexist institutions.[58] Ultimately, as Krizsan et al. 2012 note, there is 'growing complexity in the institutional arrangements designed to address inequalities'.[59] To ignore these nuances is to ignore the state of the real world and its effects on women who are myriad in their diversity. Just as we cannot assume that institutions are gender neutral, we cannot assume that gendered institutions are not also raced, heterosexist, or otherwise.

FI analyses to date have not just struggled with analysing the layering of different kinds of inequality (racial, gender, so on), as an IFI approach would seek to address. FI approaches have also struggled to analyse the layering of the same kinds of regressive policies, practices, and rules on top of each other. This is another underresearched element considered in this book. Whilst the concept of institutional 'layering' has been used to understand the layering of progressive gender equality policies and rules on top of pre-existing rules,[60] there remains a gap for conceptualising the layering of *regressive* institutions. Given the complex and multidimensional contexts in which gendered institutions operate, applying the concept of layering to understand multiple sites of regressive rules, norms, and institutions could be of major benefit to theory. It could also help in addressing issues of causal complexity, the idea that social phenomena is often the result of different, sometimes overlapping, combinations of conditions.[61] Discovering and outlining the layering of regressive institutions across contexts or sites could prove revealing for understanding the interrelated nature of formal and informal gendered institutions—a recognised site of further desired research.[62] This concept of layering will be explored throughout this book, as a key part of understanding the gendered institutions at work in international affairs. It represents another major contribution to the FI and IR literature, as well as providing insight into the gender complexity of other fields of heavily internationalised work.

Finally, the durability and 'stickiness' of institutions has remained a core concern of FI and this research that warrants further investigation. Contributors to Waylen's book[63] *Gender and Informal Institutions* highlight that while formal institutions may change, informal institutions in particular are frequently defined by their stability, 'stickiness', and endurance.[64] The durability of institutions remains a core concern of this research. However, recognising gaps and spaces of institutional malleability, Cornut[65] argues that rather than viewing the diplomatic practices of international affairs—practices that are often more informal, than formalised—as fixed and inflexible, they are more fluid. This fits along the lines of Zygmunt Bauman's[66] notions of liquid modernity, whereby he argues that structures and institutions (formal and informal) are somewhat less stable. Institutional durability and change is therefore perhaps best summed up by North, who notes that institutions have a 'tenacious survival ability'.[67] This survival ability does not preclude institutions from change, although it does suggest that enduring threads of continuity remain. In the context of this research, I draw both from concepts of instability and stability to argue that gendered institutions in international affairs endure through adaptation. Inequalities evolve as institutions change. I will return to this central theme throughout the book, as well as these three gaps in FI theory in the development of the theoretical frameworks later in this chapter.

Situating Intersectional Feminist Institutional within the Field of IR

Few FI analyses exist in the field of international relations (IR), yet their approaches fit comfortably within it—both remain focused on power relations. Within IR, as late as the mid-1980s, women were invisible and feminist scholarship was largely excluded from discourse, which Pettman identifies was a 'normalised absence'.[68] Until recent decades, 'gender was not considered a relevant or useful analytical category in IR'.[69] Now, feminist analyses of IR are increasingly mainstream within the discipline. Following the seminal work of Charlesworth, Chinkin, and Wright,[70] Tickner,[71] and Enloe,[72] scholars and advocates have increasingly drawn attention to and explored the relationship between women's rights and the opportunities offered by international law, policy, and relations. Feminists have highlighted links between masculinity and power in international relations,[73] characterising states as like humans—with the weaker more often associated with the feminine.[74] IR theorists, from realist and liberal perspectives, have also concerned themselves with questions around differences in actions and influence between male and female actors, as well as what are the dynamics of women's roles in international organisations and international decision-making.[75] Neo-institutionalist sociology and constructivist IR approaches that centre on the rise and diffusion of norms have gained traction in the literature, which has remained historically dominated by rational and materialistic perspectives of what gets done and how.[76] Theoretical questions across the IR spectrum require much-needed empirical evidence, and both studies on gender in international affairs and FI theoretical approaches remain marginalised within the field.

In existing studies globally, the status of women in this this field has been analysed from United States perspectives (for example, Morin;[77] Shoemaker and Poire;[78] Shoemaker and Park[79]), European perspectives (for example, Aggestam and Towns;[80] Towns and Niklasson;[81] Niskanen and Nyberg[82]), and increasingly perspectives from Brazil (for example, Farias and do Carmo[83]), Indonesia (for example, Dewi and Rachmawati[84]), Japan (for example, Flowers[85]), and Turkey (for example, Rumelili and Suleymanoglu-Kurum[86]) among others. Per such studies, the status of women is far from ideal, with women marginalised not only within the field of diplomacy, but also within the scholarly field studying it.[87] Chappell[88] begins to apply FI theory to international organisations, such as the International Criminal Court, and Rossetti[89] begins to apply feminist neo-institutionalism to Australian diplomacy, with other studies drawing on institutionalist literature to understand gender, race and diplomacy. Yet the application of FI theory to wider IR and diplomacy studies remains an opportunity for further research. This is a site where this book makes significant contributions, particularly in applying FI theory across multiple intersecting international affairs agencies.

Scholarship internationally includes studies of gender in individual Ministries of Foreign Affairs (MFAs) and within diplomacy more broadly (see for instance: Crapol;[90] Jeffrey-Jones;[91] Neumann;[92] McGlen and Sarkees[93]). Since Morin[94] studied 50 years of US Foreign Service envoys, repeated studies have found that women have been posted to less significant posts, often in lower status positions and lower priority countries. Towns and Niklasson's[95] pioneering research analysed almost 7,000 ambassadorial appointments globally to test whether similar patterns of gender segregation exist as in other institutions. They found that 85 per cent of the world's ambassadors are men, and that female ambassadors are less likely to occupy high-status ambassadorships than their male colleagues. They acknowledge that women are reaching leadership in international affairs, particularly in ambassadorial and diplomatic positions, yet they confirm that women's prospects for leadership are worse than men's, and that diplomatic communities continue to reproduce the link between men and power that is predominant in IR. While their study does not cover why the patterns continue despite the abolition of many discriminatory practices, and rise in gender equality initiatives globally, this is a crucial next question this book helps understand.

Towns and Niklasson's global comparison of gender in diplomacy is joined by other comparative studies, including their own of women's representation to militarised and violent countries,[96] Niskanen and Nyberg's[97] comparative case study of women in MFAs in Norway, Denmark, Finland, and Iceland, and Bashevkin's[98] comparison of foreign policy leaders in the US. Yet very few studies address international representation across different aspects of diplomatic leadership, moving away from studies solely of MFAs, or 'big picture' comparison.[99] McGlen and Sarkees's[100] study remains one of the most important studies on this topic, presenting critical insights into the lives and experiences of foreign policy 'insiders' across the US Defense and State Department. Drawing on Duerst-Lahti[101] and Powell,[102] they claim that research must look at three different variables affecting individuals in organisations: societal, organisational, and individual factors. These elements are combined into the theoretical framework developed later in the chapter and build on the gap in FI identified earlier: the underresearch phenomenon of how gendered institutions (rules, norms, behaviours, practices) are layered across sites or contexts, which is particularly relevant for international affairs research.

Other gaps that become clear from the literature is that while MFAs might lead and coordinate a country's international relations, they are dependent on the working of multiple international-facing government agencies and their representatives, which highlights the need to capture new and rising forms of diplomatic action, including police-led and defence-led diplomacy. In fact, while research on defence diplomacy is growing, the research appears to have entirely overlooked the gendered dimensions of defence, policing and other forms of state diplomats or envoys. Yet increasingly international affairs is the responsibility of myriad international-facing or internationalising departments—leaders across politics, diplomacy, security, trade, policing, immigration, border protection, business, and education. In Australia, this is reflective of interdependencies within the core executive of government, as well as the globalisation and technological changes, and is not a trend isolated to Australia.[103] As researchers have extended work on women's representation to male-dominated arenas of diplomacy, so this book seeks to extend it further beyond MFAs to demonstrate consistencies across a broader set of international affairs leadership. This is crucial, as globalisation continues to relentlessly transform historically domestic agencies to ones increasingly internationalised. Ultimately, the application of FI approaches to IR and to this study of international affairs agencies therefore fills multiple gaps: the paucity of cross-comparative research on gender and diplomacy; the paucity of research across different institutions in international affairs beyond the MFA; and the layering of gendered rules and institutions across contexts.

Gendered Nature of Diplomacy, National Security, and International Affairs

Rosetti notes that diplomacy is both a primary international institution, and one that has largely been considered within the IR field as 'gender neutral' despite evidence to the contrary.[104] By seeking to understand individuals working at the front end of international affairs, the gendered nature of diplomacy is a principal concern of this research. Connell finds, 'gender, like other social structures, is multi-dimensional; it is not just about identity, or just about work, or just about power, or just about sexuality, but all of these things at once'.[105] To speak of diplomacy (in both its specific application and more broad understanding across international-facing agencies) as 'gendered' then refers to the fact that like other aspects of our lives, diplomacy operates within specifically gendered understandings and constructs, with access to power and resources often dependent on, or influenced by, gender. Considering the historic literature to date, this could not be more true.

One of IR's pre-eminent theorists, Francis Fukuyama, notes that pursuing women's inclusion in international politics will make states weaker, arguing that 'as women gain power in these countries... [they] should become less aggressive, adventurous, competitive, and violent'.[106] Women's exclusion from decision-making in IR is justified by the perception that women are a 'security risk',[107] with 'international relations... such a thoroughly masculine sphere of activity that women's voices are considered *inauthentic*'.[108] When Neumann[109] speaks of diplomats as the 'hero', he also argues that these conceptions are deeply gendered, with the diplomatic and hero script best filled by the traditional male civil servant.

Until recently, the Foreign Service, as well as security spheres typically within the military, remained patriarchal strongholds as the most male-dominated spheres within the state.[110] Enloe[111] notes that men are presumed to be the diplomats, and Tickner states that women's leadership has historically been constrained by the widely held belief 'that military and foreign policy are arenas of policy-making least appropriate for women'.[112] Women have historically remained underrepresented for every period in which we have studied the topic.[113] While women occasionally served in formal diplomatic roles, particularly when royal courts reigned supreme, their influence is documented largely through their informal representation.

During the nineteenth and twentieth centuries, the focus of diplomacy became more professionalised and bureaucratised.[114] During this period, women's exclusion from international affairs became deeply institutionalised—'women were expressly and officially barred as a sex from holding diplomatic positions'.[115] Within security agencies, women were completely barred from combat positions, and, where they were found, was generally within gender-segregated units (during war times) that at times have been dismantled completely (post-war).

Eagly and Karau[116] argue that the domination of men within specific fields of work effects the tendency to attribute gender characteristics to those roles and occupations. Correlating with men's historic dominance within most roles in international diplomacy and security, IR leadership is generally associated with masculinised attributes. For instance, Ticker notes that 'strength, power, autonomy, independence, and rationality... [are the] characteristics we most value in those whom we entrust the conduct of our foreign policy and the defence of our national interest'.[117] Boyce and Herd find that 'the underlying stereotypical perceptions of leadership in the military are masculine in nature', stereotypes also extended to policing and enforcement.[118] Even those fields now perceived as more humanitarian and 'soft', such as immigration, remain to exhibit hypermasculine stereotypes around enforcement, judgement, and protection. Stereotyping, assumptions, and expectations about the gender 'appropriateness' therefore infiltrates many fields of work, with role congruity theory or social role theory highlighting that women are likely to be employed in relatively low status positions, with lower opportunity for advancement, and perceived lower levels of achievement and competence. Eagly and Karau note that role congruity influences: '(a) perceiving women less favourably than men as potential occupants of leadership roles and (b) evaluating behaviour that fulfils the prescription of a leader role less favourably when it is enacted by a woman'.[119]

Building from Enloe's findings of international affairs as a world deeply guided by norms of masculinity, Neumann[120] notes that differing masculinities also exist within a hierarchy in diplomacy. In this way, hegemonic masculinity[121] both legitimises men's dominant position in the field and justifies subordination of women and men along lines of gender, as well as ethnicity, sexuality, ability, and class. Masculinities and femininities that do not conform to the hegemon are likely to experience differential treatment based on whether their identity is perceived as 'legitimate' or not. As Krook and Mackay note, 'constructions of masculinity and femininity are intertwined in the daily culture or 'logic' of political institutions', influencing accepted and appropriate behaviours in the field, as well as 'who' can occupy the field.[122]

In characterising identity within diplomacy, Neumann's work *The Body of the Diplomat* found that women represented two different femininities and hierarchies for understanding their roles: 'as a diplomat that happens to be a woman' and 'as a woman who happens to be a diplomat'.[123] Neumann asserts that these characterisations are due to inherent tensions between the status of being a 'woman' and a 'diplomat', and that women felt they had to make a strategic choice to identify and privilege one status over another. Neumann found that there were hefty career costs associated with identifying as women-first-diplomat-second, as it reproduced stereotypes and was 'professionally wasted and even counterproductive'.[124] Neumann also notes that 'given that general social discourse operates on a hierarchical principle with males being privileged, the woman-first-diplomat-next confirms and perpetuates that hierarchy, to her own loss as well as to the loss of women who embody other femininities'.[125]

As Tickner states, 'so long as women are seen—by politicians, career diplomats, media editors, and other women—first and foremost as wives, the sexist barriers will remain high and the normalisation of masculinized diplomacy will remain entrenched'.[126] Yet in the past, Sawer[127] notes that early

Australian women politicians were expected to identify as woman-first-job-next. Sawer notes of these women, 'their first commitment was to traditional gender roles in the home, and... housekeeping the state could only come later and never at the expense of the primary role'.[128] This places women's identity in a bind. For those who identified as diplomat-first-woman-next, costs still existed as 'making male diplomats your circle of recognition and insisting that as a diplomat, you are just the same as the boys, means to accept playing and being umpired on terms that are masculine, and so not your own'.[129]

Edwards et al. sum up the implications of this in the Australian Public Service context:

> Two factors at work crystallized around the commitment of women to their families: either women choose to place a priority on their family responsibilities over the demands of their career or assumptions are made about their reliability, availability and/or commitment. In both cases, [women] miss out on opportunities to take-on challenging and high profile work, which is needed to develop their experience and reputation to progress their careers.[130]

In US and EU-based research on women in international affairs careers, workplace culture for women in government agencies has changed for the better, and there are more women in leadership.[131] However, women often do not get the support they need, and organisational environments are experienced differently for male and female staff. Though women's representation has improved over time, social isolation continues, and women possess weaker professional networks that are important for career progression and insider knowledge on specific tasks and responsibilities.[132] Women are still excluded from widely evidenced 'old boys clubs' and networks that are depended on for information, rumours, social support, and assistance for new jobs or postings. Neumann[133] also noted that once tokenism had given way to mass recruitment of women into international representations, homosocial interaction increased, to the exclusion of women. This is not helped by the fact that women are often horizontally segregated, restricting them to particular policy portfolios.[134]

If we understand institutions as difficult to change,[135] historic accounts of women in diplomacy and international organisations should provide an apt background for contemporary gendered rules as explored in this research. Morin's[136] study analysing 50 years of US Foreign Service envoys is one such critical study and demonstrates diplomacy's reliance on the unpaid labour of diplomatic spouses. She found that women ambassadors often had to hire extra help to enable them to complete their diplomatic duties—such as hosting events and functions which were traditionally the role of the 'trailing spouse'. This work, although unpaid, was (and remains) expected as part of the 'package' of being the partner (traditionally, the wife) of a diplomat.[137] As a result, one of Morin's most interesting findings was that women ambassadors lack a 'wife'. Women with wives will be explored more later in this book.

Morin also asserted that gender makes little difference to women's leadership in the Foreign Service, which contrasts much of the literature since then and even some of her own findings. Morin found that women political appointees were more likely to have children and be in priority postings, as opposed to women career diplomats who were generally posted in lower priority posts, and of whom almost none had children—a deliberate choice made 'convinced they could not have both'.[138] Despite the assertion by Morin that gender makes little difference in diplomatic practice, the diplomatic practice had considerable effects on women's career and family options.

The language used by Morin and her participants also reveals gendered 'rules of the game'—what is required to be an international representative. Morin mentions that the women were 'good athletes', had 'high energy', 'reported being tomboys' as children, had prevailing physical and moral 'courage', were 'risk takers', and 'pragmatic' in their decision-making.[139] Morin also notes that her participants were taller than the national female average and attractive—'good brains went along with good physical endowments'—a statement which reflects the researcher's perspective at the time as much as the field's.[140] In Morin's study, the more masculine attributes of the women studied come into focus, reinforcing links between leadership and masculine archetypes, as studied by Rost.[141] One woman devised 'a black evening costume that closely resembled formal male attire, with a long black skirt in place of trousers, so as to be less conspicuous at diplomatic functions'.[142] Another woman was widely disregarded both within her own service and her host country (who were reportedly humiliated by being sent a woman ambassador) as she was 'the antithesis of the soft-spoken, subservient woman then admired'.[143] These messages reinforce a pattern of masculinised attributes being associated with diplomacy, and that, where a woman's identity is permitted, it should be in the form of the archetypical *subservient* woman.

The 'genderlessness' of women in diplomacy or their categorisation as a 'third gender' is also a theme that features throughout the literature and data. One of McGlen and Sarkees's participants state:

> The ladies I speak to about it, say if they can be regarded as a third sex or something they can get by in the Middle East. Because that's the only way. If they are regarded

as women, then men in those countries go to put them off somewhere. And they can't be regarded as men, so they have to be regarded as something else present in the discussion.[144]

This will be revisited in later chapters.

Overall, Rossetti[145] argues that the growing number of women entering the Foreign Service is beginning to challenge the gendered nature of diplomatic and security leadership. Yet as Cassidy[146] notes, that there is no steady upward trajectory, nor no single experience women share once they enter the diplomatic realm globally. The literature on women's experiences in international affairs agencies to date therefore highlights opportunities for this book to contribute to more up-to-date data on women's representation, as well as accounts of women's experiences and how international institutions are changing as more women crack the diplomatic glass ceiling. To this end, this book provides a wealth of new data on gender in the international affairs institutions of Australia.

Locating Gender in Australian International Affairs Agencies

The rapid prioritisation of women in Australian foreign policy—and gains made—warrant further investigation of what is known and still left unknown. Like much of the world, a gender imbalance exists in Australian international affairs, with women remaining underrepresented at senior levels across virtually all sectors in Australia.[147] This is nothing new. Australia recruited its first women diplomats in 1943, six years after the first Australian overseas representation was established in its own right in 1937.[148] Yet the Marriage Bar restricted women's potential advancement until it was abolished in 1966—coincidentally making it the first Western foreign service to lift the bar.[149] The bar required that married women were to only be employed as temporary staff, often meaning that they had no means to accumulate superannuation or experience to count towards promotion. In many cases, it forced women to resign on marriage, and during APS downsizing in the 1950s, resulted in the retrenchment of many women before men. Towns and Niklasson state of this phenomena globally: 'While the formal Marriage Bar on female diplomats may have been lifted in most states, in practice, the combination of life as a Foreign Service officer and marriage (especially with children) continues to be particularly problematic for women'.[150]

The shortage of men on the home front during World War II allowed new opportunities for women to serve in war bureaucracies. At this time, the Women's Auxiliary Australian Air Force (WAAAF) was formed (1940), as well as the Australian Women's Army Service (AWAS, 1941) and Women's Royal Naval Service (WRANS, 1942). Women's recruitment as diplomats followed in 1943. Like women's largescale entrance into the workforce during the Wars, World War II also provided many opportunities for Indigenous, black and ethnic minority representation in some countries. In the United States (US), women and African Americans gathered intelligence on behalf of the US, whilst in Australia, despite not having citizenship status, thousands of Aboriginal and Torres Strait Islander people served in the Australian Defence Forces from the 1860s (and possibly earlier).[151] Even so, like the gendered exclusions witnessed elsewhere in international affairs, racialised norms, beliefs, and practices are evident.

These early efforts were followed by periods of little to no recruitment of women across international affairs, and it was a period where women faced various forms of discrimination, as well as horizontal segregation into 'soft' policy areas such as human rights, cultural relations, human resources, administrative and consular work.[152] Diplomatic experts at the time called for the need to recruit the 'very best men available', with the service in the capital noted as 'privileged', 'competitive', and dependent on the strength of personalities to drive the post-war international agenda.[153] Many international postings were deemed unsuitable for women based on safety or strategic reasons, with leading male Australian political figures securing most international deployments.[154] McGlen and Sarkees talk about the 'evidence' used to keep women from foreign political posts, such as 'the cultural stereotypes of other nations'—a notion that has, until recently, continued to hold sway.[155] In 1973, six years after the Marriage Bar was lifted, women received equal pay under law, flexible working hours and paid maternity leave, which helped remove other barriers to women's advancement. It was not until recent decades that many of the affirmative action policies and gender strategies were embedded across government—and equal pay remains as abstract now as it was almost 50 years ago.

The sector is not small, though, and women's roles not meagre. Australian Public Service (APS) employment accounts for over 242,000 jobs, 60.4 per cent of which are now occupied by women.[156] Equality is explicitly part of Australia's international mandates, including the supporting of human rights, gender equality, democratic principles and the rule of law, international security, and open and transparent global markets.[157] Additionally, the principle of 'merit' is significant to APS appointments, underpinned by legislation and deeply engrained in decisions surrounding recruitment and progression.

Like more global constructions of merit, merit in Australia is typically understood as gender neutral. Yet merit has specific implications, especially in public service, assuming that 'those with the requisite training, experience, and personal motivation will succeed in a meritocratic society, while those who fall behind have only themselves to blame'.[158] In Australian journalist Annabel Crabb's 2021 TV Show *Ms Represented*—dedicated to telling the stories of Australia's foremost female political leaders—Margaret Reynolds, a former senator, comments that merit is 'something than men invented when women came on the scene'.[159] Whilst clearly social commentary, a critical appraisal of merit, its origins, and its applications is warranted. Pre-eminent Australian researcher and government advisor on merit and promotion in the workplace, Clare Burton, presented cornerstone research on merit in Australia in 1988. She found that not only is merit subjectively assessed, but also 'that men are perceived to be more able, to have more natural ability in a range of areas, than women'.[160] This issue remains three decades later.[161] Simpson, Ross-Smith and Lewis agree, stating that 'formal procedures based in merit can "hide" or justify difference in outcomes and cannot guarantee gender-based "fairness" . . . This may be because formal procedures may be circumvented by informal practices'.[162] This reinforces how informal norms and processes within organisations can derail meritocratic outcomes and the formal processes of merit. It also highlights gaps in understanding how ideas of merit and achievement are perpetuated in international affairs agencies.

Empirical studies of women in international affairs remain marginalised and infrequent within the Australian context, except for a few recent book chapters, interviews, and studies (see Westendorf and Strating;[163] Lowy Institute;[164] Stephenson;[165] Rossetti;[166] Conley Tyler;[167] Conley Tyler et al. 2014;[168] Harris Rimmer;[169] Hewitt;[170] Shepherd and True[171]). Melissa Conley Tyler, Emily Blizzard, and Bridget Crane begin to explore Australia's 'missing' women in international affairs in their 2014 paper, presenting important pre-cursor research to this. They debunk theories that women are less motivated[172] or lack interest in 'hard' international affairs.[173] Instead, they offer four reasons for the continued underrepresentation of women in leadership: direct discrimination, indirect discrimination, family commitments and socially constructed gender roles.

Firstly, direct discrimination includes historic institutions such as the Marriage Bar and other practices that normalised bias and discrimination against women, particularly prior to the institution of anti-discrimination legislation. This direct discrimination has resulted in 'women who today would have acquired the necessary seniority, experience and qualifications to occupy senior positions in international affairs' being lost to the field.[174] Historical discrimination has a legacy effect on institutions globally today.

Secondly, indirect discrimination is the result of laws, policies or programmes that are seemingly gender-neutral, but have gendered effects. Indirect discrimination may persist due to a failure to recognise women and men's different experiences. This is evident in the Australian Federal Police (AFP), where the 2016 *Cultural Change: Gender Diversity and Inclusion in the Australian Federal Police* review found that women have different experiences to their male counterparts, despite men's belief that their experiences were the same.[175] DFAT's *Women in Leadership Strategy* also notes that 'the department's culture constrains women's choices and is not applying the merit principle fully or making the most of its talent', which aligns with Burton's findings on merit.[176]

Indirect discrimination may also be the result of informal power structures within departments. Embassy Magazine's analysis of foreign diplomats internationally found that 87 per cent of respondents agreed when asked whether diplomacy was a man's world.[177] Within the AFP, women experienced difficulties 'fitting in' to the male-dominated organisational culture, feeling pressure to 'prove themselves' in a sexualised environment.[178] Over half of women in male-dominated departments that were identified in *Not Yet 50/50: Barriers to the Progress of Senior Women in the Australian Public Service*, felt excluded from informal networks important for career progression.[179] 'Boys clubs' and similar informal exclusionary networks can be particularly challenging within the field of international affairs due to the dominance of masculine norms within the field.[180] Further, Conley Tyler, Blizzard, and Crane find that 'where senior managers and decision-makers share group characteristics— typically white, Anglo-Celtic, heterosexual, able-bodied, middle-class men— it can create an exclusionary culture'.[181] This presents considerable challenges to individuals who differ in one or more of those aspects.

Thirdly, family commitments were found by Conley Tyler, Blizzard, and Crane to negatively impact women's opportunity to form part of senior positions in international affairs. Because women continue to carry the burden of greater responsibilities for caring duties within the home, the hours in which women can undertake paid work are restricted and it is more difficult for women to pursue jobs in other locations.[182] For women in the APS, Edwards et al.[183] found the absence of available and affordable childcare to be a key barrier to career progression, which has implications for internationally deployed women in which access to reliable, safe, and affordable childcare may be more difficult to negotiate. Additionally, the Community and Public

Sector Union[184] found that 40.5 per cent of women believed that taking time out for family reasons would damage their future careers. While flexible work arrangements affect both men and women, women are disproportionately affected and tend to be overrepresented in part-time and flexible work.[185] The practical considerations involved in relocating to a new country imply that there is an even greater need for flexibility in work for women.

Conley Tyler, Blizzard, and Crane's final reason for the low representation of women in Australian international affairs was socially constructed gender norms. As set out earlier, diplomacy has specific scripts, norms, and expectations of its actors, which are characterised by gendered differences. Lee-Koo[186] finds that within IR discourse in Australia, masculinity is associated with power, autonomy, rationality, and public space, while femininity is associated with weakness, dependence, nurturing, private spheres, and emotion. Not only do these constructs have an impact on who is seen as capable of occupying leadership positions and representing 'Australia', effecting vertical segregation, but they also have the outcome of horizontally segregating women into policy and portfolio areas. Not only are all these four reasons significant in the Australian context, but they are also significant globally.

When viewing the Australian case through the established literature, a few further salient factors explaining women's underrepresentation in international affairs can be found. *The Review of Employment Pathways for APS Women in the Department of Defence* states that 'strong internal group culture and structures has led to development and implementation of *localised, disconnected practice and process*'.[187] FI highlights that institutions 'travel'—that is, geography and different portfolios across the agencies may affect the local informal gendered rules and norms, regardless of what the formal rules delineate. This reinforces the difficulties in implementing 'whole of organisation' policy across divisions, agencies, or posted countries. It also reinforces the need for a theoretical framework that advocates for a holistic, layered understanding of inequality challenges across multiple contexts, as will be put forward throughout this book.

Additionally, agency structure influences women's underrepresentation. Defence and the AFP, as highly structured military and paramilitary and hierarchical organisations, could be expected to present further barriers for women seeking leadership than DFAT and Home Affairs. This is based off existing research on military and enforcement agencies, with McGlen and Sarkees[188] finding that organisational structure influenced gender ratios within the organisations, as well as hierarchical structure and leadership, division of labour, and the degree of centralisation of power. Later chapters will address the validity of this expectation.

Diversity beyond gender markers also remains a key concern across government, with Conley Tyler[189] highlighting four challenges to the greater inclusion of Indigenous Australians within DFAT. She argues that direct discrimination, indirect discrimination, family and cultural responsibilities, and social constructs all affect Indigenous Australians' career progress, mentoring and retention. Australia only appointed its first Indigenous Ambassador, Damien Miller, in 2013, and appointed its first female Indigenous Ambassador, Julie-Ann Guivarra in 2018. Further challenges may exist for Indigenous Australians wishing to represent Australia internationally.[190] Yet considerable gaps remain in understanding CALD, sexually diverse, disability, and other intersectional experiences of diplomacy beyond gender, again providing an opportunity for this book to reflect on how the intersections of gender, race sexuality, class, rural and regional upbringing, education and more relate to whom is chosen to represent the nation, and how this might influence their experiences of international affairs.

This gap is not just limited to Australia. Historically, the role of ethnic minority candidates in British international affairs was 'near non-existent' even until recently.[191] Traditional methods of recruitment, security vetting and background checks factored heavily into explicit and implicit discrimination 'against those from non-Oxbridge backgrounds', with a small exception for specialist linguists or clerical grades.[192] Some of the limitations were the result of nationality rules, yet latent racism and monoculturalism also prevailed. In the related field of intelligence, whilst there was some flexibility for candidates with dual nationality from Commonwealth or English-speaking countries, the growth of the 'wrong sort of British subject' led to curbs in security departments.[193] In this research, there was a noted a reluctance to appoint candidates with an accent (meaning, non-Australian or 'foreign' accents), with ethnic diversity in national security agencies often perceived to be a 'security risk', and staff facing various forms of overt and covert comments and discrimination based on ethnicity.[194]

Whilst there have been several biographical accounts and historical analyses of sexuality in national security, particularly the military, overall, there remains a dearth of literature on sexuality and international affairs. Particularly given changes in social attitudes towards same-sex marriage equality and growing rights for transgender people across some countries globally, this represents a missed opportunity to understand the degree to which diverse gender identity and sexual orientation in international affairs is supported or challenged, and the nature of policies, practices, and experiences that go alongside it. Additionally, given the 'Lavender Scare' moral panic during the mid-twentieth century which saw the overt homophobia and many homosexuals' expulsion from US government service, as well as 'lesbian witch hunts' in Australia, criminalisation of homosexuality, and longstanding police brutality, the barriers to accessing international affairs are likely higher. LGBTIQ + and ethnically diverse communities may have more to fear than most from national security communities and the vetting requirements in international affairs. This calls for deeper understanding and knowledge, so as not to repeat past mistakes in practice, as well as understand enduring sites of contention and reform that this book seeks to uncover. This up-to-date Australian and intersectional approach to gender and diplomacy is direly needed.

The Theoretical Frameworks

The exploration of FI earlier in this chapter highlighted three key theoretical gaps to which this book aims to contribute: around intersectionality, the layering of gendered institutions, and evolution of inequalities. Addressing these gaps, I have developed three frameworks for analysis. First is an intersectional feminist institutional (IFI) framework; second is an IFI framework for studying international institutions; and third is a framework for understanding inequalities' evolution as institutions change.

Intersectional Feminist Institutionalism (IFI)

Central to the IFI framework is an analysis of the gendered nature of institutions. However crucially, other aspects of identity, from race, ethnicity, class, ability, sexuality, and so on (as defined by the researcher) should inform the research design and analysis at all possible stages. In this research, the IFI approach informed the institutional histories analysed, the data gathered, the individuals interviewed, the approach to analysis, and the overall book now produced (with not just a gendered analysis, but also race, ethnicity, and sexuality in particular featuring throughout). IFI neither seeks to constrain researchers to just analysing gender, nor does it implore them to undertake an exhaustive intersectional account. Rather, it seeks to rectify white feminism's blindness towards race and ethnicity and dismantle the heteronormative, binary approach to gendered institutional studies, drawing from Kimberlé Crenshaw's[195] understanding of intersectionality and aspects of queer and race theories, and building on Krook and Nugent's earlier intersectional institutionalism. Throughout this book, contributions are made around queer women in international affairs in particular, with novel findings developed around the intersection of gendered and heteronormative hierarchies in diplomacy.

A Framework for Studying International Institutions

The quandary of how to research institutions deeply international and multidimensional is also a core concern of this book. I propose the following framework in Figure 2.1 to guide an intersectional analysis of gender in international institutions. This framework derives from a combination of theory, which highlighted salient gendered institutional contexts, and insights gained during pilot background interviews, which highlighted gaps in existing theoretical models, where they existed.

I identity four core sites as influencing gendered international institutions: the field of work, the domestic and host country contexts, the agency or organisational context, and the individual or family context. This covers all three aspects that McGlen and Sarkees[196] argue research on women in foreign policy should assess—societal, organisational, and individual. Yet it has further broken-down factors and extended analysis to capture important differences. For instance, if one studies the impact of 'society', which society do they study? For actors in international affairs, home society and host society are specific environments that deserve complete analysis. The field of international affairs is neither a society nor an organisation, but like many fields of work it is still a relevant unit of analysis complete with distinct histories, norms, and beliefs, and should be differentiated from other contexts. The individual is also analysed in this research, including analysis of family contexts—because whether and how women deployed internationally was always dependent on their family circumstances, and what other social supports they had.

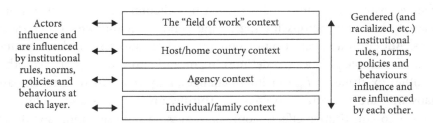

Figure 2.1 A layered framework for international institutions

While not exhaustive, each of these sites present critical insights into norms, behaviours and practices that either hinder or support women in international affairs. The framework also acknowledges the co-constitutive relationship between institutions and actors. Not only do institutions work to support or hinder (gendered, etc.) actors, (gendered, etc.) actors also exert influence over institutions, changing them both formally and informally through their presence and the enactment of new rules and norms. Additionally, gendered institutions in one 'site' or context frequently influence other contexts, and vice versa. This framework is posited to provide an effective rubric for measuring gendered institutions across international affairs agencies globally, allowing analysis of multiple core sites of institutional change and resistance.

An Approach to Studying Institutional Change and Inequality

In applying the above framework for analysing international institutions throughout the book, a few further factors rose to the fore. Crucial to this research, the institutions studied are undergoing seismic shifts and changes, brought on by the increasing internationalisation of many forms of government that has both centralised power for militarised agencies and dispersed power for diplomatic agencies—at least in the Australian context. As these institutions are in states of change—of diminishing status or increasing leverage, for instance—the impact this change has on gender dynamics has been considered. As institutions adapt to social mores and introduce formalised gender equality and other policies, institutions undergo change.

How do you apply a fixed IFI framework for analysing international institutions to contexts undergoing changes, sometimes rapidly so? In this book, understanding institutional history, stability, actors (including critical actors), and the timing of changes is crucial. Firstly, history is posited to continue to play a significant role in upholding gendered institutions across institutions, particularly given the 'stickiness', durability, and difficulty to change institutions addressed earlier in this chapter. Secondly, institutional stability has implications for ingraining gender equality and other measures. Adoption and rejection of policies in short succession, the introduction of multiple policies (sometimes in contradiction) on top of each other, or other machinery of government changes, may create inconsistencies and gaps that are important to analyse. Thirdly, given actors and institutions have a co-constitutive effect, women's increasing representation should influence institutions. Additionally, the presence, or absence, of critical actors to advocate on behalf of gender equality is important to assess whether new institutional rules are taken up, to what degree, and how quickly. Finally, timing refers to wider social movements and changes that may strengthen (or weaken) gendered change initiatives, as well as the lag between implementation of progressive policy and outcomes. Each of these factors is analysed alongside women's experiences and statistics on gender and representation, to contextualise the gendered rules and practices in use.

On top of this, through mapping institutional change (as represented by time, norms, policies, and practices) against inequalities faced (gender, racial, sexuality, class, ability, and so on) we can gain insight into the ways in which inequalities evolve as institutions change. This framework for identifying gendered, racialised, heteronormative institutions, sensitive to time and other forms of institutional change, is a core contribution to studying international affairs, international institutions, and institutions undergoing transition.

Ultimately, the literature on gender and international affairs to date makes space for deep research on gender and other inequalities as they apply to diverse international affairs agencies undergoing sometimes rapid change. The literature makes space for this book to extend analyses of gender and international affairs that are typically made of one institution (for instance, diplomacy or the military) to encompass a comparison of four (across diverse international-facing portfolios including diplomacy, defence, policing, intelligence, and home affairs). The book aims to be more comprehensively intersectional, extending the application of FI theories across multiple layers and contexts. And ultimately, this book provides a wealth of new data on gender in international affairs institutions in Australia—with lessons learned and ramifications extending well beyond Australian borders.

3
Who I Researched and How I Did It

> I got pregnant and had my first baby . . . when I told them I was pregnant they threatened to send me home . . . I said, 'well, good luck, give it a go. Try and send me home if you like'.
> —Jane, Department of Foreign Affairs and Trade, 15 November 2015[1]

International affairs could be a disastrous thing to research during COVID-19. Fortunately, I had touched down back in Australia just prior to the outbreak occurring, allowing me to have completed my world tour across more than 10 countries, speaking with over 80 leaders in international affairs and those who support them, bunkering down in embassies and high commissions, and traipsing across different national security quarters. Yet even without COVID-19 impairing my research, researching international affairs is still difficult—from gaining access to elite international institutions to navigating the sensitivities of gender, race, and sexuality in research. It was my genuine desire to see the best out of the institutions I study and at times work with that has therefore necessitated my approach to this book. Seeing myself as a critical feminist friend to the institutions studied, this chapter explores how I did the research.

Being a Critical Feminist Friend

Drawing on the work of Louise Chappell and Fiona Mackay, the critical feminist friend approach I used recognises the aspirations and dilemmas for feminist researchers 'entangled' in the international organisations they study, arguing that 'critical friends' can be at once engaged and critical.[2] This is a line that can be difficult to balance at times. There is an imperative to present a true account of the status quo and analyse without reservation the intricacies of gendered (and racialised, and so on) discrimination at the frontlines of international affairs. Yet there is also a necessity to get to know those researched over a long period, and, at least in my case, an opportunity to eventually conduct consulting or other forms of work alongside them. The entangled nature of my research, other work, and life with some of the institutions studied has necessitated full transparency and a focus on building trust as a critical friend—someone who can both be relied on for the work required, whilst also able to deliver on the requirements of ethical and unbiased research. There are considerable benefits that a critical appraisal of institutions such as this can bring, but many challenges to navigate too.

The notion of being a critical friend is not always typically encountered in research yet lends itself to the feminist methodologies employed in this book, which above all seeks be emancipatory. The approach stems from the ability to ask 'provocative questions', analyse data through a different lens, and critique work as a 'friend'.[3] Common features of a critical feminist friend approach include the researcher's relative autonomy, expertise, 'close distance', shared goals, and 'a commitment to understanding of contingency and contextual entanglement'.[4] The approach provides a way to navigate the political and ethical tensions that 'relations of proximity' introduce into research,[5] given the natural challenges, opportunities, and compromises feminist 'insiders' face in their research. Scholars now generally accept that 'improvements in women's lives rest, for the most part, on engagement with and entrance into institutions'.[6] In short, we cannot be mere passive observers analysing and debating gender relations in isolation from the institutions and organisations we study.

Yet the dilemmas of this closeness include that privileged access to agencies may be given at the expense of relative autonomy. Chappell and Mackay note that it is rare to be given access to international organisations (government or otherwise), and 'rarer still to examine institutional change from the inside'.[7] After gaining access to the agencies, trust, time, and 'institutional churn' all factor as considerable challenges.[8] Continued access to the same institutions may also be threatened by the findings—whether perceived as favourable or not, too critical, or not critical enough. Researchers can also develop a sense of loyalty to the agencies studied, which presents dilemmas in disseminating findings, even if findings have been openly disclosed and approved by participants. Researchers may find it difficult to speak hard truths and may face co-option by those researched. Such challenges can be difficult to negotiate and rarely have a one-size-fits-all model of approach.

In this research, the critical feminist friend approach influenced not whether or how much critique and analysis is offered, but to what end. Collaboration— a value closely associated with feminist research methods—was sought at times and reinforced that researching institutions often requires genuine partnership at some level. This may include employing methods such as aligning researcher and agency goals where possible, as well as humility, awareness, sense-making, and reflection in undertaking the research.[9]

Ultimately, the research approach draws on international standards for best-practice feminist research, including Ackerly and True's critical international relations (IR) approach, which is based on five points that feminist critical IR research should cover. It should:

1. be grounded in observation of human experience, key material developments, and processes of historical change;
2. evaluate current practices and policies from the perspective of how they are constructed;
3. draw out the emancipatory potentials of existing social formations, the processes of social learning of which they are the result, and the implications of both for the transformation of the world order;
4. reflect on the very process of theorizing and role of the intellectual or scholar in society; and
5. be ongoing.[10]

Intersectional Feminist Institutional (IFI) Research Design

Feminist analyses of international affairs question what issues and types of knowledge we count as important, legitimate, or authoritative when investigating international politics—and provide ways for accounting for them.[11] In IR, this is particularly important given the rise of new challenges, from climate change to COVID-19, and the potential to rethink old, seemingly intractable challenges through different methodological approaches. The value of using a feminist approach to the research is that without it, we do not always see 'other' or alternative worlds of international politics as they are 'methodologically obscured' when not looked at through a gendered lens.[12] Therefore, following calls for empirical research in international affairs,[13] grounded in human experience,[14] this research is specific in its choice to study *women's* leadership and experiences. Tickner identifies that the history of international relations is the history of *men* in international relations. As Tickner states:

> Since knowledge about the behaviour of states in the international system depends on assumptions that come out of men's experiences, it ignores a large

body of human experience that has the potential for increasing the range of options and opening up new ways of thinking about interstate practices. Theoretical perspectives that depend on a broader range of human experience are important... as we seek new ways of thinking about our contemporary dilemmas.[15]

While Chappell[16] argues for the study of 'gender'—inclusive of men and women (or anyone not defined by the binary)—in comparative studies of politics, she and Vickers[17] do acknowledge that research focussing on women remains a gap. As Chappell goes on to say, 'it is essential that we do not lose sight of women as a category of analysis... to do so leaves men in control of formal political institutions'.[18] Additionally, Ramji-Nogales[19] notes that the study of the complex hierarchies within the category of women grows increasingly important. Binary narratives of men and women have largely consumed IR, which leaves little room for analysis of the intersection of gender with other categories (ethnicity, sexuality, class, and so on). Ramji-Nogales highlights that, more than anything, a focus on women results in a process of inclusion in the research.

The focus on women, yet also on diverse women and an inclusive approach to women, therefore underpins this research. Because intersectional analyses have not yet been mainstreamed in IR or FI research, intersectionality is insufficiently understood in producing solutions for women's equality in leadership—also remaining a gap in the FI theoretical field, as noted in the previous chapter. This research therefore puts women's voices at the forefront of analysing leadership, employing a feminist approach that is aware of the intersection of inequalities produced by gender, class, disability, sexuality, and ethnicity. Employing intersectional feminist approaches allows this research 'to uncover and remove the blinders that obscure knowledge and observations concerning human experiences and behaviours that have traditionally been silenced by mainstream research'.[20]

During the research, I was conscious that 'the researcher's positionality (in terms of race, gender, nationality, age, economic status and sexuality) may influence the data gathered'.[21] I used reflexivity to identify power relations, exercises of power, and their effects on the research process, which was critical to be accountable for the knowledge produced and understand how the way I framed the research and questions may have affected the data gathered.[22] The IFI research approach therefore shaped the way I asked questions: how I introduced the research topic and myself mattered.

For instance, I used interviews as an opportunity to share my own personal credibility, as well as the research context and the 'safety' of the interview space. Creating a 'safe' space was important, particularly as not just sexism but racism, homophobia, and other forms of discrimination and harassment may have factored into women's stories. To establish the space as safe, I would often mention my own work in the fields of gender equality, lesbian, gay, bisexual, transgender, and intersex (LGBTI+), culturally and linguistically diverse (CALD), or other inclusion and would always use the language of 'diverse' women, and the diversity of their experience. Sometimes, in addition to my gender, I would further disclose elements of my background to establish a safe environment. This contributed to a kind of 'embodied intersectionality' approach to research. My personal identity as a young queer woman researcher who had been involved in international public diplomacy efforts with the associated agencies, and whose life had been affected by various aspects of disability, gender, and sexuality, brought a very specific understanding and ability to connect and explore the research.

Without my positioning as a researcher whose lived reality is affected by race, gender, class, education, sexuality, disability, and so on, I may not have received access to some of the data I gathered. While much of the objective of research and evidence gathering is that it should be able to be undertaken by anyone, and the results gained would be the same, the reality is that researchers can influence the research undertaken.[23] As much as it was important to display credibility when gaining access to the diplomatic and security field, my credibility or embodiment of identity was also important in gaining access to participants' perceptions, narratives, and emotions. This is not to say it would be impossible to gain the same data I gathered without being 'me'—however, it does acknowledge that who I am was important to have some of that data revealed, and some of those stories shared. As a sort of insider, this presented me with the ideal opportunity to explore how the intersection of women's diverse identities affected their experiences and pathways to leadership.

Yet it also carries a warning: namely, that this should not provide me with a (false) sense of familiarity with participants' lives, who are as complex, unique, and ever-changing as my own.[24] This highlights the multiplicity and fluidity of identity. Regardless, embodiment of experiences relatable to the participants aided them in sharing stories they thought I would understand, whether that was both of us sharing a history working in the same country or region or the world, or sharing common sexuality or gender, and by extension, implicitly understanding some of the unique challenges of that experience. I believe this resonates within the field of IR, which has not only failed to represent women equally as researchers within the field, but also traditionally failed to consider the experiences and perspectives of women. No doubt the two are related.

The IFI approach also affected the research more generally, compelling me to follow a mixed method approach that sought to understand gender (and race, and so on) from a multifaceted, holistic perspective in international affairs. A mixed method approach informed analysis of the case agencies, comprising in-depth qualitative interviews with women leaders, quantitative data analysis on gender over the last 34 years, observation, and document analysis. The literature, critical feminist friend approach, research questions, and the quest to discover detailed, substantive understandings of women's leadership in international affairs guided the choice of methodology and case location. Such a rigorous methodology provided many opportunities for theoretical and empirical insights into the gendered nature of institutions in diplomacy and security, as well as important opportunities to triangulate the data. The mixed methods research approach chosen reinforces a feminist tendency towards 'face-to-face, qualitative and interactive methods', yet also recognises the benefits of quantitative data, particularly in uncovering trends and findings that would have remained obscured without holistic analysis.[25]

The primary data for this book comprised in-depth interviews with 57 women in executive level (EL) and senior executive service (SES) level positions, as well as named interviews with Australia's first female Prime Minister, Julia Gillard, and first female Foreign Minister, Julie Bishop. I focused on interviewing those who are or have represented Australia internationally in the last 10 years at the highest levels, and I spent extensive time in the field learning from women both in their domestic and international postings across more than 10 countries and three regions, allowing observation to complement the interviews undertaken. The research also involved a further 27 informal discussions with former heads of departments (men and women), politicians, human resources managers, and other related individuals within the agencies to establish context, test ideas, and guide the research direction.

Analysing quantitative data from annual reports and the Australian Public Service Employee Database (APSED) *Yearbook Statistics* since 1984 provided important trend data across 30 + years, breaking down gender, rank, and international deployment across the agencies. Textual and document analysis of surrounding policy informed an understanding of the formal rules, their implementation, successes, and gaps. The combination of the mixed method approach, plus self-reflexivity and triangulation of the data (including with external sources), was an essential part of the process, allowing me to explore knowledge in ways that reduced distortion and elevated truths.[26]

Data Collection: On-Ground, In-Person, and International

Throughout the research, data was collected through (1) qualitative interviews and (2) quantitative statistical trend data of women's representation in the agencies over the last 30+ years. This has enabled findings to be triangulated and explored in a multimodal, holistic manner, as explored in this section.

Qualitative Interviews

Within the context of international relations, 'global leaders are those people who most strongly influence the process of global leadership', and in the case of international affairs agencies, involves leadership in both domestic and international spheres, often cross-cultural.[27] Leadership has historically been gendered, focusing on notions of the 'hero' and masculinised attributes around strength, courage, determination, and vision. Rost's[28] study of 221 definitions of leadership concluded that definitions of leadership can be seen as rational, hierarchical, management-oriented, quantitative, cost-driven, technocratic, male, short-term, materialistic, and pragmatic. Leadership has also had a propensity towards the public realm—while women may have historically wielded influence in private or domestic spheres, this has not always been seen as 'leadership'.

Leadership is not just concerned with formalised roles and processes, yet its value is frequently equated with male-dominated public realms and formalised positions of power and influence. Hanna Fenichel Pitkin's[29] seminal work distinguished representation as formal (institutional position and authority), descriptive (the nature or representativeness of a person), substantive (acting on behalf of constituents), and symbolic (assigned meaning and legitimacy). Formal representation within Australian international affairs, depending on the level and position, can rely on public elections (such as electing a minister or prime minister), political appointments (as in the case of a minister or prime minister appointing departmental secretaries or a politically appointed diplomat), and merit-based appointments to roles and positions of leadership. Further, informal influence, vision, courage, and action is not restricted to those in formalised leadership positions and may provide influence in myriad ways not formally documented by studying leadership.

This book recognises that women's leadership manifests both formally and informally within international affairs and may be expressed in ways that are different to prevailing masculine stereotypes. However, the scope of the book focuses on the narratives of women participants based on their *formalised* positions of leadership, as there are clear power differences bestowed by role and title. Women's descriptive underrepresentation is therefore a key concern. Role and title appear to have considerable influence in diplomatic and security spheres, which remain heavily influenced by hierarchy and status.[30]

In-depth qualitative interviews with senior executive women leaders form the primary data collected for this book. As Jacoby states, 'interviewing provides access to people's ideas, thoughts, and memories in their own words rather than in the words of the researcher'.[31] Through conducting interviews, experience is understood as a 'source of legitimate knowledge', which raises certain inherent dilemmas, such as the tendency to equate experience with truth. Interviews therefore reveal narratives, which are not only powerful in themselves, but can be analysed alongside other forms of evidence as produced by discourse, document, and statistical analysis.[32]

Formal interviews with 57 women leaders across the four case agencies took place from May 2018 to May 2019, and informal discussions for background with a further 27 men and women from June 2017 to December 2019. Informal pilot backgrounding discussions were essential and allowed me to narrow down critical issues prior to undertaking the main data collection period, assessing potential relevant and irrelevant factors. This was particularly important as gaining access to elites and international institutions can be difficult and limited, and I needed to ensure that my research focus, questions, and theoretical framework was robust. This pilot period allowed me to have an informed insider perspective from the outset. As Chappell and Mackay note, gendered 'rules are often taken for granted—usually submerged and barely visible—and therefore difficult to study'.[33] Therefore, this methodological choice enabled me to understand institutions and actors from multiple perspectives. Those consulted during this period were typically individuals in a position relational to the agencies, such as former secretaries, human resources teams, research and communications teams, and diversity and inclusion strategists within the agencies.

Inevitably, I could not conduct research at every agency or department involved in international affairs. However, recognising Cohn's evaluation that 'national security discourse and policies are created by the workings of many complex social organisations', I chose Australia as a leading case globally, and four of Australia's most salient agencies to international relations based on their roles and their ease of access—as covered in Chapter 1.[34] All four case agencies have headquarters nationally in the Australian Capital Territory in Canberra and have overseas representatives in Australian embassies, as well as embedded units in host government offices, and representatives at international organisations such as the United Nations and other fora.

I undertook data collection both domestically and internationally. My fieldwork domestically was critical to gain the perspectives of those in the highest positions of power within their agencies. These individuals are typically Australia-based with sporadic international representation. Australia-based research was also highly accessible, as internationally deployed staff tended to return home between deployments, providing plenty of opportunities to connect with recently returned staff. From Australia, in-person interviews were undertaken in concentrated blocks in Canberra and telephone or Skype interviews were undertaken on and off over the data collection period with internationally based staff. My fieldwork internationally was undertaken to round off the data collection, allowing me to undertake a percentage of the interviews in-situ. I also undertook informal discussions and observations on-ground across Japan, Vietnam, the United States, India, Hong Kong, Singapore, Taiwan, Cambodia, Laos, and Brunei—with the ability to negotiate further access a key contribution of the research. This allowed me to gain an observational understanding of the workings of embassies, as well as in-country relationships and dynamics that could not be gained from a distance. It gave context to the often highly guarded and elite spaces in which international representatives work and enabled me to begin to understand aspects of their lives, like isolation and disconnection from home and host counterparts, as well as from family and other support networks. It also gave insight into the bilateral and multilateral relationships of some of Australia's most important allies: the US as a key strategic power; and those in the Indo Pacific region particularly, given Australia's policy orientation towards Indo Pacific engagement.

Purposive sampling was deemed the most appropriate method to gain participants, as in similar studies (see Corbett and Liki,[35] and Spark, Cox, and Corbett[36]). Purposive sampling involves a 'practical sample with which to carry out an in-depth and detailed study' of a specific target population.[37] This approach ensured homogeneity among participants—that they occupied a certain level of occupation or hierarchy in their organisations. Purposive sampling is an 'organic practice, which grows and develops throughout the research', and is 'shaped and formed by what the researcher wants to achieve analytically'.[38] Participants were recruited per the following criteria:

- that they identified as a woman (a language choice to include both cis-gendered and trans women, although to the researcher's knowledge no transgender women were able to be found for the final dataset);

- that they occupy or occupied an EL or SES level position in one of the four case agencies in the last 10 years;
- that their position was international-facing; and
- that they had been internationally deployed or are involved in international diplomatic or security representation.

The requirement to be international-facing helped me to characterise those interviewed as international affairs workers, and all participants studied were characterised by their 'whole-of-life' commitment to their jobs because of the circumstances of their international relocation or representation. Further, the Vienna Convention on Diplomatic Relations establish many of the rules of their international engagement and characterises the forms of their diplomatic or official international representative action. Participants generally formed part of the following cohorts: senior overseas representatives in DFAT (heads of mission (HOM), heads of post (HOP), consul generals, deputies and special ambassadors); Defence Attaches (DA) and DA staff deployed internationally (across the Australian Defence Force (ADF) and Department of Defence, including International Policy Division); A-based Australian Border Force (ABF) and Home Affairs portfolio (Immigration and Customs) staff; and staff deployed in International Operations (IO) in the Australian Federal Police (AFP).

The problem of selection bias was mitigated by focusing on individual women selected from government employment databases to reflect different levels of senior leadership, roles, and portfolios. Even where agencies provided lists of potential women to interview, I did my own research to ensure I approached a range of women across a range of portfolios, experiences, ages, and rank. Further, a network strategy was used to gain participants. I initially contacted participants via email, and on occasional relied on 'snowballing'.

I determined the number of people I interviewed by both the availability of participants and the saturation level:[39] when there was enough data to replicate the study, little new information was attainable, and further coding was no longer feasible. I initially aimed to interview at least 10 women per agency; however, due to the potential of this research to capture these women's experiences in many cases for the first time, I also conducted interviews with individuals who contacted me wishing to participate (providing they met the criteria). In the end, I formally interviewed 16 women in DFAT, 11 in the AFP, 14 in Defence, and 14 in Home Affairs, plus further interviews with the two former politicians.

As a form of ethnography, the interviews drew out experiences which were compared against each other, accounting for the various contexts of the women's work domestically and internationally. This kind of insight into 'everyday diplomacy' is a robust methodological choice to understand 'the ways individuals and communities engage with and influence decisions about world affairs'.[40] I used a semistructured interviewing technique, which I chose because of its capacity to provide insights into how the research participants viewed the world.[41] An interview guide was compiled using main questions or topics, yet the process remained flexible and able to be adapted per participant responses. Participants were questioned about their career path; employment challenges and opportunities; their leadership role; their experiences of international deployment and representation; negotiating the difference in gender norms and experiences in domestically and internationally in countries they may be based; their perceptions of the importance of women leaders in international relations; and any advice that they would give to other women aspiring leaders.

I conducted only one interview per person for most interviews, with subsequent emails to clarify points or gain feedback on theories developed. I interviewed five participants multiple times, as part of a process to gain a deeper understanding of agencies with which I had fewer interviews. This dataset allowed me to gain data across different portfolios and types of work (service lines) within the agencies. While a representation of participants was sought across the different divisions or service lines, in some cases only one or two participants were interviewed per service line or division. Where this happened, further corroboration was sought through the established data or informal background discussions.

I carried out all interviews one-on-one, and where possible undertook face-to-face interviews, as they generally allowed me to establish rapport and trust quicker and gain a more collaborative research feel. For instance, when I conducted interviews face-to-face in an overseas embassy, I had lively discussions and was given the opportunity to tour the premises on many occasions. I was also able to employ some observational methodologies by doing this, which helped me to understand the circumstances of interviewees better. In many cases, prior to meeting an interviewee in person overseas I would have an initial phone or Skype call to introduce myself, which both helped to organise the interview and to establish rapport and trust. From experience working alongside DFAT and representing Australia in an international capacity prior to this research, I had a level of 'cultural and relational understanding' of the workplaces and international context.[42]

Interviews ranged between half an hour to two hours long, with most taking an hour, and were located in the participants' location of choice, mostly their offices, with occasional meetings in other meeting rooms, libraries, or cafes. Halvorsen[43] notes that a source of error can be that the context in which interviews take place affects the conversation. In some circumstances, basing the interviews within agency offices may have had the effect of limiting what the women were willing to discuss. Likewise, in cases where no other meeting space was available or suitable, we used cafés as a safe third space (not being a work or private, home context). These spaces were generally comfortable locations for the interviewees, who felt that the noisiness and business of the space were private enough for them to speak candidly. However, they did present challenges to transcribing the interviews later.

All participants gave informed consent, when the participants were first contacted and again prior to the interview taking place, where the participants signed information and informed consent sheets or otherwise gave their verbal consent. To respect the privacy, anonymity, and confidentiality of participants, I contacted and liaised with interviewees directly until after participants had access to the information and consent form, at which time some interviewees scheduled their interviews with the help of their executive assistants. Names of participants have not been used in this book to maintain confidentiality, which was an important consideration for many. In the text or references, participants are referred to by pseudonym, agency, and date of interview—for example, Anna, DFAT, 21 June 2018. Participants were largely concerned about being named due to the perceived affect this might have on their careers. In fact, only the most senior women leaders, who had reached the peak role in their careers, were unconcerned about being named. Likewise, the two politicians interviewed—former Prime Minister Julia Gillard and former Foreign Minister Julie Bishop—agreed to be named due to the significance of their roles and the importance of recognising their roles in Australian international affairs. In their case, I gained additional informed consent. Named participants had the opportunity to review and approve their quotes in situ in the book prior to submission. Interviews were transcribed ready for analysis, either by myself or by a paid transcription service, Pacific Transcriptions.

Practically, I felt that reflexivity assisted in mitigating dilemmas whilst conducting the research, including issues around subjectivity, bias, and framing. Reflexivity—a process of self-awareness—is critical in feminist research, as 'any researcher's critical consciousness is constrained by the limits of their knowledge, culture and experience, and also by their personal skills, powers of empathy and political openness to silences and exclusions'.[44]

Subjectivity and bias are implicit in conducting qualitative interviews, no matter how objective an interviewer may attempt to be.[45] Interviews require reflexivity in thinking about and acknowledging how the researcher's own assumptions may affect the research. There was a temptation to validate the women's experiences by outwardly agreeing or disagreeing with their understandings of gender in their field, or experiences of discrimination and harassment (or lack thereof). Before and after interviews I would take time to reflect on how I was going to (or did) position the research, as well as how I acknowledged and responded to women's experiences—a process of 'sense-making'.[46] I noticed that over time I became better at concealing my reactions and felt less temptation to automatically validate an interviewee's perspective. By the end of the interviews most participants did want to know whether their experiences resonated more broadly, and so I did have an opportunity officially after the interview had finished to share more about the research and its findings without influencing the women's stories in advance.

Quantitative Trend Data

Quantitative data on agency, gender, rank, role, and international deployment from 1984 to 2021 represents the second major dataset analysed in this book, allowing a historical, trend data analysis of international affairs. There were considerable difficulties in gaining access to data due to inconsistent reporting methods, gaps in the data, and limited accessibility. The primary sources analysed include:

1. Australian Public Service Employee Database (APSED) Yearbook Statistics, accessed under a Request For Information (RFI 763) which compiled data on gender and rank, by agency, from 1984 to 2018.
2. Agency annual reports from each agency studied. This includes data from 2000—2018 for DFAT, Home Affairs and Defence, and from 1984—2018 in the AFP, due to its exclusion from the APSED dataset. DFAT annual reports for 2011-2012 were missing, and AFP annual reports from 1990 to 2003 were missing and unable to be sought by the AFP Freedom of Information (FOI) team, as they had not yet been fully digitised. Not all agency annual reports recorded data on gender, with the ADF only recording this data since 2012.
3. Agency websites. Particularly for DFAT and the AFP. DFAT's Australian ambassadors and other representatives page was analysed and gender data collected at multiple points throughout the research.[47] The AFP publishes data on international representation on their website, updated yearly; however, this data was pure percentage data, with no numerical data accessible.[48] It broke international representation down by gender, but not by rank or role.
4. Data requests made directly to the agencies.

Data Analysis: Themes, Narratives, and Trends

This book compares descriptive statistics, descriptive analyses of institutional structures and rules, and thematic analyses of interviews. Descriptive analysis involves using current and historical data to identify trends and relationships. Although descriptive analysis is not often able to point to causal relationships, it can be particularly important in identifying phenomena that has not been previously studied (or for which there is limited up-to-date research). Descriptive analysis has been described as understanding 'what is' and mapping the status quo of an issue, context, or phenomena.[49] It is therefore an essential baseline analytical tool for understanding this topic of women's representation and gender equality in Australian international affairs—a subject requiring initial groundwork, mapping, and uncovering of conditions. In this book, descriptive analysis of statistics from 1984 to 2022 on gender and representation, plus descriptive analysis of individual agency structures and rules, has been undertaken to identify overarching trends, which can be supplemented by and explored deeper through interviews.

Thematic analysis was used to analyse interview transcripts and notes taken throughout the research process, using two steps as described by Baumgartner and Schneider[50] involving: (a) identifying emerging themes by coding the transcript data for each research question; and (b) compiling prevailing themes into a matrix. I evaluated themes for both internal and external homogeneity, described respectively as the extent to which data coalesces in a meaningful way within each category, and the differences between categories being bold and clear.[51] Themes coalesced around women's challenges (particularly focused on key junctures along their career trajectory, as well as wider contextual factors relevant to their agencies), opportunities (the benefits they felt their gender brought to international affairs, opportunities gained to propel their careers, or movement between agencies to more lucrative or funded areas of international affairs), and desired areas of policy change (workplace conditions, continued entrenched sexism, micro-aggressions and inequalities, and so on), which proved revealing of individuals' perspectives on their agency and the sector, as well as the relationship between statistical improvements in women's representation and women's reported experiences. Additionally, by paying attention to the language and framing used by participants I was able to understand not just what was said, but gaps and silences—subconscious ideas about the field of international affairs, how their agency was performing, or challenges still unaddressed.

Complementing this analysis, I drew on some elements of process tracing[52] to analyse the temporal sequence of events across the agencies, which was particularly useful in situating contemporary experiences within wider agency histories, as is explored in detail in Chapter 4. Given limitations in time and scope, this analysis was mostly restricted to a descriptive analysis of agency events and policies across time that related to and built upon the layering of gendered norms, rules, and processes affecting women leaders today, which does leave gaps for further research to explore in greater detail, particularly to explore causation.

Additionally, in line with the critical feminist friend method, supplementary observation as a result of 'being there' in the field for periods internationally and nationally enabled me to make sense of the interview data, the quantitative trend data, and the policies analysed.[53] Using descriptive analysis of what I observed, I was able to triangulate findings and understand insights from a position relational to those I studied.

Accessing Elites and Delving Into the Diplomatic Bubble

Focusing on those who were at the highest levels of leadership in international affairs institutions resulted in a case selection of women in Executive Level (EL) and Senior Executive Service (SES) level positions across DFAT, Home Affairs, and the AFP, and equivalent ranks across Defence—the 'leadership cadre of the APS'.[54] As stated by Mills, elites are those whose positions 'enable them to transcend the ordinary environments of ordinary men and women; they are in positions to make decisions having major consequences'.[55] Neumann asserts that being within the field of diplomacy has a consolidating or furthering effect on social status, with civil servants generally, and diplomats specifically, forming part of a social elite. Rank, as in Defence, Home Affairs and AFP military or sworn roles, heightens this 'elite' status. Implicit in interviews with elites therefore is a power imbalance, which creates several challenges, but also opportunities, for interviewers.[56]

Because of my status as a young Caucasian woman and PhD student (at the time), and the interviewee's status, which was always more senior to me and 'elite', power imbalances did exist. Some elites are often 'used to being in a position of authority, leading discussions rather than following [them]'.[57] Generally, this did not present a problem, and the women's high level of interest and engagement with the topic made most of their narratives insightful, honest, and frank. As a researcher, they also seemed to respect that

I came in with specialised knowledge, which minimised power imbalances. Because 'attempts to assert power and to change relations may have a negative effect on the study', I generally let the interview flow naturally following a semistructured approach.[58] As I was someone with very little power relationally to them, I felt that they were happy to speak honestly without consequence, and many had had media training and so were comfortable with the interview questions and format.

I was aware early of the challenges I might face in gaining access to elites, and understood that because of time concerns and the busy nature of their work, there would be difficulty in gaining access to them, and in conducting multiple interviews with any one individual. Therefore, in the first year of research, an early strategy I employed was networking and agency introductions, with the aim of becoming known and trusted. Once interviews commenced, I maintained a flexible schedule and was prepared to be persistent in following up potential interviewees—though I found interviewees relatively easy to approach and secure. I did have some links to individuals, particularly across DFAT; however, in general I relied on researching who senior women were in the agencies, and then cold contacting them through email. This enabled me to speak directly to the women themselves first (rather than go through executive assistants or secretaries), which was an important ethical consideration given participants have been de-identified in this book and agencies do not know the participatory status of their staff.

Credibility and connections were important in gaining access to participants for interviews, in alignment with the literature.[59] On occasion, I relied on the knowledge and help of my supervisors to speak to contacts already known to them. Once I had established credibility in one agency, I was able to establish credibility more quickly across other agencies and their staff. Personal connections allowed me to speak to very senior individuals quicker than I might have been able to otherwise, and this snowballed quickly into opening access to other individuals.

Throughout the course of the interviews, I noticed that those who spoke most freely were largely in their last position before retirement or moving on from the agency and were generally at senior levels of their careers and in SES or equivalent ranks. I often found that they asked more questions about my own career ambitions and what was next for me—and many stated that they wanted to be part of the project in order to 'give back' to the next generation of women coming after them. Lower ranked participants (EL1 and EL2 levels particularly) were more guarded in what they spoke about, and often would write to their agency to confirm that they had permission to speak to me, regardless of the approvals that I had already gained and told them about. On occasions, some of my interviewees would discuss the research with their colleagues. In some circumstances, if they were not able to participate but knew someone who would, they might forward my email directly to that colleague. In these cases, I did notice that participants were more guarded in what they spoke about, and they may have felt more obligated to participate by being asked by a colleague. This may have added to what Dexter[60] found: that elites, who often have more conservative perspectives, may not be as forthcoming when interviewed by academics who are often perceived as more liberal.

For those who were closer to my age, participants often spoke more openly, perhaps as it was perceived we shared a kinship or understanding as young women. In these cases, the interview almost took on a gossipy form—it was more relaxed and colloquial, and often rapport was quicker to establish. Further, some power imbalances were minimised by being of the same gender, and I felt that there was a kind of mentorship being offered by some of the women. Cohn[61] found that as a young woman interviewing elites in the military, she was able to ask 'naïve' questions and receive honest, straightforward responses. Similarly, I tried to treat each interview as if it were the first I had done, and not bring prior knowledge to interviews so as not to lead participants. When themes started to recur, I was then able to continue to dig deeper and test theories; however, I felt that this kept the integrity of listening to women's voices and letting their experiences come to the fore without my leading.

With that said, Cohn states: "There was an "I" who asked the questions, and inevitably, who I am shaped not only what I noticed and was able to hear, but also what people would say *to* me and *in front of me*".[62] In some cases, an interviewee would withhold their opinion on a topic, yet often the silences, and reading in between the lines, helped me to understand their gaps. Some women, although happy to participate, had more of an agenda than others did—for instance, if they were in a senior administrative or managerial position, they might give me a more established narrative about the agency. I felt that much of what they did or did not tell me was dependent on their position in the agency, seniority, and stage of career, as well as my status as an 'outsider'. Because Kezar states that as there is 'virtually no way for the interviewer not to impact the nature of information shared', I found that establishing an environment that was secure, had protocol, and established confidentiality early encouraged elites to share openly.[63]

I found that interview structure mattered. I would always start by asking participants to tell me about their personal life history and career path since leaving secondary school. I found that this enabled them to get into the rhythm of sharing their lives and was a friendly subject. The first half of my interview would be taken up by this topic, over the course of about one to three questions. Interviewees responded better to guided questioning than might have come with a stricter and more structured interview. The interview adopted a conversational tone which helped to build rapport and trust. By the time I got to the critical questions around the gendered nature of international deployments and their gendered experiences within the agencies, participants had relaxed into the interview more. I felt this made their answers more open and honest, particularly where they had to be conducted over the phone, which was more difficult to establish rapport than in in-person interviews.

I noticed that in some circumstances, if I mentioned at the start of the interview how a participants' agency was responding to gender equality, I set the interview up and potentially biased the results. On two occasions, I distinctly remember making a comment to the effect of how their agency was better at gaining representative leadership than other agencies. I felt that the entire interview then took a different path to the other interviews—more scripted and less open or critical. After this occurred twice, I realised my mistake and was more conscious of what I revealed about agencies in my future interviews. Employing reflexivity and sticking to an initial script and structure helped to mitigate my giving away too much information too early that might influence what we spoke about.

I noticed that the two politicians formally interviewed, Julia Gillard and Julie Bishop, were already retired or were about to retire by the time we conducted interviews. Although I approached (at the time) Shadow Foreign Minister Penny Wong, Foreign Minister Marise Payne, and Defence Minister Linda Reynolds, none of these politicians gave me an interview, despite some initially agreeing. This may be due to their busy schedules or could be indicative of the political and sensitive nature of the topic, in which many participants were anxious about revealing their stories of differential gendered treatment. For instance, my interview with former Foreign Minister Julie Bishop was conducted in her last sitting week in parliament. After retirement, she commented in the media that during her time in politics she realised that she had experienced a kind of 'gender deafness', which may have affected our earlier interview and the information shared.[64]

Overall, it became clear that many participants drew on deep courage to participate. This reflects the status of discussions about gender in the field—it remains a contentious topic. Acknowledging gendered treatment is seen as weak or damaging to the women's careers. Fear of repercussions resulting from speaking out clearly remain to affect women. Even so, fewer than five individuals did not answer, or refused to take part in the research. This is indicative of participants' commitment and ambition to see progress, often driven by the work they were doing and the opportunities it afforded. It demonstrated that a desire to see change was more important than the risk of speaking out.

Ethical Clearance

Access to international affairs agencies can be difficult, with ethical clearance arrangements varying by agency, revealing elements of agency culture and approach to information. Prior to commencing fieldwork, I sought to have casual conversations off-the-record with academics and individuals who worked with or had knowledge of the agencies and international context for work. This background information helped to shape what questions would be useful to ask, which agencies were going to be most pertinent to the research, and which groups of people would be best placed to participate. Before commencing interviews, ethical approval was then sought and gained through the Griffith University Human Research Ethics Committee (GU 2018/059). Some of the agencies required extra ethical or approval processes. Initial approval to conduct the research was sought from DFAT and the AFP through direct contact with senior leadership or agency gender teams. For Home Affairs, contact was made with the Strategic Research and Communications team, which assessed the research proposal, helped to collate raw unpublished data, and called for expressions of interest within the main divisions of the department: Immigration, Customs and the Australian Border Force.

For Defence, secondary ethical approval was required. The Defence ethical approval process took nine months to complete, by which stage I had gained unconditional ethical approval through the Low Risk Ethics Panel (Number: 098/18). As part of Defence research protocols, after gaining ethical approval, my contact in the International Policy Division (IPD) sent out an expression of interest email to everyone who might fit the research criteria, with instructions for them to contact me directly. This way, Defence was able to ensure that those who fit the research criteria had the opportunity to take part in the research, whilst protecting their anonymity insofar as the agency did not know who then participated in the research.

4
Historical Developments in International Affairs and Deep Insights Into the Case Agencies

> I have found myself in meetings in Border Force in Australia and through my career in Customs where I have felt like the lone woman in the room. You know, it's confronting.
> —Lucy, Home Affairs, 2 May 2018[1]

Hocking[2] notes that ministries of foreign affairs (MFAs) have been undergoing a 'state of relative decline' over the past decades, with Dittmer arguing that they are 'less an all-powerful agent of world politics and more like a tail being wagged by two different dogs'—the state and the global diplomatic community.[3] The role of MFAs in diplomacy is changing—not just by necessity as has been the case under COVID-19,[4] but also by other influencing factors like globalisation, technological changes, and new security threats.[5] MFAs' roles as the premiere international agencies of the state are also declining—with the state increasingly reliant on multiple agencies implicated in international affairs to carry out its objectives.[6] The trend to military-led diplomacy has increased post-September 11,[7] furthering the tenuous position of MFAs at the forefront of international decision-making. Not only has it resulted in countries like the US or Australia's defence and security agencies undertaking a greater role in international affairs, but it has also resulted in the development of police-led and defence-led diplomacy initiatives that increasingly encroach MFA's prior territory. This has resourcing ramifications that are fundamentally transforming the way in which international affairs is done in some countries globally.[8]

Equally, women's greater presence within MFAs, and more generally, is changing the scene. The gradual increase of women in international affairs follows the lifting of bans on women in the Foreign Service in many countries, a gradual reclassification of roles, shifting social norms, the introduction gender targets and specific hiring and promotions processes, and a wider push within international affairs to demonstrate leadership in gender equality.[9] Despite potential impacts from COVID-19,[10] opportunities appear to be increasing for women seeking an international career.

How do we reconcile these changes, to understand the nature of gender in international affairs and the challenges remain? Tracing trends in the wider international affairs field, women's treatment and representation, and the detailed histories of the case agencies allows us a glimpse into the status quo and how we got here. As international affairs institutions undergo change, gendered, racialised, and other inequality dynamics also change and warrant the closer exploration that a deep historical analysis in this chapter will provide. Ultimately, by doing so, we can gain better insights into how inequalities evolve as institutions change—a core theme of this book.

The Australian Cases: Institutional History and Cultural Relics

Agency history is integral to understanding women's contemporary status in international affairs, following Cassidy's[11] research that found that institutional origins relate to the obstacles women continue to face. Given gender inequalities pervade the history of international affairs, it is expected that historical legacies would drive contemporary gender norms and be key to understanding why women leaders remain underrepresented (or unequal) in international affairs. Overall, all agencies everywhere started out gender unequal (and often, racist, homophobic, and so on), and over time have developed cultures and policies that have resulted in more, or less, equal gender representation, and more, or less, visibility of on-going gendered challenges.

Yet in studying the Australian case, rather than these cultural differences determining substantial differences in women's challenges across institutions—for instance, whether women experience particular instances of discrimination—agency history and culture are more marked in determining whether these challenges are *more visible* or *less visible*. Agency history and culture also determine what enforcement mechanisms are used to maintain a pre-existing gender order and help us to understand how and why inequalities evolve as institutions change. Whilst each agency in Australian international affairs maintains that their cultures are exceptional and different—particularly DFAT and Defence—in reality, they demonstrate the *same* underlying gendered challenges that may only *manifest differently*. This has significant—and troubling—ramifications.

Setting the Context

Defending sovereignty and advocating for myriad state interests on the global stage has occupied governments and ruling empires for generations. Whilst most nations have long histories of diplomatic conduct and negotiation (sometimes by force) with other states, Australia's recent colonisation and gaps in our knowledge about Indigenous diplomacy before it produces a unique picture. Australian international affairs agencies as we know them emerged at the turn of the twentieth century. They were established within a complex web of colonial and post-colonial politics, emerging national identity and gender norms, and international institutions that were in various stages of ascension and failure in the lead up to the world wars. Australian women were the first in the world to gain full political rights. Australia was seen as a world leader and 'advanced' because of it.[12] However, women were not always able to exercise these rights, as many norms (and laws) across family, religion, and society clearly delineated roles and responsibilities for women. Their roles as wives and mothers came first[13] and so-called equality remained truly unequal. Indeed, the Commonwealth Franchise Act (1902) that made Australian women the 'freest of the free' also stripped Indigenous Australians' voting rights.[14] Therefore, at the turn of the twentieth century, Australian women's engagement in international affairs focused on engagement with civil society and reform organisations—largely 'informal' roles removed from the power and prestige of formal positions of engagement.[15] Even as recently as 2013, women's main role in international representation remained as 'supportive unpaid spouses' and gendered and racialised dynamics remain.[16]

Few accounts exist of Australian international engagements prior to British colonisation, let alone the gendered dynamics of such relations. As recently as the sixteenth to twentieth century Indigenous Australians maintained trade with Makassar Indonesians, and international trading routes likely predate this.[17] Despite this history, Australia's place on the world stage was only formalised under British Colonial rule, a rule that at the time was heavily patriarchal and paternalistic. Now, Australia is recognised as a federal constitutional monarchy guided by a parliamentary democracy, the rule of law, guaranteed freedoms, and adherence to international human rights laws and conventions. Australia has a comprehensive workplace anti-discrimination legislative framework, which in theory should make it achievable to attain gender parity in Australian international affairs. Once the subject of the repressive and racist White Australia Policy (the Immigration Restriction Act 1901), Australia is now noted the most diverse multicultural society in the world, exceeding even the United States, Canada, the United Kingdom, and New Zealand with over half of Australians born overseas or with a parent born overseas.[18]

Despite this cultural heterogeneity, the APS, and wider society, subscribes to predominantly Western, individualistic values and to a meritocratic understanding of career advancement and leadership.[19] As in other Western liberal states, particularly those with Westminster systems, 'the bureaucracy has developed, over time, a strong underlying commitment to the norm of bureaucratic neutrality'.[20] Yet as Chappell notes, 'the norm of neutrality is profoundly gendered'.[21] Additionally, there is an enduring imbalance in leadership and a prevailing and significant gender pay gap across almost all fields of work[22]—one that worsened during COVID-19. Australia's political climate has been critical of women in the past few years, evidenced, for example, by the high-profile misogyny against former Prime Minister Julia Gillard.[23] Women have been continually marginalised within Australia's bilateral relationship with its foremost allies, with 15 white Australian men recognised as part of the hundred-year anniversary of the US-Australia Alliance 'mateship' campaign in 2018—and no women.[24] Public debate and media coverage of gender inequality reached a crescendo in 2021 followed by allegations of rape and sexual harassment in parliament, a flood of women parliamentarians in elected in the 2022 federal election, and the drafting of a new Parliamentary code of conduct that followed. Australia is now experiencing a highly changeable political and governance environment for women leaders.

While overt barriers to women's rights, equity, employment, and leadership are largely nonexistent (even illegal), latent forms of bias and discrimination remain embedded within organisations and wider society. As Neumann states:

> When a law or set of laws is changed, even if it happens as a result of an erosion of the social and metaphysical grounds upon which it rests, those grounds may still have a lingering presence in discourse and so remain a precondition for action in lieu of legal purchase.[25]

But why? Australian international affairs agencies now exist within complex and complementary legal and policy environments, which should provide some guarantees around equality. The following list is not exhaustive however does map some of the key legal and policy frameworks within which the agencies studied operate. Each agency is guided at national and international levels whilst also having specific agency policies, some more holistic, detailed, and up-to-date than others.

International Legal Framework
- Convention on the Elimination of All forms of Discrimination Against Women (CEDAW)
- United Nations Security Council Resolution 1325 (UNSCR1325) on Women, Peace & Security

National Legal Framework
- Sex Discrimination Act (1984)
- Workplace Gender Equality Act (2012)
- Equal Employment Opportunities Act (1987)
- And intersectional acts like: Racial Discrimination Act (1975)

Foreign and Defence Policy Framework
- Australian Foreign Policy White Paper 2017: 'Australia's foreign policy pursues the empowerment of women as a top priority' (Commonwealth of Australia 2017, p. 43).
- Defence White Paper 2016: 'Gender equality and increasing female participation in the Defence workforce and in senior leadership roles is fundamental to achieving Defence capability now and into the future' (Commonwealth of Australia 2016, p. 23)

Australian Public Service (APS) Policy Framework
- Australian Public Service Commission (APSC) Diversity and Inclusion Strategy
- Australian Public Service Gender Equality Strategy 2021–2026, replacing Balancing the Future: The Australian Public Service Gender Equality Strategy 2016–2019 (lapsed)
- Gender Equality Action Plan (lapsed)

Agency Policy Framework and Networks
DFAT
- Women in Leadership Strategy (2015)
- Gender Equality and Women's Empowerment Strategy (2016)
- Cultural and Linguistic Diversity (CALD) Strategy 2018–2021
- Lesbian, Gay, Bisexual, Trans or Gender Diverse and Intersex (LGBTI) Workplace Strategy 2018–2021
- Indigenous Peoples Strategy 2015–2019 (lapsed)
- Disability Action Strategy 2016–2020

Home Affairs
- Gender Equality Action Plan 2017–2020 (lapsed)

- Disability Action Plan 2016–2020 in the Australian Border Force (ABF)

AFP
- Gender Strategy International Operations 2018–2022
- International Command Gender Strategy 2018–2024
- Gay and Lesbian Liaison Officer (GLLO) network
- Malunggang Indigenous Officers Network
- AFP Ability Advisory Network
- National Women's Advisory Network
- Cultural and Linguistically Diverse (CALD) Network

Defence
- Australian Public Service Gender Equality Strategy 2016–2019 (lapsed)
- Defence Diversity and Inclusion Strategy 2012–2017 (lapsed)

Agency Reviews on Gender Discrimination and Harassment
AFP
- *Cultural Change: Gender Diversity and Inclusion in the Australian Federal Police* (2016)

Defence
- The Review of Employment Pathways for APS Women in the Department of Defence (2011)
- Report on the Review into the Treatment of Women at the Australian Defence Force Academy (Phase 1) (2011)
- Report on the Review into the Treatment of Women in the Australian Defence Force (Phase 2) (2012)
- Review into the Treatment of Women at the Australian Defence Force Academy (Audit Report) (Phase 3) (2013)
- Review into the Treatment of Women in the Australian Defence Force Audit Report) (Phase 3) (2014)

Each agency has a specifically and deeply 'layered' institutional context[26]—with new institutions layered on older policies, accreted centuries of Westminster practice, Administrative Arrangements Orders, and machinery of government changes. These formal policies are important for understanding how institutions *regulate* behaviour.[27] Yet neither women's representation in leadership, nor experiences of international affairs, are neatly tied to the formal policies and strategies that are in place. Within these agencies, it is important to remember that 'swapping female for male bodies in traditionally masculine arenas'—or indeed implementing 'neutral' or gender equality policy—'does little to disrupt either the symbolism or practices of the gender order', as the gendered dimensions of institutions are more deeply embedded.[28] As one participant noted, agencies often still look for 'the right sort of female chap', indicating prevailing gendered biases applied even despite changing agency policies.[29]

Defence has been the subject of many reviews and audits—see the Australian Human Rights Commission reviews from 2011 to 2014, plus more.[30] In fact, between 1995 and 2013 there were a total of 13 inquiries into military culture prompted by scandals.[31] Yet more than one former senior Defence official noted that each subsequent review overrode the recommendations of the prior, resulting in reduced traction, which is evident in Defence policy development and reflected in the Moran Review too where it was noted that 'there are gaps between rhetoric and what gets accomplished'.[32] Defence's website evidences commitment to diversity and inclusion across gender, cultural, and linguistic diversity, sexual diversity, and so on; however, this is not supported by formalised policy documents publicly available. Further, two of the key documents, the *Australian Public Service Gender Equality Strategy 2016–2019* and the *Defence Diversity and Inclusion Strategy 2012–2017*, have lapsed, which represents a major oversight and policy gap. Collection of YourSay Survey data was also ceased in 2019, which was designed in part to understand and address why women decide to leave Defence. Each individual service line (Navy, Army, and Air Force) has its own separate policies and practices, which highlight localised attempts to address gender inequalities operationally. However, it is likely that these localised attempts have reduced traction without the backing of overarching Defence strategies, given the hierarchical nature of Defence where chain of command matters. Further, the disparate nature of policies allows for inconsistencies, with policies lapsed or not renewed at times.

Of the other agencies, the AFP's International Operations (IO) division has its own Gender Strategy separate to any AFP-wide policies—suggesting a developed policy framework for women leaders deployed internationally. Home Affairs until recently had the least number and depth of policies on gender and diversity inclusion, including having a four-year gap between reinstating gender equality strategies from 2013 to 2017. Yet it also has the highest percentage of women in international representation, which perhaps indicates the *lack of need* to introduce policies due to informal rules and norms that were already more gender equitable. Finally, the Department of Foreign Affairs and Trade (DFAT), on surface levels, appears to have the best-developed frameworks for gender and diversity inclusion. However, while it has multiple and specific policies promoting diversity throughout the agency, not all are current, including major ones around Indigenous inclusion—which is interesting to note, given Foreign Minister Penny Wong's 2022 commitment to a First Nations foreign policy agenda in government.

These policies set the agenda and parameters for action around gender and diversity inclusion. In many cases, they have explicit aims to transform organisational cultures to become 'more supportive' of women. They provide scaffolding, giving women policy-backed support for their representation and participation. Yet many are largely aspirational and not prescriptive. While the policies suggest a feminist turn in international affairs, in the context of a broader shift in direction across Australian business and public services, women's experiences are a far more useful indicator of policy traction. Some agencies, like DFAT, have already attempted to understand women's qualitative experiences through instituting 'think-ins' led by the Women in Leadership Secretariat. However, most of the findings of these 'think-ins' remain inaccessible to the public, which both contributes to a lack of transparency and obscures the insights gained. What the Lowy Institute[33] makes clear is that gender in Australia's foreign policy apparatus is amid change.

Prior to delving into each of the agencies in the next section of the chapter, it is noted that departmental change through Australia's machinery of government occurs frequently, particularly following an election.[34] Therefore, the exact name and makeup of a department represents a glimpse into history only at a certain point in time. For instance, when this research commenced in 2017, Home Affairs did not yet exist as an agency. Yet within the Australian Public Service Commission's (APSC) own Statistical Yearbook, previous departmental structures have been subsumed under their contemporary titles—for instance, all previous Immigration and Customs data is now condensed under the 'Home Affairs' category. Within the context of new departments being made, old departments being disbanded, and departments often merging, the institutions (rules, norms, and practices) guiding these departments are often in a state of change, and the policies layered. This highlights even more so the importance of tracing the agencies *historical forces* and *structure and leadership* to better understand organisational culture and gender relations—two key elements of analysis informed by McGlen and Sarkee's research on international affairs agencies that will be employed in the following sections.

Eliteness Eroded in the Department of Foreign Affairs and Trade (DFAT)

DFAT is Australia's core diplomatic and foreign policy agency, guiding much of the policy landscape and priorities adopted across the other agencies in international affairs. Recognised as a Male Champion of Change for his leadership in instituting the *Women in Leadership Strategy* and *Gender Equality and Women's Empowerment Strategy*, former secretary of DFAT, Peter Varghese, identified gender diversity as one of five issues challenging Australia's diplomatic effectiveness internationally.[35] Yet the focus on gender has been relatively new in the agency's history, as explored in the next section.

Historical Forces

The Department of Trade and Customs and Department of External Affairs were amongst the first of seven Commonwealth Departments established at Federation, yet Australia only established its first diplomatic missions to foreign countries in 1940. In 1987, the Department of Foreign Affairs (DFA) and the Department of Trade (Trade) merged into a single department, currently recognised as the modern-day DFAT. Prior to the merger of DFA and Trade, DFA was criticised as not matching the change in Australian society with regards to staffing.[36] Amongst criticisms were what Harris argues was an assumed dominance of staffing from private schools, noting that the service was becoming 'increasingly out of touch with technological, social and other changes'.[37] This fits within international diplomatic studies that characterise the field as high prestige, but also out of touch with changes across wider society, and in part explains the increasing focus on professionalisation that has since dominated the department and wider APS.

Yet gender appeared not to be a relevant enough category of analysis to mention, with Harris's study of the agency failing to make any gendered analysis nor mentioning the heavily male staffing composition in leadership. The historical Marriage Bar had done much to restrict women's access to diplomatic careers, particularly in terms of progression. Australian High Commissioner to Cyprus, Trevor Peacock, noted in 2012 that

> the marriage bar reflected the views that a married woman should be supported by her husband, and that married women took men's jobs. It was also argued that recruiting women was an inefficient use of resources—why employ women when they would marry sooner or later and have to resign? The resistance to appointing married women rested on claims that there would be no place for a male spouse at an overseas mission and that it would be socially inappropriate—if not scandalous—to post a married woman without her husband.[38]

Peacock's assessment of the period is reinforced when he quotes a Trade Official of the time:

Women could not mix nearly as freely with businessmen as men do; they could not withstand the fairly severe strains and stresses, mental and physical, of the trade commissioner's life, and 'a spinster lady can, and often does, turn into something of a battleaxe with the passing years—whereas a man usually mellows'. Tellingly, the [Trade Official's] greatest concern was that women recruits 'would take the place of a man and preclude us from giving experience to a male officer'.[39]

While Australia was the first nation to lift the Marriage Bar in 1966, the change in policy did not result in an automatic change in attitudes, and it was nearly two decades before women began entering DFAT as graduates in equal or greater numbers.[40] Even so, elements of the *Immigration Restriction Act* (1901) were still in place, so the abolition of the Marriage Bar was limited in its effects to the predominantly middle- and upper-class white women who had access to government employment at the time.

Barriers included negative attitudes about the professionalism of women officers and the predominance of a 'male culture' and male domination within the organisation that inhibited women's abilities to operate freely. In 1971, the first woman head of mission (HOM) was appointed, Dame Annabelle Rankin, a political appointee, to the Australian High Commission in New Zealand. In 1974, Ruth Dobson became the first career diplomat female HOM, appointed as the Australian Ambassador to Denmark just over 30 years after first joining the service.

In 1984, a survey of officers found that over half felt that being a woman had affected their career, institutional barriers to promotion and postings affected their career progression, and negative assumptions about their ability to manage family and their career were common. One former Ambassador and former Governor of the State of Queensland recalls being told at that time that she needed to choose 'whether she was a mother or an officer, reflecting a then prevalent view that it was not possible for women to be both'.[41] At this same time, only two women (out of 52 overall roles—three per cent) were employed in the Second Division (now SES) in Foreign Affairs, while women represented 44.5 per cent of overall employment.[42] This gap between women's overall representation and their representation in leadership is a theme that will be returned to later—and demonstrates a pervasive diplomatic glass ceiling.

Following the 1984 passing of the *Sex Discrimination Act*, in 1985 DFA introduced an equal employment opportunity (EEO) program. Amongst some of the first aims of the program was *reducing* the number of posts unsuitable for women officers—which is striking in that its initial aims were not *eliminating* the number of posts deemed unsuitable for women officers, as is the case now. Initial attempts at EEO were not truly equal. By the time of the 1987 merger, one of the hallmarks of diplomacy—its prestige—was starting to shift with the abolition of separate career structures for diplomatic policy staff and administrative staff. This abolished the 'perception of an exclusive caste'.[43] As the department has become more professionalised and bureaucratised, it has also developed as a Canberra-based public service career. This is a distinctive shift from diplomacy of the past, in which 65 per cent of positions were based internationally in 1984, compared to 2018 in which only 24.9 per cent of positions are based internationally.[44]

In 1996, the Department's first childcare centre in Canberra was introduced, aimed at addressing long work hours and a lack of work-life balance that characterised employment in the agency. The introduction of the centre followed a 1994 follow-up survey, in which male spouses accompanying women internationally were raised as a challenge in terms of: finding work for the spouse; financial income losses; social expectations that the man of the house should work; and the 'double burden' placed on women to manage the post and the house. Spousal challenges remain a core issue today. Positive findings of this survey included that women diplomats believed they were more ethical, more consultative, and better managers of their staff. They also felt they had wider access to contacts in their host countries by virtue of being female.

2013 heralded a significant change for DFAT, in which the incoming Abbott Government restructured Australia's overseas aid and development initiatives, abolishing the Australian Agency for International Development (AusAID), and merging many of the previous AusAID staff with DFAT. The absorption of the Department of Trade (in 1987) and AusAID (in 2013) to make modern-day DFAT represent two of the greatest cultural shifts the agency has seen.[45] Each of the three parts—foreign affairs, trade, and aid—had specific organisational cultures, norms, and practices. Participants still refer to staff from these different departmental mergers as 'tradies' (those from Trade), 'foreign affairies' (those from DFA), 'wasAiders' (those who were part of AusAID), and 'preFATers' (those from DFAT prior to the AusAID merger). Esther (not her real name) noted:

> There was a lot of 'us and them' in DFAT for years. The trade people used to call them the 'foreign affairies' and they would look down on the 'tradies'... for a long time there was a sort of delineation of jobs you might get overseas... if you're a tradie, then you'll only get trade jobs anywhere, go to Washington as head of the trade section, but you won't go somewhere as ambassador.[46]

Prestige and status were important to the department, with the 'foreign affairies' named 'purists', versus 'tradies' who dealt with 'the smutty, commercial part of a relationship' between states. Not only did 'tradies'—characterised by participants as not as skilled in the 'art' of diplomacy—have classist connotations, names like 'wasAiders' were generally used derogatorily. As a microcosm of intradepartmental relations, nicknames are employed partly in jest, and partly as a method of maintaining the overarching order of divisions in which one's background pre-determined status within the Department.

The merger of Trade and DFA also had specific gendered effects. Overall, Trade was described by participants as more masculinist, and men represented 61 per cent of Trade's total workforce in 1985, as opposed to 55 per cent of Foreign Affair's total workforce at the same time. Further, the leader of the National Party often held the trade portfolio ministerial role—a role in which women have never yet held. On the other hand, the 2013 AusAID merger had the effect of rapidly increasing the proportion of women in the Department, increasing women's representation by 5.2 percentage points in just one year, when women went from representing 52.3 per cent of the agency to 57.5 per cent across 2013–2014. Concerns flourished that these AusAID staff were unskilled (in the art of diplomacy), reaching high-level diplomatic postings overseas before it was merited. A different kind of gendered impact arose from the merger.

Dana describes the prestige associated with the traditional Foreign Affairs portfolio, noting that one of the things that drew her to the work was 'the prestige factor, or at least there was at the time. Now that the walls have sort of opened up a bit that has lessened'.[47] Pure foreign affairs was the bastion of prestige, whereas the humanitarian side of international affairs was 'soft' and has 'lessened' the exclusivity of the organisation. This is also interesting to note considering that the 'soft' policy areas around humanitarian topics have traditionally had greater representation of women, reinforcing that the prestige and exclusivity of DFAT diplomacy was a *gendered exclusion*. In fact, some participants interviewed recalled the day AusAID employees merged with DFAT and staff walked into their new offices in the RG Casey building in Barton, noting that some DFAT employees stood on the towering platforms above the entrance and shot imaginary machine guns at the new arrivals and mimicked tipping buckets of water over their heads. If nothing else, this reveals workplace behaviours sometimes exclusive, competitive, and protective, if not outright aggressive.

During the mergers, in reconciling employment policy differences, DFAT was noted to take the 'lowest common denominator' approach on several critical issues.[48] For instance, some fertility provisions that were guaranteed under the AusAID structure were removed under the DFAT structure. One participant described how AusAID provisions covered women returning to Australia for fertility treatment. In contrast, DFAT 'never had that, and so they've now caught up to the lowest common denominator'.[49] Attempts to regain policy support were met with misunderstanding (deliberate or otherwise). Dana stated:

> What [the women] were asking for was support for at least what was covered under the APS here [in Australia] ... where the executive landed on it was to say that any woman who wants to come back from posting early in order to have children or for fertility reasons won't have their careers negatively impacted, which wasn't what women were asking for ... [women were] saying women are career oriented, they want the opportunity for posting, it's important to their career, *of course* their career should not be negatively impacted when coming home early, that was a given ... so it's a situation where [the Department effectively said] 'dear women, if you want to do this sort of thing which we say we do want you to do, leave these hard-fought career opportunities early' [ignoring the requests for support made].[50]

This example highlights the impact of dominant cultures during machinery of government changes, demonstrating that 'good' policies on gender may drift or be completely removed during departmental shifts.

Now, not only are there growing numbers of women overall and in leadership, but there is also a rhetorical shift away from some of the prestige factors of the past: private school educated, connected, upper-class, white, and male. Is this a positive change? In many ways, yes. However, these changes are also coinciding with the agency's diminished role in international affairs. The Lowy Institute[51] identified the shrinking of DFAT's overseas network by over 30 per cent between 1987 and 2013. They note, 'although the government sector as a whole flourished, growing nearly 60 per cent between 1997 and 2013, DFAT staffing remained virtually unchanged'.[52] Additionally, 'since 2009, the Lowy Institute has consistently argued that Australia's Department of Foreign Affairs and Trade (DFAT) has been under-resourced over a period of several decades. As a result, its overseas network has thinned out significantly'.[53] The context is therefore complex. Just as women are beginning to gain traction in the traditional diplomatic side of international affairs, DFAT is losing strategic power to militaristic agencies, and withdrawing from maintaining a presence in the world. One participant commented on the beginning of this trend in the late 1990s:

> The Liberal government came in and there was a real freeze on public service positions and movements. So, this was the start of DFAT starting to get very little funding and very little emphasis. A lot of funding was going into security agencies and not much into diplomacy. You can make a gender story out of that if you wanted to, I think it's actually very significant.[54]

This puts some of the more recent progressive changes in question. Has DFAT been able to gain more women and institute more progressive policies only because it is no longer the premiere arena for Australia's international affairs? Like McGlen and Sarkees's findings in the US, recent developments have seen an increase in funding and strategic importance within the 'harder' security and enforcement agencies (Defence and Home Affairs particularly) and a decrease in funding for DFAT.[55] DFAT's 'shrinking' coincides with a more enforcement-based, 'hard' approach to Australian foreign policy led by military leaders and a securitised approach to affairs. In McGlen and Sarkees's study, they attributed this trend both to politics and the functions of the departments, 'with [foreign affairs'] relatively passive role of observation, reporting, negotiation, and advisement', as compared to the military's primary function of action.[56]

Yet the rising influence of 'hard' military agencies and decline in funding—and potentially influence—of 'soft' foreign affairs agencies is particularly relevant given that 'the public perceives women as better equipped to handle the 'soft' issues in politics and management... not the 'hard' issues involving conflict'.[57] In fact, whilst Lee-Koo notes:

> Commitments to the participation of women, enhancing women's leadership, promoting gender equality, and the provisioning of resources to achieve and measure progress toward these goals is evident on a number of fronts... the traditionally masculinist policy areas of bi- and multilateral trade, foreign investment, war fighting, military procurement, and weapons trading remain largely untouched by the move toward pro-gender norms.[58]

The power shift to 'hard' international affairs is therefore gendered. Indeed, as my own subsequent research has found, 'whilst symbolic status and material resourcing fluctuate in Australia's international affairs, where the funding is greatest, the proportion of men is highest'.[59] This has major ramifications for women in DFAT, who have now achieved parity (or near to it) at a moment when Australia is 'out of line' with international trends in diplomatic spending, with the Lowy Institute[60] claiming Australia is operating with a 'diplomatic deficit' and Oliver[61] arguing Australia is in diplomatic 'disrepair'. This has real implications for women's career paths and opportunities in foreign affairs, with women's progress to leadership positions in diplomacy limited by the declining functional power of those positions — a diplomatic glass cliff.

It is within this recent context of fluctuating funding, prestige, and power that policies such as the *Women in Leadership Strategy* (2015) were launched. The strategy established the Women in Leadership Secretariat within DFAT, which sits within the executive branch, directly below the Secretary, suggesting that it has the commensurate power (symbolically, if not substantively) needed to enforce the strategy and guarantee accountability. So far, the *Women in Leadership Strategy* has had marked success in achieving its short-term targets of 40 per cent by the end of 2018 for SES band 1, reaching its end-2020 target of 40 per cent women at the SES band 2 level (48.4 per cent) and was close to reaching its end-2020 target of 43 per cent women at the SES Band 1 level (42 per cent). The Strategy, and *Gender Equality and Women's Empowerment Strategy*, build on previous policy commitments by DFAT including the creation of the Ambassador for Women and Girls (in 2011), changed in 2020 to the Ambassador for Gender Equality, which until recently was held by DFAT's first Indigenous woman ambassador, Julie-Ann Guivarra.

These recent developments suggest that formal policies with measurable and time-limited objectives, that are enforceable by a body with the requisite power to implement policies, have been successful at increasing women's representation in leadership. Additionally, critical actors (like DFAT's secretary, formerly Peter Varghese, a Male Champion of Change, then three-times female secretaries in Frances Adamson, Kathryn Campbell, and Jan Adams, as well as the Ministerial leadership first of Julie Bishop, then Marise Payne and now Penny Wong) have reinforced women's leadership at the highest levels. As mentioned in Chapter 1, when analysing women deployed internationally in senior leadership at the start of 2017 and again at the start of 2018, women's representation increased by 14.6 per cent representation.[62] This, and DFAT's ability to achieve its initial targets, highlight institutional success in some key areas.

Yet despite this, one of the most notable features of modern DFAT gender relations is that women's strong representation overall and in leadership has not correlated to gender equality in experiences and opportunities. In fact, as explored later in the book, the progress made by the agency obscures persistent gender inequalities that remain. Participants' contemporary experiences highlight covert or more 'genteel' forms of gendered challenges and even toxic masculinities that have altered, but not necessarily reduced the inequalities experienced. Rani noted that gendered challenges are 'increasingly pushed underground and subdued. There will be some people you can never change and they might just not say it out loud but they are still secretly saying these things'.[63]

Participants highlighted a shift to 'underground', more covert forms of discrimination and 'toxic' forms of workplace masculinity. Toxic masculinities refer to hegemonic forms of masculinity that subordinate women and others who do not fit the archetype.[64] Whilst toxic masculinity is more commonly associated with militaries, 'genteel' forms of toxic masculinity recurred throughout the more diplomatic or bureaucratic nonmilitary agencies studying, seeming just as pervasive, only more difficult to identify. Participants recounted colleagues within their agencies knowing exactly what to say, and how to say it, which meant that gendered behaviours were often harder to spot (and therefore harder to believe). Despite the policies that now exist, participants still reported keeping lists of predatory men in the department to avoid, and while some men championed doing the 'right' thing, they persisted in gendered treatment anyway. Women still did the bulk of the 'organisational housework'—clearing out rooms after meetings, providing baked goods for organisational morning teas,—and the progress made in the department often meant it was harder to have the inequalities that endured recognised. Tick-box inclusion exercises remained common, across a range of diversity groups.

These enduring forms of covert, 'genteel' gendered behaviour in diplomacy are consistent with findings globally. Barrington,[65] for instance, highlights that while attitudes have evolved in the Irish MFA, covert forms gendered treatment, unconscious bias, and sexism in the media's treatment of women diplomats remains. Further, Barrington notes that while an equal number of, or more, women are not being recruited into the department, leadership remains stubbornly out of reach. Cassidy echoes this, arguing that 'while the nominal participation of women within the diplomatic sphere may be increasing, the substantial nature of their role within the service has not progressed at the same pace'.[66] MFAs globally are acknowledging that most formal barriers are gone, and that (male) colleagues are often acutely, distinctly aware of the 'right thing' to say and do. Yet distinctly gendered treatment in experience and senior representation remains. The question to consider is: How much do these covert forms of genteel toxic masculinities extend beyond Australia or global cases, and into other forms of work?

Structure and Leadership

Additional to the history of DFAT canvassed above, contemporary agency structure and leadership informs women's experiences and underrepresentation in international affairs. The degree and centralisation of decision-making, level of hierarchy, and structure of leadership impact on the 'gender ethos' of an organisation.[67] This ethos or context frames gendered institutions—rules, norms, and practices—that affect women leaders. McGlen and Sarkees highlight how 'some types of decision-making structures are more conducive to women's power than others', mapping out four key structures that aid women in foreign and defence affairs leadership.[68] Decision structures that produce a more favourable gender ethos include those that:

(1) have nonrigid procedures that downplay rightful participation based on position and include individuals expertise;
(2) tend to de-emphasise and personalise the power of the secretary;
(3) are least centralised and hierarchical; and
(4) have more women involved in communication surrounding decisions.[69]

McGlen and Sarkees propose that the more linear and rigid organisational charts are, such as those of all the case agencies, the more hierarchical an agency. They also note that rigid and hierarchical structures tend to favour more male dominated departments. These centralised decision-making structures generally benefit women only when women are within the decision-making positions.

DFAT is a hierarchical organisation, with the hierarchy becoming steeper towards the top. Canberra, state and international offices all have specific chains of command. Consistent with the rest of the APS, staff in DFAT, whether posted internationally or not, have clear ranks. Unlike some of the more militaristic or paramilitaristic agencies however, these ranks are not physically visible on employees (in the form of a uniform or 'stripes', for instance), which may reduce hierarchy and rank friction—allowing for a 'flatter' structure in practice. APS ranks 1–6 form most of the workforce, followed by those in the leadership pipeline in EL Bands 1 and 2, and SES Bands 1, 2, and 3.

Until 2021, then-Secretary of DFAT, Frances Adamson, prioritised gender equality and took a 'leadership by example' approach. Not only was she the first woman Secretary of the department, but she instituted a female majority of Deputy Secretaries for the first time in the department's history. Her position as Secretary, the presence of her Deputies, and a female Minister for Foreign Affairs in Julie Bishop and later Marise Payne, was significant. In the US, the Olmsted report concluded that 'the single most important factor in achieving equal employment opportunity in the Department of State is the commitment demonstrated by the Secretary of State and the Under Secretary for management".[70] As Australia's former Foreign Affairs Minister Julie Bishop notes:

> I always think that when a women is the first to fill a position, she has the responsibility to make sure that it's easier for other women to follow, not harder. So, I'm particularly pleased that my successor is a woman, Marise Payne. Australia now has the second female foreign minister, so it's not such a novelty. I think that is a responsibility that all women have. Once you have that position—a position that has not been held by a woman—you must try and make it easier for the next woman to achieve it.[71]

The actions of critical actors have been important at each of the significant gender milestones achieved by the department. On viewing the success of the Department of Treasury's gender strategy, DFAT undertook the task of implementing the *Women in Leadership Strategy*. Yet the agency had been characterised by a lack of action on women's representation in the preceding years. It took the steadfast working of individuals—mostly women—within the department to lobby and push the executive into action. It also involved a threat of loss of key women to get the required uptake. This fits with Acker's[72] findings of the most successful gender change initiatives, which often require *coercion or the threat of loss*, as well as support internally within the department as well as externally within society. Julienne detailed what this process looked like from the inside:

> We had adopted a little girl in November . . . and [the Department] called me and said, I want to promote you into this job but you have to come back [to Australia]. I said, I didn't want to come back because I had this arrangement, I'd uprooted my family . . . I was on mandated adoption leave at the time in any event, so legally . . . I was protected. Anyway, I did have a pretty open conversation . . . about, this is why you don't have many women in leadership roles in the organisation, because it becomes very difficult when you have to make these choices . . . there wasn't an organisational fix, it was a personal fix, which then led me when I went back to think that we needed to do something about improving women in leadership credentials . . . All of that research pointed to one absolutely critical factor for success, and that was that any initiative like this *had to be led from the top*.[73]

This narrative reinforces hierarchy: changes required top-down instigation. The *Women in Leadership Strategy* is now regarded as one of Varghese's foremost contributions to the Department as Secretary. It took the leadership of Varghese to institute, which reinforces the hierarchical structure of the agency. However, it would not have been possible without the dedicated internal lobbying of individuals within the Department too—internal support that Acker reinforces as crucial for organisational change.

Varghese was clearly a critical actor in beginning to transform the gendered institutions within DFAT, launching the *Women in Leadership Strategy* in 2015. Yet *who* he was, was also important. Julienne stated:

> The terrific thing, of course, was that it was Peter Varghese that led this. It wasn't Julie Bishop, it was Peter Varghese and he was a bloke. Not only was he a bloke, but he was a very well-regarded, clever thinker bloke. The fact that he was doing this management stuff on women sends a really strong message. The fact that Frances was able to come in and ramp it up ... that's powerful ... I think it will be very hard to undo after Frances, I really do. It's better, in my mind, that it started under Peter then continued with Frances. That was a better sequencing. Because if Frances had started it and some man had come in and said, 'oh, *that's women's business*' ... the fact that she came in behind Peter and said, I know where you're going, I see what we're doing and I'm going to take it up a notch and get it done ... you couldn't get better than that.[74]

Perceptions of not being 'a woman who only cares about women' recurred throughout the research as being important to the legitimacy of leadership in the Department. Likewise, having a male critical actor introduce the Strategy lent weight and a perceived 'gender neutrality' to the issue that was needed to see its uptake within the still male-dominated DFAT leadership. This indicates differences in the perceived weight of women's voices versus men's within the Department, highlighting that for this policy to 'work' within DFAT, it needed to come from the epitome of what it meant to *be* DFAT—in this case, a 'very well-regarded, clever thinker bloke'.

In placing DFAT relative to the other agencies studied on a continuum between a traditional military to a traditional diplomatic international affairs agency, DFAT is characterised as the most traditional diplomatic organisation studied, with all its staff professional public servants and its structure guided solely by the *APS Act* (1999). This delineation is useful to situating the agency relative to the other agencies compared, particularly when it comes to understanding the statistics later in this book. Overall, DFAT's structure and leadership reveals a hierarchical organisation. Critical actors have been essential to implementing gendered change in institutions, and strategies and policies for gaining women's representation, to date, have largely worked. The gender of critical actors, and sequencing (male instigated, followed by female leadership) has been crucial to ensuring specifically gendered policy is naturalised, neutralised, and normalised within the agency. The implication is that while women cannot introduce gender-specific policy without being perceived as a 'woman who only cares about women', they have an important role in ensuring its on-going implementation.

More Than a Golden Handshake: Defence

McGlen and Sarkees note that 'the right to participate in the making of a country's foreign policy has been conditioned by the ability to fight in a country's wars'.[75] Smith states that, 'for thousands of years, war has been the preserve of males'.[76] The premise underlying global militaries is therefore heavily gendered, and Australia is no different.

Historical Forces

Broadly regarded as one organisation known as 'Defence', the Australian Defence Force (ADF—the military body with Army, Navy and Air Force service lines) and the Department of Defence (DoD—a civilian, public-sector department) are a diarchy, part of a long standing, strong tradition as one of the most masculine portfolios of the state. Defence is a key and growing portfolio for Australia, with many reviews and inquiries identifying Defence as one of the most critical contributors to the delivery of Government capabilities, particularly around protecting and advancing Australia's national and strategic interest.[77] Its role has been further substantiated following Australia's 2019–2020 summer bushfires and COVID-19 response, as well as the establishment of the new Space Command in 2022, all of which have drawn Defence into a wider scope of security threats.

The inclusion of women is therefore a growing priority for the agency, which is not only under pressure to deliver gender equality on moral grounds, but strategic too. The Australian Human Rights Commission notes that the ADF 'must address the problem of a shrinking talent pool, the significant cost of unwanted departures, the lack of diversity at leadership level and its desire to be a first-class employer with a first class reputation'.[78]

Until recently, women could not serve in combat roles, and generally were employed only within 'soft' staffing and administrative areas or gender-segregated service lines. Therefore, women's greater inclusion in Defence has been made possible by two significant changes over the past few decades: the changing technology and characteristics of war; and changing social and cultural norms, attitudes, and institutions.[79] Technological advancements in the defence industry, as well as the changing nature of warfare along chemical, cyber, and nuclear lines, have reduced barriers raised by physiological differences. In contemporary combat, operation of weapons is less about sheer muscle power than about technical skill and training. These changes have resulted in a reduction in physicality as a barrier to combat roles, and therefore, progression to more senior leadership. For these very reasons, the Air Force has historically recruited more women than other service lines and opened a greater range of positions for their employment—it has a larger need for technological and administrative corps than actual combatants.[80] On the other hand, tasks with greater technical and specialised skills, as well as operational planning roles, have largely excluded women and continue to do so, if not by design, then by unconscious bias and gender stereotyping that maintains men as the most skilled in operational planning areas.

Responding to these technological changes (as well as social), since 2011, the Australian Government endorsed Defence's plans for women to serve in combat roles. However, the historic combat ban has influenced women's pathways to leadership. As Bridge notes, it 'placed a ceiling on promotion . . . barring women from prestigious and elite positions by restricting leadership positions—especially where combat experience is a prerequisite'.[81] The exclusion of women from combat and largely the wider activities of Defence has therefore been predicated on (a) physicality, (b) social and cultural institutions, and (c) by virtue of the first two points, gender. The art of fighting wars, the brute strength required to wield weapons, and even the 'band of brothers' mentality have all worked to create military spaces as spaces of exclusion of women.[82] Smith notes, 'differences in physicalities—whether real or perceived—have thus helped to make the military calling an essentially male preserve'.[83] This trend continues in the modern Australian military, reflective of persistent and stubborn informal norms that continue to equate the military with the male.

Social and cultural institutions have also prescribed Defence as the antithesis of what it means to be woman. Many social and cultural institutions globally, as well as within Australia specifically, have foregrounded women's roles as mothers, daughters, nurturers, and carers.[84] Their many virtues are extolled as being peacemakers and creators—'*women* are not supposed to be violent'.[85] They are positioned as oppositional to the warring aggression and patriarchal strength needed to ensure the protection of Australian national interest and way of life.[86] The many objections raised against women joining the armed forces in the first place were heavily based around 'the popular image of woman as the passive, nurturing mother of the race [which] does not easily mesh with the combat soldier, an aggressive, killer male'.[87] Opponents 'have expressed fears that women's lack of capacity (physical and psychological) for combat roles will reduce the effectiveness of military operations, will distract men, will incite public outrage and disrupt male bonding'.[88] Throughout this research, narratives of the 'killer' and the 'protector', the 'patriarch' and the 'powerful', continued to permeate Defence norms and ideologies, reinforcing role segregations that have continued to see women predominate in caring roles within the agency—health, human resources, and support.[89] As Elshtain identifies, while women have 'beautiful souls', men make wars.[90]

The physicality associated with Defence activity, and the social and cultural institutions that surround it, are gendered. Yet Smith finds that only *particular groups* of men can undertake the functions of Defence too. Smith states:

> Young men are selected and trained to be warriors, sometimes from a very early age. In addition to learning military skills, they are imbued with the ethic and values of the warrior: loyalty, courage, self sacrifice and a sense of *esprit de corps*. The last-mentioned, in particular, creates a sense of difference from the rest of society, a belief that those in the military are members of an elite responsible for vital roles in that society. A central part of this military ethic is the belief that war and soldiering are the business of men. In the military class customs, traditions and taboos emerged to reinforce this attitude. It became unthinkable to have women in combat: at best this would be distracting, at worst subversive of discipline and *esprit de corps*. The place of women was to provide support, comfort or diversion for those in uniform.[91]

Women's presence was viewed as fundamentally reducing the capabilities of the military at this time—a subversion of the basis of military hierarchy and command, discipline, as well as being sexually distracting.[92] Notions of eliteness are consistent across DFAT and Defence despite their different masculine archetypes. Eliteness connotes exclusion that furthers the denial of access to women. While access to these military spaces of exclusion may be historical, the notion of exclusion has persisted due to the enduring *and* adaptable nature of institutions, and history's role in forming agency culture, norms, expectations, and rules from the start. Exclusion, like inequality, evolves.

Historical gendered institutions have a compounding impact in Defence, for which identity, actions and beliefs are strongly tied to tradition and history. For instance, each year, Australian public holidays recognise war and military personnel. Remembrance is a key theme of Anzac Day, a day that broadly commemorates Australians and New Zealanders who died in all wars, conflicts, and peacekeeping operations. History and tradition underpin the annual Anzac Day observances and days like it, reinforcing lines of continuity in terms of identity, culture, and behaviour.[93] The actual acts of past wars, as well as the acts of remembrance were, and continue to be, gendered, with Dwyer noting that fiction and narrative surrounding the Wars have 'been used to promote exemplars, to marginalise and exclude alternative versions of masculinity, and to subordinate the feminine'.[94] Women, Indigenous people, and people with non-Anglo-Celtic backgrounds who fought (and died) in wars remain underrecognised, and accounts of war 'heroes' are mostly accounts of 'the manly Anzac', with men portrayed as 'ungendered representatives of humanity . . . [with] the "ungendered norm" equated with male experience'.[95] The sacred and hallowed nature of days like Anzac Day, and the re-enactment of war tragedies and stories of bravery and strength, add a further layer to Defence's history. Remembrance strengthens 'old' military narratives and ideals that continue to influence women's place and treatment within Defence as marginalised, separate, subordinate, and inferior. As will be explored later in this section, challenging these old norms is viewed as 'sacrilege' and can result in these norms embedding deeper.

Women's participation in Defence is tied to the rise of the world wars and the need for nursing and support across clerical, administrative, transport and communication tasks.[96] In the build-up to the Second World War, auxiliary units were established, enshrining women in segregated portfolios and women's roles as different. Even though many women were given considerable duties and rank during the War, with even Indigenous women serving within these auxiliary units and women 'found employed in practically every job for which they were physically capable', this was quickly reversed in the post-war period, highlighting women's roles as largely temporary and exceptional.[97] They were not embedded in the cultural make-up of the agency and service lines, but rather were neat appendages that could be discharged when no longer required. Women could occupy some roles throughout the military, but it was never at the exclusion of men doing so.[98] This 'separateness' of women within Defence was actively supported. Bomford notes:

> Women entering a profession traditionally associated with the image of man the aggressor and armed protector were only acceptable within the institution itself, and to the broader community in Western society in general, if they maintained their stereotypical gender role, which in the 1950s was to support men by performing the sedentary, routine 'housekeeping' tasks in the army.[99]

There were clear and strict rules around what women could or could not do. They could join the corps, so long as they were 'plum', and not poor-quality applicants 'dissatisfied with their lives' and for whom the service offered 'higher social status, greater economic security, companionship, even . . . a substitute family'.[100] They could be drivers, so long as they had 'the right temperament'.[101] Women could be re-engaged in the service, so long as they were not overweight, with some participants recalling being called too 'podgy' for Defence service. When women signed up to join army rifle clubs, it was found not 'appropriate or necessary' for women to learn to shoot, with any memberships or access to resources immediately withdrawn.[102]

The reliance on stereotypical roles and duties also flowed into stereotypical looks, with women encouraged to emphasise their femininity through dress and comportment. While men were selected for traditional masculinised strength and physicality, women were selected based on their pleasant, womanly, and feminine appearance—delineating very different roles for very different physical attributes. Although the military tended to attract women who were more 'masculine' in discourse and appearance,[103] some participants' recalled being asked to dress and behave more 'womanly' so that they were not mistaken as lesbians. A number of participants recalled their male colleagues seeking women out as sexual 'conquests', with any women who refused to sleep with them perceived as 'uncontrollable', or queer. Participants reported that those who were homosexual were often removed from the service, and so heterosexual women would often help to cover for gay and lesbian women who were closely watched and often under intense scrutiny. Those who were perceived as 'uncontrollable' (often, they lived off campus or refused to have sexual relations with their colleagues) reported being given longer hours and more demanding work, often in administrative or organisational roles away from the operation duties of the ADF. These mechanisms at multiple levels of appearance, comportment and behaviour were used to maintain the existing gender order, as consistent with other studies.[104]

Bomford notes that, since the 1950s, women have been criticised for being 'less useful because they did not serve as long as men and could not fulfil the same range of duties as men'.[105] This criticism fails to recognise the overt discrimination and formal and informal restrictions on what roles women could fulfil. In the 1960s and 1970s, the male dominance within the military slowly began to shift, much like other areas of society. Major social changes regarding the equality of the sexes, including substantial legal gains around equal opportunity and freedom from discrimination, had begun to shift attitudes and employment in Defence, particularly with the growing stature of second-wave feminism, the anti-Vietnam War movement, gay liberation, Indigenous rights, and various worker movements. Changes in broader society are important causes of institutional change, not just within Defence, but also across all the agencies studied.

Although Defence has been slow to take up many of these wider societal shifts due to some of the abovementioned engrained institutions and an inherent conservativism, the agency is not immune to change. The nature of the work ensures that the agency requires large numbers of new recruits, as well as their retention under challenging and exceptional workplace circumstances. Demographic pressures over the past few decades have therefore opened new opportunities for women, as agency growth and turnover require broader recruitment than past all-male conscription or volunteering.[106] Indeed, in 1982 Cynthia Enloe noted that 'military personnel planners have pushed for greater use of women not so much because they have 'seen the light' and are on the verge of giving up patriarchy, but because they are worried about manpower shortages'.[107]

At this point, it is worth briefly exploring some of the core historical circumstances that inform the current operation of the three service lines—the Army, Air Force, and Navy. Each service line is distinct from the others, which reinforces the fact that generalisations about Defence must be undertaken with care, and nuances explained. Chain of command and military structuring ensures that overarching ADF principles guide each of the services. Yet each service also has its own organisational structures, policies, and practices, highlighting the 'layered' institutional context and complexity of Defence.

Of the three, the Army has the lowest overall representation of women, with women in 2022 representing only 15.11 per cent of personnel.[108] Women were historically segregated in the Army, as part of the Women's Royal Australian Army Corps (WRAAC) from 1951 to 1984. When the WRAAC was established, Bomford notes that 'a women's corps was the only way women would be accepted in the army', with women's integration into the Army defined by constant negotiation for ideological and professional space.[109] Women were only permitted to go on deployments from 1992. Prior to that, women were deployed at 'home' only, and there were no women in operative units. However, time in combat remains to be the most important element to career progression. Because women were only permitted in combat recently, there is still a lag and roles continue to be recruited based off ideal forms of hegemonic masculine physicality, with informal gendered norms guiding career appointments and deployments.[110]

The Air Force, on the other hand, had the highest representation of women in 2022, representing 26.14 per cent of personnel—largely because of different norms around physicality and the duties required to be an Air Force pilot.[111] However, leadership remains elusive for women—out of the 53 generalist star ranked officers in 2012, there was only one woman (1.9 per cent).[112] The initial gender-segregated unit was the Women's Auxiliary Australian Air Force (WAAAF), followed by the Women's Royal Australian Air Force (WRAAF) established from 1950 to 1977. WRAAF was earliest segregated unit to be disbanded out of the three service lines. Disbanding these gender-segregated units has been an important marker of progress, as prior units were temporary, limited in their operations and opportunities, and inferior to the men's equivalent—a result of not being the part of the 'real' work of the mainstream service lines.[113] Yet like the other service lines, the conditions of service were heavily gendered, with unequal pay formalised in policy (generally two thirds to three quarters of the male pay rate) and combat bans for women similarly applied as in the Army.[114] Time in operations—piloting planes—count most towards career advancement. Because members are trained through ADFA before commencing down their own service lines, many of the gendered norms and cultures in the wider ADF are also found in the Air Force.

As of 2022, women in the Navy represent 23.49 per cent of personnel.[115] Women were only sent to sea from 1984 onwards, because the Women's Royal Australian Naval Service (WRANS) regulations were repealed on incorporation into the Permanent Naval Forces.[116] However, the core component to career progression in the Navy is in operations—with the aim to deploy at sea captaining warships. Women's historical exclusion from deploying at sea has considerably restricted women's progression to leadership, resulting in a significant lag for women attaining these roles. Additionally, when ships are not engaged in actual warfare, a critical issue reported by participants was keeping members safe from themselves on ships—pastoral duties. Drugs and alcohol present key problems for warships, particularly in periods after docking at port for supplies. Given the majority male workforce and the entrenched gendered nature of the Navy, issues with drugs and alcohol likely increase instances of sexual harassment and assault—with research from the US indicating that out of any military installation, sexual assault was most likely on a Navy ship.[117] The isolated nature of ships presents clear challenges for women negotiating a male-dominated work environment, under the pressure of war-readiness, and in circumstances that are physically bounded at sea.

The final division to be discussed is the culture and work environment of the Department of Defence (DoD). Unlike the three military service lines, those who work in the departmental side are largely (although not exclusively) civilian staff, with a greater degree of lateral recruits from other APS agencies and a bureaucratic structure that more closely matches the rest of federal government (and some of the other agencies studied). When the bulk of this research was undertaken in 2018, women represented 44 per cent of overall employment and 32.6 per cent of SES positions.[118] In 2022, women represent 46.7 per cent of those employed overall, and 51.5 per cent of the Senior Executive Service—a 5 percentage point increase on the prior year, and almost 20 percentage point increase from four years ago.[119] Even so, military norms and identities still affect the departmental side of Defence. Military experience or high levels of experience and networks in DFAT, the Department of Prime Minister and Cabinet, or the Defence Minister's office still counts as important for the most senior roles.

The opportunities for leadership and new challenges in the ADF and the DoD are extensive, with myriad options for different roles and duties. Strong bonds and tight 'family' units are a large part of each of the three service lines and Defence in general, with participants' identities more closely entwined with their workplace and career. This has the result of both facilitating relationships that are robust, loyal and tight-knit, and by that same nature, places individuals at the mercy of their colleagues to a higher degree than a standard, non-Defence job might do—particularly for those in the ADF, those deployed internationally, or on operations. The three service lines do not tend to cross over; however, there are opportunities to work across the agency in Joint Operations Command (JOC) positions, in staff colleges, or in divisions such as the International Policy Division (IPD), where military personnel and civilian staff work together prior to overseas deployment as attachés and staff.

In Defence, as a matter of policy and practice, careers are managed within the three service lines of Navy, Army, and Air Force, with entire tomes written on career trajectories, and substantial resourcing and staff to help oversee career development. This has obvious benefits for both men and women in the service. However, career managers and supervisors are not free of bias, with the Australian Human Rights Commission[120] finding a tendency for career managers to not select women for operational planning roles, which has affected women's career progression. Poor communication between individuals and career managers adversely affected women and often slowed their career trajectory. This was the case with participants in this research, some of whom reported missing out on key professional development opportunities as they were 'about the right age' to get married or have children.

Defence has also experienced several high-profile cases of sexual assault and rape. For instance, the 2011 Skype sex scandal perpetrated by a male Australian Defence Force Academy (ADFA) cadet against a female cadet, or the 2013 'Jedi Council' of 171 male Army personnel distributing explicit emails sexually denigrating women, highlight on-going cultural issues.[121]

After analysing hundreds of articles, military expert Megan Mackenzie found that military sexual violence is consistently justified by the Australian media and military leaders as a result of 'young soldiers' uncontrollable natures', indicating worryingly pervasive and damaging gendered norms that remain despite recent reviews and cultural change initiatives.[122]

In response to the scandals, the Australian Human Rights Commission launched a series of reviews into both the DoD and the ADF. Canvassing discrimination, bias and harassment, the reviewers found: the lack of a critical mass of women, stemming from recruitment and retention issues; rigid career trajectories; difficulties combining work and family; and 'a culture still marked, on occasion, by poor leadership and unacceptable behaviour including exclusion, sexual harassment and sexual abuse'.[123] Gendered differences in experiences are evident: while 88.9 per cent of men in starred ranks have children, only 22.2 per cent of women do. Furthermore, ADF workplaces are 'highly sexualised environments', with a high tolerance for 'sexual and sexist jokes and sexually suggestive banter, emails or SMS messages, inappropriate comments or sexual advances'.[124] This produces a workplace environment that evidences considerable forms of 'toxic' masculinity—defined as 'an extreme expression of hegemonic masculinity, which promotes masculine supremacy, strict gender roles, and devalues women'.[125]

While culture change recommendations like those in the Phase 1, Phase 2, and Phase 3 Reviews aim to tackle these and other issues, inconsistency across policies and service lines, and distinct service line identities, hamper the ability of these formal institutions to produce lasting change. Following the Phase 2 review, Defence instituted a yearly *Women in the ADF Report* coinciding with the release of each Annual Report. Yet as of 2022, Defence ceased publishing *Women in the ADF* supplementary reports alongside their usual annual reports. Whilst the *Women in the ADF* reports had substantial gaps and only offered limited transparency on women's representation, their absence in the 2022 Annual Report is noted, with only limited data on gender, ethnicity, and disability included more generally. On top of this, historical gender segregation, horizontally and vertically, continues to effect women, siloing their opportunities with women overrepresented in health, logistics, administration, and support roles, and underrepresented in engineering, technical, security and combat roles. Additionally, women's enlistment rates are falling.

As the primary international-facing envoys for Defence, Defence Attachés (DA) and staff form the cohesive unit primarily analysed for this research. DAs are recognised as 'diplomatic representatives who build military-to-military relationships between nations and facilitate Defence policy objectives overseas'.[126] DAs and their staff form a distinct, comparable group to understand women's experiences and representation in Australian international affairs, leading diplomatic work and negotiation from the Defence portfolio. However, unlike within DFAT, these diplomatic postings have not been high prestige or high-status roles important on the path to career advancement. While both civilian and military staff can form the staff of DA offices, only military staff are deployed as the top representative—the DA—meaning that the unique cultures and histories of the service lines (canvassed above) are integral to understanding women's opportunities to be a DA.

As noted, ADF staff generally have clear pathways to leadership, with transparent career trajectories and ranks. This is not the case with attaché positions, as Sarah noted:

> With the breakdown of forces, you'd expect 50 per cent to be Army, 25 per cent Navy, 25 per cent Air Force, that would be a reasonable breakdown. That's not always how it looks. That's because there is no set path for Defence Attachés. There's so no set path for international representation in other agencies either but there's definitely no set path for Defence. So previously, there's been a lot of chance involved, oh you're the right person, at just the right time, you vaguely understand this or whatever.[127]

Until recently DA positions were colloquially known as the 'golden handshake', a position traditionally given to individuals transitioning out of the ADF and into retirement.[128] Following greater prioritisation under the Chief of the Defence Force (CDF) Angus Campbell, the role of the DA has grown in importance. Danielle explained:

> [Now] we're trying to tell people that taking a Defence Attaché role is excellent and we want good quality Defence Attachés . . . [but] you've got to remember, Defence didn't value Defence Attaché roles. We used to give it to our retirees, because the problem with the Defence Attaché role is that they were they were out of mind, out of sight. You weren't working for the generals who were making the promotion decisions, so we weren't getting good quality people wanting to be DAs because you didn't get picked up [for promotion] if you were a Defence Attaché.[129]

There are therefore several factors behind the current gender imbalances in DA roles, in which women represent just 17.2 per cent of all positions in 2019, down from 18.8 per cent in 2017.[130] These include that most roles may have traditionally gone to Army personnel, the service line in which women are least represented, and these were not always high prestige roles on the path to career advancement. Women often did not have the opportunity to reach the top positions from which DAs would be appointed prior to retirement. Participants noted that even if women were at the right rank (generally at the Colonel equivalent rank), with the opportunity to apply for DA roles, if women did want to progress their careers then the DA role may not have been a help, but a hindrance. Danielle went on to explain:

> The Defence Attaché job was seen as a sidewards move and your career would cease right? ... I don't think the job has ever not been attractive to women, but I think it comes back to [the fact that] we didn't have enough women to apply for the role, [and] that's why there weren't a lot of women. Now more and more women are becoming Colonels, you're seeing the percentage of women asking for Defence Attachés roles increasing, I would like to think. And like I said, now they've changed the dynamic that it's not an end to career ... we are now valuing people.[131]

While not exhaustive, this section has provided a brief historical backdrop of the DoD as an APS department and the three service lines as military bodies of the ADF to give context to women's underrepresentation in leadership, and generally throughout the agency. Defence identities are steeped in a heavily gendered history. As well as remaining the agency with the lowest representation of women, Defence (particularly the ADF) exhibits worrying instances of overt toxic masculinity. With new technological advances that make the taking and sharing of images and video particularly easy, some instances of sexual harassment and abuse have intensified.[132] Formal institutional shifts stipulating recommendations to improve gender relations appear to be limited in their effect so far—largely due to inconsistent and lapsed policies that allow deeply embedded sexism and misogyny to flourish under a lack of enforcement. Yet given the hierarchical and top-down chain of command structure of Defence, could the 'right' policy be all that is needed to bring about gender equality? Or is institutional change in the agency more complicated? The next section will cover agency structure and hierarchy to demonstrate significant limitations on the power of critical actors in Defence to enforce gender equitable policies and practices.

Structure and Leadership

Defence has one of the most complex and hierarchical structures studied. Analysis of their organisational chart highlights a multilayered organisational structure with multiple chains of command. Defence has chains of command according to location (localised chains of command where staff are deployed or posted), different civilian and military chains of command (which sometimes overlap), different chains of command for the service lines (Army, Air Force, and Navy) and for those posted offshore, external chains of command to DFAT heads of mission (HOM) or heads of post (HOP).

The APS side of the DoD follows the same structure as DFAT in terms of APS, EL and SES-level ranks. The ADF operates under a second ranking system, where rank O9 correlates to SES Band 3 (the Chief of the Defence Force), O8 correlates to SES Band 2 (Major General, Rear Admiral, Air Vice Marshal), O7 correlates to SES Band 1 (Brigadier, Commodore, Air Commodore), O6 correlates to EL Band 2 or leadership pipeline (Colonel, Captain, Group Captain) and O5 correlates to EL Band 1 or leadership pipeline (Lieutenant Colonel, Commander, Wing Commander).

Formally, each military rank has an equivalent and equal civilian rank. However, practically, rank is not equal across military and civilian sides of Defence. In Defence, further to the usual intersectionalities found in any organisation, whereby gender, sexuality, ethnicity, class, and disability can all effect opportunities for leadership, employees are further divided by their civilian or military status. As one participant from McGlen and Sarkees notes:

> The military themselves have discrimination against civilians, whether they're male or female, because most civilians have not been in operation. So there is a bias or perception that civilians don't know what they're talking about. Then when you put the women on top of that, it makes it even a little worse.[133]

McGlen and Sarkees describe this civilian and military status as an individual's 'surface credibility'. Military members have a surface credibility that civilian employees lack. This hierarchy of credibility underpins access to power and resources and highlights deeply gendered lines of segregation across the agency. Given that women are more represented in the civilian DoD (in 2022, at 46.7 per cent), rather than the military ADF (in 2022, at 20.1 per cent), a lack of surface credibility has compounding effects on gender. Rebecca elaborated on being part of the DA staffing corps as a civilian:

> You're always going to be the one civilian in a room full of military, maybe sometimes two of you. If you have a commander who supports you and your role, your life is significantly easier. You become acutely aware of how military hierarchy works. When the commander says, 'I like this person, work with him or her'—it happens. If you have a commander who's like, 'I kind of think you're a bit of a waste

of time. I don't like civilians, and, you know, I feel like you're here to monitor me'—then the job becomes very painful.[134]

Lee, also a civilian, further commented on the inequality of rank across the two sides of Defence:

> For my work I was dealing with our Special Forces area who are entirely all male-dominated. It's the, you know, kind of the maleness of the maleness in the ADF. I would have conversations with them and hang up the phone, and the Chief of Staff at the time [who was ADF] would look at me and she was like 'so, are they going to do what you've just asked them to do?' and I said 'probably not'. So, she would then ring them up and because she was the rank higher than them, there was an automatic 'ah man!' [response indicating that they have to follow her orders]. So that was an interesting [thing]. You know, I don't think it has anything to do with the fact that I was female, although they probably [just thought] I'm a civilian, I don't do operations, what am I talking about? Stop bothering me.[135]

This example highlights the importance of being able to 'pull rank' in international environments. Rank gave women traction that otherwise could not be gained. However, one of the core issues in this example is that the participant was employed at the highest APS rank that can be sent overseas. In other words, without the help of the military Chief of Staff to ensure that her requests got through to Special Forces, this participant would not have been able to do her job as she was required. Civilian status evidently matters, as the participant recognised; however, gender is also likely to have played into her experience. It suggests that women can only gain the respect and authority needed to lead if they are (1) military personnel and (2) more senior than those they are trying to direct. Women face challenges on both fronts.

On the topic of rank, critical actors are particularly significant in Defence, where rank equals the power to make change, and leadership is rigidly top-down. Former Chief of Army David Morrison demonstrated the considerable effect of critical actors in changing gendered institutions. In 2013, in response to the revelation that dozens of men had been involved in hundreds of explicit emails denigrating women, Morrison filmed a powerful three-minute-long address to 'sexist soldiers' calling upon personnel to 'respect women or get out'.[136] Morrison's video was one of the most public and acclaimed attempts at establishing new gender norms and cultures of respect in Defence. The action sent waves through the Defence community and onlookers internationally, eventually leading to Morrison winning the 2016 Australian of the Year Award for his commitment to gender equality, diversity, and inclusion.

Because of Morrison's role as the Chief of Army, he was in the unique position to send a strong message around gender in a way that had not been done before (or since).

However, despite Morrison's acclaim and his success at prompting a review of norms and practices, the public stance taken through the video and later the Awards ceremony has not been repeated with other leaders. In fact, Morrison drew considerable criticism over the whole scenario: from the fact that Catherine McGregor, Australia's highest profile transgender woman in Defence (and also a contender for the Australian of the Year Awards), wrote his speech; to the petitions calling for his resignation and condemnation after speaking about gender equality (and not veterans' welfare) at the Awards ceremony; and for his insistence on the use of nongendered language in Defence workplaces (seemingly incompatible with the informal values critical to Defence).[137]

Critical actors are important in Defence, and rank is important to ensuring that critical actors are heard and have the power to implement change. However, Morrison's case demonstrated that critical actors were *as limited or constrained* as any other rank within the agency when it came to advocating strongly for gendered change. These constraints do not seem to be usual for such an 'authoritarian institution' in which chain of command matters and top-down leadership sets the agenda and parameters for action. Yet according to former Deputy Secretary of Defence for Strategy and Intelligence, Hugh White, the ADF can be 'a bit out of touch and bit inclined to believe they should not be in touch with current values' around gender equality.[138] The issue of gender equality appears anathema to Defence identity, with Morrison's public pro-gender equality actions at times almost sacrilegious.

Morrison's case demonstrated that there were ramifications to being 'too public' or to pushing things 'too far' when it came to advocating for gender equality. In fact, it seems that the negative backlash that Morrison drew after his very public stances on gender has served as a warning for any leaders coming after him. Morrison 'broke' the rule by publicly condemning ADF treatment of women and broke it again by prioritising gender over other topics—like veterans' affairs. Waylen finds that sanctions and enforcement for broken rules include 'shunning, social ostracism or even violence', to which I would add invalidation and discrediting.[139] Morrison's example demonstrates that informal rules continue to have immense power over Defence, and despite any rhetorical or policy commitments to equality, gendered divisions endure. Additionally, the power to enforce rules relating to gender within the agency is not just limited to those in the agency—current serving members or staff—but also includes those external to the agency—veterans and the public. The example illustrates the (in)ability to change norms and introduce new forms of thought within the agency. When the actions of the highest ranked (and male) member of the Army are 'policed', then it suggests a damning narrative for lower ranked (and female) members to drive institutional change.

Related to the complex chains of command and authority, women's place and power within Defence is restricted by the types of positions and specialities that they hold. As noted, the staffing group that is the focus for this research, DA's and staff, are charged with Defence diplomacy and negotiation. In contrast to those engaged in warfare, strategy, and operations, this group represents Defence staff tasked with applying Australia's foreign policy objectives within a Defence environment. These policymakers and Defence 'diplomats' are drawn from both civilian and military pools, yet all of the most senior roles, including DA roles, are military roles and generally SES or equivalent positions.

One civilian participant explained her role as a support staff to a DA:

> We were tasked with supporting the commander to do any international engagement activities, as well as managing the equities and reputation of Defence in the region, sort of as Defence rather than as the ADF—so the broader organisational stuff. We had this quirky management arrangement in that we were force-assigned and thus technically subject to military discipline and the command of the commander. But we also had a boss [in Canberra], actually in International Policy Division . . . when things were happening in theatre that we didn't think were entirely kosher, we could raise it in theatre and say, 'this is not in line with what government wants you to do'. If that didn't get us any traction, we could exercise the judgment to come back [to Canberra], and elevate the issue and say 'you guys need to be aware that this is happening. You need to reach in, and we need to step away. And you guys need to come in over the top and see what's going on'. . . . So there's this inherent tension between a military understanding that we can have an effect if you just let them go and do something, and what is often the burden on the civilian part of the organisation, which is 'yes, but it's not worth it'. . . . You advise on often fairly common sense stuff to us, but you have to translate it into the language and mindset of an operator who sees a military objective and the way to achieve that objective—which is often, 'send those people with those guns to that thing to take that hill, and then they can do that. What's the problem right?' So you [establish the] context [in which the military can operate in alignment with government objectives].[140]

For one military participant, DA, structure, and chains of command looked different:

I find as a Defence Attaché here, you're given a budget, you're given strategic guidance, and it's probably the most autonomous role I've ever had ... and don't get me wrong I still have to get guidance from back in Australia, but you get to implement a program and see change. And, in 20 years time I can go, that's the program that I started. [It's] essentially having an idea and creating it. And everyone goes 'that's what Colonel's are for'. Yeah, but in Army headquarters in Canberra, as a Colonel, you actually have to have 5, 10, 20 people sign off on, 'I want to travel to Canberra tomorrow'. You know what I mean? So it is different.[141]

Interviews therefore demonstrated that even though Defence's organisational chart formally recognises the civilian Department equally to the military ADF, only military personnel occupy the most senior DA roles, and power tensions exist between civilian and military personnel. The two women's experiences set out above are very different, clearly demonstrating the level of authority and power military versus civilian employees can wield internationally. For civilians, opportunities for leadership are reduced—more so internationally than at home, where civilians can continue to rise to the rank of Secretary (although no woman has ever done this yet). Because of women's low representation in the military, the most senior, prestigious, and powerful international roles in Defence continue to largely exclude women. This is consistent internationally, too.

In fact, a commonly circulated poster within the department is the 'International Faces of Defence'—a pictographic A3 poster of all the Australian DAs across the world depicting on average three women in a sea of 45 mostly white older men. Gabrielle discussed it: 'I would like to think that naturally, based on merit, we would have a 50% [balance] ... and it really annoys me because there's what, I don't know, three women on there?'[142] The overall structuring, traditions, and culture of Defence (derived and handed down from US and UK equivalents) creates a military ethos, even in the civilian side of the DoD. Military values, norms, and behaviours 'travel' and extend to the civilian DoD—enforcing a culture more associated with the military and masculine ideals than a more bureaucratic approach across the agency. One of the final implications of this hierarchical structuring and chain of command is that this structuring has gendered effects. More hierarchical organisations are associated with greater instances of sexual harassment and discrimination, resulting from power differentials. As McGlen and Sarkees find:

In most instances hierarchical organisations are seen as impacting negatively upon women, for a number of reasons: because women generally are not a part of the elite group that dominates these hierarchies; [and] because women are not seen as having the characteristics necessary to sit at the top of the pyramid.[143]

Overall, Defence is characterised as the most militaristic agency studied, as compared with the four agencies.

This section has reinforced the conclusion that the gendered institutions in Defence are enduring. There appears a lack of formal enforcement of gendered change programs, such as recent cultural change recommendations that are superseded before any substantive action can be implemented and enforced. Yet strong informal enforcement of 'old' norms and ideals appears to have a powerful effect in discouraging women (and men) from speaking out and making gender dynamics public. Power differences between civilian and military staff amplify gender hierarchies, resulting in women being systematically underrepresented and underpowered. As constraining this structure appears to be, it is the case agency with the best-developed career progression delineated for staff. This seems to indicate that, in principle, women may have better career advancement prospects than other departments—provided they can outlast sexual harassment and abuse that is amplified in military organisations. The global ramifications of this will be explored later in the book.

The Dark Side: Home Affairs

The bulk of the functions of the Department of Home Affairs (Home Affairs)—a new department which now includes national security, intelligence, law enforcement, cyber security, aviation and maritime security, transnational and serious organised crime, crisis coordination, immigration, customs, and border protection—were the roles of several departments in the past. History is therefore particularly important to understanding the historical antecedents of Home Affairs and how it has impacted the modern agency's composition and culture.

Historical Forces

Home Affairs has a wide geographic spread, operating both in Australia and through 69 international offices.[144] Home Affairs diplomacy involves supporting the aims and objectives of 'team Australia' and the government of the day. Home Affairs staff form the second largest contingent in Australian embassies across the world, although are the least studied agency in Australian international affairs and frequently overlooked as a serious player. They support the operations of DFAT and the AFP, as well as facilitate relationships and negotiations between host and home governments. Out of the agencies studied, Home Affairs (its component parts and predecessors) have endured the most machinery of government changes. This has resulted in an organisational environment that is semiregularly re-assessed to integrate disparate policies and rules from departmental mergers.

The modern Home Affairs did not exist at the start of this research, as it was only established on 20 December 2017, adding a slate of security and intelligence agencies to its existing Immigration, Customs and Border Force portfolios. It is the newest addition to the research. Since the merger, Home Affairs now has several portfolio agencies under its departmental structure, most of which are new. These new portfolio agencies include: the Australian Border Force (ABF), Australian Criminal Intelligence Commission (ACIC), the Australian Security and Intelligence Organisation (ASIO), and the Australian Federal Police (AFP). These portfolio agencies fall under the overarching command of the Department, but are also semi-independent statutory agencies, with their own chains of command and operational policies, practices, and culture. For the purposes of this research, study of Home Affairs has remained focused on the core three portfolios of Immigration, Customs, and the ABF, as these provide better insight into the enduring institutions and experiences of those in the agency. These three divisions represent the most on-going, essential, and long-standing make-up of the Department in recent years.

Over time, the component portfolios of Home Affairs have developed an increasingly international and enforcement-based, securitised focus—a product of globalisation, and one that has been controversial, particularly given the previous history of the agency as a nation-building agency. Elements of the agency now have significant 'sworn' (uniformed, ranked) populations, such as the ABF and the AFP. Tracing the history of the Department and its predecessors is significant, not just for understanding the gendered impact of institutions, but racialised impact. In fact, the Department of Immigration was established in 1945 under conditions that were overtly racialised—being at the forefront of negotiating race and what it meant to be Australian. The Department oversaw developing, implementing, and enforcing policy in alignment with the government of the day's priorities.[145] The history of the Department is therefore closely entwined with Australia's national identity, given its role in stipulating the laws and conditions migration: who can *be Australian*. Coinciding with the Federation of Australia in 1901 was the introduction of the *Immigration Restriction Act* (1901), later known as the White

Australia Policy, enforcing strict language and other tests on whom could enter Australia. In combination with later policies, such as the *Naturalisation Act* (1903), the Department was at the centre of restricting migration and citizenship from anywhere essentially non-European, specifically banning those of Asian, Pacific Islander, and African descent. Combined with Australia's colonial history that claimed Australia as 'terra nullius' (unoccupied or uninhibited), Australia's national identity and the history of the Department is one that has largely sanctioned racialised (and racist) policies and attitudes (whilst at later times, being at the forefront of advocating for multiculturalism). These raced rules and policies were co-constitutive, both responding to wider social sentiments amongst the largely European colonial population and stipulating a maintenance of that status quo generally, and in prestigious (exclusionary) government service of the time.[146]

The Department's history is also one with a similar early relationship to gender as Defence had,[147] with the staffing population initially largely ex-military: 'In the first years, the great majority of officers who joined the Department of Immigration were returned soldiers, sailors and airmen. It was often called "an ex-servicemen's department".'[148] Settling and helping new arrivals assimilate became a large part of the department's work, yet all the leaders and most of the workforce at the time were male. Jordens's book *Alien to Citizen* notes how women were mostly employed in providing assistance services to migrants.[149] They were employed specifically in the Social Welfare section of the department and were noted for representing the 'compassionate face' of the Department.[150] In fact, the agency's own summary of the history of migration, notes that ' "the Department of Immigration reflected the culture of the society from which its officers were drawn" . . . Power within the Department resided with men in positions with responsibility for implementing government policy—the migration planners and selectors'.[151] This highlights early horizontal (across different portfolios) and vertical (across different ranks) segregation throughout the department, in part by accident and in part by conscious design.

By 1975 the Department had grown to over 1500 staff, with 197 staff posted in 34 overseas offices. Of this time, one worker based overseas stated: 'This work is not glamourous but necessary. Public opinion is rarely kind to the Department. Those with intentions to migrate who are not approved see us as frustrating and heartless bureaucrats'.[152]

Overseas representational work at this time was described in the Department's history as uncomfortable and often dangerous. Although a gender breakdown of representatives from this time is unavailable, based off the experiences of women posted overseas in government at this time, it is likely to have been a difficult working environment for women. In wider employment, unease existed over the 'proper' role of women in the workforce, and gender segregation remained an enduring feature.[153] Elements of this continue, with one participant highlighting how

> it's a high-risk role to be in because it's highly visible. So, if you do it poorly everyone is going to notice, and the impact, risk, and the effects of the risk of that are high. So, if you don't do well, everybody notices, and it can become an issue across government.[154]

Even so, in the Department's (2015) publication *A History of the Department of Immigration: Managing Migration to Australia*, women posted internationally in the early period are the only voices quoted on their experience as posted officers. This suggests that women were not uncommon in deployed posts, and their voices had a good chance of being recorded and heard.

After machinery of government changes in the 1970s, the institution began to shift, both relating to gender and race. The firsthand experience of migration to Australia became increasingly important to the Department, and by 1978 nearly a third of staff came from a migrant background.[155] During this time, a 'respect for cultural diversity' became formal policy.[156]

In the 1990s, further structural changes gave the Department and customs officers enforcement powers. From this time, enforcement and protection became more important—a key shift in the agency. Enforcement and protection are duties traditionally associated with male agentic attributes and forms of hegemonic masculinity that are aggressive, use excessive force, involve abuses of power, and are threatening and hostile.[157] One participant noted of this time:

> I'd been teaching for three years, and then joined the public service. I thought I'd gone back to—I don't know what, I had no idea the culture, the service in 1985 was so bad. Just the intimidation . . . it's just a blokey law enforcement environment. But I ended up, after being trained for a year, [being] thrown into this workplace where it was [an] open floor office. When you walked in it was mainly men and you would get wolf whistled or commented at about what you're wearing so you had nowhere to hide. And then [you had to] sit with the blokes in the open office, at a desk opposite some bloke who was smoking. In those days there was office smoking in there. So, it was just really hostile, really hostile. Then I eventually one day got the slap on the bum from some guy, so, it's like they're just physically threatening environments . . . I never forgot that . . . that's been with me the whole

way through. I don't know, it gives you a bit of determination, self-assertiveness to deal with difficult situations. It's like nothing is going to be as bad as that.[158]

The organisational culture at the time was heavily and overtly gendered, often sexist, and an uncomfortable environment for those participants who experienced it. Women's place in the Department, hierarchical structuring, and social norms of the day reinforced considerable instances of sexism and harassment, which participants noted resulted in culture and power dynamics often exclusionary to women.

Even so, as a humanitarian-based 'soft' portfolio area, Immigration was reportedly considerably more gender equal than many APS government departments at the time. The Department tended to attract more women and retain more women to higher levels of leadership. In fact, the first female federal secretary of a department was Helen Williams, Secretary of the Department of Immigration and Multicultural Affairs from 1996 to 1999— the only female departmental secretary for almost two decades, who recalled being asked to 'play mother' by then-Treasury secretary.[159] As the first federal department to promote a woman to its highest rank, this does indicate that the agency had enough female representation normalise women's leadership and had the pathways to make career progression possible. This has not yet been achieved in Defence or the AFP and was only recently achieved in DFAT. Unlike many other federal departments, Immigration has not to this day developed the same level of gender equality policies and strategies. However, it appears that there was *less need to*—women were adequately represented, even if they continued to face gendered challenges. This is a key point that I will return to later in the book. Women's experiences indicate enduring gendered institutions that manifest differently and perhaps less visibly for periods of the Department's history. Yet as became clear through this research, differential treatment remains to this day, enduring by adapting over time.

By the early 2000s, the department was increasingly weaponised as part of Prime Minister John Howard's pitch to win elections, both under mandates of stopping 'illegal' migration and countering terrorism. By 2005, the Department became the subject of intense scrutiny and criticism, resulting in two key reports: the Palmer Report and the Comrie Report. Criticisms included that the agency had developed rigid and narrow thinking, as well as a culture of denial and self-justification at the heart of several key mishandlings of cases. Intense scrutiny and low public attitudes have been a legacy of the Department which handles some of Australia's core questions around national identity and who has the right to seek asylum, *be Australian*, and represent Australia and its values.[160] Gradually, successive recent governments have shifted the primarily concern of the Department from nation building to border protection and enforcement, often marked by fear mongering and 'othering'. Indeed, under Operation Sovereign Borders, Australia was found by the United Nations to be engaging in illegally turning back boats of asylum seekers and refugees. The Department has been at the centre of a number of high-profile cases involving border protection, with a hallmark initiative of the Department—offshore processing of asylum seekers—deemed a 'cruel, inhuman or degrading treatment' and unlawful under international law.[161]

The 2012 *Australian Public Service Commission Capability Review into the Department of Immigration and Citizenship* (predecessor to Home Affairs) found significant gaps in the support for EL and SES managers. It found that, like DFAT, the Department had trouble with HR management, induction, training and on-going mentoring and support. A high proportion of staff (33 per cent) did not believe recruitment decisions were based on merit (compared to 25 per cent in the wider Australian public service), which is worrying given the pervasiveness of unconscious bias and gender discrimination in workplace appointments generally.[162] As of 2012, the Department maintained heavy internal recruitment for senior executive roles, with 79 per cent of SES band 1 roles and 100 per cent of SES band 2 recruited internally. With the recent amalgamation of agencies under Home Affairs, the agency has seen an increase in ex-military and AFP staff.[163]

Additional to what was happening with Immigration, Customs' history is also entwined with DFAT. It retains many similarities in terms of early historical forces canvassed above in DFAT's history, such as a heavy male domination within the workforce and horizontal and vertical segregation. For a brief period, Customs was also covered under the Department of Police and Customs, and many masculine norms of law enforcement are also present its contemporary structure. One participant, Lucy, talks of her experiences on joining Customs in the 1980s:

> Traditionally it was quite a blokey work environment . . . I joined as a customs officer because they were recruiting and changing their profile. So, I started in an environment where it was a male dominated policing kind of environment. Women worked in the public service in the typing pool. It was a 20-year journey of creating credibility of women being able to do other jobs, which was a bit of a hard slog.[164]

Like Defence, building credibility was a key part of women's narratives amongst participants. There were assumptions around who could do what work, with some roles and portfolios understood as inherently more suited to men than women, and vice versa. Considering that women retain the lowest representation in the most masculine, enforcement-based division of the Department—the ABF—building credibility, particularly in 'hard' portfolios, continues to affect women.

Formally created in 2015, the ABF represents the youngest section of Home Affairs, and its founding reflects the most recent a major change in the Department, from a past more bureaucratic agency structure, to one that has become increasingly paramilitaristic. Unlike Immigration, Customs and the ABF have more in common in terms of departmental culture and experiences. The ABF's culture is informed by AFP and Defence cultures, with a large proportion of staff from enforcement and Defence backgrounds. Participants commented frequently about the then-Minister and Secretary's preference for ex-AFP and ex-ADF staff, noting that the ABF often accepted those who had been 'kicked out' of their former departments because of behavioural issues— highlighting a degree of personalisation and politization in appointments. The cultures of the ABF and Customs is therefore closely related to the departmental cultures of Defence and the AFP—on occasion marked by overt hostility, aggression, and 'bolshie' male-dominated cultures. While the ABF was reportedly established with a gender equal leadership team in 2015, five years later women only represent on average a third of those posted internationally. In 2019, Home Affairs returned the lowest levels of staff engagement and satisfaction of any agency in the APS.[165]

This is particularly troubling. While Home Affairs has the highest representation of women in leadership overall and amongst those posted internationally, the youngest division of the Department, ABF—which was initially gender-equal—now has the lowest representation of women internationally in the Department. Informal gendered norms and rules of enforcement-style agencies—as well as leadership in the form of Ministers and the Secretary, and cultural relics from the AFP and Defence enforced by ex-AFP and Defence staff—have eroded initial attempts at gender equality. Even though women and men may have been equal in leadership, masculinist norms and behaviours 'won'—they have prevailed over alternative, gender equal or more feminine norms. The equilibrium of such paramilitaristic enforcement agencies remains unequal.

As leadership tensions and a leadership spill threatened in federal politics, Prime Minister Malcolm Turnbull announced the government would create the 'super ministry' Department of Home Affairs in 2017, appointing former police officer Peter Dutton as Minister.[166] Though the remodelling of the Department was widely questioned and criticised, the decision to combine portfolios had been raised as a possibility since September 11, 2001, with the changing nature of terrorism beyond a purely law enforcement issue, to one of national security requiring the joint operation of multiple actors. According to its first Secretary, Michael Pezzullo, the agency is therefore the 'third force of security' in foreign affairs, alongside DFAT and Defence—an ambition that demonstrates the Department's size and contemporary ambitions as much as that of its leader, who has taken a proactive approach to departmental growth.[167] As of the 2017–2018 amalgamation, the agency has become increasingly 'hard': enforcement, intelligence, and security focused—becoming the 'dark side' of international affairs as one participant named it.[168]

The effects on women in the department are significant. For those in the ABF and Customs side of the Department, the merger was experienced as overwhelmingly positively. Apart from the usual difficulties in reconciling different agency cultures and chains of command, participants reported being largely satisfied and happy with the new departmental make-up as it offered new opportunities and was a pro-active and positive workforce to join. One participant noted that, coming from the Customs side, the merger was experienced as 'a bit more of a blip than sort of a big deal'.[169]

The experiences of Immigration staff (the 'soft', humanitarian side of the Department) were starkly different. Many reported the merger as marking a mass exodus for some of the most senior and qualified women in the Department. Button comments that the Secretary, Pezzullo, 'made life intolerable for a lot of senior people. He came prejudiced; he had already made up his mind the place was incompetent'.[170] Even more worryingly, some participants reported a rise in depression and anxiety because of the merger and the culture shift within the agency. They even discussed colleagues who had suicided. Lorelle explained:

> When we merged, it was just horrendous. I'm just surprised more people didn't commit suicide. It was shocking. I had people dropping left, right and centre. The way I was treated by, now, people who are ex-departmental people, was absolutely shocking, was terrible ... [the Home Affairs merger was] like any other takeover. There are winners and there are losers. People would say I was a winner out of all of that, but I've got the scars to prove it, and ... I think, Secretary down, everybody's got the scars to prove it. It was a pretty traumatic process.[171]

There was a significant gendered price that came with the merger. Immigration was women-dominated and Customs and ABF were male-dominated. For Customs and ABF women interviewed, the merger was difficult, but generally not experienced as more than a 'blip', and the pros far outweighed the cons. For the Immigration women interviewed, they left the Department, or remained, 'scarred', or, in some instances, reported their colleagues' (male and female) suicides. Indeed, both *The Sydney Morning Herald* and *The Age* uncovered a 'troubling culture' inside the ABF, marked by bullying and harassment, mental illness, and a 'string of suicides'.[172] A joint investigation by *The Sydney Morning Herald* and *The Age* found that leaked ABF files show one in five staff were bullied of harassed. While Home Affairs now has the highest representation of women in leadership and in international representation across all the agencies studied, these statistics mask significant differences in women's experiences depending on which part of the department they are from. These nuances will be further investigated in the following chapters. They reinforce that each agency does not represent a monolith of a single experience or pathway. Rather, there are significant nuances within the agencies, as well as across them.

Overall, Home Affairs highlights considerable similarities with the other agencies in terms of its male-dominated history. Women have never been equally represented in the SES in the Department, despite women representing, at its peak, over two thirds of the Department in 1996 and coming close—49 per cent—in 2009 prior to a continuing decline in representation ever since. Gendered challenges appear to have always been there, despite the Department's higher representation of women. Perhaps more subtly and invisibly, gendered challenges have endured—at times more covert than others. The establishment of new portfolios like the ABF appear not to have embedded gender equality in international representation, despite a more gender-equal start. Further, the agency is becoming increasingly enforcement-oriented—signalling the potential for greater, not fewer, gendered challenges to come.

Structure and Leadership

The complexity of Home Affairs' structure, culture, and leadership, combined with growing militarism and a relative lack of formal policies (until recently) promoting gender equality, has allowed hegemonic forms of masculinity to flourish and informal norms of enforcement to predominate agency culture. The agency's contemporary structure is complex, with tiered chains of command spanning an immense department and mix of organisational structures and hierarchies within. Hierarchy is important to the agency, with sections of the Department falling under 'sworn' populations that are ranked and uniformed, and other sections conforming more to generic public service—un-uniformed with standard APS rankings. The complex and interlayered nature of the Department both disperses power across portfolios and centralises it. While the super-ministry includes many agencies that have largely retained their own statutory independence, the power of the current Secretary, Michael Pezzullo (whom Button describes as a 'military-minded former Defence bureaucrat'[173]), and outgoing Minister, Peter Dutton (a former police officer, since replaced by Clare O'Neil in the 2022 federal election), increased as they maintained authority across multiple new agencies in a 'united front'.

Given that critical actors can play an important role in both instituting progressive gender policy and resisting or stymieing gendered changes, the positioning of the Secretary and former Minister Peter Dutton is important. Like Varghese in DFAT, Pezzullo is a 'Male Champion of Change'. In fact, in a key speech to women leaders within the department, Pezzullo called for an 'insurgency and revolution' to disrupt the history of male dominance in senior positions.[174] The way in which he speaks about women's leadership is revealing for his rhetorical support:

> Some people need to employ different tactics to own a room or an issue. You don't have to have the loudest voice. You don't need to put ego into every sentence... You need to disrupt the very system itself by creating new solutions to problems that largely men—because most of the senior leadership positions are still owned by men—are charged with.[175]

Participants noted that Pezzullo's leadership was important and they felt safe and respected as leaders—with Pezzullo's female deputies even referred to as 'Charlie's Angels'. However, wide discontent was recorded amongst the participants, particularly for those who had not made it during the merger and reported extreme difficulty operating in a bullying and a toxic workplace environment. The Department has a patchy history regarding institutionalising gender equality strategies too, with large periods of absence in formal policies. In the context of APSC commitments to gender equality, as well as women's overall domination in the Department (but not in leadership), this appears to be a critical oversight. Inconsistency hampers the ability of the Department to enforce policies on gender equality. Because of the centralisation of many portfolio agencies' power under Home Affairs, the stance that Home Affairs takes on gender equality is also important more broadly for sending a message to a range of critical intelligence and security agencies—many of which who do not have the same level of women's representation or the same level of transparency and reporting (the intelligence agencies in particular).

Gender equality is not the only subject of the Secretary's rhetoric, however. Defence and the focus on maintaining a 'hard' security-focused departmental orientation is also glorified. Talking about what it takes to get leadership roles in the Department, Penny noted:

> The Secretary has set that tone at the top, glorified someone who's worked at defence, because he thinks that's the pinnacle. They do have some great qualities, but like I said before, not everyone. It's just, if you've worked in Defence, it's this assumption that, oh, you're brilliant. You'll be able to do this, this, and this. It's like, 'oh, come on, give your own guys a go'.[176]

In terms of 'setting the tone' for the background and attributes valued in Home Affairs to reach leadership, there are evidently gendered effects of the privileging of individuals from Defence and AFP backgrounds, and the move from 'planning the nation's future to policing its frontier'.[177] One participant noted that because of these cultural shifts, there are 'a few more controls and restrictions around what we do',[178] with Pezzullo claiming that 'the department of immigration (sic) of our collective memory and imagination will be no more'.[179]

Increasingly, the agency is seen as paramilitaristic in relation to the other four agencies studied, with higher power and priorities placed on security, intelligence, and border protection than past nation-building exercises. Leadership is increasingly characterised and valued according to norms of authority, discipline, and command common in law enforcement and military agencies. This has gendered effects on women, for whom representation in the Department is falling. Immigration women in particular were affected by the 2017 merger, with many key women in the pipeline leaving the agency and those who remain reporting worrying concerns of mental illness, 'scarring' and suicide amongst themselves or their colleagues.

Police-Led Diplomacy: AFP

Police forces have not always been considered to play a key diplomatic role, however this is changing with a greater focus on collaborative police-led international efforts. This section details the historical forces behind the Australian Federal Police (AFP), finding that both its internationalization and an approach to incorporating gender have been engrained from the start.

Historical Forces

On 13 February 1978, a bomb exploded in a garbage bin outside the Hilton Hotel, the venue for the Commonwealth Heads of Government Meeting (CHOGM), killing three people and injuring others. Without clear legal or constitutional authority, Prime Minister Malcolm Fraser and New South Wales Premier Neville Wran deployed nearly 2,000 heavily armed troops. Over the following 18 months, Fraser used the Hilton Hotel as a pretext to expand the powers and resources of the police and security apparatus. No genuine inquiry was ever made, 'despite evidence pointing to the possibility that the crime was committed by the security agencies themselves'.[180] It was this very incident that sparked the establishment of AFP.

Combining the Commonwealth Police, the ACT Police, and the Narcotics Bureau, in its current form the AFP is critical to addressing transnational crime, cybersecurity, narcotics and trafficking. Whilst not traditionally viewed as an international affairs agency, substantial numbers of AFP employees are engaged in United Nations mission work, and the AFP engages in 'police-led diplomacy' both embedded within international governments and embassy posts. Former AFP Commissioner Andrew Colvin noted:

> [Police-led diplomacy] utilises law enforcement links more broadly to build upon, and find common bilateral and diplomatic ground when more traditional exchanges present barriers ... what country doesn't want to cooperate on combating terrorism, organised crime, child sex tourism, cybercrime and the like?[181]

In an increasingly securitised global context, the AFP is one of many traditionally domestic agencies now internationalised, with one of the agency's key priority areas the contribution to Australia's international law enforcement interests. This more international orientation is recent and has grown post-September 11, 2001.

Initial leadership of the AFP was military-influenced, with the first two Commissioners from an Army background, and the agency described as distinctly masculine. One participant stated:

> Over that period of time [in the last 30 years] there has been significant challenges. (1) as a female in the workforce but (2) the challenges that every individual has reconciling their own personality types and the way that they operate against a culture that exists in what is a quasi-military style organisation ... when I came in, it was highly male centric in everything from the way that we operate to the culture

at that low level that you see in any organisation—but a very, very male centric environment.[182]

The AFP was also uniquely structured. It was established by the Australian Federal Police (AFP) Act 1979, quite separate to the APS Act—the Act that continues to guide the other three agencies' civilian divisions as well as AFP staff who merged from the Narcotics Bureau. Now that it is a portfolio agency of Home Affairs, this makes for a complex institutional background.

To date, only men have occupied the role of Commissioner, yet in 1982, only three years into operation, women formed the majority of recruits in an AFP training course, where there were 16 women and only seven men part of the intake.[183] Women formed 25 per cent of all police recruits who graduated in 1983–1984, which increased their overall population to 2.7 per cent of sworn police—evidencing critically low retention of women. At this time multiculturalism was also beginning to enter the force, with 6 per cent of recruits born overseas and 13 per cent of recruits with parents born overseas.

The AFP is a substantially younger organisation than the other agencies. The AFP was created in a time when social justice and issues of equity and equality were being implemented across government service, and some of the AFP's initiatives clearly reflect that. Even so, the 1990s highlighted gendered issues that had been simmering within the agency and were increasingly constraining women. Carmel Niland and Associates[184] completed an audit of the agency's Equal Employment Opportunity (EEO) Program to find that it was an excellent policy in theory supporting an equal workforce. However, despite this, the agency's ability to meet the objectives were poor—the enforcement mechanisms were weak. This is a very clear case of how formal policies were strong and supportive of women, and yet failed in application due to informal norms and behaviour within the agency. The report found that AFP's culture produced 'a climate conducive to sexual and racial harassment', and the legal obligation to eliminate workplace discrimination and harassment to be poorly understood.[185] Given that law *enforcement* was the guiding mandate of the agency, the fact that enforcement of policies relating to gender equality was weak indicates a significant inconsistency in the agency. The lack of enforcement of pro-gender policies is indicative of will, rather than ability, to enforce.

The agency culture at this time, and since the establishment of the AFP, was distinctly bullying, sexist, and overtly discriminatory towards women. One participant who had been in the agency almost since foundation and promoted only once in that period recalled being berated in the first few years of her service for putting her hand up for promotion. On placing her paperwork on her (male) boss's desk, her boss walked up to her in a line-up of staff, ripped her application up in front of her face and yelled crude expletives about her gender. Another participant commented how the early days 'was all like bravado and swearing all the time and that sort of thing', with humiliation, harassment and discrimination embedded in the psyche of the agency.[186] The overt hostility witnessed by participants demonstrates extremely gendered informal institutions and a culture marked by visible, tangible, and physical exclusion. Social attitudes and the greater emancipation of women was a mainstay of wider society by the end of the century, yet the AFP remained marked by considerable gendered challenges.

September 11, 2001 marked a critical juncture for the agency, with the largely domestic-facing agency shifting to its contemporary orientation focused on strategic policy advice on issues relating to national security, law enforcement and international matters affecting the Commonwealth, with international engagement permeating all aspects of AFP operations.[187] In fact, from the very first year of the AFP's establishment, Commissioner Woods noted that 'accepting the increasing complexity of crime and the threat imposed by international criminals, it may not be unrealistic to foresee a day when Legal (Police) Attachés may be seen as a necessary adjunct to all overseas Missions'.[188] Legal (Police) Attachés formed part of Australia's overseas embassies from establishment, although the role of the AFP in Australia's international relations and foreign policy was still evolving. In 1999, women represented six out of 62 overseas-posted staff (sworn and unsworn), filling 9.6 per cent of roles. It was not until the early 2000s that the AFP's international footprint grew rapidly and began to reflect the international affairs role that the agency has today. Key events post- September 2001 led to large numbers of AFP staff deploying internationally, from the placement of 100 AFP members in Indonesia at the peak of the response to the Bali bombings, to the creation of the International Deployment Group (IDG) in 2003–2004 to deal with the joint operation of Army and AFP personnel in Regional Assistance Mission to the Solomon Islands (RAMSI). At this time, the International Network also expanded offices to 32 posts across 26 countries. By 2004–2005, up to 500 IDG personnel were in missions across the Solomon Islands, Papua New Guinea and Timor-Leste.[189] These two types of international postings form the basis of AFP overseas representation, with mission work comprising largely of multilateral United Nations missions' assignments, and the International Network forming AFP work across embassies and posts.

Within the agency's contemporary context, former Commissioner Andrew Colvin committed to achieving a 50:50 gender balance within the next decade, heralding a range of new strategies to increase women's overall representation and their representation in leadership. Yet even months into the new Commissioner Reece Kershaw's appointment, two of the most senior AFP women left the agency, leaving (for a time) senior executive leadership devoid of women. As at time of publication, the AFP's Chief Operating Officer and Deputy Commissioner Operations have been replaced with women.

Following the 2016 report, *Culture Change: Gender Diversity and Inclusion in the Australian Federal Police,* the AFP has increasingly sought to reform elements of its culture, presenting the current timing of this research in a critical time of transformation.[190] As of 2014–2015, the IDG released its first Gender Strategy, and the division (now named International Command) is now on its third iteration, *International Command Gender Strategy 2018–2024* (replacing the second iteration, *International Operations Gender Strategy 2018–2022).*[191] The fact that the AFP has a specific gender strategy (and is in its third iteration) for its international operations is significant, demonstrating formal commitment to extending gendered change to international affairs, matched only by DFAT's strategies. Further, renewed focus on gendered differences throughout the agency and even the establishment of an all-female recruitment round demonstrate a dedication to institutional change, particularly around gendered cultures, as well as bullying.

Yet bullying remains one of the most significant reported workplace issues, with the agency experiencing at least six suicides since 2017, two of which were undertaken in the armoury of the AFP's federal headquarters. Just prior to the most recent suicide, in December 2019, former AFP staffer Julie Woodward sent a 56-page suicide letter to the AFP and Australian news outlet news.com.au detailing the substantial systemic bullying and physical and sexual harassment she and other colleagues had endured.[192] A further 100 whistleblowers came forward and a petition was launched calling for a federal inquiry into bullying in the AFP—which has not yet been actioned. These incidents indicate a toxic culture within the agency. Given the gendered challenges and entrenched sexism and misogyny within the agency, bullying is likely to have increased effects on women, and was a persistent feature throughout interviews.

The AFP demonstrates considerably more instances of gender discrimination and continued marginalisation within the department than might be expected given its (relatively) recent establishment. In the AFP, gendered informal institutions associated with policing as a profession appear to be crucial to the exclusionary, bullying, and misogynistic norms and behaviours in practice since establishment. These norms associated with the *profession generally* have informed the individual circumstance of the AFP. Even though it was established in a key period of gendered institutional change in wider society, with the introduction of EEO policies and other measures, the agency appears to be informed by 'old' policing norms rather than changing 'new' social norms. This might explain why the ABF (previously canvassed) has *regressed* in terms of its gender representation since its establishment. In these agencies, what it means to be a 'law enforcement agent' or officer of the law appears to be more important than the formal policies around equality within the agencies *or* changing social norms in wider society. What it means to be a police or enforcement officer is gendered, based in old 'traditions' around men as the 'defender' and 'enforcer'. To be a police officer is to be male, 'blokey', 'bolshie', aggressive, hierarchical, and authoritative.[193] Policing in Australia is characterised by 'an aggressive patrol style, abuse of power, excessive force and an emphasis on arrest and charge', and typically associated with a male-dominated policing culture. Gendered social and professional norms and institutions are therefore enduring in the AFP.

Added to that, in some cases, instances of exclusionary behaviour and bullying have intensified. Many participants reported that often (male) colleagues viewed the participants' career progression as only the result of targets and being the 'token', and not because of their 'merit'. The participants themselves viewed their career progress as the result of a hard, unending battle in which their achievements and 'merit' was infrequently rewarded, and when it was, it was well overdue.

While participants reported that the agency has markedly improved in terms of transparency as a result of the 2016 report *Culture Change: Gender Diversity and Inclusion in the Australian Federal Police*, gendered challenges endure. Women continue to be significantly underrepresented, as will be explored in the next chapter on demographics. Issues around horizontal and vertical segregation, plus discrimination and harassment, remain, and the ideal police officer continues to be inherently male.

Structure and Leadership

Analysis of the AFP's structure and leadership demonstrates an agency guided by hierarchy and rank, which has inherent positives and negatives for women. Highlighted earlier, the structuring between the *AFP Act* and *APS Act* presents one such point of tension, particularly regarding mobility across agencies. Lateral mobility is often key to leadership progression, particularly for women seeking more women-, and family-, friendly employment. While the 'sworn' nature of police officers restrict lateral recruitments at rank from the outside into the AFP, technically it should be easy to transfer to a new department at rank for those wishing to progress their career from the AFP to a new agency. Yet because the AFP falls under the *AFP Act*, participants highlighted that transferring out to general APS or other work would mean that they would lose portability of superannuation that was provided in their conditions under the Act. This presents a big disincentive for women particularly, given that women receive on average only one third of the superannuation payout of their male colleagues.[194] Legal structures therefore present challenges around lateral mobility and retention. For women who wish to transfer out of the AFP to a more family-friendly organisation or better work hours, or for whom the nature of the work or gendered challenges in the work become too much, the financial ramifications are significant.

As a uniformed agency, the AFP's structure is both hierarchical and rigid. It is characterised as 'paramilitaristic', closer to a military structuring than DFAT or Home Affairs more generally, on the spectrum ranging from military to diplomatic international affairs institutions. Like Defence and the ABF canvassed prior, rank is clearly visible, represented by uniform stripes, stars, and badges. The overtly physical nature of hierarchy creates a structure in which chains of command are significant and gendered: top-heavy and male-dominated. McGlen and Sarkees note that this kind of structure 'can generally advantage women only if women populate the crucial positions'.[195] Yet analysis of the organisational chart highlights a structure that while highly ranked, is simpler than the other agencies. This may be reflective of the agencies' size and its relative scope, which is action and enforcement oriented.

Like each of the other agencies, critical actors are also important in the AFP. In the 2016 Elizabeth Broderick & Co. review, the authors found that 'the AFP must capture the breadth of talent and expertise available in the Australian labour market and reflect the diversity of the Australian community'.[196] Women's experiences of leadership were found to be different to men's, despite a belief that their experiences were equal. Gendered challenges were found to be amplified in remote work, which suggests that women deployed in international positions face significant and differential treatment. Because of AFP's hierarchical and ranked structuring, and the ingrained nature of gendered cultures, movements for gender equality have required the leadership of critical actors, particularly the Commissioner. The former Commissioner Andrew Colvin's leadership on gender recurred regularly in the interviews, suggesting that his stance was a lived commitment. One participant noted:

> The AFP is undergoing an incredible reform and I think that our agency is in a really positive place because of the reform agenda that our Commissioner [Andrew Colvin] has currently put in place ... Andrew commissioned the [Cultural Change]

report, he welcomed the outcomes of the report. I don't think for a lot of the senior management at the time there would have been very palatable outcomes because there was and there will always be the existence of harassment and the like within an organisation, or lack of opportunity—but he welcomed it. He put in place [measures], he made commitments, he personally models it and it's about that leadership [by example].[197]

Increasing women's leadership has been prioritised for its utility as a central part of this reform agenda. Gender equality (1) strengthens capability and operational effectiveness; (2) contributes being a leading law enforcement agency; (3) creates an inclusive culture aligned with the vision of the senior leadership; and (4) ensures the AFP is able to meet the uncertain challenges of the future.[198] The aims of reform and critical actors is not without challenges, however.

Like the example highlighted earlier with the former Chief of Army David Morrison, agency culture also affects the Commissioner's ability to see through the reform efforts. One participant, Delilah stated:

It's a difficult cultural change for a policing organisation to go through... we've got these policies in place now that back you up though like the international [gender] strategy, the engagement strategy and that sort of thing. We can say, well, no, this is what the Commissioner wants, so this is why I'm making this decision and this is what is fair for us. So that's kind of it's good to back you up but, look, it's not without its negativity from people basically, their reluctance to change, so it's been challenging.[199]

While hierarchy and rank are important to being able to implement policy decisions in the AFP, across the more militaristic or paramilitaristic agencies studied, a core objection to gendered change that was raised during this research was prioritising *operational needs* above gender equality (as if they are mutually exclusive). Operational needs may be well justified in emergency situations, as what is most important is that the agencies are able to act in a timely manner and in the best way possible to ensure threats to life or national security are addressed, and government outcomes and objectives are met. During terror attacks, war, criminal, or other operations, at any moment, a situation could turn deadly. The precariousness of the work is not to be underestimated, and staff put their lives on the line every day to ensure that agency and country objectives are met.

Yet because of this, tackling so-called real problems—'real' cases and immediate operations—is prioritised over dealing with more intangible and ephemeral issues, such as problematic gender relations within the agency. Additionally, blind promotions processes, as well as multilayered interviews and testing, were introduced as a way of curbing bias in promotions. However, these policies were tested and changed and tested and changed in rapid succession, impairing the ability to reach the outcomes and targets desired. Indeed, participants noted that there was an instability in diversity and inclusion policies, which would change from one year to the next. Considering this, one participant noted:

> It's not that we need to scrap these initiatives, it's just we need to revisit how they're being delivered. But, like anything, people have kneejerk reactions like, 'well, that didn't work'. I think there's such a push for change that when the result isn't immediate people are quick to criticise initiatives that, [and change that]... [but,] I think, [it] needs more bedding down.[200]

Frequent change resulted in policies aimed at equality and addressing discrimination and disadvantage having less perceived credibility. It made policies more difficult to navigate and enforce. Further, frequently changing policy placed women in a difficult situation. Not only was it more difficult to navigate career progress, but staff distrusted the system used to produce the new results, which also effected women's credibility as the 'right choice' for the role in the eyes of their colleagues. Instability in the rules and processes therefore appear to have disadvantaged women, discredited their achievements, and even harmed the credibility of policymakers, with the effect of eroding the authority of their rank (at least on this issue).

Overall, the AFP's history, structure and leadership highlights enduring policing institutions that have normalised a masculine, bullying and in some cases a misogynistic workforce. Recent policy changes are evidently gaining traction across the agency, gradually improving women's representation and access to opportunities. However, the actual experiences of women are still poorly understood, and tracing history to the contemporary day indicates prevailing discrimination and harassment are part of what is already a difficult and stressful job. The former Commissioner Colvin's commitments highlight an agency proactive in changing, yet whether, and to what degree this progress is continued under the new Commissioner is yet to be seen. Further, a question remains whether these reform efforts will result in a truly equitable force, or not. Like in the other agencies studied, gendered inequalities have adapted to new policy and cultural environments, evidenced by continued substantial entrenched cases of harassment and bullying despite formal institutional changes.

Overarching Trends

Analysing historical forces, leadership, and structure across these international affairs agencies indicate that the gendered challenges in Australian international affairs agencies shift and evolve over time and alongside institutional change. There have been many pockets of progress, and policies aimed at producing equality are beginning to work, particularly with regards to women's representation, as will be further substantiated in the next chapter. But there are also gaps. Policy development is not consistent across and even within agencies, key reporting mechanisms (like the *Women in the ADF* reports) lack depth and consistency, and there are still gendered dynamics to what critical actors can and cannot do around substantive, systemic reform.

Whilst each agency spans a different portfolio of international affairs expertise, agency histories demonstrate far more similarities in background than at first blush, with many being influenced by early military and policing cultures, and all starting off as almost exclusively male-dominated. For some, particularly the more militaristic and paramilitaristic of agencies studied, the gendered challenges remain quite visible and overt. For Defence, the AFP and some of the more paramilitaristic parts of Home Affairs, this is the case—with public reviews reinforcing high levels of discrimination, sexual harassment and lagging statistics still found in my research, years later. The militaristic and paramilitaristic norms associated with Defence and 'sworn' policing and border force portfolios have proved hard to shift, with entrenched cultures privileging male physicality and masculine leadership norms prevailing. Uniformed contingents provide women with a 'surface credibility' that unsworn and nonmilitary individuals do not have, which can both benefit sworn and military women, whilst further effecting nonuniformed women's ability to utilise their power and authority.

Yet for the traditional diplomatic agency of DFAT, the overtness of gendered challenges is no more—in fact, policies aimed at producing equal representation in leadership have had strong success. For my research participants, there were notable improvements. However, increased representation was also not necessarily correlated with gender equality—micro-aggressions, differences in power and opportunities, and paternalistic behaviour still occurred. Gendered challenges were more likely to be 'underground' and covert, at times described as more 'genteel' forms of toxic masculinity than might be witnessed in militaries. Indeed, the types of gendered challenges at play in DFAT become clearer later in this book, where it is revealed that whilst women may have achieved parity or near parity in senior leadership, they are still more likely to be posted to lower status countries, in lower prestige roles.

Further, by analysing DFAT's stagnating and shrinking funding, status and power alongside women's increasing representation, as I have done separately in an article on the *diplomatic glass cliff*, it is clear that 'women's newly made gains in representation are constrained by the shrinking functional power of the roles and institutions they occupy'.[201]

The chapter therefore highlights several things. Firstly, despite improvements, international affairs agencies remain pervasively gendered, and much of this is influenced by institutions' early composition, norms, and history. To a degree, international affairs institutions are path dependent—how they started, matters to what is valued and normalised today. Secondly, the major differences across the agencies are not in whether gendered challenges exist, but to what degree, what shape, how visible these challenges are, and what policy options are chosen in attempts to rectify imbalances. The degree and shape of inequalities is impacted by many things, from institutional male-dominated histories of the agencies to prevailing contemporary norms associated with the line of work (role congruity theory), and the success (or not) interventions have had. The ability for critical actors to push for progress or stymy progress or even be limited and 'policed' themselves when attempting to make positive change for gender equality is different across the agencies, again constrained by the weight of institutional history and prevailing norms. The policy options chosen, including how much power, resources, transparency, and accountability involved, then has an impact on what success is possible. An analysis over time and across agencies demonstrates that for gender equality policies and strategies to work, they rely on having dedicated and multilevelled political will (across the department and Minister's office), legitimacy and credibility, institutional power and authority, resources to enact, monitor and evaluate change, transparency about progress or lack-thereof to date, and accountability mechanisms, for instance aided by clear reporting, targets and quotas. My analysis has also shown that success is often ultimately nested: equal or near-equal representation may be achieved in leadership or overall, but cultural patriarchy or inequality can still prevail.

This reinforces an early claim of this book: the gendered aspects of international affairs institutions are somewhat durable and stable, yet changeable enough that inequalities evolve over time, just as institutions change over time. The ramifications this has for other states and indeed other fields of work are significant and highlight that women's increasing representation does not automatically correlate with a reduction in gendered (and other) inequalities. It further highlights that visibility or invisibility of gendered challenges may impact on women's representation, which I will explore later in this book. These questions are worth considering in the following chapters which will explore who gets to lead internationally, where they are represented, and what are their experiences.

5
Which Women Lead International Affairs?

> I do find though as a diplomat or as representative of your country, you don't have gender... I'm Australia.
> —Sunny, Department of Foreign Affairs and Trade, 15 October 2018[1]

International affairs has long been the preserve of men. However, it has also been the preserve of *certain types* of men, remaining a bastion of prestige, social class, heteronormativity, and cultural homogeneity. Spike Peterson notes the state exercises power not only through its claim to legitimate violence, but also through state activities, routines, and rituals that constitute and regulate 'acceptable forms and images of social activity and individual and collective identity'.[2] Who can represent the state is an exercise of authority and state control, and as many feminists argue, the personal is political.[3] This section therefore goes beyond Enloe[4] and Neumann's[5] question, 'where are the women?' to ask, 'which women?'.

Research on ethnic diversity and diplomacy contributes strongly to this question of *who* is chosen to represent the state. Lequesne argues that contemporarily, there are two explanatory variables that stand out explaining why ethnic diversity has become a concern of MFAs in Western Europe. Firstly, is legitimacy, with increasingly ethnically diverse populations triggering concerns on how MFAs can and should 'change their existing image as being aloof from the reality of society', and not merely 'corpratist fortresses dominated by white men from wealthy families'.[6] Secondly, is the image that states project in the international system, with ethnically diverse MFAs helping to 'consolidate the image of a country as open to the "other"'.[7] Despite this, legacies of slavery, colonization, and racism impact some states' abilities to represent their constituents, and although affirmative actions are common in some states, others rely on indirect policy instruments to support more ethnically diverse workforces (or do nothing at all).

Other aspects of diversity are also important. Germany highlights the fact that as of 2022, they employed 300 federal foreign officers with a severe disability, one third of which are stationed abroad.[8] Yet research on disability and diplomacy is almost completely absent, as is literature on rurality and representation in diplomacy—something of particular importance to large countries with substantial rural populations. There is slightly more on LGBTIQ + diplomacy, with Janoff[9] and Rainer[10] exploring how diplomats and states' foreign policies engage on LGBTIQ + rights. Yet my own research on experiences and positionality of LGBTIQ + diplomats finds that queer women in diplomacy experience deep exclusion in diplomacy, often invisible despite their highly visible roles.[11] Standfield[12] explores diplomatic competence through an intersectional lens to argue that gendered, raced, and classed power shapes who is recognised as competent or virtuosic in diplomacy, whilst Neumann[13] argues that diplomacy is divided along class and gendered lines, with civil servant masculinity continuing to 'rule the roost'.

Ultimately, because employment opportunities are unevenly distributed across class, gender, sexuality, (dis)ability, and ethnicity,[14] it is expected that the participant demographics expose the gendered (and racialised, and so on) nature of international institutions too. This section will uncover participant demographics with regards to ethnicity, sexuality, class, education, rural and regional upbringing, relationship and familial status, rank, years in service, and (dis)ability. In doing so, it seeks to understand who represents the state internationally, pushing analysis beyond solely gender to the intersectional dynamics of international representation. It also seeks to give life and colour to those interviewed, and prompt reflection on the intersecting ways in which representation is evidenced and discrimination repeats in international affairs.

Where Are the Women of Colour?

One of the most striking initial findings when assessing participant demographics was ethnic diversity—and specifically, the lack of it. Race and ethnicity are core concepts to international affairs, as international representation requires individuals to authentically conform to the values, citizenship, and embodiment of the nation they are charged with representing. Indeed, Sasson-Levy[15] argues that militaries are never organised by gender or by race or ethnicity alone—rather, they are always designed at the intersection of race and ethnicity and gender, creating ethno-gendered groups and identities that are constructed and reaffirmed through formal policies that result in individuals experiencing their work in different ways, with different forms of convertible power post their discharge or retirement, and different relationships to the institution of citizenship. All these factors seem equally true for the international affairs agencies studied. No policy papers or formal strategies across international affairs delineate what 'representing the nation' means, beyond the requirement of citizenship. However, not everyone who is a citizen of the nation can represent the nation. In this research, not all Australians can represent Australia, with 'white masculinity' historically remaining at the centre of the Australian state.[16]

Australia is a migrant colonial nation whose Indigenous inhabitants were largely and gravely internally dispossessed and, in many instances, decimated.[17] Determining modern-day international representation is therefore complex. In the fledgling Australian state after federation, diplomatic and international representational posts were largely filled by 'new' Australians of Anglo-Celtic heritage, or British personnel. Gradually, this has begun to change, following shifts in the composition of the Australian population. Discriminatory or explicitly racist formal institutions, such as the Immigration Restriction Act 1901/White Australia Policy have now been dismantled. Yet it was only recently that Indigenous Australians had citizenship conditional on renouncing their heritage and only had conditional voting rights up until a 1977 referendum—several years after the White Australia Policy was abolished in 1973 and the passing of the Racial Discrimination Act in 1975. As Mercer notes, 'it must never be forgotten that Australia stands alone as the only country in the former British Empire to have denied its Indigenous people the right to self-determination'.[18] Therefore, while the Commonwealth's 1948 Nationality and Citizenship Act instituted that all who were born in Australia were legally citizens, in practice this legislation was an 'empty vessel' and Mercer argues that Indigenous Australians still remained largely 'citizens without rights'.[19] Historic discriminatory policies have influenced the circumstances and opportunities for Indigenous Australians and other ethnicities to represent Australia internationally.

Yet there are signs that things are changing, with the 2022 federal election seeing the first nonwhite, nonstraight, nonmale foreign minister in Penny Wong—a distinct difference from the past. Born in Malaysia, Penny Wong is Australia's first queer woman of colour Foreign Minister. Not only is her appointment historic, but her policy platform is too: she has committed Australia to following a distinct First Nations foreign policy agenda. Whilst the detail of this agenda is still under consideration, First Nations foreign policy scholar James Blackwell[20] argues that in international affairs, 'we are too often treated as subjects, not participants. And we are sometimes not even treated as subjects in international affairs', highlighting ongoing inequalities across not only diplomacy and defence representation, but also across foreign policy think tanks, universities, and development agencies. Therefore, despite the Labor government committing to a First Nations foreign policy and a vote on a Voice to Parliament that would enshrine Constitutional recognition enabling Aboriginal and Torres Strait Islander people to provide advice to parliament on policies and projects impacting their lives,[21] inclusion remains patchy, incomplete, and not guaranteed.

Contemporarily, Australia is recognised as 'strikingly culturally and ethnically diverse', yet international affairs institutions remain stratified along lines not just gendered, but also racialised.[22] Only 14 per cent of total participants interviewed identified as being from an 'ethnic' background—a limited and at times problematic delineation indicating their minority ethnic status in Australia. Data on ethnicity and employment is not always kept by the agencies, particularly given Australia's comprehensive anti-discrimination framework that makes the collection of data on ethnicity subject to strict regulations. However, the Australian Human Rights Commission found that, despite individuals from Anglo-Celtic and European backgrounds representing only 76 per cent of the Australian population, they are overrepresented in leadership, comprising 94.6 per cent of all Senior Executive Management roles.[23] Further, individuals of Anglo-Celtic or European heritage comprise 99 per cent of State and Federal government department heads.

The underrepresentation of culturally and linguistically diverse (CALD) individuals goes beyond race and ethnicity, to skin colour. Australians of Anglo-Celtic (white) background form 58 per cent of the population. Although individuals of (largely white) ethnically diverse European descent represent 18 per cent of the Australian population, they form 18.9 per cent of leadership.[24] While (largely nonwhite) non-European individuals of Asian, Middle Eastern, North African, and other non-European backgrounds form 21 per cent of the Australian population, they form only 5 per cent of leaders. Similarly, while Indigenous Australians form 3 per cent of the population, they are represented in only 0.4 per cent of Senior Executive Management. These trends hold for the international affairs agencies studied. Indeed, whilst Aboriginal and Torres Strait Islander people form 3.5 per cent of the Australian Public Service in 2022, they only form 0.007 per cent of the Australian Signals Directorate, part of the Defence Strategic Policy and Intelligence Group.[25] Intersectional analysis highlights how marginalised statuses (for instance, race or gender) 'act independently and combine additively to shape people's experiences'.[26] This may explain why CALD women of colour remain particularly underrepresented in international affairs leadership despite the gains made for many women across the agencies.

Across the participants, ethnic diversity was least represented in leadership within DFAT, and most represented in Home Affairs, followed by Defence. This aligns with the discussion in the previous chapter on history, which found a high proportion of CALD individuals employed within Home Affairs due to the needs of the immigration portfolio. Out of all the participants studied, only one spoke in accented English. On speaking to senior leadership across the agencies, one senior advisor explicitly stated that accented English is a 'no-go' for Australian international representation—that rather than discrimination or stereotyping based on ethnic background, it was often based on accent. Accent also denotes social class, with Colic-Peisker and Hlavac noting that 'ethno-cultural, educational, socio-economic and occupational attributes of a speaker are almost always reflected in his/her speech', and that there exists an 'accent ceiling' in which accented language is a 'marker of foreignness' that may detract from individuals' merit in the employment market.[27] This may have a duplicative effect on women, particularly in the high prestige diplomatic corps.

Accent was just one part of the 'informal criteria' required for diplomacy. During backgrounding discussions, it was reinforced that there was also an idea that a person had to be an authentic representative of the state. In the case of Australia, that meant being 'essentially Australian', a phrase that was connoted with sportsmanship and being a general all-rounder. The values and language associated with the informal criteria of diplomacy were typically masculine and spoke of an era of colonial Australia steeped in Anglo racial archetypes.

Inversely, CALD representation in Home Affairs (and to a lesser extent, Defence) is likely higher due to the nature of the work and the operational requirements involved. Having gained a 'critical mass' of not only women, but also CALD representation throughout the Department, has likely normalised a greater degree of diversity in leadership. Further, the needs to (a) ensure they had 'culturally fluent' staff in Home Affairs and (b) ensure they had enough recruits necessary for operational requirements in Defence, has likely resulted in an increased proportion of CALD representation overall in these agencies, as well as in the sample interviewed. However, it does raise the question, is CALD representation encouraged only when there are specific operational requirements (for language skills or cultural interpretation, for instance) or grave threats to life (on the frontlines of defence, for instance) in international affairs? If so, the implications are clear for international affairs: ethnic diversity is premised on utility and not mainstreamed in the same way that gender diversity is now being encouraged. Interrogating the co-option of ethnically diverse communities based solely on utilitarian aspects of inclusion is needed.

Even so, across all agencies, there were clearly benefits to CALD representation. In many instances, CALD representation meant greater language skills and cultural competency. One participant from Home Affairs explains, 'I was born and raised in the Philippines, and they really latch onto that and they go, "you understand us, but you're Australian still"', indicating a special relationship or quicker rapport developed based off a perceived mutual understanding.[28] Another participant noted, 'in diplomacy . . . [CALD] people bring . . . cultural understanding readymade because they've had to grow up in the crazy Greek community in Melbourne. They bring language skills, all of that'.[29] Talia in Home Affairs noted the special understanding that her Maori New Zealander background brought to her work:

> I researched and I found out it was a matriarchal society that I was posted to. I ring the old ladies in New Zealand because I am part Maori and I said I have to go to [this location] to work: (1) can I have your permission to go and do that, and (2) how would I manage best to obey the courtesies of that island. And then four days later they'll ring back and say oh, what we think is we'll ring such and such and then we'll give you a letter and then before you go you should speak to her son who speaks really good English, and then when you get there you'll make time and won't have any meetings for work until you meet and have a cup of tea with [this lady], you'll meet all the ministers' mums, then they do their bit and you'll be able to do what you need to do for your work.[30]

This suggests that the cultural knowledge available to representatives of diverse ethnicities may act as a crucial positive for work in the field. It was evident from Talia's narration that the standard norms of diplomacy and negotiation may not have been appropriate in some circumstances, and that because of her cultural background, she was able to access knowledge, customs and networks that might not have been otherwise available.

Despite the benefits that CALD individuals bring to the field, there were also noted 'security concerns' associated with CALD diversity. During background research, ethnic diversity within Home Affairs was canvassed. I asked about the ethnic diversity of leaders, to which one respondent replied 'well that's a security concern, isn't it?'—what appeared to be an attempt at a joke that touched more deeply on entrenched beliefs within the agency and wider society. This theme of CALD identity being a 'security concern' was repeated across Defence. Rebecca spoke about the additive layers of identity that influence on leaders' experiences:

> So I'm also not a person of colour, so I don't stand out that much. I've only got the gender hurdle to get over. My last name is pretty foreign, you know, we have a bit of a giggle about that and people move on. But I'm not being approached, unlike many of my close friends, to be on the cover of yet another brochure, because they're the Asian female. They get so sick of it. One of the things that's happening, which I think is quite interesting at the moment, is because of the paranoia around China in Defence circles, people of Chinese descent, whether or not they were born in China, speak Chinese or anything—if they look Chinese, there is a growing sort of sense of 'oh we should be a little bit suspicious and careful of you, right?' 'What was your name again?' That sort of thing. 'Oh are you from China?' I think that that's pretty hateful.[31]

Across the sample, one participant identified as Indigenous. In Larkin's[32] study of First Nations representation within the APS, he notes that the cumulative effect of a racial hierarchy within agencies sustains a racial division of labour within the APS. Considering that it was only in 2018 that DFAT posted its first Indigenous woman ambassador, Julie-Ann Guivarra, it seems that barriers clearly remain for CALD women, particularly women of colour and First Nations women. In fact, intense feelings of tokenism existed for participants who identified as CALD, particularly in a policy environment that defaulted to viewing them as 'disadvantaged' because of their ethnicity. One DFAT participant noted: 'The problem with diversity policies is it starts from a premise of disadvantage. So the premise on cultural and linguistic diversity is if you are a CALD person you are by definition disadvantaged. So our policies will be aimed at alleviating disadvantage.'[33] When I attended one official embassy event, two CALD people of colour, one woman and one man from Home Affairs and DFAT, bumped into each other, turned to me, and laughed as they explained they were the diversity hires for the embassy. What was perhaps meant as a light-hearted joke turned out to be a distinct, and even isolating observation. As just one example of informal behaviour in embassy settings, there was evidently a shared experience of tokenism, marginalization, and isolation that formed part of individuals' experiences.

In Britain, traditional methods of recruitment, security vetting, and background checks still factor heavily into explicit and implicit discrimination 'against those from non-Oxbridge backgrounds', with a small exception for specialist linguists or clerical grades (Lomas 2021, p. 9). Although research on the impact of recruitment, vetting and background checks for ethnically diverse communities is largely missing, latent racism and monoculturalism prevails in the Australian agencies. Relatedly, the value and authority that participants brought to negotiations often began from a place of having to prove themselves, and was perceived, explicitly, as 'not equal' to the representation of a straight white man in the same position. Internally to agencies and externally to the world, women were perceived as less authoritative, less senior, and less legitimate as leaders—even in the same rank or role as men. Women of colour felt they had to work twice as hard again to be recognised. Lyn summed up her experience:

> I'll never forget, in one country, which I shall not name, but they had a stream of very excellent women high commissioners year after year and the prime minister, male, said to me, 'when are we going to be upgraded?' I said, 'Excuse me?' He said, 'Well, when are we going to get a man high commissioner?' He was having a go, but for him to have raised it, he was also a bit sincere, you know, why do we—when are we going to get a real ambassador.[34]

Women's 'outsider' positioning was repeatedly reinforced by participant experiences. Trying to combat the biases or assumptions of international counterparts was difficult, however. Unlike agency-based discrimination, there is little recourse to combat discrimination and harassment in the international field. This is particularly so because much of the work of international affairs is based around minimising diplomatic incidents—potentially reducing the chance of justice (at least publicly) for women 'when things go wrong'. Yet it does reinforce an existing gender order in which women, particularly women of colour, are at the bottom. Language like 'real ambassador' suggests that only men can do the work and embody what it means to be an ambassador, and that women are just 'pretend playing' in the role until the next man comes along. This evidently affected women's perception of their own ability to fulfil the role too and may be additively experienced for women of diverse backgrounds, with one LGBTI+-identifying participant noting:

> I don't think it's necessarily because of my gender or my sexuality or my ethnicity, but . . . I spent a lot of time worrying that I wasn't ambassadorial enough, I wasn't like some of the people I'd seen in DFAT, particularly the men I have to say, because there's more of them to look at.[35]

Queering International Representation

LGBTI+ communities have long histories of being policed, marginalised, and made invisible—perhaps nowhere more than on the international stage. Yet norms around sexuality and international representation exist just like the gendered and racialised norms around 'who' can represent the nation. Indeed historically, LGBTI + individuals have been viewed with caution and suspicion, as security risks typically excluded from sensitive diplomatic positions.[36] Sexual identity placed individuals especially at risk of being blackmailed, and the loyalties of LGBTI + individuals in diplomacy and security were questioned, perceived as being part of a transnational cosmopolitan community.[37] In Britain, the Cadogan report on security argued that sexuality was a 'mark of unreliability' that would 'undermine the ability of the department to manage Britain's diplomatic relations'.[38] Further, security vetting placed many barriers for LGBTI + international affairs workers, with homophobia and transphobia in wider society and in law an inevitable influence on background checks that sought to find and restrict so-called sexual deviance.[39]

For Australia's first openly gay diplomat, Stephen Brady, and noted gay senior diplomat John Dauth, queer identity had marked impacts, affecting individuals' abilities to take the posts they wanted, in some cases requiring them to take 'lesser' posts in an act of 'career suicide'. Yet for most of the international and Australian histories of LGBTI + people in diplomacy, the focus has almost exclusively been on gay men, with the issue of queer women only raised in the context of equality. For instance, in discussions in the UK, the question was framed as: if gay men were barred from international appointments, should queer women also be barred?

While the field of political science and IR has marginalised 'queerness', both remain centrally focused on power and the (re)production of power relations.[40] As Marinucci argues, 'the oppression of women and the suppression of lesbian, gay, bisexual and transgender existence are deeply entwined'.[41] In fact, sexuality had a deep impact on participants interviewed, with four out of the total 57 interviewees openly identified as lesbian or gay. Considering women's underrepresentation across diplomacy globally, and the low proportion of LGBTI + women in society and the agencies, the sample size is roughly representative and included individuals of diverse ethnicities and urban or rural upbringings. While all women were 'out' (their sexuality was publicly known), the degree to which they were 'out' depended on the audience and their host country.

For instance, depending on a host country's legal and social acceptance of homosexuality, differential treatment, harassment, and discrimination was common, with queer women often experiencing a profound form of exclusion. Their experiences were summed up as thus: '[being] LGBTI+ is harder offshore where the environment does not sustain [you]—where it's illegal or where you're very much frowned upon'.[42] The experiences of queer women envoys were affected by their ability to be 'out' but did not depend on it. Individuals may have been 'out' within their agency or to a select group of colleagues, yet not 'out' more broadly. Or, they could have been entirely 'out' to the world. If they were 'out' entirely, they were often subject to greater overt instances of homophobia or heterosexism—name-calling, bullying, isolation, and physical threats or violence—both from within their agency and from the field or host country. If they were not 'out', or only partially 'out', they still experienced instances of homophobia and heterosexism; however, this was often coupled with the burden of invisibility and lack of recognition, both of themselves or of their partner and relationship.

The ability to gain the required visa was often an issue, with considerable delays and highly unusual instances of visas being dealt with by the host countries' foreign affairs department rather than the immigration department. Due to visa requirements, queer women who represent Australia in some host countries recounted bringing their spouse as a 'member of the house', rather than being included on a spousal visa as usual. As one participant states: 'Before [Australia] had [legalised] gay marriage, I think we had something where if the other country kind of recognised same sex relationships, the same sex partner could go in on that visa, but otherwise you go in on a member of the household domestic visa'.[43] Participants reported instances of colleague's spouses deploying as 'maid' or 'chauffeur', which had ramifications on whether they could claim spousal financial benefits. Further, in emergencies, generally only those on spousal or family visas were evacuated—not those on household or staffing visas. Navigating visas and benefits had significant financial and social ramifications for individuals, which also has ramifications on the wider attraction and retention of staff. Substantial improvements have been made in recent years, with departments extending allowances to spouses regardless of their visa status. However, as long as LGBTI + individuals in the field remain closeted or only partially out, visas remain an issue.

For individuals posted from more security and enforcement style international affairs agencies, the challenges at post were viewed as even more difficult. Whereas homosexuality has been comparatively more accepted in traditional diplomatic spheres, military and paramilitaristic organisations throughout both Australia and internationally exhibit many examples of highly institutionalised homophobia and heterosexism. In the military, this has historically been experienced through 'don't ask, don't tell' policies in the US; however, the lines of homophobia went even further in Australia, where a total ban on gay men and women in the military existed until 1992. In fact, gay men and women served at a time when their identities were illegal, and 'lesbians were punished as deviants who might somehow contaminate the services'.[44] Australian policing agencies were often on the forefront of historical persecution of LGBTI + individuals.

The experiences of queer women in this study highlighted the gendered reliance on spouses at post. The presence of male 'trailing spouses' at posts is still disruptive for diplomacy, with many women in my research talking about the inability or unwillingness for their male partners to take on the expected (but largely unrecognised and unpaid) roles of hosting and maintaining the diplomatic home, as well as the men not knowing what to do with themselves or their time. Having two women posted together—as ambassador, commander, defence attaché, and as spouse—was in some ways therefore more traditional. Indeed, women with wives were perhaps a better fit for the traditional roles of diplomat and spouse rather than the role reversal of heterosexual envoys with a female diplomat and male spouse. Queer female diplomats (with spouses) can do the work that straight male diplomats with wives can do. Yet this was also deeply conditional—on things like the political and social context of the country posted to as well as on whether the couple was 'out' or not, and willing to fulfill this heteronormative model of diplomacy. The nuances of this finding will be explored later in the book.

Additionally, because the ideal diplomat remains the heterosexual, (white) man in Australian international affairs, sexuality was also a salient factor for heterosexual women who represented a deviation from the masculine norm in international affairs. In Defence, Aria notes:

> When you look at close girlfriends and I who are still single, there is a view that we must all be lesbians... actually we're not [lesbians] ... but I mean I've been accused of being a lesbian for a long time, particularly within the Army.[45]

For some participants, the correlations between them having short hair, no children, and no partner (or a combination of the three) and being a woman in a significant position of leadership, led to them being repeatedly perceived as queer. Mostly, this was received good-naturedly and did not affect their work. However, the way participants were perceived by the outside world and their counterparts is significant for understanding the nature of gender in international affairs. Even if not queer, women were frequently typified to be queer. This is emblematic of 'othering' experienced by women leaders and diplomats for whom international affairs continues to reinforce specific gendered and sexual power dynamics that support gender inequality and heterosexism.[46] It reinforces the 'deeply entwined' nature of the oppression and suppression of women and of 'queer'.[47]

Additionally, for LGBTI + participants, although 'queerness' was inherent in their experiences, like Christo's[48] findings, their status as women generally preceded their sexuality. Gender and sexuality produced related, but also distinct experiences. While gender is often based off socially constructed differences—many of which are physically 'obvious'—sexuality is often invisible, and therefore the need to identify as LGBTI + or queer differed from participant to participant. Sexual identity was therefore an integral part of participants' identity, but not always one they could promote or announce. As discussed in Chapter 2, Neumann's *The Body of the Diplomat* found that women represented two different femininities and hierarchies for understanding their roles: 'as a diplomat that happens to be a woman' and 'as a woman who happens to be a diplomat'.[49] For those who were openly out and were sought for specifically LGBTI + related initiatives or events within their agencies or in-country, the hierarchy for understanding their role followed more of a 'queer and woman-first-diplomat-next' identity format. In almost every other circumstance, their gender and sexuality were downplayed, following a role-first-woman-next pattern, with their sexuality often left out entirely. Often, the decision to remain partially in the 'closet' was based out of fear that coming out would limit their career options, damage their reputation, or put them physically at risk on their postings or even in their agencies. Not only was this reflective of their experiences, but was also mirrored in the interviews, with participants often only mentioning their sexuality near to the end of the interview, after trust and rapport had been established, and a key part of their experience was evidently missing from the narrative discussed to that point.

Inability to identify, or ability to identity their queerness only in certain contexts, highlights international affairs as a space more hostile than not to queer women's identities. In fact, many of Australia's first female diplomats are reported to have been queer, perhaps as they were not affected to the same degree by the Marriage Bar or children as their heterosexual peers were, although there is very little transparency and visibility about early sexuality in the service. It appears only welcoming of diverse women conditional on a large variety of external factors—highlighting what Altman and Symons[50] note as a conditional acceptance of queer identity. It is also likely that this conditional acceptance is experienced by queer men and straight women too—given the widespread othering of 'difference' across the agencies. As well as being influenced by gendered and racialised institutions, international affairs is clearly heteronormative and heterosexist—basing its presumptions and practices on the experiences of heterosexual actors and privileging those experiences in action.

A Class of Its Own?

Ministries of foreign affairs have often been considered 'elitist' institutions, whilst policing and military establishments have their own social class histories, in the Australian context as somewhat more socially open, yet classed nonetheless.[51] Class was therefore pervasive across the agencies, but not homogenous. DFAT embodies many traditional diplomatic values, particularly around 'elite' private school education, dynastic ties and an association with upper-middle class, genteel, and 'cultured' norms. Variation to this was noted, for instance Anna spoke about not being part of the 'DFAT dynasty', equating employment in the agency to that of being born into a royal empire: 'I was very much middle class, mum's a teacher, dad's a teacher . . . I'm public school, [rural] university [educated]. I'm not what some people associate with our diplomatic service and nor what some people sometimes expect'.[52] Government service has typically been associated with the upper-middle classes and professionalism, and was on occasion historically associated with favouritism, nepotism, and cronyism as mechanisms to get the top jobs within public service. A prohibition was only placed on patronage and favouritism in the Australian Public Service in 1999,[53] whilst Matheson asserts that staff selection in the Australian Public Service has historically exemplified 'social closure', particularly based on educational credentials or lack thereof.[54] Leadership positions or international representation, moreover, was associated with the elite. Indeed, in many instances globally diplomacy was sponsored by the individual, meaning only those with the finances and influence wielded diplomatic roles.[55]

Within the modern agencies, the increased professionalisation of government in favour of merit-based appointments, rather than politics and connections, has had an impact, increasing the diversity of representation across class divides. However, class lines have not been entirely blurred, and class is experienced in different ways across the agencies. Participants from DFAT reinforced the most prestigious class connotations, as opposed to the AFP, Defence, and elements of Home Affairs, which had more working-class connotations and participant profiles.

Class was also related to educational attainment. Participants in DFAT and Home Affairs had undertaken the most education, while many participants from Defence had joined the agency for its embedded education opportunities, with previous tertiary education not a condition of entry. Across all women listed on DFAT's Ambassadors and overseas representatives page online in 2018, all (100 per cent) had at least a bachelor's degree. Of these women, over 80 per cent had a second degree, generally a master's degree, diploma, or certificate, generally but not always in a specialised, related field. Most had studied some form of international relations, law, politics, or history.

Therefore, in my dataset, participants who studied topics that differed from this felt they stood out. For instance, Bel commented that 'It's not a very kind of conventional [career path]—I didn't go and do law or politics at one of the Australian sandstone universities'.[56] There was less focus on higher education in AFP, and participants demonstrated the considerable success that could be reached regardless of educational background. One AFP participant noted that 'I was a senior in 1990 in Queensland . . . I was the only one in my immediate family to make it past Grade 9'.[57] Class and educational attainment were often entwined—while level of education attainment does not prescribe class, it is often indicative of class.[58] Prior to 1995, individuals did not have to have a university degree to apply for a job with the AFP. Many senior level leaders who have been part of the AFP since before 1995 therefore do not have university degrees, which is a significant difference to some of the other departments, notably DFAT. Another senior AFP officer discussed what is important in her job, and how challenges are navigated:

> I have not got a degree. So is education a prerequisite? It's not . . . sometimes it is the old common-sense factor . . . in almost 28, 29 years, I've gone with my gut . . . I think if you haven't got that . . . please don't deploy offshore [laughs] . . . Policing in any given day, is any given situation, and you cannot predict it . . . you are usually unarmed, you're using your mouth and you are in a situation that could go pear-shaped within two seconds. So how do you prepare for that? Sometimes you can't. So every day you just go there and you hope for the best. Especially when you're in offshore in mission component areas and so you have to be able to cope.[59]

Rural and regional upbringing versus urban upbringing also factored into participant demographics. Overwhelmingly participants came from 'rich' urban centres, predominantly Canberra, Sydney, and Melbourne. Yet of all the participants, just over 10 per cent disclosed they were from rural or regional backgrounds and were evenly split across the agencies. In most cases, this backgrounding played a significant role in their identity, and in many cases was reiterated by the participants themselves as an important part of diversity within the agencies. It was also an important part of their narratives around resilience and what made them capable in the work they did. Odette from the AFP noted, 'I'm finding in all my learnings at the moment, the more resilient people are those that had a country upbringing'.[60]

Family and Baggage to Follow

It is well-recognised in the literature that many of international affairs' earliest representatives were single women or those without children. This is partially a result of the marriage bar, as well as influenced by the difficulties experienced by women in undertaking both the bulk of domestic labour and intensive international representation at the same time. Not all participants disclosed marital status and whether they had children; however, of those who did, 32 (55.2 per cent) were either married or in a relationship and 16 (27.5 per cent) were single having divorced or never married. 10 (17.2 per cent) did not disclose and were not questioned on this—a specific methodological choice to allow the women interviewed to raise the elements of their journey that had been most important (rather than asking and making assumptions around the impact of family and children). From my sample, women in DFAT and the AFP were most likely to have children, and most participants from these agencies did have children. In Home Affairs and Defence, under half of the participants had children. Even so, it is worth noting that 46 per cent of Defence participants reported having children, which is more than double the average for women generally in the ADF. This might signify that those with children may be more likely to pursue a 'diplomatic' Defence role or that the Defence Attaché role is more family-friendly than general ADF service. Alternatively, it could just reflect a correlation made in this small sample size.

Spousal status and children were key considerations regarding deployment and leadership. Most participants with children took their early career posts when their children were at pre- or primary school age and most women took their senior-career posts when their children had finished secondary school or commenced university. Interestingly, marital or relationship status did not always equate to greater support for the women on their deployments. For approximately half of the participants who had spouses, their spouses accompanied them on posting and were able to provide crucial supports for them, their role, and their children. Yet for the other half of participants, their spouses *did not* accompany them on post. This occurred even if the woman was deployed and took their children with her, leaving her effectively 'single' at post and often still in charge of raising their children. One participant commented, 'I'm a strong advocate for helping women to have children [with them on their posting] because to me that's extremely hard, *especially when you're married*'.[61] She highlighted that whilst female spouses often provide core personal and professional support for men, male spouses often do not fill these same roles for women. Often in these cases, the husband (it was always a male spouse), would not accompany the woman.

One Defence participant provided further insight into the challenges that deployment raises for relationships, commenting that it is good practice for women in Defence to gain a partner early in their career. It was reported by the participant to be more difficult to get a partner later as they generally did not understand relentless and all-consuming nature of the work.

If a participant's child(ren) remained in Australia while she deployed internationally, often the spouse and wider family were very supportive in maintaining the home, and regularly visited the women at post or in a third country 'holiday' location. Returning to the family after post was a considerable challenge for many, for whom their family and partners had 'got on with life' as usual and both parties experienced tension on returning to the home dynamic. Out of the agencies, the AFP had best-developed institutional supports for individuals returning from post to re-integrate without causing family disturbance, often taking participants through a short one- to two-day period of re-integration before releasing them back to their families. Trends around family and children will be further analysed in Chapter 7 on women leaders' experiences.

Geographic Reach and Patterns of Deployment

The women researched for this project were truly international in terms of the breadth and depth of their postings. Participants had been deployed in every region of the world, across a wide range of postings. In most circumstances in Defence and Home Affairs participants could not simply choose their preferred country of deployment. However sometimes, such as in the civilian side of Defence, women could register expressions of interest only for the countries they wanted. For those who could choose their country of deployment, gendered considerations (how gender equitable a country was, personal safety, freedoms) were a key consideration in determining whether they took up opportunities or not. Particularly for those with children, the choice was explicit. For others, factors like the type of lifestyle, level of domestic support (for instance, the ability to have domestic help), and spousal opportunities for their partners weighed considerably into their choice—all of which will be explored further later in the book.

A small number of countries were considered 'no-go' countries for participants interviewed, including Saudi Arabia and Pakistan. Several countries were highly contested as countries participants would willingly nominate for, including Papua New Guinea (PNG), Afghanistan, and a few other

Middle Eastern countries. For instance, participants question the level of safety and perceptions of women in power in PNG. One participant noted:

> PNG has a culture of . . . there's high levels of family violence, there's traditional norms that essentially mean that currency is paid for brides, and high levels of just general sort of community violence. And definitely for women there's a higher security risk. Personally, I wouldn't go out of the compound or out of a secure area and just go walking in the streets. But if my male six-foot partner had to cross the street, I feel like he would be safe enough to do that. Whereas I wouldn't. So there is definitely a culture where there's gender bias and gender inequality.[62]

Despite this, PNG was the fifth-most deployed to country, and most participants who had spent time there had greatly enjoyed the experience on a professional level, even with safety or other concerns. This may reflect the fact that Australia has a large presence in PNG, and that there are many early career posting opportunities for junior staff—as well as it being considered a post in which junior representatives could 'cut their teeth' and prove their strength in complex contexts.

Additionally, even countries such as the United States (US) were warily regarded. For instance, due to political circumstances, queer participants were affected by the 2018 decision of the US State Department to stop issuing visas to the same-sex partners of foreign diplomats sent to the US or the United Nations in New York unless they are legally married.[63] Participant sentiment amongst the LGBTIQ + participants reinforced that no location was entirely 'safe'. Rather, safety was marked more by safety within participants' own agencies, reinforcing findings that agencies (not host countries) matter most to women's treatment internationally.[64] This could be reflective of those interviewed, and where they had been posted. However also highlighted the intense precarity of international deployment for gender and sexual minorities.

The women interviewed had represented Australia in over 40 countries (excepting Julie Bishop as foreign minister and Julia Gillard as prime minister who represented Australia extensively, with Julie Bishop visiting 105 countries for instance, some multiple times). Over the entire career span of participants, the following countries were most deployed to: China (11 times); US (9 times); United Nations in New York (6 times) and Afghanistan (6 times); Papua New Guinea (5 times); and the UK, Japan, and East Timor (4 times each). A range of other countries were deployed to three or less times across the interviews.

Out of the agencies and women studied, women deployed the most in DFAT (averaging 2.8 deployments), followed by Home Affairs (averaging 2.6

deployments), AFP (averaging 2.1 deployments), and Defence (averaging 1.5 deployments). Generally, those in senior SES ranks had deployed the most, with women in EL or leadership pipeline roles having deployed the least. The AFP was an exception: those in EL level positions in the AFP deployed on average 3.25 times, whereas those in SES level positions only deployed an average of 1.8 times. This could be a result of the fact that international roles within the AFP were generally restricted to EL levels until recently when international roles at an SES level were introduced.

In cases across Home Affairs, AFP, and the civilian side of Defence, women would opt out of career advancement in favour of overseas postings. For them, the ability to regularly post overseas was more important than career progression, which often offered less, or no, postings at more senior levels. In these agencies in particular, postings were not always seen as a career positive, with the choice often being made between posting or promotion a 'double-edged sword'.[65]

Correlating with the desire to research women in leadership, most participants were of senior rank and years of service. Most participants were in their mid-late stages of their career, with experience ranging from five years to over 40 years in their respective agencies. Fewer years in service generally correlated with lateral transfers. Additionally, out of the total 57 formal interviewees, 31 (54.3 per cent) were at SES or equivalent ranks, and 21 (36.8 per cent) were at EL or equivalent ranks, three with undisclosed ranks, and three not ranked (the former ministers and one political appointee). Participants at SES or equivalent rank represented 86.7 per cent of DFAT participants, 42.8 per cent of Defence participants, 42.8 per cent of Home Affairs participants, and 54.5 per cent of AFP participants. Senior positions correlated strongly with years in service, reinforcing that international affairs leadership remains to follow specific pipelines requiring deep operational and organisational experience that may disadvantage lateral transfers or those who specialise, rather than general or operational streams of work.

Straight, White, and . . . Female?

This section highlights several trends. Firstly, the oppression of women is fundamentally entwined with the oppression of racial difference and LGBTIQ + identity. Colonial structures reinforce patriarchal hierarchies in international affairs, and heteronormativity reigns. Secondly, the fight of women's greater representation in international affairs has often been siloed and one-sided, with women's multiple identities not always supported in the same ways.

Thirdly, there are the beginnings of many positive changes. The commitment to First Nations foreign policy, the professionalisation of the workforce beyond traditionally elite and class-exclusionary cohorts, and the beginnings of more family-friendly policies across the agencies suggest that in the decades to come, we will see further shifts and opening within international affairs.

Yet while the moral and utilitarian imperatives around representing the nation fully across gender, ethnic, and other dimensions are clear, encouraging intersectionality reforms in international affairs is not entirely unproblematic. As Cynthia Enloe states of the military, 'the newest maneuver has been to camouflage women's service to the military as women's liberation'.[66] Therefore, there is serious doubt whether it is possible to transform international affairs, if its primary aims are the maintenance of colonial and imperial sovereignty, interests and power structures and the organized use of violence to achieve national objectives devised by groupings with few women and marginalized groups represented. At the same time, whilst MFAs and other organisations continue to be at the forefront of international affairs, they should be diverse. Even if a more diverse workforce does not result in the complete remaking of the sector, it is still important to fight for the right for women and historically marginalized groups' inclusion in international affairs. The task is therefore to both disrupt the instrumentalist way in which international affairs views diversity, whilst also holding the promise that such institutions can indeed be transformed.

Overall, in this study participants were largely white, middle-class, and heterosexual—like their female counterparts in the US, Canada, Sweden, and the United Kingdom. While most women did have a partner and family, it was striking that this percentage was not higher, which suggests that leadership remains to impact on participants' choices and opportunities around spouses or children. From demographics alone it is clear that 'rules' exist around who can represent Australia overseas, with women of colour and those from sexually diverse backgrounds least represented. Whilst no participants disclosed a disability, further research into diverse representation in international affairs—and its barriers—is needed.

6
Where Are the Women in International Affairs Leadership?

> We're not talking about digging a ditch here. We're not talking about heavy labour. We're talking about international relations and there's no excuse for it. There can be no excuse for it to be male dominated.
> —Grace, Department of Foreign Affairs and Trade, 5 October 2018[1]

At a global level, women's underrepresentation in international affairs is pervasive, unrelenting, and seldom overcome. Underrepresentation is evidenced across diplomatic missions, the United Nations and other international organisations, military bases, political meetings and negotiations, think tanks and the corporate advisory community, and even academia.[2] Women's underrepresentation and inequality in international affairs is therefore all-consuming.

Even so, this book has indicated how Australia is in many ways leading the charge—the gap is closing, and in cases rapidly. This section therefore seeks to quantify and detail women's representation in the Australian case, particularly given the rapid changes that occurred even during this research. The Australian foreign policy think tank Lowy Institute[3] found that gender diversity in the Australian international affairs field lags significantly behind the Australian Public Service (APS). Overall, women remain underrepresented, and more militaristic agencies are generally considered the worst performing—with militarism frequently noted as oppositional and antithetical to feminism.[4] However, breaking down data on gender by rank and comparing it with opportunities for leadership and international representation over time reveals substantial original findings on women's representation in Australian international affairs—some particularly counter-intuitive and surprising.

In this chapter, trend data from the last 30 + years is analysed, followed by statistics on (1) overall representation, (2) SES (and equivalent) leadership, (3) EL (and equivalent) leadership, and (4) international representation. Data on international postings, unless otherwise stated, remains focused on women in SES and EL positions to accurately portray women's *formal leadership* in Australian international affairs. A range of datasets have been accessed, over a range of periods, to obtain the most accurate account of women's representation across the agencies. To reveal the most rigorous and thorough account of gender across the agencies, I have endeavoured to reduce inconsistencies in reporting methods and gaps in the data.[5] However, given some of the gaps in knowledge and restricted access to some forms of data, there were considerable difficulties in compiling this dataset. This data represents a significant new contribution to the literature, including analysis of previously unpublished datasets.

Tracing Women's Representation in Australian International Affairs

Women's overall employment in the agencies studied has grown steadily over the last few decades. From 2000 to 2022, women's representation has increased the most in DFAT and the civilian side of Defence, where women's representation increased by 14.1 per cent in the Department of Defence (from 32.6 per cent to 46.7 per cent) and 14.6 per cent in DFAT (from 44.9 per cent to 59.5 per cent). In the AFP, data is only available since 2011, where women's representation has increased by only 0.7 per cent (from 38.1 per cent to 38.8 per cent). Similarly, ADF data is only available from 2012, where women's representation increased marginally better, by 5.3 per cent (from 14.4 per cent to 19.7 per cent). Home Affairs is the only agency that has experienced a decrease in women's representation from 2000 to 2022 of –5.3 percentage points in Home Affairs (from 57.7 per cent to 52.4 per cent), yet women remain in the majority. Women are a minority in the ADF, AFP and civilian Defence, and the least progress has been made in the AFP.

Developments across the agencies are therefore complex. Whilst representation continues to skyrocket in DFAT and the civilian side of Defence, women's representation is going backwards in Home Affairs, and women still have not cracked the glass ceiling to make it to equal representation in the SES. Indeed, women form the majority of roles from APS band 4 to EL 1, but not above. Women's declining representation in Home Affairs begun with the merger in 2014–2015 that saw the Department take on an increasingly securitised role and creation of the Australian Border Force (ABF). Women's proportional representation dropped by 7.1 per cent in just one year in 2015. One participant, Penny, comments on the changed gender balance, particularly in the enforcement side of the agency and since the merger into Home Affairs. She noted: 'I don't think it's jobs for the boys here, what I think is, it is jobs for Defence and jobs for AFP. Let's bring in anyone with that kind of background, they're going to fix things'.[6] However, on reflection, she noted that 'to a certain extent, it is jobs for the boys', given the male domination in Defence and the masculinised values of those departments.

Besides some major changes over the years that have contributed to women's fluctuating representation, as explored in the chapter on history, there are a few other noteworthy points to consider in mapping women's underrepresentation over time. *Women in the ADF Reports* were instituted in 2011, requiring Defence to account for gender data in annual reports. Two years after this new gender data-gathering was mandated, women went from representing only 15.0 per cent of the ADF in 2013 to 18.3 per cent in 2014. However, these gains were almost completely reversed by the following year, when women represented only 15.3 per cent of the ADF. No reasoning is given in the annual reports for this decrease in representation; however, the 2014 ADF *Audit Report* released by the Australian Commission for Human Rights urged the service lines to 'be vigilant against a backlash directed at women as a result of the cultural change process'.[7]

The *Audit Report* provides clues as to why a reversal may have occurred, including that the gender reforms were seen as giving women 'special treatment', 'lowering standards' on an exclusive force, or 'undermining merit' in the selection process. All the above hints to a cultural context reluctant to change despite (or because of) increasing numbers of women. Additionally, it is possible that highlighting the gendered challenges in the agency gave some individuals pause to reflect—that the act of documenting challenges highlighted how gendered and sexist these 'normalised norms' really were. This theme arose throughout the interviews, with women reconsidering their career options particularly after reports were released highlighting gendered issues. Further, as previously mentioned, the frequency of reports and audits on Defence seems to have lowered the traction made on gender equality. It is likely that this enabled the agency to make only partial change—well-designed policy implemented with no intention of truly being fulfilled. During periods of instability such as these, Mackay[8] finds agencies more likely to revert to old practices and norms—a combined effect resulting from resistance to both 'newness' and 'gender'.

Where Are the Women in Leadership? 147

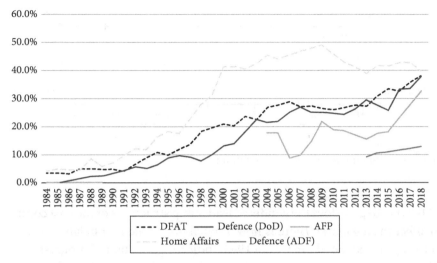

Graph 6.1 Representation of women in SES positions, 1984–2018

Data source: Agency Annual Reports and APSED RFI 736 data. AFP data points from 1990 to 2003 were not able to be found by the AFP when the Freedom of Information division conducted their search. Defence data points prior to 2013 are unavailable, as 2013 marks the first Women in the ADF Report—the first time this type of gender data is publicly available.

Unlike the relatively steady increases and decreases witnessed in women's overall representation, women's representation in senior leadership since 1984 has fluctuated considerably (see Graph 6.1).

In analysing the data in Graph 6.1, over the last three decades all agencies have made significant gains for women in the highest echelons of leadership. For instance, up until 1984, only men occupied the highest division of employment (Division 1) within the APS, and *women were not even included as a category for analysis* within Division 1 positions in tables in the APS Statistical Yearbook. Within Second Division employment (now the SES), in 1984 women were severely underrepresented across the portfolios of Defence (0 per cent), Foreign Affairs (3.8 per cent), Immigration and Ethnic Affairs (8.6 per cent), and Trade (2.3 per cent). In real numbers, Second Division leadership comprised no women in Defence, only two women in Foreign Affairs, two women in Immigration and Ethnic Affairs, and one woman in Trade. Considering the Marriage Bar, many Australian government agencies developed distinctly masculine identities, with leadership compositions that were almost entirely male, as evident from early data (1984–1989 in particular) in the gender breakdown in Graph 6.1. This stands in vast contrast with women's contemporary representation in all of the agencies studied.

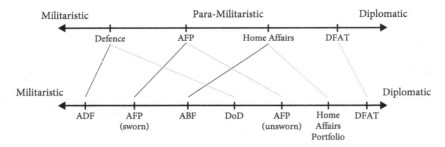

Figure 6.1 Militaristic-diplomatic continuum

To what degree does the gendered leadership structures of the past continue to affect the agencies? There is now a much greater gender balance across all of the agencies than there was in 1984, indicating substantial progress. Home Affairs was quickest to gain greater gender equality, almost reaching parity in leadership in 2009 (when women represented 49 per cent of the agency's workforce). Yet all agencies are now on an upwards trajectory for women in SES *except* for Home Affairs—why? Each agency is layered with formal policies aimed at gendered change and that change is occurring. However, there is an enduring underrepresentation of women and stubbornly persistent gendered challenges remain.

Given that considerable differences exist within agencies, the following datasets disaggregate women's representation by dividing the case agencies into their sworn military and civilian populations. Disaggregation reveals findings that aggregated data would obscure, improving the accuracy and rigour of statistical analysis. Following earlier research dividing the case agencies along a militaristic-bureaucratic continuum,[9] the agencies have been divided along a militaristic-diplomatic continuum in Figure 6.1. All professional, civilian, or unsworn divisions are characterised as more traditionally 'diplomatic' in structure than their relevant military or sworn divisions. The ADF is characterised as most militaristic, followed by the AFP (sworn), the ABF, the Department of Defence, the AFP (unsworn), the Home Affairs Portfolio and lastly, DFAT. In the following graphs, Defence is broken into the ADF (military) and the Department of Defence (DoD –civilian), the AFP into sworn and unsworn populations, Home Affairs into the Australian Border Force (ABF, predominantly sworn) and the Home Affairs Portfolio (predominantly professional, Immigration, and Customs), and DFAT remains undivided. These characterisations reflect how each portfolio is divided within their own agency annual reports. Disaggregating the agencies for this section reveals major differences in military and sworn populations versus civilian or unsworn populations.

Where Are the Women in Leadership? 149

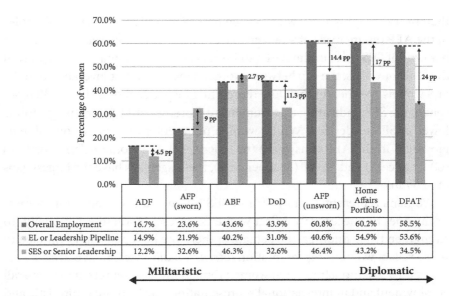

Graph 6.2 Representation of women in the agencies (disaggregated), 2017, 2018
Data source: Agency Annual Reports and APSED RFI 736 data. Data compares 2017, 2018 data to reflect the most consistently updated datasets.

Graph 6.2 details the percentage of women (1) employed overall in the agencies, (2) employed in EL or equivalent roles, and (3) employed in SES or equivalent roles along this disaggregated continuum, additionally highlighting the percentage point difference between overall representation and SES leadership.

Graph 6.2 demonstrates that the less militaristic, paramilitaristic and more traditionally diplomatic an agency is, the more it evidences a 'glass ceiling' form of gender imbalance, whereby 'discrimination actually *increases at the top* of the hierarchy'—in SES roles in particular.[10] The graph shows that in 2017, 2018 women remained the least represented in overall employment in ADF at 16.7 per cent, followed by AFP (sworn) at 23.6 per cent. Women's representation in the ABF is at 43.6 per cent and 43.9 per cent in the DoD, both within the acceptable range for gender parity. Women form the majority of overall employment within the AFP (unsworn) at 60.8 per cent, Home Affairs Portfolio at 60.2 per cent and DFAT at 58.5 per cent. Analysing SES leadership, women in the ADF represent 12.2 per cent of senior leadership, which is 4.5 percentage points lower than their overall representation and demonstrates that women are least represented in ADF SES equivalent roles out of all of the agencies studied. Yet analysing women's representation in AFP (sworn) and ABF roles, women have *higher* representation in SES roles than their overall employment, with women representing 32.6 per cent of SES roles in the AFP (an increase of 9 percentage points) and women representing 46.3 per cent of SES roles in the ABF (an increase of 2.7 percentage points). From the DoD onwards, the gap between women's representation overall and in the SES widens. Women in the DoD represent 43.9 per cent overall, and 32.6 per cent of the SES, indicating that women are represented 11.3 percentage points lower in SES leadership. Whilst women represent a majority of overall employment in the AFP (unsworn) (60.8 per cent), the Home Affairs Portfolio (60.2 per cent) and DFAT (58.5 per cent), these agencies have the largest gaps in SES ranks.

Women's representation in EL and SES (or equivalent) leadership domestically does not necessarily reflect women's representation internationally. To strengthen these findings, the data must therefore be further substantiated to solely reflect women's representation *internationally* (see Graph 6.3).

Graph 6.3 demonstrates that women remain the least represented in overall employment and in international representation for the more militaristic and paramilitaristic agencies—ADF (16.7 per cent, 14.6 per cent respectively), AFP (sworn) (23.6 per cent, 20.1 per cent respectively), and ABF (43.6 per cent and 30 per cent respectively). While woman represent a majority in

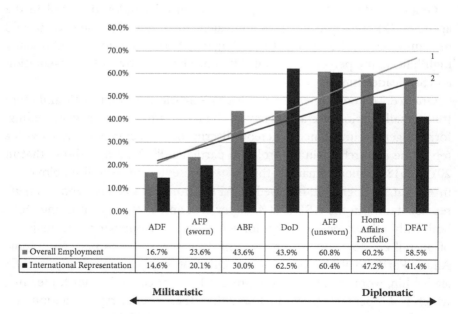

Graph 6.3 International representation of women in the agencies (disaggregated, with trend lines), 2017, 2018
Data source: Agency Annual Reports and APSED RFI 736 data.

international representation for DoD (62.5 per cent) and AFP (unsworn) (60.4 per cent), this percentage decreases for the more bureaucratic agencies of Home Affairs Portfolio (47.2 per cent) and DFAT (41.4 per cent). Applying a linear regression to compare trend data across the agencies, the original findings illustrated in Graph 6.2 are reinforced in Graph 6.3. Women in the most militaristic and paramilitaristic agencies are (a) least represented internationally (trend line 2), but are (b) most proportionally represented. The gap between trend line 1 (overall employment) and trend line 2 (international representation) increases as the agencies move towards a more traditionally diplomatic structure. The gap, once again, is the largest for DFAT.

There are some important nuances in this data that are captured in Table 6.1. Table 6.1 documents the percentage point difference between women in overall employment by the agency, and: women in EL or equivalent; women in SES or equivalent; and women in international representation.

Table 6.1 demonstrates that *in only three occurrences* do women have a higher chance (proportional to women's overall representation) than men (proportional to men's overall representation) of reaching leadership or overseas deployment. In the first occurrence, AFP (sworn) women have a 9 per cent increased chance, proportional to their overall representation, of reaching SES leadership. In the second occurrence, ABF women have a 2.7 per cent increased chance, proportional to their overall representation, of reaching SES leadership. This is a significant finding, highlighting women's increased chances for achieving SES ranks of leadership in the AFP (sworn) and ABF.

Table 6.1 Representation of women proportional to overall representation, 2017, 2018

Agency	Overall % of women	% point difference for EL or leadership pipeline	% point difference for SES or senior leadership	% point difference for international representatives
ADF	16.7%	-1.8%	-4.5%	-2.1%
AFP (sworn)	23.6%	-1.7%	+9.0%	-3.5%
ABF	43.6%	-3.4%	+2.7%	-13.6%
DoD	43.9%	-12.9%	-11.3%	+18.6%
AFP (unsworn)	60.8%	-20.2	-14.4%	-0.4%
Home Affairs Portfolio	60.2%	-5.3%	-17.0%	-13.0%
DFAT	58.5%	-4.9%	-24.0%	-17.1%

Data source: Agency Annual Reports and APSED RFI 736 data. Militaristic-diplomatic characterisation in descending order, from most militaristic to most traditionally diplomatic.

The third occurrence is in the DoD, where women have both a higher chance than men of deploying internationally (representing 62.5 per cent of deployments) *and* a higher chance of deploying internationally compared to their overall representation (an increased 18.6 per cent chance from their overall proportion of 43.9 per cent). This indicates very good chances for civilian women to be deployed internationally, compared to civilian men *and* compared to their overall gender ratio in the Department. However, there were only *eight* international posting opportunities available for Defence Attaché (DA) civilian staff in total for that year. Civilian staff continue to have the least prestige, authority and power compared to military staff when posted overseas. Therefore, the area in which women have had the highest initial chance of attaining international representation, compared to men, remains largely unfulfilled because of the lack of opportunity and the limitations of civilian status.

There are three further core findings that Table 6.1 illustrates. Firstly, women in DFAT—as Australia's primary international affairs agency—are expected to have an easier pathway to international representation, due to the nature of the work. In fact, women form most of EL positions (53.6 per cent) in DFAT. However, a stark gap remains between women's overall representation (58.5 per cent) and their representation internationally (41.4 per cent), with women having a 17.1 percentage point decreased chance of international representation compared to their overall representation. Women in DFAT experience the *lowest* chances of gaining international representation (proportional to overall representation) out of all the agencies studied. An even bigger gap remains for women who seek SES leadership (representing a decreased chance by 24 percentage points). This means that women in DFAT have both the lowest chance of gaining international leadership and the lowest chance of gaining SES representation (proportional to women's overall representation) out of any of the agencies studied. As will be discussed later in this chapter, the gap between employment and opportunity for SES and international representation has remained consistent for almost two decades in DFAT, even despite women's increasing leadership.

Secondly, while agencies that are more traditionally diplomatic or less militaristic may be more female-dominated in terms of pure numbers, this evidently does not prescribe nor proscribe leadership or international opportunity. As explored in Graph 6.1, trend data demonstrates that women's representation in leadership is generally increasing (with the exception of Home Affairs in recent years). But the data explored subsequently demonstrates that while women in the Home Affairs Portfolio and DFAT are not the minority (at 60.2 per cent and 58.4 per cent respectively), they form part of a consistently marginalised majority. In those agencies, women's representation lags considerably behind in SES and international roles.

Thirdly, this table reinforces findings made in Graph 6.2 that the most militaristic and paramilitaristic agencies more proportionally represent women internationally and in leadership. This trend broadly holds over the entire 1984–2018 period for which data is available, highlighting that these findings are not simply one-off conclusions, but are indicative of a longer-standing trend.

But why? Two themes emerged from the research that explain this. The first is structure, with Defence and the AFP generally providing structured opportunities for women to progress from one rank to the next, as discussed in the chapter on history. The second theme that explains these results is the overtness of gendered rules in more militaristic agencies, which provided a kind of visibility or transparency of gendered challenges—something I argue has a significant effect on women. For some, the overtness of gendered challenges acts as a disincentive for pursuing more militaristic agencies as career choices, evidenced by the lower levels of women overall. For others, the overtness and visibility of these gendered institutions enables women to navigate them more successfully. In fact, participants in this study commented that they knew what to expect in terms of gendered challenges, and therefore how to work around it, unlike some of their colleagues in more bureaucratic agencies for whom the challenges, and career paths, were more obscured—indicative of more 'genteel' toxic masculinities and covert forms of gendered discrimination and bias. Thus, both the structure and visibility of gendered challenges contribute to women's most proportional representation in more militaristic agencies, and least proportional representation in more traditionally diplomatic agencies.

Despite these differences, a Catch-22 remains for women. By numbers alone, more international postings exist in more traditionally diplomatic agencies and women have a lower chance of getting them. Less international postings exist in more militaristic and paramilitaristic agencies, but women have a higher chance of getting them. Disaggregating the agencies in this section has proved particularly revealing, substantiating earlier findings and uncovering important distinctions in women's representation internationally. For instance, while women are the least represented internationally in ADF DA and staff roles (at 14.6 per cent), they are most represented internationally in DoD DA and staff roles (at 62.5 per cent). Without disaggregating the data, this finding (and others) would be statistically obscured. It is also important to note that once the agencies are aggregated back into their four core identities—Defence, AFP, Home Affairs, and DFAT—in no agency are women represented equally to men internationally yet.

The next section of this book will break down women's representation across each of the agencies to understand these nuances more.

DFAT

After approximately three decades of gender parity in recruitment, it was only in 2018, shortly after the *Women in Leadership Strategy* was introduced, that women finally verged on parity in international leadership positions in DFAT. The change has not been a gradual 'fixing' of a leaky pipeline, though, with the recent more rapid increase in representation coinciding with targets set in the strategy. An initial analysis might suggest that if gendered institutions have been barring women from leadership over the past three decades, they are not as 'entrenched' as it would seem—evidenced by the rapid almost-doubling of women's representation in senior international leadership in the last few years. Yet when we look at the data in Graph 6.4, this rapid change is not as striking as it would first appear.

Graph 6.4 shows that women formed most of the Department since 2006 (50.3 per cent) and a majority of EL positions since 2014 (51.8 per cent). Women's representation in SES leadership continues to lag behind the most, with data in 2021 showing women's representation at 45 per cent (although

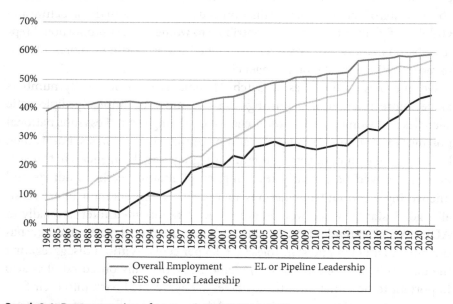

Graph 6.4 Representation of women in DFAT, 1984–2021
Data source: APSED, RFI 763—Statistical Yearbook (1984–2021).

is up considerably from 34.5 per cent in 2018, when the bulk of the following data was collected, as previously covered in Table 6.1). Interestingly, for over three decades a relatively consistent gap appears to exist between women's overall representation and their representation in SES leadership, whilst the gap between EL representation and overall representation appears close to closing.

What is striking is that women in 2018 only had a *0.6 per cent increased chance* of getting an SES position than they had in 2000.[11] Women's chances of getting a Head of Mission or Head of Post (HOM/HOP) role have improved from 2000 to 2018, by 10.8 percentage points. However, a significant gap remains between women's overall representation in the Department and their representation in HOM/HOP positions: a 29 per cent average (mean) gap over time.[12] Likewise, a similar gap exists between overall representation and the SES: 25 per cent average (mean) gap from 2000–2018. Therefore, while there are more women are in SES and HOM/HOP positions than ever before, and this continues to improve into 2021 and beyond, women's representation in leadership is still not keeping pace with women's overall representation. This is illustrated in Graph 6.5.

Graph 6.5 highlights further changes over 2000–2018. Three years on from the introduction of the *Women in Leadership Strategy*[13] in 2015, the gaps between the overall percentage of women employed and those in SES, EL, and

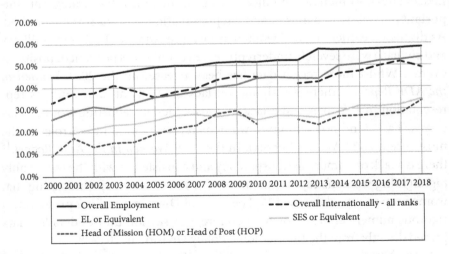

Graph 6.5 Representation of women in DFAT, 2000–2018

Data source: APSED, RFI 763, Statistical Yearbook (1984–2018); Department of Foreign Affairs and Trade (2000–2010, 2012–2018). DFAT annual report for 2011 was missing, hence 2011 data on women's overall international representation at all ranks, and representation as Head of Mission (HOM) or Head of Post (HOP) is absent.

HOM/HOP positions—gaps that had remained relatively consistent across the preceding years—begin to close in 2018. This suggests that these changes are a direct result of the targets set in the Strategy (as well as the critical leadership and enforcement ability of the Secretariat)—highlighting formal institutional success in reaching targets for women's representation. Yet the Department appears to gain more women in leadership positions only by maintaining an ever-increasing majority of women in overall employed staff. This raises an interesting question: If women's overall representation in the Department stayed the same, would women's representation in leadership also stagnate?

The trend data in Graph 6.5 suggests rapid changes and improvements in representation for women. However, it also suggests a culture in which women's accomplishments and work is less visible and rewarded. It reinforces the fact that women remain a marginalised majority within the Department. In turn, this obscures the gendered barriers that remain. The initial cause for optimism in DFAT hides more nuanced findings that suggest that women remain critically overlooked and marginalised in the most important duty within the agency—representing Australia internationally.

Defence

Like in DFAT, women's admittance to decision-making roles, strategically important portfolios, and international representation remains severely limited. As discussed earlier, in 2017 women as Defence Attaché (DA) staff (military and civilian) were severely underrepresented at only 18.8 per cent of positions overall. Whilst more recent data has been released in the 2021 *Women in the ADF Report*,[14] there is a significant lack of clarity around women's representation in DA roles and a lack of consistency in reporting from a year-to-year basis (and no mention of women's representation in DA roles in the most recent 2022 Annual Report). In the 2019 *Women in the ADF Report*,[15] there is a lack of numerical transparency and consistency, with the report only highlighting women's representation in DA roles in a graph (indicating that women represent a decreased 17.2 per cent of DA roles) and not presenting a rigorous numerical breakdown. Therefore, this section utilises detailed data gained directly from the International Policy Division in 2017.[16]

Even though women have more proportional opportunities for leadership and international representation in Defence (as highlighted in earlier graphs), an imbalance exists at the more granular level. Women represent 30.7 per cent of the lowest ranked E8/E9 ranks and 9.1 per cent of O4 ranks—none of which is yet at EL or SES equivalent ranking. In fact, women only represent 13.7 per cent of EL equivalent positions (O5 and O6 ranks) and form *no* part of the top two tiers of SES equivalent positions internationally (O7 and O8 ranks). According to Kanter's (1977) definitions of tokens being a minority less than 15 per cent, women in the most senior levels of international Defence diplomatic representation (SES and EL equivalent roles) exist in an environment in which women constitute tokens. As tokens, McGlen and Sarkees note that women often must develop 'alternative coping mechanisms'.[17] This was consistent across Defence participants interviewed, who evidenced considerable resilience and varied methods to minimise the negative effect of their gender on their experiences, noting that the challenges they faced were relentless.

Breaking this data down by gender and role reveals further findings. Women remain least represented in the DA roles from the Navy and Army (0 positions). Women are more represented in Air Force and Military Attaché roles (AFA, MA), at 33.3 per cent and 50.0 per cent respectively; however, women are only represented in these roles as *assistants,* not full attachés. Similarly, a greater number of Defence Administrative Assistants (DAA) are women, representing four roles (26.7 per cent)—but these are precisely roles that it is expected women would be siloed in, administrative and assisting positions.

Women's exclusion from combat until recently is likely to have resulted in some of the skewed statistics—affecting women's low representation in SES or equivalent leadership and DA roles. McGlen and Sarkees note flow-on effect for women that the US combat ban had:

> They are excluded from the most important and key line jobs in the military. The exclusion of women from combat and the restrictions put on the positions they can assume because of the need to reserve slots for men, limits the upward mobility of women in the military and thus the Department of Defense.[18]

While these trends hold, there is a degree of nuance. As noted earlier, women are most proportionally represented in leadership positions in Defence—as compared to their overall employment—out of all the agencies studied. This suggests that while Defence's considerably more male-dominated and masculine culture inhibits women, structured career progression and visibility of these gendered challenges has resulted in women and men gaining opportunities in a relatively proportional way *no other agency achieved.* This has significant ramifications, suggesting that if more- militaristic agencies in international affairs can increase their overall proportion of women employed, these agencies may be better structured to give women opportunities for leadership and international representation than any other.

Home Affairs

Women's representation in policing, intelligence, border force, customs, and immigration portfolios has seldom been analysed internationally. Yet in the Australian context, the data proves revealing. In 2019, women's overall representation in Home Affairs was at 53.7 per cent, compared with 47.1 per cent at the international A-based representational level—highlighting a relatively comparable and gender equal representation. Yet women's leadership follows the same pattern set out by Towns and Niklasson,[19] who found that women were least represented in higher status roles. Indeed, higher status positions correspond with lower representation of women in Home Affairs. Additionally, despite evidencing the most gender equal international deployments of all the agencies studied, the highest prestige posts (for instance London and Washington, DC) are occupied only by men in the most senior ranks of leadership, reinforcing Towns and Niklasson's[20] findings that women are less represented at the most prestigious posts or in the most important countries.

Looking to leadership, women represent 48.1 per cent of EL roles in the Home Affairs Portfolio and 56.2 per cent of EL roles in the Secretary's Office. Women are lower represented in SES roles, at 38.5 per cent in Home Affairs Portfolio and 38.0 per cent in the Secretary's Office. Women form only 30.0 per cent of EL roles in the ABF (with no data available on SES, A-Based international positions for the ABF). Women form most of the deployments in only one area, EL roles in the administrative side of the Secretary's Office. This aligns with the literature that women often remain siloed in 'soft', humanitarian, and administrative roles in international affairs.

Analysing trend data in Graph 6.6 shows that from 1984 to 2018 on women's representation in (1) overall employment, (2) SES or senior leadership, and (3) EL or leadership pipeline roles has fluctuated.

Graph 6.6 demonstrates that since 1994 Home Affairs has been a female-dominated agency, reaching its peak in 1996 at 68.4 per cent women employed across the Department. Yet this has steadily decreased ever since, and since the 2015 merger and creation of ABF, women's overall proportion in employment and in EL positions have also decreased. While EL and overall representation is now stabilising, women's representation in SES roles continues to decline from its peak in 2009, when women almost, but not quite, achieved parity at 49.0 per cent of the agency.

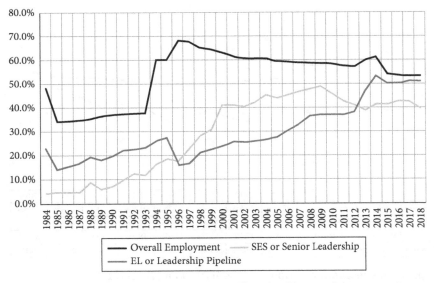

Graph 6.6 Representation of women in Home Affairs (and former departmental configurations), 1984–2018

Data source: APSED RFI 763 Yearbook Statistics 1984–2011. This data was collated by APSED, so while it is statistically rigorous, earlier data (particularly pre-2015) does not represent the modern configuration of Home Affairs.

Even more confoundingly, whilst women's overall representation rapidly increased from 1993 to 1994, the share of women in EL positions rapidly decreased just after this, from 1995 to 1996. Home Affairs is perhaps clearest at demonstrating that institutional progress around women's representation has no steady upwards trajectory.

AFP

Since very early in the AFP's history, women have formed a substantial, and sometimes majority, of recruits. Over most of the last decade, sworn women have slowly increased their representation in the AFP, most evidently for SES positions, as represented in Graph 6.7.

Graph 6.7 covers the AFP's (sworn) representation of women (1) in overall employment, (2) in EL or equivalent, (3) in SES or equivalent, and (4) in international representation. Out of all the agencies, women's representation in SES leadership is increasing fastest in the AFP. Incredibly, in 2018, women are represented in SES leadership 9 per cent higher than their overall representation, representing 23.6 per cent of overall employment and 32.6 per cent of SES

160   The Face of the Nation

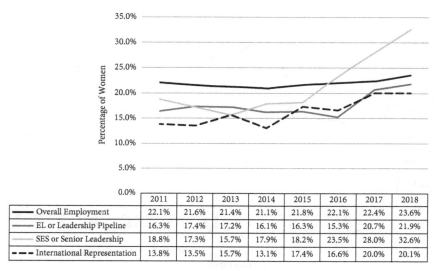

Graph 6.7 Representation of women in the AFP (sworn), 2011–2018
Data Source: Australian Federal Police (2011–2018) Annual Reports.

positions. Most of the growth over this period happened between 2015 and 2018—coinciding with the release of the *Cultural Change: Gender Diversity and Inclusion in the Australian Federal Police* in 2016.[21] This reinforces the effect of formal policies and the will of critical actors for driving change, particularly in women's representation in senior leadership.

However, Graph 6.7 also demonstrates that women remain chronically underrepresented across the AFP. Women's overall representation in the agency only increased by 1.5 percentage points from 2011 to 2018, from 22.1 per cent in 2011 to 23.6 per cent in 2018. This increase is marginal and insubstantial when compared to the policy commitments and affirmations driving gender equality within the agency. Additionally, progress for EL and international representational roles has been inconsistently achieved over this period. While the AFP may be doing well at advancing women from EL to SES positions, attraction and retention remain issues.

Like the DoD, civilian unsworn and professional women have a higher chance of being represented internationally, than gaining EL or SES leadership (see Table 6.1). On average, women represented 53.8 per cent of all unsworn international deployments and 59.5 per cent of the unsworn workforce from 2011 to 2018 (their mean or average representation). While this signifies that unsworn women do have a good chance at international representation, like in Defence a small minority of roles are reserved for the professional, civilian unsworn population. In fact, in 2018, 80 per cent of international representatives were sworn police and only 20 per cent were unsworn, which suggests that overall, unsworn women have low opportunities for deployment. EL and SES leadership remain to be the most elusive for AFP (unsworn) women; however, by 2018 represent near parity—with women representing 40.6 per cent of EL roles and 46.4 per cent of SES roles, compared to 60.8 per cent overall and 60.4 per cent international representation. Again, women's relatively high representation in unsworn international deployments is constrained by the low availability of unsworn international roles.

Divided by Gender, Status, and International Appointments

It is not just pure representation by virtue of seniority or international representation that matters to the study of women's underrepresentation. Rules-in-use are described by Ostrom as a distinctive ensemble of 'dos and don'ts that one learns on the ground'.[22] Lowndes[23] argues that gendered rules distribute power by assigning actors to roles, specifying access to organisational resources. Distribution of power and roles was seen in participants' debates about their career trajectories and reinforced the Lowy Institute's[24] findings that women were often concentrated around 'soft' policy areas and away from operations. Career management had considerable positives for ADF women, providing clear, transparent pathways to the next rank and type of role. This was similarly the case for AFP women—particularly after the *Cultural Change* review. However, some participants expressed the issue of being career-managed out of the operational roles critical for career progression. Unconscious bias was identified as a major barrier for women, whereby career managers tended to assign operational jobs to men, giving women fewer opportunities to be involved in operational planning. A lack of operational planning experience was considered 'career suicide', with chances of reaching leadership very low.

Accordingly, women are highest represented in largely nonoperational roles, which reinforces horizontal segregation. Indeed, in the most recent *Women in the ADF Report*,[25] women remain highest represented in Health and in Logistics, Administration and Support, and lowest represented in Engineering, Technical and Construction, followed by Combat and Security. Whilst APS service has similar formalised pathways across (not necessarily within) agencies, careers are not managed to the same formalised degree. The APS Integrated Leadership System (ILS) and newly formed APS Academy also places the burden of career development on individuals, rather than agencies, which is problematic given that women often only apply for roles if they meet all criteria. Women are frequently appointed on experience, men on potential.[26]

Decisions around whether to specialise or remain a generalist further dominated women's experiences across the agencies. Most participants began in generalist work streams. Yet many noted a tendency to specialise amongst their female colleagues—particularly in human resources (HR), capability or acquisitions. This resulted in a quicker initial career trajectory, but longer-term career damage. The choice between specialising or staying in generalist operational streams was one with heavy consequences across the agencies. Specialisation had many positives for women, including quicker career progression and greater flexibility than operational roles. However, inevitably these niche roles or corporate governance roles placed limits on women's progression—eventually taking them out of key streams needed for international opportunities and senior leadership. One AFP member talked about the choice between generalist and specialist streams when she stated:

> For me that breakthrough moment was when I was working in surveillance. I wanted to go on the Executive Development Program at the Institute of Police Management. I wasn't getting on it. All of my performance reviews [would] say, oh you're an incredibly strategic thinker, you should be doing X and you should be tracking towards management. I kept applying for this program and couldn't get on. I had a manager who turned around and said to me, 'you're in surveillance'. I said but that shouldn't make any difference—this is for future leadership, this is for this, that and the other. He said 'you're in surveillance'. I said but boss, I've got this and you're always commenting on this, I should—he said, 'you're in surveillance'. So I took a $30,000 pay cut [to leave specialist surveillance and join operations].[27]

At the time, the participant was the only woman in surveillance, so it was not an area where women were traditionally siloed, out of operations. However, as an isolated case, the participant was one of few women in the AFP at this time. Surveillance was a role that did not require as much of the 'hands-on' physicality that is involved in generalist police work and could therefore be undertaken in much more flexible circumstances, for instance around family duties. The role may have been quite a good role for some women, considering women's work conditions in other streams, plus the extra duties that the women often bore at home, from domestic chores to childcare and eldercare. However, it was also clearly considered a sidestep to the operational work and career development that 'really mattered'. Participants recounted that these specialist roles often had more limited resources—particularly in terms of power, opportunities for personal and professional development, and career progression to senior levels.

Women in agencies without formalised career management still experienced career segregation and were often employed in roles perceived as 'soft', such as human rights and public diplomacy in DFAT, immigration in Home Affairs, surveillance in the AFP, or HR management or administration across all the agencies. This also reinforced profiling particular roles for particular genders, as one DFAT participant noted of her work in economics and trade, 'it was a little bit unusual for that to be a woman, frankly, a girl that was doing that'.[28]

Access to resources and opportunities had big effects for women seeking international representation. Alongside Towns and Niklasson[29] uncovering a gender imbalance in ambassadorial appointments globally, the authors also found that 'women are less likely than men to end up as ambassadors in countries with the highest economic and military status'.[30] For diplomats and ambassadors employed by DFAT, a similar finding exists, with the Lowy Institute[31] finding that Australia's largest and most strategically or economically important posts are much more likely to be headed by men.

Women have traditionally had higher representation in International Governmental Organisastions (IGOs)—organisations that mostly have explicit values around gender equality and leadership compared with many host countries. As of 2020, 75 per cent of Australia's senior representatives to the United Nations (UN) are women (down from 100 per cent in 2018).[32] Women represent Australia in 33.3 per cent of IGOs outside of the UN—including the World Trade Organisation (WTO), Organisation for Economic Co-operation and Development (OECD), and Asia Pacific Economic Cooperation (APEC). This is down from equally representing these roles in 2018. Further, in 2022 women represent 50 per cent of specialist ambassadorships (among roles: First Nations People; Arms Control and Counter-Proliferation; the Environment; Regional Health Security; People Smuggling and Human Trafficking; Cyber Affairs; Gender Equality; and Counter-Terrorism), which is a significant improvement on their 2020 representation of only 28.5 per cent of specialist ambassadorships and 2018 representation of only 17 per cent of roles. Yet appointments appear to continue to be gender segregated around 'feminised' and 'masculine' portfolios—with only women so far holding the role of Ambassador for Gender Equality, for instance.

As of 2020 women predominate in only one area of leadership appointments, where they represent 57.8 per cent of Deputy Head of Mission roles. Women's representation gradually falls, the more senior and high status the role. Women do have better representation in roles that are part of the pipeline to senior leadership; however, overall, women are still not accessing the top roles equally. Additionally, women are yet to occupy posts in London and Washington, DC, two of the most strategically important posts.

Similarly, of the top five Defence attaché (DA) posts—the United States (US, 13 positions), the United Kingdom (UK, 8 positions), Indonesia (6 positions), and Papua New Guinea and China (4 positions each)—only Papua New Guinea has equal representation of men and women attachés, and only China has more women than men. In every other post, women are underrepresented—sometimes severely so, representing only 15 per cent of US positions, 12.5 per cent of UK positions, and 33 per cent of Indonesian positions. Is there a gender story here? If the number of DAs deployed to a location is indicative of the importance of that country to Australia's defence relationships, then women are less likely to be deployed to Australia's highest-ranking Defence deployments. Out of these countries, it is also clear that Australia's closest allies (the US and UK) have both the highest number of attachés accredited to their post and the lowest proportion of women. On the other hand, the countries that are more likely to be perceived as 'threats' or relationships to be managed, have a higher representation of women.

In fact, arguably Australia's biggest relationship to be managed—China— has majority women in leadership. While it is possible that this is merely coincidence, considering the overtly gendered nature of Defence and its mostly male deployments, it appears more than coincidence. In fact, during the bulk of this research taking place (2017–2019) all agencies studied had a gender equal or a female majority senior leadership team deployed in China and Hong Kong. It is impossible to infer anything concrete from this; however, it does raise questions around the deployments seen as most appropriate for women, a topic also raised by some participants who saw it as a strategic move to negotiate an at-times tense relationship. At a point in time where interactions with China grow increasingly sensitive, is this indicative of a 'glass cliff', whereby women are likelier to achieve leadership roles during periods of crisis[33]—when the stakes are highest? Alternatively, is it emblematic of women's perceived strength in pacifying and peacemaking, a diminutive female representative that can appease Chinese authority when required?

If more than coincidence, the narrative might indicate that Australia's most important negotiations with *allies*—that involve strategic partnerships, threat detection and important joint security operations—are ones that require *men* to lead. Australia's biggest relationships *threats*, on the other hand, require a certain amount of management of relationships, balancing political power and military capability, and soft negotiation—negotiations that require *women* to lead. The use of women's gender could be a strategic move to appear less threatening—a strategic move to placate a volatile China. In Defence, participants commented that women tended to be more likely take the roles requiring higher diplomatic skills.

Overall, the often-subtle rules of the game had a distributive effective when it came to access to roles and resources. All agencies evidenced horizontal as well as vertical segregation. It was clear that because of this horizontal segregation (out of key operational areas needed for progression), women also became more vertically segregated.

Overarching Themes and Trends

There are direct correlations between militaristic versus more traditionally diplomatic international affairs institutions and women's representation. Yet the correlations are not simplistic. Core findings include that militaristic agencies have lower proportions of women overall, in leadership, and in international representation, consistent with the literature. However, inversely, one of the core original findings of this book is that militaristic agencies also offer women opportunities for international representation and leadership that either more closely matches or exceeds their overall staffing population. Women's representation in more traditionally diplomatic agencies is least proportional to their overall representation. Further, a significant and enduring gap has remained over the last few decades.

On introduction of formal policies across a number of the agencies, rapid changes can be seen. For instance, since DFAT's *Women in Leadership Strategy*[34] in 2015, there have been substantial increases in women's representation which indicate formal institutional success. Yet the entrenched and continuing gap between overall representation and representation in the SES is worrying. The fact that women's international representation (relative to opportunity) has stagnated for almost two decades is significant. It suggests that even in agencies with the highest representation of women, informal institutions remain, making women a marginalised majority. This is consistent with the literature too, which finds that existing discussions 'centre around the narrow belief that gender equality will be achieved once nominal equality is achieved'.[35]

On the other end of the militaristic-diplomatic spectrum, gendered divisions in labour and rank remain deeply embedded in Defence. However, the rigidity and hierarchy of the agency does not follow the simplistic pattern put forward by McGlen and Sarkees,[36] who find that military structures only benefit women when women are in the most senior leadership positions.

Rather, while Defence struggles to attract and retain their female staff within the ADF, when they do, women are generally able to progress to EL equivalent and SES equivalent leadership much as their male counterparts would (and not because senior women dominate or even occupy many senior roles). In fact, the 2019 *Women in the ADF Report* notes that women officers do spend more time at rank thank men; however, this is marginal—six years at rank for women, compared to five and a half years at rank for men. For other ranks, excluding the SES equivalent, the comparative time at rank was the same for men and women—five and a half years.[37]

Whilst women remain severely underrepresented in DA and staff roles, they are represented more proportionally than the other agencies have been able to manage. Much of this can be attributed to the positives of structure: career management and consistent professional development; clearly laid out manuals describing progression points and career options at early and yearly milestones; and a strong respect for rank and hierarchy which aids women in overcoming gender bias in order to exercise authority once they are in leadership. The visibility of gendered challenges appeared to make those challenges easier to negotiate, as will be discussed later in this chapter. The caveat is that women remain completely *unrepresented* in SES positions in the DA and staffing roles. Defence is also yet to have women in the role of chief of one of the service lines, or as Chief of the Defence Force (CDF). This suggests that there are clear limits to how far women can go in leadership, reinforcing gendered differences in career opportunities and the continued sway of 'old' historical norms around 'who' can represent Defence.

The frequent machinery of government changes in Home Affairs and increasing paramilitarisation of a once-more bureaucratic agency has resulted in a complex institutional context. ABF maintains near parity in EL and SES positions, which does suggest that more gender-equal institutions are possible under the creation of 'new' agencies. However, considering that women in this section of the agency are lowest represented overseas, it is worth considering whether the 'newness' of the agency has really helped in establishing and maintaining a more gender equal agency. Rather, the norms of physicality and enforcement, like seen in Defence and the AFP, appear to have transported across as gendered, particularly in what it means to *be* and *represent* the 'face' of Australia internationally. The decreasing representation of women more generally in the department is worrying, and appears tied both to the agency's increasingly masculinist, enforcement nature, and inconsistencies in formal policies guaranteeing gender equality.

Finally, the AFP has taken an unusual approach to addressing the gender imbalance within the agency, with critical leaders both pro-actively commissioning the *Cultural Change* report and pioneering efforts such as an all-female recruitment round. Women have the highest opportunity for SES leadership out of the agencies studied, relative to opportunity. Like Defence, women tended to be more proportionally represented in leadership and international representation—showing that there are considerable positives to the structured opportunities of these more militaristic agencies, as well as positives of the visibility of gendered challenges that remain. Yet similar to Defence and Home Affairs, women are better represented in the professional civilian or unsworn side of the agency, rather than being part of sworn policing and operations. This is clearly a disadvantage for women, whereby fewer roles exist for unsworn members internationally or in leadership.

Overall, the statistics reinforce firstly that significant progress is possible, and is happening. The statistics also reinforce that women remain underrepresented; however, there are nuances across the agencies once data is disaggregated. The chapter adds to global findings reinforcing that the nominal participation of women has not equalled substantive changes in their roles—findings we can now extend beyond diplomacy[38] to other areas of international affairs. Secondly, because nominal changes do not automatically equal gender or other forms of equality, the gender of not just diplomacy,[39] but also of international affairs institutions, remain a core concept to address. The establishment of the AFP or the ABF in more 'gender equal' times, and indeed with gender equal recruitment or leadership on conception that has now regressed or not been maintained highlights this concept. There is an equilibrium in international institutions—even new ones—which is gendered. International affairs remains masculine and masculinised. Finally, women's substantive representation has evidently changed over time, in most cases substantially from almost zero representation in senior leadership only ~30 years ago, to verging on parity or exceeding their overall representation in agencies contemporarily. Yet still horizontal and vertical segregation remains, and gendered experiences ensue. The major gains for women's representation in leadership and internationally have not overcome the overwhelming effect of history. The gendered history of institutions matters to international affairs, and it is clear that representation is only one part of the gender equality puzzle to address.

7
How Did You Get There?

Career Paths and Leadership

> It's not all clinking champagne glasses with dictators . . . but that is very much part of my job.
> —Rani, Department of Foreign Affairs and Trade, 1 February 2019[1]

Statistics on women's representation say little about their experiences or the pervasively gendered differences in international affairs. This chapter therefore explores what women saw, heard, felt, and experienced on the world stage, to better understand the depth and nature of progress, as well as ongoing gender and other inequalities in international affairs. Understanding the world through their eyes, gendered institutions 'travel' with participants as they experience their deployments. Complex and multifaceted norms and rules at every turn affected women's experiences, ultimately highlighting international affairs as reliant on multiple forms of gendered sacrifice across contexts.

To explore this, the chapter has been divided according to three critical times in women's experiences: their pathways to posting, their experiences once on posting, and their return from posting. This chapter addresses what happens, and why, women may leave their jobs, as well as briefly summarising the values and characteristics important to participants' successful international deployment. Through researching women leaders who have made it into leadership, this chapter highlights the institutional rules and norms that endure, as well as how they might be navigated.

International representatives across the four case agencies exist in a challenging environment, undertaking challenging roles, for men and women alike. The Australian Public Service Commission (APSC) states:

> Australian officials overseas are seen at all times as representing Australia both in the performance of their official duties and in the manner in which they conduct

themselves as private individuals. Regardless of their official roles or responsibilities, their status as foreign officials means their actions will be subject to *greater scrutiny and public interest* than they would be at home. Australian officials abroad may also face dilemmas in the area of personal conduct which do not arise in Australia—whether in social, cultural, financial or personal settings.[2]

Therefore, international affairs requires an extraordinary commitment from posted officials. No role could be summed up simply as 'a job', as responsibilities closely entwine with individuals' entire identities and lifestyles in what might be considered as 'total institutions'.[3] International experiences are characterised by a high level of mobility; an ability to work independently of the agency headquarters, representing both the agencies' and Australian national interests; and a requirement for high level of executive decision-making on important national topics spanning a wide range of issues, both inside and outside their particular area of expertise.[4]

Beyond the general challenges experienced by all international representatives, there are gendered differences in experiences. For some aspects of life, the gendered challenges faced by women, such as the 'double burden' of work inside and outside of the home, were translated directly to their international environment. Yet participant experiences also reinforced the uniqueness of the field of international affairs; a context deeply layered, complex, and teeming with multifaceted gendered, raced, and heteronormative rules. The chapter contributes to understanding why women still experience gendered challenges despite seismic changes over recent decades and explores to what degree these challenges are shared across agencies.

Pathways to Posting

Analysing women's pathways to international deployment aids in understanding the rules and practices that determine who, when and in what circumstances an individual can come to represent the state internationally. This section is broken up into three parts: understanding women's career entry and progression, how individuals gained their postings, and the factors that participants considered before applying for or accepting a posting. It delves into how women 'got to' their leadership positions. It also demonstrates the salience of individual circumstances to the decision of whether, when and where to post, and inversely, how little the actual role or host country context appeared to affect women's decisions, unless it was related to personal safety. While opportunities for posting are increasingly 'merit-based' (problematic as the concept of merit may be), informal connections and operational requirements continue to influence who is chosen for the highest prestige roles. Gendered challenges within agencies, as well as gendered expectations at home, in the field, and host/home societies, continue to affect women's opportunities.

Strategising Around Difficulties on the Path to Progression

Most participants joined their agencies as graduates in graduate programs, and many in the AFP and Defence came through recruitment processes that began in secondary school. None of the AFP participants had been lateral recruits from other agencies, with traditional employment pathways—joining as a graduate and working their way up—dominating the experiences of sworn participants. DFAT participants had the most lateral transfers (37.5 per cent), often coming from related federal departments (like Prime Minister and Cabinet, Trade (pre-merger), a state Supreme Court, or international divisions of domestic-facing agencies). Lateral recruits were generally at an EL level when they transferred, although most noted that their career trajectory slowed after joining the agency.

Career trajectories were largely the result of gradual career progression. In general, DFAT participants had the slowest career trajectories out of the agencies, which could be a result of the smaller or stagnating budget, as well as the increased talent pool because of the AusAID merger. For ADF participants in Defence, their careers began in the Australian Defence Force Academy (ADFA). Similarly, AFP (and recently ABF) staff commenced in their separate training academies. These training facilities inculcated strong discipline, groupthink, and masculine-informed rules of enforcement. Most undertook generalist pathways initially, although the training process often detailed future pathways across different divisions or streams of work—providing an early idea of future career progression and options for advancement. For civilians in the other agencies, participants would often start in graduate programs for their particular areas—Trade, AusAID, Customs, Immigration, and so on—with initially little work across portfolios. This process has changed over time, with graduate positions now generalist in the first year, with compulsory rotations to different portfolios offered over the second year of their program.

When strategising their career paths, participants generally advocated for planning. However very few participants did this—which could be emblematic of the time they commenced their careers, in which transparency in career progression was not mandated. More commonly, participants demonstrated an aptitude for taking risks and following opportunities when they were offered. In DFAT, an inverted T or 'upside-down T' of experience was sought—a broad base knowledge of a range of topics, with deep specialised knowledge in one or two areas.[5] Similar trends existed across the other agencies, except for Home Affairs where a greater degree of specialisation was found—Immigration, Customs, and ABF staff did not tend to cross over and get experience outside of their job area. Whilst participants from DFAT and Defence generally joined the agency for the international opportunities, those from Home Affairs and the AFP often did not even know that their agency ran international deployments until many years into their employment. This could also be an effect of the fact that prior to September 11, 2001, these agencies were less engaged internationally.

Career progression was often a troubling time for participants—a time at which they were more at the mercy of their (mostly male) superiors and often had—or felt they had—little recourse when things went wrong. The APSC and agencies themselves do have appeal processes; however, women were often disinclined to use them, also suggesting that they were not very unionised either. Although most acknowledged that times have now changed, almost all SES-ranked participants had experienced engrained and challenging instances of sexual harassment, discrimination, or humiliation on their way up the ranks. In the Navy for instance, as junior seamen (there being no term for seawoman), women experienced being 'kicked around the bridge'. One participant, Andy, highlighted how it was

> not very long into my career and any confidence I'd had in terms of leadership had been eroded, because when we trained as seamen officers in those days we'd be what's called 'kicked around the bridge'. You were humiliated, very bad for morale particularly if you weren't very good at the job, and I'd have junior sailors and they would say 'oh we feel really sorry for you'. I felt terrible. The seaman officer in terms of the way we trained, they'd think the ship revolves around them, because they are the principal warfare officer. But, the attitude and the way they trained people in those days was pretty bad.[6]

Given the 2021 March for Justice and 2022 drafting of a Code of Conduct for parliament after reports of high-level sexual assault was made public by former staffer Brittany Higgins, there is a current high level of awareness of the prevalence of sexual harassment and abuse that occurs in government.

There are many indicators that assaults remain common, yet underreported, with the 2021 Jenkin's Review[7] into Australian Parliament finding the following:

> While we heard of positive experiences of work within the Parliament, there were others who shared experiences of bullying, sexual harassment and sexual assault. Too often, we heard that these workplaces are not safe environments for many people within them, largely driven by power imbalances, gender inequality and exclusion and a lack of accountability.

Age was also a factor that affected women's career progression. The Australian Human Rights Commission hints at considerable informal rules in Defence, whereby 'there are unwritten, but strong and broadly understood, organisational expectations about the age range within which certain promotional pathways and/or types of experience are to be attained'—which, if missed, makes it much harder for individuals to progress.[8] Similar age-related promotional pathways were evidenced in the AFP—where, if participants missed advancing to a certain rank by a certain age, it was assumed that they must have been deficient in some manner. This further held back their careers, with women blamed in a Catch-22 situation for their lack of advancement at similar rates. This compounded disadvantage as women were more affected by career breaks to have children and care for children and aging parents, often unavoidably slowing their career trajectory. In Defence, norms existed around when was most 'acceptable' (and potentially least career damaging) to have children, which was generally around the mid-late twenties, with one participant noting that her having children at age 29 was considered 'late'.[9] Yet these periods often coincided with key times when women would be experiencing their first international postings or crucial promotional opportunities. Women's career and life options were therefore often informally policed by colleagues and agencies (not to mention societal and family norms)—with a result that many of the earliest female Australian international representatives had no children, and the choice to have children for many women since is one that comes with a gendered toll not shared by male colleagues. Indeed, both of Australia's first female Head of Missions (HOMs), Dame Annabel Rankin and Ruth Dobson, remained unmarried and childless. Contemporarily, neither former Prime Minister Julia Gillard nor former Foreign Minister Julie Bishop had children or married, although men in similar diplomatic and foreign policy political roles almost always did. Perhaps tellingly of queer women's ability to 'fit in' to predominating heteronormative roles in international affairs (as explored in the previous chapter), current Foreign Minister

Penny Wong both has a wife and two children, reinforcing the participant sentiments that women need wives in international affairs.

Politicised, Instable, and Obscured: Navigating How to Get an International Posting

On average, participants across all agencies had been employed for at least two years before deploying on their first posting. Participants were generally required to spend a few years back in Australia or Canberra after their deployment and before undertaking their next posting—unless they were following their partner on a deployment, in which case each person would generally take turns at taking the deployment, while the other worked remotely (or took leave) from their new post location. Opportunities to gain an international posting were generally advertised (by country location, rank, and role) within the agencies and required an 'opting in' process. Across most of the agencies (DFAT excluded), the prestige or status of the post was generally informally known, rather than formally ranked. This had gendered ramifications, as only those 'in the know' or connected enough to senior leadership would fully understand the status or prestige of a post—particularly where multiple roles might be offered at the same level across very differently ranked countries. Women remained less connected with those in positions of power within the agencies, particularly in agencies that remained most male-dominated.

Most international representatives deploy at the level they are currently at, with some deploying as stretch assignments, and some deploying as a downgrade to their current rank if they are seeking a particular role or status of country. Appointments are chosen partly on merit and partly on operational requirements, such as the ability to speak the language and the agencies' capacity to fill the position they are leaving. Yet as discussed, women tended to occupy lower status positions than men when posted, and tended to be posted to lower status countries, echoing Towns and Niklasson's[10] findings that women are less likely to be appointed to high status countries. In DFAT however it does not appear to be because the prestige and rank of countries is not known, as all are formally ranked: 'It's highly structured, everyone knows the rank... Head of Mission and Head of Post jobs get advertised on rank, and the rank is related to their importance to Australia and the significance in the size of the embassy and the job'.[11] Since this ranking is known, it suggests that women are either not applying for the highest prestige or ranked positions, or they are not getting them. Given Conley-Tyler, Blizzard, and Crane[12] and Westendorf and Strating's[13] studies on the topic, which debunked the myths that women are less interested in Australian international affairs and apply for roles at lower rates than men, the latter case seems more likely.

In DFAT, many of the highest status, highest prestige posts are political posts—suggesting that these postings still rely on political background or expertise, rather than the professionalised diplomatic expertise of career diplomats, which, by definition of their appointment, are bipartisan and a-political in approach. This has a gendered impact, as women remain a minority of Australian political leaders. In fact, from 2007 to 2019, only two out of 17 (11.7 per cent) of political diplomats were women—Amanda Vanstone in Italy (2007) and Patricia Forsythe in New Zealand (2019).[14] Men continue to dominate all the other political posts over this time, including nine out of 10 of Australia's top strategic posts (Washington, DC, Chicago, Houston, New York, London, Brussels, The Hague, and Tokyo, with New Zealand only in 2019 receiving its first female political appointee and the Holy See receiving its first female Ambassador in 2016). Washington, DC is not only the peak international posting for Australia, but it remains underpinned by ideals of masculinity—a role that has never been held by a woman, and as earlier mentioned, involved a highly controversial 2018 mateship campaign celebrating individuals core to the US-Australia relationship—none of whom were women.

Despite a few legacy political postings remaining, the trend towards greater professionalisation was evident across all agencies. In the AFP, deployments had moved from a network-based approach of 'who you know', to a professionalised, merit-based approach. One participant, Laura, noted:

> You don't get tapped on the shoulder; you apply through a process and it's based on the merit at the time as to who they select. I was just very fortunate; I left it so long in my career that I was still picked up, albeit at the last highest rank that you can go.[15]

This had positive effects on the women interviewed, particularly as women benefit from de-identified, merit-based selection processes—such as those recently introduced in the AFP that aim to remove unconscious bias in selection panels. In the AFP, the inconsistency of these policies however did appear to be undermining progress, as noted by Jacqueline:

> It's a little bit confusing at the moment. So they've got a people taskforce now and they're looking at promotion and recruitment processes because it appears to be causing quite some angst. In the round that I went through, it went for a ridiculously long period of time and it was almost tortuous because they went to such extremes

to say it's a blind application process. They had like, 600 apply, narrowed it down to, I don't know, 300.... They had a panel of four that had independently reviewed applications and they then only had like, a 5% variation. And then a batch went through the assessment centre. And then we did these assessments and exercises where you're writing reports, doing the psych testing, you're doing presentations—and then we still went on and we did the interviews. And it just went on and on. It must have been a very demanding and costly process... I think it had some unintended consequence where they set a benchmark, perhaps, that's not really practically sustainable. And so, when they've modified that people have challenged the process since, and other processes.[16]

Participants reflected on how the instability of these new processes (formal rules) created an environment of angst and disharmony. In the place of stable new rules, 'old' elements of organisational culture were reverted to, akin to Kenny's[17] findings of institutional erosion and drift, and Chappell and Mackay's assertion that informal rules 'preserve the gender status quo, or gendered logic of appropriateness, in the face of reform efforts'.[18] This was also an issue for participants in Home Affairs, where inconsistencies between policies across the agency—resulting from the merger—made progression more difficult to navigate. Additionally, policies did not always protect participants, with another participant, from Defence, given an international posting only to be asked to step aside for a man in the agency who had threatened to leave if he was not given that role. This highlights that posting and promotions remain far from gender neutral and professionalised, despite rhetoric to the contrary.

Gendered Factors Determine Which Posts to Apply for and Accept

Participants considered several core factors in the pre-deployment period. In order of importance for the majority of participants, these included: family considerations around children, family considerations around their spouse, the role and type of work, and the country of deployment. However, this ordering was not homogenous across participants, with LGBTI + participants more likely to rank the country of deployment as a higher consideration, mostly out of concerns about the legality of homosexuality, perceived safety, and treatment they might receive in-country. The overall low level of concern for the host country highlighted that women remained most concerned about their gendered treatment and experiences from their own agency, rather than their post location.[19] The only exceptions to this occurred in extremely gendered cases where safety and the cost to women's freedom was more gravely impacted.

Unpacking the top four factors participants considered prior to posting, the first was around children, often concentrating on timing. As one AFP participant mentioned:

> Over the years, [the AFP] have expanded offshore, grew the international network, and then you sit back in your career and you think, okay, I'd love to do that but then the timing's everything. I had young children, and it was very hard. I also had a husband who had a career. And then I went through a divorce, which makes it even harder. You're bounded by where your children are and then the schooling age of your children as well... So I literally waited until I could—until my last child was in Year 12, to apply to go offshore.[20]

Of those who had children, most participants would either deploy prior to their children reaching adolescence, or after they finished secondary school. The life of an international representative was generally not compatible with the needs of family, particularly during adolescence and the needs of secondary education. In many cases the ability to have domestic help overseas weighed as a significant consideration, particularly if women did not have a partner who would be primary carer. Jacqueline in the AFP noted:

> From a personal point of view, what I was trying to get was a posting where I could have domestic support with my daughter. And that never panned out. America was an expensive exercise... a friend of mine who had long service leave came over for four months to help me get set up because she had previously been a single mother offshore with a different agency. And I ended up having a team at the time that helped me out with childcare, but there was no like, having a nanny, it's just not affordable over there. And now, I don't have any kids living with us, I've got three step-kids now but the three of them—three of our four are all adults. And now I have a live-in helper... Could have used that 10 years ago.[21]

It is significant to note the extent of support required to make a posting work—features often rendered invisible in analyses of international affairs. In men's careers, these realities are often further externalised, with the burden of setting up home and childcare remaining the domain of wives. Historically in the US, a diplomat's performance review included reviewing and grading the performance of his wife. In the absence of women having their own wives (which is a separate theme, to be returned to later) to absorb this externalised cost, participants drew on friends, colleagues, and extensive familial networks to 'do' deployment. Posts remain structured around heteronormative, nuclear family models that assume copious lengths of unpaid labour and support (frequently borne by women), to function—reinforcing Enloe's[22] findings around the invisible work of women needed to maintain the functioning of international affairs.

Spouses were generally the second top consideration prior to applying for or accepting a posting, with post location largely dependent on whether the spouse could also work whilst there. If they could not, that post location was almost unanimously not applied for or accepted. If participants did still apply for that posting, the spouse was more inclined to remain in Australia. Participants discussed the concerns of their partners; that they would not have anything to do, or that the financial loss of both income and superannuation would be too much. This is a very different model to traditional diplomacy whereby the male representative would be accompanied by a female 'trailing spouse' who was not employed outside (or, formally, inside) the post, even if expected to do significant 'wifely duties' of hospitality and representation.[23] Cangia notes that trailing spouses therefore have a 'precarious privilege'.[24]

Participants noted that women are often still expected to leave their job or not work if they are a 'trailing spouse' at post—but that the reverse remains almost entirely unfulfilled for men. Further, it demonstrates that it may be more financially viable to be a single-income household only if the single income is the *man's* income—a reality that women continue to experience a gender pay gap in almost every sphere of work, worsening through COVID-19.[25]

In many instances, male spouses would not accompany their female partner, mostly due to career aspirations and commitments at home. This was particularly the case for the spouses of DFAT participants, who were more reluctant to move with the rest of their family, often resulting in participants representing Australia as the highest representative at post, whilst also providing the full-time care to children who had come with them. One DFAT participant, who at the time was HOM, summed up the issues of spouses at post:

> My children were one and three when we went to [our posting], and my husband wasn't there. He was commuting between Canberra and [us] and I had the children with me so that was, I think there were all sorts of challenges there because I mean a number of things. First of all, the issue of what does your spouse do ... and I don't think it matters what gender you are, although traditionally it's been more likely or common for the female spouse to follow the male rather than the other way around. One thing I noticed when I was filling my two head of mission postings, was ... most of the male heads of mission had spouses with them ... whereas none of the female

or very few of the female heads [did] . . . the second thing of course is when you've got small children, there's heaps of childcare. So often when you're in a developing country, you're very dependent on the availability of child care, and for domestic staff to help you look after the children, so I think that's another thing. The third thing I would say would be the allowances that they pay you . . . they're never going to compensate for the loss of income, for the lack of career advancement and all that kind of thing [for spouses], so I think those are systemic issues . . . I don't think there is an easy solution.[26]

In Defence and the AFP, fewer postings were accompanied—referring to a deployment that allows a spouse and children to accompany the representative on international posting. So, by virtue of policies, most women deployed alone. If Defence or AFP participants had children, their spouses were more likely to remain at home with the children; and they were often the primary caregiver and so did not engage in paid employment. Within these households, the role of spouse was particularly supportive, demonstrating that a supportive spouse did not necessarily have to go on posting.

For those who were seeking to deploy with their spouse, participants expressed that the time it took to consider the posting opportunity could have been expedited with more attention to spouses. For instance, one participant from the AFP stated:

If you have somebody who wants to deploy, male or female, and their spouse is AFP and they have the right skillsets, make it easier for them to work and organise it for them so they don't have to go through all this to do it themselves. Because if we could deploy and straightaway they said, we're offering you the posting, but we guarantee [your spouse] will get work, I could have made that decision as soon as I got the offer from the AFP. I said to them 'I can't accept it yet, I need to speak to [my spouse] and we need to talk to some people about getting him some overseas work' . . . If the spouse doesn't want to work its fine, that's cool. But if they want to do some type of work and they've got the right skills—and most of them will have, most of them will have some skills in whatever area they're from—speak to them about it then give them some opportunities . . . don't make assumptions on behalf of partners and spouses, pick up the phone and speak to them.[27]

International posting opportunities were almost never exclusively individual decisions for the participants, because of spouses and children. At this individual level, women were the main caregiver in most circumstances, which affected their ability to commit to roles without extra levels of support—domestically, and through their workplace. For participants without children, there was a greater level of freedom in their individual decisions; however, their workplace would often make presumptions about their likelihood to get married or have children soon, or whether they were queer. Formal institutions and policies prevent workplaces and managers from asking questions around marriage or children, and from discriminating on this basis. However, the participants' experiences highlighted that questions around children and marriage were still a regular occurrence—and one restricted mostly to women in the agencies, not men. The participants' experiences, particularly around spouses and children, highlight international affairs as a state action reliant on externalising costs borne predominantly by women. This reinforces that while social norms may be somewhat changing, women's role as the diplomatic *and* domestic housewives remain. The implication of this was that for women with female spouses, provided they were 'out' and able to be visible in their post locations, they were generally very highly equipped to deliver on this diplomatic double burden.

The third factor most considered by participants was the type of posting and role. Participants generally sought out work that was interesting and challenging first, considering second whether the role would progress their career. This indicates that job satisfaction was often more important to individuals than career ramifications—and postings did have significant career ramifications. These included that it took women from the pipeline to leadership positions and placed them 'out of sight' of supervisors and promotions teams for a period of years, reduced their training opportunities, resulted in a loss of networks within the agency at home, and so on. One Home Affairs employee noted that once she went on international posting:

> Five and a half years went past, I didn't get one lick of training. No development, no nothing, you just have to work at your job for that three year posting. So, if you apply for something [a promotion], they will say to you, 'okay, you've won the job, you're fantastic. Report for duty next Tuesday'. So, you either can't take up the role [because you're overseas], or you take up the role, and you come home early from posting, which was always seen as something negative. That's like the worst of the worst [with both career and personal ramifications].[28]

For the AFP and Home Affairs, postings were markedly less important to their overall career progression within the agency, with many noting that it was a choice between posting or promotion—you would not get both. Similarly, in DFAT, participants were unlikely to receive both a promotion or a posting at the same time; however, rank and prestige generally built on the previous posting, with women tending to gain subsequent higher prestige posts. In

Defence, several participants received both posting and promotion at the same time, although this was generally after nearing the end of a successful posting. The recurring reality was that women who sought deeply international careers often would not progress at the same rate as their domestic-bound colleagues, and even in DFAT where posting did result in progress, women remained chronically underrepresented in *senior* international affairs leadership.

The final main factor women considered prior to applying for or accepting a posting was the country of deployment. As canvassed earlier, there was some concern about which countries of deployment would be dangerous or disrespectful to women—with international postings ranked from A-F on a hardship scale (although it is unclear to what extent these rankings account for gender in ranking 'hardship'). However, participants mostly considered country of deployment in terms of the lifestyle it would afford. In particular, the following concerns were raised: whether they might have access to low-cost domestic help, whether they would have to live in a walled compound or in accommodation of their choosing, if there were environmental concerns such air pollution, what schooling systems were available for children, and how safe it was for themselves or children to walk around streets and partake in everyday public life. Many women noted that despite many of these concerns being shared concerns between themselves and their partner, the onus often fell to them to do the research and organisation—particularly around childcare and education. This is indicative of the diplomatic mental load borne by women.

While participants received many negative comments around having young children at post or giving birth at post, there were considerable benefits for the women themselves. Living in compounds attached to embassies was considered a major bonus by some, particularly for participants with young children. One Home Affairs participant noted: 'We lived on compound, and so it was really great... I breastfed both my children until they were 18 months old. Not many people get to do that. So, I'm not bitter at all. I'm in fact very grateful'.[29] Lifestyle, therefore, was a key factor influencing women's choice to apply to and accept certain deployments.

Overall, it was striking that considerations like the role description and professional opportunities were often 'given' factors, taken for granted, and therefore not always a main concern to women deploying internationally. The opportunity that international roles might provide was a consideration subsidiary to whether the opportunity was even possible, logistically, in the first place. Participants felt this to be a consideration unique to women across the agencies and highlights substantial ways in which international affairs institutions are gendered across multiple contexts determining women's ability to deploy.

Experiences Once on Posting

International posting is often the end or overall goal of representing the state in international affairs, and therefore is a critical period for understanding why women remain underrepresented or otherwise face inequalities in experience on the world stage. This section explores (1) the gendered rules that define deployment and (2) the experiences while on post. More than any other agency, the extraordinary demands on Defence personnel are noted. Discrimination and harassment are just the start of the physical threats women in Defence experience. Sexual assault and death are real and tangible concerns for deploying personnel, who are more likely to be deploying into war or conflict-affected areas, and for whom their role as a Defence leader is both high profile and exposed. Indeed, prior to deploying with Defence, training centres on not if you are sexually assaulted, but when. Being captured by rogue actors in the host country was specifically noted as worse for women, for whom gendered treatment is significantly worse.

Gendered Rules Define Deployment

Beyond those in DFAT—employees who are 'naturally' considered diplomats—each of the other agencies have specific understandings of what 'diplomacy' involves in their agency. Defence diplomacy involves supporting ambassadors, supporting NATO missions, and force protection, with the core duties surrounding understanding and communicating security threats. Home Affairs and the AFP work to support ambassadors, yet also facilitate safe border crossings, intelligence gathering, negotiating key issues such as human trafficking, terrorism, and drug offences and international criminal investigations, as well as maintaining the overall safety and security of Australia from an international standpoint. These specific scripts and modes of behaviour inform how diplomacy and deployment is 'done' across the agencies, informing the 'do's and don'ts' of the field. They are often specifically gendered—following a 'logic of appropriateness' that suggests that institutions constrain certain actions (and actors) whilst encouraging others.[30] The demands and requirements are often exceptional compared to domestic representation. International affairs is unique: duplicating and magnifying many of the gendered challenges across multiple contexts, from the individual level to agency, home and host society, and diplomatic field.

Postings were often characterised by a range of practices and behaviours that had specifically gendered implications and informal rules around them. For instance, one participant noted: 'We talk about Asia, you can't—to be honest, can't rely on going to strip clubs and drinking beer until three in the morning to build those relationships. So I think that the way we [women] engage is different'.[31] Excessive drinking and masculinised forms of entertainment characterised many deployments. An inability or unwillingness to participate in after-hours drinking engagements was common amongst participants. However, it was also recognised as an important part of work across the agencies, often a source of relationship building, important negotiations, and insider information to assist the work of international affairs. Participants were caught in a Catch-22 situation, whereby the informal rules dictated that much of the important work of diplomacy happened in these casual, relationship-building settings—at bars, while playing golf, at solo dinners. Yet informal rules also dictated that it would be inappropriate for women to partake in such settings or occasions.

Flexibility was also important, with diplomatic work requiring almost total flexibility from participants, without giving much formal flexibility in return. Formally, flex-time and part-time work was often prohibited across the agencies. For instance, in Home Affairs, 'flex-time is available to all APS Level 1–6 Employees, other than . . . *those employed at overseas posts*'.[32] Those in EL and SES levels were not entitled to flex time domestically or internationally. The Secretary may approve paid adoption or foster leave or supporting partner leave '*with the exception of Employees on an overseas Posting*'.[33] In Home Affairs' Workplace Determination, the entitlements as part of the overseas conditions of service are 'determined by the Secretary from time to time', indicating that not only are they not clearly transparent, but that there is flexibility in the entitlements.[34] This could result in inconsistently applied entitlements, which has gendered ramifications considering the latent discrimination and bias found within the agencies and society more generally. As the Thodey Independent Review of the APS noted, many APS systems and entitlements are fragmented and incomplete.[35]

In Defence, because recruiters and career managers had generally not done part-time work themselves, they rarely saw it as being possible for roles they were recruiting for, which tended to affect women more than men. In fact, the Australian Human Rights Commission found that 'there are deeply held beliefs within the ADF that many roles cannot accommodate flexible working arrangements', a trend that appeared particularly true for deployments.[36]

For those in the most senior ranks of leadership, particularly within DFAT and to a lesser degree the other agencies, there was considerable freedom despite policies—'you're running your own shop'.[37] Many were able to take engagements from home or work flexible hours, often working in the morning, with time off to pick up children, feed, and bath them in the evening, before returning to work late at night. This was also a convenient way for participants to ensure that their local time zone matched with Canberra for any required meetings back home outside of their usual work hours.

Some leaders influenced the informal norms around flexibility too. One participant in Defence noted that in her role in workforce retention:

> I would say to my guys [the managers she was responsible for supporting], 'the answer is going to be "yes" you are going to accept that flexible work arrangement and you can sign whatever you like, but if the answer is going to be 'no' then you need to come and talk to me'. So I guess [I was] enabling them to make the easy decision but then getting them to seek help when it's the harder decision.[38]

While the formal policies granting flexible and part-time work did exist, rules-in-use indicated that managers were not often willing to agree to flexible work arrangements. This participant therefore demonstrated her ability to influence and change the rules-in-use to encourage a workplace that normalised the granting of flexible work arrangements where there was previously low up-take.

Unfortunately, participants who did seek to change informal norms often did so in isolated cases in the context of the wider organisations. As the *Phase 2 Review into the Treatment of Women in the Australian Defence Force* highlights, variability amongst supervisors' willingness to approve flexible work arrangements remains a key concern.[39] For women in pipeline leadership roles, deputy roles, or those part of larger Australian contingents, there was often far less flexibility. This often also coincided with critical periods in participants' lives: largely when they were amid raising young children. Gender, age, and stage of life intersected to add or lessen challenges for participants.

How diplomacy was 'done' was therefore largely predicated upon informal engagement and negotiation opportunities that had significant implications for women. While diplomacy requires a lot of flexibility, flexibility was rarely formally guaranteed. There were ways around this. If women were the most senior official at post, then given the physical distance away from Canberra headquarters, they had greater flexibility to determine their schedule. As women remain least represented in the highest ranks of leadership and deployment, women's ability to wield this flexibility was often constrained by a lack of opportunity.

Externalised (Gendered) Costs Underpin Experiences on Post

Sacrifice and commitments external to the specifics of the job—what might be seen as 'externalised costs'—dominated challenges on post. The top core themes revolved around: (1) maternity and motherhood; (2) post reliance on spouses and wider family support; and (3) the challenges that therefore arose of being the 'single' female diplomat. A further externalised cost was (4) the gendered experiences of differential treatment, harassment or discrimination received *in-country* (from country counterparts, or own agency colleagues).

Firstly, each agency has historically had difficulty in appropriately responding to and managing pregnancy and parental leave in international deployments. This overwhelmingly affected women. Inability to take flex time resulted in years of leave without pay, particularly around crucial childbirth and child-rearing years. Considerable 'cultural issues' with pregnancy on post remain across all agencies, with women often thought by their colleagues to be taking advantage of the system.[40] One participant who became pregnant on her first posting noted:

> I got pregnant and had my first baby . . . when I told them I was pregnant they threatened to send me home. At that stage there was no real leave provision for women . . . I worked with two guys whose wives were having children and they weren't being sent home . . . there was that threat to me and in fact, my equal opportunity representative, who was herself a woman, also told me that she wouldn't have gotten pregnant on posting. So the person who was the worst to me was in fact the other woman in the office . . . I said, 'well, good luck, give it a go. Try and send me home if you like'. So I was given the very generous provision of two and a half months off . . . it's pretty hellish actually . . . I can remember, you know, going into the bathrooms and crying from exhaustion and breastfeeding and all the rest of it.[41]

Many described being among the first cohort of women pregnant or child-rearing at post, noting the significance and rarity of this happening. Informal rules around motherhood and pregnancy were clear and enforced by both men and women: posting was not a place to get pregnant or have a child, particularly if you had any career ambitions going forward. This rule was often enforced by social ostracism as well as women being moved out of core operational or engagement roles, into administration or work with lower chances of progression. In many cases, high levels of resilience and determination was required of these women. Later, these same women frequently became advocates for changes to maternity and parental leave policies in their agencies. However, without the support of the highest officer at post (the High Commissioner in the above example's case), it is difficult to tell whether the women would have been able to continue their posting and pregnancy together. This reinforces the importance of critical actors and 'sponsors' within the agencies, that may have helped women stand up against discriminatory or unfair policies and practices. Critical actors also translated to critical gatekeepers, with one participant commenting:

> When I had my first baby and I went back to work, my then boss who was actually a very nice person, said 'well I suppose you won't be interested in overseas postings or short-term missions now'.... when I got promoted to the senior executive service, my boss said 'why do you want to be in the SES when your husband's a doctor?'[42]

These narratives reinforced gendered stereotyping of roles and types of work suitable for women, as well as reinforcing gender norms inappropriate in a modern workplace.

Tragically, miscarriages and stillbirths on post were also very specific gendered experiences. One woman posted to a conflict zone in the Middle East recounted sitting on the doorstep of the local hospital having miscarried after no medical evacuation services were available—conflict had just broken out. With no counselling available at the time and limited personal support on post, this was a very heavy burden to bear. Difficulties in navigating medical facilities further amplified challenges.

Many changes have now occurred across the agencies, and in the last few years during which this research was conducted. These changes are likely the result of both policy and critical actors. For example, after years of not having gender equality policies across the agency, Home Affairs now has gender equality policy and following this, has abolished its previous policy on maternity leave, whereby leave was not granted to those on deployment overseas. Now, no mention is made of restricting women from taking maternity leave when posted overseas.

Even so, women (and men) who are deployed internationally often do not get the same provisions as those awarded to Australia-based staff. In the AFP, the standard enterprise agreement (which does *not* cover those deployed internationally) accounts for maternity and parental leave provisions.[43] Within overseas conditions of service manual, no mention of maternity and parental leave is made at all—leaving formal policy unclear on whether maternity leave provisions exist overseas, and if so what kind of leave is possible. In the absence of formal, supportive rules and institutions, agencies are more likely to regress to 'old' norms, which suggests that it may be very difficult, if not impossible, to undertake maternity leave whilst posted overseas with the AFP.

Overall, it appears that the Australian standards for public sector employment are to be upheld and met in every regard except for those in international representation. There are some likely reasons for this, in that international deployments are expensive, and spending must be justified to taxpayers. However, it raises an important issue, which is that Australia's representation on the world stage is only possible due to various institutionalised forms of externalising costs onto employees. The brunt of these costs is borne by women, regardless of whether the employee in question is a man or a woman. This is because most domestic work, caring work (of children, elders, or other dependents), and unpaid diplomatic labour is carried out by women—regardless of whether they are the trailing spouse or the HOM. As one participant said:

> [The agency] has to own the fact, as a department, that part of our job is to entertain. Part of our job is to meet with people and have a drink with them in certain countries or whatever. Part of our job is to do things out of working hours and that might mean that we have to provide support [for this]: that might be financial, so whether it's allowances for people to hire babysitters or nannies... support for example that allows us to do that sort of a role.[44]

Reliance on women at post to 'do it all' had clear gendered effects.

Children were far from a negative from an agency point of view, though. Despite the extra work and care required by individuals with children, children also represented a positive in terms of adaptability and adjustment. Having children helped posted couples and singles to gain a strong network, sometimes more quickly than if they did not have their children with them—akin to Marriott's[45] findings. One Defence participant noted:

> Children give you almost instant membership to a particular group of [staff] for which children all go to the same school, the parents all get together and talk, and so that provides a community right there. Whereas if you don't have children... that isolates you even more and even if you want to catch up with, you know, some of the

women or the men who have children, you do feel like you're imposing a little bit on their time because they've got the kids, it's hard to find day care or babysitters when you are overseas [and people don't really speak much of it].[46]

Children have always been part of international affairs and diplomacy in various ways, and they are evidently critical members of deployed family units.[47] Yet agency and whole-of-government support does not fully account for the sacrifice, and costs, associated with childbearing and childrearing, which has gendered impacts on women particularly. As one participant said:

The idea that you should just change people's attitudes would still not fix the fact that [my husband] and I have made a sacrifice in terms of time spent with our children. That is a sacrifice, which you can't just say 'well that shouldn't be the case—that's a family choice'—it's a miserable family choice, I think.[48]

The onus is on agencies to ensure that women with families, not just men with families, are supported—because while men with families can externalise these costs onto (female) spouses, women often cannot externalise these costs onto (male) spouses.

The second challenge that affected women was therefore the agencies' assumed reliance on spouses and wider family support to ensure that posts worked efficiently and effectively. Tied into the above findings, participants commented on the types of support required from spouses. Jane commented how after getting pregnant and giving birth on post:

What made it possible is that my husband took the first year off and studied. It's been a genuine partnership, which is also very unusual in DFAT ... if I look at most of my friends, that hasn't actually been their experience. If I look at a lot of successful women in the department, a few of the most successful either have wives—women with wives, which is a very successful model, I can tell you—or women whose husbands have deliberately chosen to be the supporting.[49]

Like other diplomatic studies on the importance of 'trailing spouses', international representative work often requires the work of not one, but two.[50] Yet participants described instances when their husbands refused to accompany them on posting to pursue their own career at home. They described instances of representing the highest rank at post, yet still being expected to go home to let the tradesperson in to check on the fire alarms, even though their husband was on posting with them, at home, and unemployed at the time. One woman even described her husband divorcing her as soon as she achieved a higher rank—believing that wives should not occupy a higher position than their husbands should in the same agency. Each instance had similar themes: that overall, men's work (and even 'nonwork' in the case of some who were unemployed at post), was more important than that of their spouses.

Selena noted that when it came to organising diplomatic dinners or functions at home, 'often we used to sort of joke "I need a wife". I mean if my husband wasn't there, or even if he was, he didn't take any interest anyway. So I had to organise everything'.[51] As Jane said, 'Men whose wives are happy to come with them fare better than women who may not have a trailing spouse option, and even if they do have a trailing spouse option, their spouses and they engage socially around that differently'.[52] It was not simply that male spouses cannot or refuse to do the work of a diplomatic trailing spouse—although male spouses were perhaps better at not agreeing to undertake much of the unpaid supportive work required of spouses at post. Men were seen as being both incompetent at the work and unwilling to make the financial sacrifice of being an unpaid host. Financial resourcing therefore became a big concern of women interviewed, who were often effectively required to do twice the work for half the pay, unless they identified as queer and *did* have a diplomatic wife or female spouse to help them share the burden. Indeed, while diplomatic missions have traditionally relied on unpaid labour to carry out much of the core organisational housework, participants argued strongly that these roles now needed to be adequate funded. As one participant noted:

> I have a big house here and I'm meant to use it to entertain and have lunches and dinners and everything else. That is a full-time job, organising. In a country like [this], you can't just pop to the supermarkets to buy ingredients for breakfast, to actually have a household run properly takes a lot of work, if you want it to run at a representational level. There is a big reliance in the DFAT system on the women, female spouses—I shouldn't say that—diplomatic spouses to make that work for them. And traditionally those spouses have been female. I don't even have a husband, I have to have staff that can do that stuff. But I spend a lot more time thinking that I know the other ambassadors wouldn't because they'll have someone who can do that for them... picking the menu, making sure that the table's been set and they've placed the cutlery the right way, that stuff matters to people unfortunately. You have to get your protocols right... it's not as easy as it might seem, so some of the systems in our own system are still a little bit antiquated in that sense.[53]

In these cases, not only were (out) queer women and their wives best equipped to manage the 'diplomatic double burden', but they also remained most affected by invisibility and homophobia. In fact, without agency recognition and support, three out of the four queer-identifying participants noted that they or their colleagues were more likely to experience challenges. Interactions that were reported included homophobic and sexist comments, a lack of understanding or recourse after homophobic incidences, particularly if there was a feeling of being 'tolerated' rather than actively supported by the agencies, and bullying.[54] Further, all participants spoke about issues surrounding visibility and acceptance: navigating to whom they could be open and out (which had effects on access to allowances and visas), and the impact of entrenched, crushing, and long-term invisibility on mental (and physical) health.

Ultimately, 'the days of having people whose spouses are happy to work [free for the post] are changing'.[55] How agencies attract a range of family types was therefore an important consideration participants raised, so that Australia does not just have 'a reputation of single people'.[56] For many there was a strong feeling that postings would not be possible without the support of their spouses, which raises the important question of remuneration for spouses, and support in the absence of spouses. This is particularly timely, given that:

> DFAT has recently changed the allowance structure and removed the allowance that allows you to employ a housekeeper. I think that's a very regressive step for women and for single parents because it means that, effectively, if you're a woman you are financially penalised overseas because you have to pay out of your own pocket for that extra help that allows you to get your job, not out of the allowance that DFAT provides for you . . . I think other people have provided DFAT with that feedback, but I think that that single change put us back quite a long way from a posting perspective.[57]

Several participants also spoke of their experience of being trailing spouses themselves, where they had accompanied their male spouse on his posting. One noted:

> When you talk to anybody about these things, there's this big thing of like 'oh God, I'd give anything to be a trailing spouse'. 'God, I'd love to sit around and do nothing all day and just go to women's groups'. I'm here to tell you it's the worst time of your life. You lose your identity, you just go 'hi, I'm the wife of blah-blah'. The attitudes in the community haven't changed so much that they don't associate you with those things because when you're an expat you're there for a reason, so what's your reason? You're either working or you're there with someone who's working . . . I lost all my long service leave, every time I went on a posting with my partner, you know, it's a big hit . . . I didn't get promotion opportunities, I didn't get

posting opportunities—you're uprooting your life away from friends and family, you're uprooting your career, you're dependent on one person, not just through your identity but often just for the conversation because we don't know anyone for a long time. There are no supports in place for you to—you know, to help you—not necessarily formal ones in place to help you find your way out there.[58]

Clearly, there are considerable financial and career ramifications for individuals, not to mention loss of self-esteem and identity on post. These may be greater for men who are trailing spouses, for whom historical notions of being the 'bread winner' and provider may be more confronted by the loss of identity and self-worth. This was a significant reason why male spouses tended to stay home, alongside their lost career opportunities and financial ramifications. Across the interviews, it was rare for male trailing spouses to not work.

For men who did accompany their partner on post, it was generally a significant positive, particularly if they also worked in government. One participant commented how:

I experienced a bit of resentment because my husband's career, far from being diminished by the posting, actually took off. He got promoted and I didn't. I'm still at an EL1 [level] at this point and my husband left Canberra as an SES Band 1 officer . . . During that time he was promoted . . . So his career has been stellar, and I feel like he was benefiting from the posting because he was using his intercultural experience to great effect and I was not benefiting from my posting in that same way. So that was kind of an interesting dynamic because I've never experienced—I never expected that would be the result. I thought we were going for me, for my career, and it turned out that he was the one who was actually having all the benefits.[59]

Given that post reliance on spouses and familial support was such a crucial element of most participant's experiences, the challenges of the third theme, being single while at post, were clear. The challenges centred around (1) traditional notions of diplomacy as a two-person job (paid envoy and unpaid supporting spouse), and (2) international affairs' reliance on externalising costs as explored above. Many challenges around entertaining and completing the work of diplomacy centred on women's experiences in DFAT; however, the feelings of stress and isolation resulting from not having a supportive partner at post were present across all agencies studied.

Some issues were more trivial than others, for instance: 'You'll get invitations to dinner and it will say "To the honourable so and so and spouse" and you have to say, "look, I don't have a spouse," and then you've wrecked their numbers setting a party table'.⁶⁰ For others, experiences coalesced around the isolating nature of the work. Being single was the first thing that one participant raised, noting, 'it is a reasonably solitary existence and you can't go trawling the bars to pick anyone up' (Participant 1, DFAT, 21 June 2018). Participants expressed frustration that they did not have a partner who could be there as *confidant* or someone to share the stress and burdens of the day. Aside from these two themes, many of the issues of being single at post were related to the amount of work that was required. As Rani discussed:

> If I had a partner it would be easier. And my partner would be doing all the things the Head of Mission partners are meant to do, which is being sort of in charge of the embassy family, setting up family day—it's very much geared to having a male ambassador with a female partner who wants to be the ambassador's wife.⁶¹

For others again, even though they were now single, previously having a spouse at post had not necessarily changed the amount of work they were required to do. Leila is now divorced after having been previously married. She stated:

> I have to run this huge house on my own. I would do anything to have a professional wife to help me with my events and decorating and floral, because I have to think about all that on my own. I bet you if I was here with a male partner, I'd still have to do that. Like the women always take the double job. When I was on a posting—in my earlier postings with my husband, he was at home all day long—I would do all the entertaining and I would cook. I would come home from work at the end of the day and I would have to cook . . . So I mean I would do that after hours. This guy was very good at sitting there all day long complaining how bored he was [and how] he had nothing to do . . . in the end the style of diplomatic life is a very old fashioned style.⁶²

Aside from the challenges around childbearing and rearing, as well as posts' reliance on spouses and families and the overall externalised costs that make international affairs 'work', women experienced instances of gender-based differential treatment, harassment, or discrimination. These included being mistaken for a secretary or personal assistant (even in circumstances where it was clear that no secretaries or personal assistants would have security clearance to be part of discussions), demonstrating how much little has changed since McGlen and Sarkees study, where participants noted: 'If they know your expertise, they will listen to you. They will ask your advice. Often if you walk into a room of strangers, however, they merely will just assume you are a secretary'.[63] Many participants experienced issues around establishing credibility—the assumption being that, by themselves, women were not credible to be in such roles. What helped women to establish credibility and authority often included uniform, particularly in the case of ADF personnel in Defence, AFP officers or ABF staff. The lack of uniform was also a clear detriment, particularly to unsworn AFP officers and civilian Defence personnel. One Defence participant noted:

> In International Policy Division everybody kind of knows what level a particular person is, where they fit, who reports to who and even the military who deal with international policy on a more regular basis get it. They understand roughly where it all falls, but when you sort of move a civilian into an area where they just don't know where that individual fits, you're challenging their sense of what hierarchy is . . . [internationally] I've felt like I've been bolted on to the area and if I had have agreed that everybody in uniform far outranks me, and I'll just sit quietly in my office and be part of the locally engaged staff, then I feel that my [welcoming] into the office would have been a lot smoother and I wouldn't have ruffled any feathers.[64]

Experiences like this resulted in the International Policy Division (IPD) developing a directive of civilian ranks compared with military ranks, particularly important for when the DA was away, and staff needed to know who did what in the interim. The participant, Lee, noted how

> that directive has never been raised since it was issued . . . so I think I'm in this awkward situation where my role, my position and my standing in the organisation has never been accepted, so I'm not really the one who can be trotting out this directive to kind of say 'right, here is where we all sit, and guess what? I'm up near the top'. It's not really a thing that you want to [say], but there has been no other leadership doing that. . . . I've looked into other parts of the embassy to try and find some, not necessarily allies, but people who I can engage with, get my work done and just, you know, kind of fall back on that 'proving yourself through your work and through what you offer' [thing]. But it's been quite challenging and has been one of the factors as to why I was planning to only do two years over here, not three.[65]

Others described being interpersonal and friendly as a tactic used to gain credibility and respect, and one that might have been easier in some instances *because* they were women, and often the first order of business was a bit friendlier—as similarly found by Morin[66] and Fliegel.[67] One AFP participant noted how 'I was rocking up saying hi, I'm Australian, love me for who I am, have a koala. I simplify that but it was about building those personal relationships'.⁶⁸ But she also described the blatantly gendered and even sexist reception many of her female colleagues endured on introduction internationally, explaining how a senior female colleague 'talked about when they were introduced to a forum, they were fresh into a post that has quite an Islamic background, [and] when she was introduced they basically put music on and she had to do a dance'.⁶⁹ Interestingly, this woman's experience demonstrates how she then quickly moved to demonstrating credibility:

> She played along because of the culture but then made the point when coming off from that, of sitting down with the three or four star general there and equating her experience to his with regard—she used to drive battleships and this is her operational experience within the AFP.⁷⁰

These experiences reinforced how many of the participants had to endure exceptional expectations that would not have been required by their male counterparts, and which often had distinctly gendered undertones of entertainment and subservience. While most were adamant that their gender was not a disadvantage to what they did, the way that others reacted to their gender was clearly stereotypical, often discriminatory, and sexist.

In fact, sexual harassment and assault were common to participants' stories, if not for themselves, then for women they knew. Most instances tended to come from within their agency however, rather than from their host country. This may be indicative of the protocols and norms of diplomatic work that aim to minimise tensions between countries, rather than creating to diplomatic incidents. More common to women's experiences on posting, particularly from their host countries, was disregard, discomfort, or even mild disapproval of women in their roles. Even so, there were overwhelming instances of women being made to feel invisible, unimportant, or inadequate. Their experiences highlighted: being overlooked during introductions; assumed to be the note-taker or junior; sat at the wives' (not decision-makers') table at functions and events; barred access because of their gender to certain military and security facilities internationally; made to perform—sing or dance—for entertainment for their host country colleagues; not invited to informal events or gatherings; not socially permitted to engage in the same range of activities as their male counterparts; more likely to be scrutinised or watched; and, despite their status and position, were still subjected to sexual harassment and, in some cases, assault.

Women were also met with curiosity and interest—sometimes as 'novel', and other times approached with respectful curiosity. While the experiences of women on posting may appear extreme, they were reported to be much better than their experiences within their own agencies. Internationally, gendered situations were often experienced once off. Within their agencies, there was a much higher chance that these gendered and sexist experiences were recurrent and regular. As one AFP participant noted:

> I remember going over to the UN working with 120 member states, going 'it can never be this hard again'. Interesting I actually found the return—I felt probably *more disempowered* and I felt *more barriers* than what I found being offshore because when you are offshore [you tend to think] it is just you . . . [in Australia,] I think it's cultural. I think systems, institutions are cultural artefacts, aren't they? Once you go offshore those cultural artefacts aren't as impressive, so I really do think it's culture that stands in the way of that here. I remember coming back and I thought, wow, I can relax now, all that diplomacy that you've got to apply in dealing with people from different parts of the world with different cultures, political agendas, regional alliances is exhausting. I thought coming back here would be simpler but in some ways it's more complex . . . I guess when you're going international and you're working, I suppose you're very conscious of those differences but I think when you're working domestically there's a lot of the unconscious biases that are playing out that we don't acknowledge.[71]

This highlights a recurrent theme across interviews: in exploring why participants thought their experiences were better internationally than within their home agency, many suggested that they expected to experience gendered difficulties in some postings overseas, and so were prepared for it. In Australia, they expected to be treated equally and be protected by the diversity, inclusion, and other equal opportunities policies, and so the disjuncture between these policies and their experiences was more sharply felt. This was a key reality of some of the formal institutional policies and supports; theoretically, they protect women and promote their equal treatment, yet in practice they are often gendered.

Overall, international representation in all agencies was reliant on externalising various costs onto their employees—notably, women as formal representatives or as wives. Not only did this make it difficult for 'single' individuals, but it placed an unfair burden on women more generally that was magnified by childcare and other responsibilities. Additionally, it has implications on the dual role expected of women in diplomacy, particularly for those women who do have wives—a theme that will be returned to in Chapter 8. While multitudinous discriminatory or sexist occasions occurred in women's experiences, women reported worse discrimination, harassment, and marginalisation from their own agencies, rather than their host location.

As will become clear in the next sections, this had significant ramifications whether, and when, women would leave their agencies.

Returning from Posting

Much of the literature on women's leadership focuses on the pathways to leadership. Similarly, in considering women's international deployment, much of the literature and this book to date has focused on being selected for international representation, with little consideration of the return from posting. However, the return from posting was a key time in participants' career journeys—it was the most likely time at which women would, or considered, resigning from their agency. The findings from this section have considerable ramifications on understanding women's retention across international affairs.

Frequently, women described that their experiences and expertise were inadequately re-integrated back into their agency, resulting in work dissatisfaction and difficulties retaining staff. As one Home Affairs participant stated, 'to come back to reintegration in Australia is probably the hardest part—the return rather than the going. I think most people would probably share the same or similar view'.[72] For some agencies, like the AFP, the re-integration process was generally reported to be a thoughtful and considered process that enabled recently deployed staff to remove themselves from what was often a stressful international setting and re-adjust back home. Among some of the formal processes were requirements that deployed individuals spend a period, usually a few days, in a third party or 'neutral' Australian space first, where the focus was on de-briefing the experience and shifting back into an Australian lifestyle. This was significant, as one senior leader commented that often when women returned to their families, it stirred tension and conflict, as there was a tendency for the women to tell their partner that they are doing this wrong and that wrong—without realising that everyone had been managing fine without them while they were away. This de-briefing time was therefore essential, with staff coached into understanding how their families coped without them and that re-integration back into the family can be a difficult process if there is an expectation that life will go back to old dynamics.

Yet there were evidently still some issues within the AFP. Individuals who were posted with their spouse (also employed in the AFP) were not offered any support for reintegrating the spouse back into a work division on return to Australia. One participant stated that when you are ready to return 'you're asked to put in the preferences of where you'll go back to and where you want to go back to. And, at that time there was no consideration whatsoever of my husband and trying to help him get a position back in Australia because they basically said well, he's not part of international'.[73] For Home Affairs, there is also a reintegration process; however, it is more of 'a commitment':

> You have a position back in your home area, which is the area which you were last working in before you went on deployment ... the onus is really on individuals to [work out] for themselves where they want to work, what you want to be doing. And most people, the majority of people, will try to line up a position through their own contacts or connections, unless they're taking a promotion on return.[74]

In fact, on further consultation with the ABF staff in particular, many participants had decided prior to returning from post whether they would leave the agency, largely because of stress about finding an adequate position on return. Recently introduced policy required staff to take a posting in Canberra on return from deployment—a strategy introduced to better utilise the new experience and expertise of staff. However, it often led to participant anxiety and discouraged individuals from staying in the agency. While participants were willing to be posted overseas, uprooting their families and lives to move to Canberra after a posting ended was an altogether different ask, and they tended to resign or apply for exceptional circumstances, rather than move to Canberra as policy required.

Despite the low uptake of this policy (and its subsequent abolition), introduction of policies like this do have merit. A core concern of most participants in Home Affairs, Defence and the AFP was having their international experience recognised and utilised on return. Many participants expressed frustration that the new skills and expertise they gained were not harnessed. In these cases, women often felt that their colleagues did not understand international deployment, viewing it as a holiday rather than the often difficult and challenging work that it was. In addition, their time away was seen as more burdensome to their career, than if they had stayed at home. This indicates difficulties that these agencies have in adequately valuing the expertise and experience of internationally deployed staff—reinforced by DA positions until recently being seen as a 'golden handshake'. One Home Affairs participant commented:

> International deployment is seen as a marking time in your career, it's definitely not something that's going to put you in a good position for promotion. They left you behind, they just left you behind. Because you've been off the chart for three years. So, I mean Home Affairs might see this a bit differently, but certainly in the

Customs days it was, 'You do your overseas posting and then you come back and you're three years behind everybody else'.[75]

After returning from posting, many participants spoke of the need to build up their 'Canberra credibility', noting that posting is a 'double-edged sword'.[76] For colleagues who had been on posting, they could understand the benefits the experience brought, but generally, it was difficult to have this international experience valued by colleagues and seniors. Upon return, this often translated into work dissatisfaction. Out of all the times women chose to quit, this was the most likely time they would leave.

This was also true for DFAT, even though participants' comments indicated that DFAT valued their postings most out of all the agencies studied. Participants' newfound skills and experiences were felt to be valued in the agency, but it did not always correspond to career progression—at least in a timely enough manner for participants. In fact, for most, the posting was viewed as the reward, with postings often setting career progression back by a few years. Defence was the only agency that did not conform to this trend, perhaps because the role of DAs is changing to be more important, high prestige and high status, with a new focus on DAs as Defence's premiere diplomatic force. With the increase in funding in Defence, some DFAT participants or colleagues reported transferring laterally to Defence, because of the better career progression opportunities Defence offered. This suggests a further drain on talent and expertise from DFAT. It also highlights that the return from posting is a key gap in talent retention, particularly for women, whom have demonstrably lower opportunities for career progression to SES ranks.

What Happens, and Why, Women Leave

Only one woman among the research participants had left her posting early. However, several participants interviewed had moved on from their roles, either to work elsewhere or for retirement. Excluding those who had retired, participants chose to leave their roles for a number of reasons. All participants noted that they enjoyed the work. However, the reasons they tended to leave stemmed from issues around being undervalued and unrecognised (and therefore not promoted). As mentioned above, timing was crucial to the decision-making process. Arguably, leaving after returning from posting is a strategic move—with women gaining the positives of posting and international experience before moving on. However, it also highlighted a deficit in their experiences on return.

Pre-departure briefings exist across all the agencies, ranging from multiple-week training sessions on everything from language to culture and politics, to year-long language immersions prior to commencing their role. However, post-departure debriefing varied considerably across the agencies. In fact, women from all agencies experienced things such as arriving back in Australia to a new office that had not been told of their impending arrival, colleagues not even realising they were away for a period of years, or no job being immediately available on their return.

Because the return period was one of the most difficult parts of posting, it was also often a time of reflection. Despite the considerable perks of the job—from international relocation to extra allowances and the privilege of representing their country on the global stage—difficulties were inherent in what were also high-stress, high-pressure jobs. Across all participants, common words used to describe the work included: 'very public', 'isolating', 'lonely', 'exposed', a '24/7 job', and 'strains relationships', with one participant noting that 'at some point it just becomes de-stabilising and absent'. The language that participants used to describe themselves included: 'resilient', 'comfortable in your own skin', and 'able to spend time by yourself', with one noting that it was 'not the job for insecure people who don't like spending time alone, I would say, because it can absolutely magnify your insecurities'.[77] This reinforces how little has changed since military researchers in the US found that the lifestyle of those deployed is typically 'unpredictable and one in which [women] must maintain a state of readiness to respond to possible deployment, extended tours, or training away from home. Keeping the "home fires" burning in her absence calls for extraordinary planning and multiple sources of support'.[78] Additionally, the volatility and high-pressure nature of the work appears to have particular ramifications for women on or returning from maternity leave: the *Women in the ADF Report* found that women were generally retained at lower rates than men were, particularly after paid parental leave.[79]

Overall, women could either choose between going on post or progressing their career. This choice to *post or progress* resulted in the women in this research (those who chose to post) often reporting a slower career progression. When combined with the high-pressure nature of the job, it often made more sense to leave and progress laterally through another agency or organisation. The ramifications were that key, experienced women were often removed from the pipeline. At some stage, the challenges became too high, and too often, and the rewards too few, and too late.

Further, Julia Gillard notes of her time as Prime Minister:

> The fashionable political analysis when I was Prime Minister was that nothing about my prime ministership could be explained by gender. That I was just being treated like every other Prime Minister . . . Now, mainly because of the circumstances in the Liberal party, there's actually a lively debate about sexism in politics . . . whether being a woman can be a problem when you put yourself forward for a leadership position. Whether there's sexism that plays out in whether or not people will vote for you. All of those things are being discussed in the way that they were just dismissed when I was Prime Minister. So that's progress, in the sense that, you don't ever fix big problems unless people are talking about them.[80]

It is likely that now, more overtly recognising gendered differences in treatment may add to women's desire to leave international affairs if it is not acceptable, up to standard or does not change quickly enough. Women may simply look for better treatment elsewhere.

Leaving their agencies did not mark the end of women's gendered experiences in the field. For those who left Defence particularly, the gendered effects were stark. From previously being in extremely high leadership roles, reporting directly to the Chief of the Defence Force (CDF) or in other executive pathways, participants who had retired from Defence felt they had little transferable power, unlike many male colleagues and contemporaries. Sasson-Levy comments on this:

> More often than not, [women's] military careers are blocked at an early stage and their advancement and promotion are curtailed and limited. Moreover, their positive military experience is not carried into their civilian life. After their release from the army, they are not entitled to the economic privileges that combat soldiers enjoy, or to their political voice and power. Thus, they are not endowed with the 'recognition and respect' (Burk 1995, p. 503) of the 'good citizen', as are their male counterparts. The power the women soldiers acquire through their military service is revealed as temporary and localized, as it does not lead them to positions of power either in military or in civilian life. Therefore, we can decipher the dual mechanism of inclusion and marginalization by which the existing gender order is preserved.[81]

Similarly, for DFAT, unless participants reached the position of 'senior diplomat' (Head of Mission or Post) prior to retiring or moving on, they reported lacking the respect or currency needed to progress their career in other ways. Unlike their male colleagues, women's power was felt to be temporary and localised. While senior men often left their agencies to pursue successful and longstanding careers and consultancies, women infrequently had the same opportunities and recognition post- their careers in their agency ending.

Succeeding in Leadership Takes More Than Skills and Experience

For those who remained employed in their agencies and are in, or on track to reaching the most senior echelons of leadership, several characteristics came to the fore. All participants had a strong understanding of themselves and their personal value, even if this was not externally validated. Participants detailed the following attributes as important to their work: emotional intelligence (which some perceived to be a natural ability for women); strong relationships; political acumen; collaborative, soft skills; discipline; and authority. This definition varies significantly to Rost's[82] more masculine archetypical definitions of leadership and is more akin to Harris Rimmer, Stephenson, and Verhelst's[83] conception of feminist stewardship, employing empathy, consensus-building, personal, everyday forms of communication, and more feminine leadership characteristics without relying on mothering tropes. The importance of relationships and having a degree of political nous was crucial across all agencies—a universal attribute.

Further, all credited changes within their agency, noting that in general, the situation for women had greatly improved. Most were quite optimistic about the future of women's leadership in Australian international affairs. Demonstrating attitudes of resilience and 'getting on with the job', Rani in DFAT noted:

> Things have really changed since I entered the workforce, you know, it really has changed. I mean, I remember going to my first interview and putting my hand out to shake hands with someone and they said 'I don't shake hands with women'. I said, 'that's a shame for you', and continued the conversation.[84]

Many of the women, particularly those who were in the most senior ranks of leadership, and generally in the later stages of their career, were confident and self-assured. Participants were largely unfazed and pragmatic about possible barriers to their leadership:

> I've honestly found that people don't naturally accept you if you're a 5 foot 2 woman, at any stage in my career, on face value . . . [but] you're definitely noticeable if you're a 5 foot 2 Australian woman walking into a room . . . and that's either

been a disadvantage or an advantage ... but in those conservative cultures that I've been in [that] don't normally hear woman's voices, I have not, in the end, had a problem.[85]

There were also differences in some of the characteristics of participants. For instance, Defence women described themselves as very practical; pragmatic; had a 'get on with it' attitude; were not likely to take things personally; were highly resilient; and were deeply values-based people. In fact, of all the agencies, Defence identity (particularly in the ADF) was deeply ingrained—a values-based identity that defined every element of their life, from work through to family. This was similar in the AFP, though to a lower degree, whereby women's jobs were more than 'just a job', but rather informed a deeper part of individuals' psyches and lifestyles. As a result, these women had extraordinary coping techniques for dealing with the relentlessness and trauma of their work. One advisor described a mantra she used to repeat to herself under stressful circumstances—be yourself, back yourself, know yourself, look after yourself. As well as these highly developed internal narratives, she reported a 'phone a friend' policy: a personal check she used to keep in balance when work became overwhelming. She noted that while it is okay to be vulnerable, once you are fragile, support systems become critical and must be built into a kind of personal protocol.

Since McGlen and Sarkees's[86] study on women diplomats and security leaders, change is clearly occurring, although much has remained the same in terms of women's experiences and overall status in international affairs. Among this research's participants, there appeared to be a greater uptake of the idea of gender equality, and perhaps more freedom for women to do something about the inequalities that remained. Conducting her research on diplomacy over the last century, McCarthy found that 'from the moment they stepped into the Foreign Office many female diplomats were profoundly resistant to the idea that they had a 'special' contribution to make as women and were sceptical of the notion that they might bring a different set of perspectives and experiences to their work'.[87] In this research that did not always seem true. In fact, for the majority of participants, when questioned on why women's leadership was important to international affairs, most replied that it was because women brought something 'different' or 'special', particularly in circumstances where they may be the first Indigenous, queer or woman of colour leading in their agency or host country. Interestingly, while most participants recognised the debate about men and women's 'sameness' versus 'difference', they asserted that women did things differently to men— adding to the breadth of understanding and experience around a topic or approaching challenges in new or different ways. In some negotiations, their gender appeared to help them deliver outcomes. As Esther in DFAT noted:

> [My colleagues] did say to each other, this really is so much easier having all the girls take care of it. I think, it's not that girls are better negotiators, but I think they are, or can be, more clear-sighted about the outcome you're looking for and the pathway to get there. Maybe I'm wrong. But there's much less ego and aggression on the table as a general rule.[88]

Further, former Foreign Minister Julie Bishop notes:

> I'm not generalising, I'm not stereotyping, but women actually bring their perspective, their experience and their leadership style. There is research that found that women tend to be much more transformational—which is the way experts describe it—in that women are more focused on the individual needs when they build a team. They're much more compassionate, they're much more concerned about the emotional well-being of people. Men are more transactional and they set standards and then they hold the whole team to account. They're not so concerned or interested in the individual needs.[89]

This more conciliatory and consensus-based approach may be particularly important for international negotiation, where the stakes and impact of decisions can be high. Yet if we accept that there are gendered differences in behaviour, there can also be profound implications for this—not all welcome. It may explain why there was a tendency for women to be deployed in higher numbers in some of the more contentious environments, like China. It also has a role in stereotyping women for particular roles and portfolios, adding to the vertical and horizontal discrimination experienced.

Detailed operational experience in their field, plus 'soft' transferable skills were also necessary. One participant noted 'I think to be a better posted officer, you do need experience, and I quotation mark this, in "the business", to actually understand [what you are doing]'.[90] Additionally, participants tended to demonstrate a strong aptitude for communications, networking and building relationships that seemed to be the mainstay of international representative work. Cindy, in Home Affairs, stated:

> I never thought about applying for [posting] because I never thought that I had the right skill sets. But through my experience of working internationally and working with the overseas posted offices, I realised that I probably had the right skill set to do it . . . people [suggest] that you had to have all of this operational experience

when in actual fact, the thing that probably put me in the best possible position was strength in relationships rather than some particular expertise.[91]

Overall, international representation and leadership took more than a combination of skills and experiences, but also mental attitude and support systems that all contributed to women's success. Whilst most women felt they were not as prepared as they would have liked to be, these key factors helped ensure that their postings were generally highly successful. However, as earlier recognised, without considerable other supports, the progress of women into leadership was not possible based on skills and 'merit' alone.

Making It to the Global Stage

Despite all the challenges outlined, opportunities also abounded, and women still seek to serve their country through international affairs. They take pride in their work, and their influence and outcomes are considerable. They pave the way not just for other women, but also for their state's place and purpose in the world. They matter. Women's experiences of leadership internationally were generally a major career boost, giving participants many opportunities for personal and professional development. Following the statistics over recent decades, opportunities for leadership have increased too. By tracing history, it is evident that dedicated attention to women's leadership and gender equality in policy and practice is increasingly mainstreamed.

Not all agencies are having the same success however, and representation alone does not equal equality. It is still important to understand what women's experiences are, and how gendered challenges overlap with other challenges, in order to identify areas for continued improvement, research and reform. It is clear that for all the progress made, international affairs remains specifically gendered.

This chapter has focused on outlining the pathways to posting, experiences whilst on posting, and experiences upon returning from posting, highlighting several crucial challenges that remain, despite many recent gender progressive changes in Australian international affairs—further evidence of gendered challenges in institutions evolve. The chapter highlighted issues around the costs of international representation that are systemically externalised onto individuals (including spouses and children)—resulting in an international affairs service reliant on feminised sacrifice. The chapter also highlighted continued issues around childbearing and rearing on post, as well as spousal support issues and agency organisational cultures that continued to place a greater strain on women, than their host countries often do.

Many of the issues found in domestic government work 'travel' with the women as they experience their international deployment. Yet women in international affairs experience both domestic and international representation in unique ways. Women remain affected by institutions at an individual level, including expectations and responsibilities within their family units to bear the burden of unpaid labour and the mental load of navigating foreign education, housing, and health systems. Women are affected by institutions at the home and host society level, requiring them to adeptly navigate different gendered, racialised, and heteronormative cultures and expectations often with little recourse in terms of any negative experiences had—for instance, conforming to gendered and racialised scripts requiring women to be subservient and entertain in some countries, or security requirements that forbid women from access to facilities in others. Women are affected by institutions across the diplomatic field that continue to view men differently to women, and result in systematic marginalisation in bilateral forums and negotiations particularly. Finally, gendered institutions at an agency level affect women. These are not only enduring, but as women have gained increased representation in international affairs, the challenges have at times changed, or become less easy to identify. That does not mean they do not exist, though, and particularly for women of varied ethnic backgrounds, different sexualities or experiences of disability, rurality, class, or education, the opportunities and challenges of deployment in international affairs are nuanced. Worryingly, women reported the most sexism, discrimination, and harassment from within their own agencies, rather than countries they were posted to, suggesting that long after women have returned from posting, challenges remain.

This does not bode well when women make the choice to leave their agencies to retire or pursue other career options. Not only are agencies failing to properly retain and reintegrate their staff on their return from posting, but also whatever power women manage to amass is largely nontransferable beyond their agencies. Some opportunities exist, particularly for women who move to new 'hard' power centres like Defence, where not only is quicker career progression possible, but where women also have better chances at leadership and overseas representation. But for the most part, women's power is seen as localised and temporary.

Despite variation in women's underrepresentation in the agencies, in deployment internationally, and in leadership, why are the challenges women face so homogenous across the agencies? International affairs agencies are not so unique and exceptional that the challenges they face are radically different from each other. Although international affairs agencies experience fewer lateral transfers than the rest of government, they do still experience them, and there is a degree of shared pathways and patterns of employment and challenges that go with them. All agencies are part of a broader government culture of representing 'Team Australia', and often when posted internationally women are posted to the same Embassy or High Commission despite their agency.

More than that, the international norms of international representation and diplomacy—norms which are reinforced by agreements like the Vienna Convention on Diplomatic Relations (1961)—cut across the agencies. There are certain unique privileges, roles, and responsibilities these agencies share in the international system, that has a homogenising effect. Regardless of what agency individuals are from, overseas they represent Australia. Not only does this homogenise the treatment they may receive from others, but individuals must also represent a homogenised version of Australia. International representation is like stepping into the uniform of Australia when overseas—because the uniform has mostly been worn by straight white men in the past, it constrains in some places and does not provide enough support in others. There may be differences along the pipeline, but once women have made it to leadership and representation, the uniform they now wear has a lot of similarities. This goes part way to explain the challenges women still face despite progress, and despite differences across the agencies. As earlier noted, at some stage the challenges became too hard, and too frequent, and the rewards too few, and too late.

When analysing the findings of this chapter together with agency histories in Chapter 4 and our understanding of demographics and statistics in Chapters 5 and 6, gendered institutions continue to constrain women leaders despite progress made. To answer the overarching questions posed in the book, the next chapter will explore why are women still underrepresented (and unequal) in international affairs.

8
Why Do Women Remain Underrepresented (and Unequal) in International Affairs?

> One truism that I believe passionately is that no nation will reach its potential unless and until it is fully engaged with the skills and ideas and energy and talent of the 50 per cent of its population that is female ... if you get a critical mass of women, you see the narrative change because women bring their experience and interests and perspective to their role and I also believe passionately that the decision-making forums of the world, whether they be in Australian Cabinet or in the Security Council, will have better outcomes if there is greater gender equality in the composition. Better processes, better debates and better level of outcomes. I've seen that personally, I've experienced it, and I believe that to be true.
>
> —Julie Bishop, 3 April 2019[1]

By now, there is a reasonable understanding of women's progress to date in international affairs, as well as the specific ways in which women continue to be marginalised, siloed, and excluded. A cursory glance at women's experiences explains much when it comes to the core question of why women are underrepresented (or otherwise unequal) in international affairs, and yet the details and nuances are worth further exploring. Feminist institutionalism (FI) asserts that institutions are often difficult and slow to change,[2] which highlights the enduring effect of historical inequalities. The abolition of many formal gendered institutions and rules, canvassed in Chapter 4, gives reason for optimism. Changes are reinforced by the increasing numbers of women in leadership across all agencies that were the focus of this research. However, as explored in Chapter 5, the increased representation of women has not necessarily been an increased representation of *all* women, with international affairs still perpetuating a straight, ethnically homogenous, heteronormative, and educated image. Further, in Chapter 6, the increasing trajectory of women in leadership is at odds with detailed data, disaggregated and analysed over time. It is also at odds with much of women's narratives and reported experiences discussed in Chapter 7, which highlight a consistent marginalisation of their achievements and roles across the agencies, and numerous, layered challenges on the journey. As Chappell and Waylen[3] note, while men's access to power has been reinforced over time, organisational rules, routines, practices, and discourse have rendered 'women, along with their needs and interests, invisible'.[4] The role that informal institutional rules play in constraining women leaders therefore remains an overwhelming factor in why women remain underrepresented or otherwise unequal. Rather than witnessing a decrease in gendered nature of international affairs institutions, gendered inequalities evolve—changing the shape, but not necessarily the nature, of gender challenges.[5]

From this case study, three factors explain women's continued underrepresentation and inequality in international affairs, that should have resonance globally:

1. the legacy of history, which continues to shape contemporary institutional identity and norms in subtle and often undefinable gendered ways;
2. the 'layering' and duplication of regressive gendered rules and norms across multiple institutional fields not only within the agency context, but also the diplomatic field, home and host society context, and individual (often familial) context; and
3. the way that this complexity and layering of rules compound to effect women at different stages of their international postings, their careers, and their lives.

This final substantive chapter brings together the findings, applying the IFI international affairs framework to answer why women remain underrepresented in Australian international affairs agencies. The chapter starts with some of the core and most surprising findings, before exploring the three factors explaining women's underrepresentation in the context of each of the agencies. The durability of gender inequality within institutions means that international affairs remains exclusive, and exclusionary. Despite progress, women remain underrepresented, undervalued and often invisible.

Novel Findings Transforming Our Understanding of Gender and International Affairs

For women in international affairs, it is not just that international representation and leadership exhibit greater challenges than domestic representation might. Rather, six novel core findings highlight the complexity of women's place in the field. These include:

1. Women are most proportionally represented in leadership and international representation in more militaristic and paramilitaristic agencies, and least proportionally represented in leadership and international representation in more traditionally diplomatic agencies. This finding adds nuance to what is known about gendered challenges in militaries, suggesting that if women can remain employed in more militaristic and paramilitaristic agencies, they will be more likely to reach leadership than women in any of the other agencies studied.
2. Militaristic agencies demonstrate overtly gendered norms, behaviours, and practices indicative of certain kinds of sexist or misogynistic treatment, or 'toxic' masculinities. This is unsurprising given the male-dominated histories of these agencies, and that hegemonic masculine archetypes remain to influence informal norms. What is surprising is that more traditional diplomatic agencies demonstrate their own kinds of 'genteel' toxic masculinities or sexist treatment that are just as pervasive, only in some cases more difficult to identify and therefore confront.
3. For the first time in history, women in Australian diplomacy have equal or near-equal representation in leadership whilst the institution they represent is shrinking—in funding, footprint, and status. Even if simply a natural shift in policy priorities, this diplomatic 'glass cliff' has specifically gendered effects. Women's increased opportunities in leadership are therefore constrained by the declining status or shrinking nature of the institution to which they are gaining access.
4. Women with wives were a better fit for the traditional roles of diplomat and spouse rather than the role reversal of heterosexual envoys with a female diplomat and male spouse. Queer female diplomats (with spouses) can do the work that straight male diplomats with wives can do. Whilst this was also deeply conditional—on things like the political and social context of the country posted to as well as on whether the couple was 'out'—it also highlights the deeply heteronormative model of diplomacy. There remains a continued reliance on and subordination of women (as wives) in the international system. International affairs agencies rely on

externalising costs onto employees, their spouses, and their families—most of these costs unpaid and taken up by women.
5. Historically, women's exclusion from international affairs has been justified based on women's perceived treatment by 'foreign' host countries. Yet women in this study reported experiencing more, and worse, challenges domestically within their agencies, rather than host countries when on international postings. This adds to the literature steadily debunking international affairs as an inappropriate place for women to work.
6. Most of the challenges experienced by women posted internationally were relatively homogenous across agencies. Despite considerable differences across these portfolios and even women's representation in leadership, women's similar experiences indicate that the gendered elements of international representative experiences are relatively homogenous. This suggests considerable ramifications for other international affairs institutions in other contexts, that warrants further investigation.

This section will briefly unpack and summarise each of these key findings.

More Militaristic Agencies More Proportionally Represent Women

A core conclusion of this research is that more militaristic agencies more proportionally represent women than traditionally diplomatic agencies do. This was an unexpected finding, yet an important one considering that the literature generally correlates more militaristic institutions with greater gender inequalities—in instances, with militarism positioned as antithetical to feminism. For instance, Duncanson and Woodward note that 'anti-militarist feminists have argued that women's military participation (however manifested) merely legitimizes an institution that is antithetical to the goals of feminism'.[6] Further, prominent IR feminist researcher, Cynthia Enloe, notes: 'So long as the military is an instrument of coercion designed to uphold a political-economic and ideological order that rests on the subordination of women, the military must not be seen as simply one more institution—like schools or business firms—where women will try to gain access'.[7]

Indeed, a central argument of this book has been that militaristic, enforcement-based agencies remain patriarchal strongholds as the most male-dominated spheres within the state.[8] This is true, based on the proportion of women employed overall in these agencies, of which women remain least represented in the most militaristic and paramilitaristic agencies—particularly, in the ADF, AFP (sworn), and ABF. Yet provided women can endure the challenges of these more militaristic agencies, their progression to leadership and deployment follows at a rate roughly comparable to their male colleagues. An enduring gap remains for women in more traditionally diplomatic and un-uniformed agencies—while women represent a majority of these agencies, they have the lowest opportunity for leadership and international representation (proportional to opportunity). These findings would have remained obscured without comprehensive trend and comparative data obtained and analysed throughout this research.

As discussed, both structure and visibility explain women's better representation in militaristic agencies. Firstly, militaristic agencies tend to have more structured and concrete career paths than bureaucratic agencies. The nature of employment opportunities and ranks in Defence and the AFP provided clearer leadership pathways and opportunities than those in Home Affairs and DFAT, where careers were considerably more fluid, flexible, and opportunistic. Secondly, the visibility of gendered rules affected how navigable agencies were for women. Not only do more militaristic agencies tend to be more male-dominated, 'bolshie', and 'blokey' environments underpinned by masculine ideals and traditional archetypes, but this is well known. There are considerable agency reviews that go into depth about gender discrimination and harassment, as well as high-profile sexist incidents, which have made gendered challenges visible in these agencies. On the other hand, gender in the more traditionally diplomatic, un-uniformed portfolios in international affairs tend to be less researched, with fewer instances of overt sexism and discrimination in the public eye, and no (public) reviews of a similar depth as those in Defence and the AFP to help reveal the gendered challenges. The gendered challenges in traditionally diplomatic international affairs agencies are more covert. Further, perhaps because of women's status as a *marginalised* majority of overall employment in these agencies, a narrative existed that the gendered issues in these agencies had already been 'solved'. This in turn has made it more difficult to have enduring challenges recognised.

Genteel Toxic Masculinities Dominate in More Traditionally Diplomatic Agencies

The consequence of this invisibility of gendered challenges in un-uniformed, more traditionally diplomatic agencies included that a novel form of toxic masculinity was evident. Toxic masculinity is defined as an extreme form of 'hegemonic masculinity' that promotes masculine supremacy, strict gender roles, and the systematic and systemic devaluing of women and men (and other genders) who do not fit the hegemonic archetype.[9] Toxic masculinity has typically been associated with militaries. However, the second novel finding is that a novel form of 'genteel' toxic masculinity was evidenced in more prestigious, elite, traditionally diplomatic international service.

In more militaristic agencies, gendered challenges were often immediately obvious and illuminatingly overt. But many participants pointed out that at least they knew where they stood (and therefore how to work around the challenges faced) in these male-dominated fields. They might have traditional forms of toxic masculinity, but at least it was visible, able to be labelled, and therefore called out.

For the elite and prestigious diplomatic corps or more bureaucratic, un-uniformed agencies, the 'rules of the game' seemed intangible and more opaque. The genteel nature of the craft of diplomacy meant that gendered challenges differed in shape, but not overall nature. Genteel toxic masculinity was reported by participants where high levels of diplomatic norms and training existed. It was defined by instances where men in power could be seen to do and say the right things, yet were *still* found to engage in discriminatory, biased, and sometimes explicitly abusive behaviour towards women. It was described as a feeling of women being listened to by colleagues, but not heard; of being placated, rather than reports of misconduct taken seriously; and of being reminded that women had already achieved equality, even when they clearly had not. Women were often praised for their organisational skills yet left with the menial note-taking duties or organisational housework. They were seen as having an affinity for negotiation and consensus-building, often placing them in difficult roles that had little prestige nor opportunities for advancement. Women were often painfully *invisible* when it mattered—putting hands up for opportunities or being recognised for work—and painfully *visible* in the case of organisational or media scrutiny.[10]

Particularly given the progress made, participants found that it was sometimes harder to have the enduring inequalities recognised or even seen. Poor behaviour by colleagues was often far more covert, pushed underground, and subdued—but remained self-declared as 'toxic', ultimately affecting women and anyone else who did not 'conform'. Their experiences were marked by slower career trajectories and systemic exclusion from power (in small ways, and larger, formal ways) that ultimately resulted in diplomatic cultures seemingly marked, on occasion, by covert forms of toxic masculinity as much as militaristic agencies remain marked, on occasion, by overt toxic masculinities.

This identification of more covert, genteel forms of gendered challenges is significant for understanding enduring inequalities despite formal institutional change and has wider implications for MFAs and other industries globally. In particular, it suggests that institutions that are seen to be doing the right thing, gaining women in leadership and having the right policies may still be the sites of pervasive gendered challenges that go un- or underrecognised. A deeper understanding of the evolving behaviours and norms of inequality are needed.

The Diplomatic Glass Cliff: Women's Representation and Diplomacy's Decline

Related to the discussion of the evolution of gender inequalities in international affairs, is the finding that whilst women have made some of the most progress in DFAT, the institution itself is shrinking. Diplomacy's decline is not new, with Hocking[11] asserting that MFAs are losing their gate-keeping role in diplomacy following a 'state of relative decline' over the past decades. Globalisation has widened diplomatic action for other actors and communication channels that do not always require the involvement of the MFA. Further, the trend towards militarism and an erosion of diplomatic power, prestige, status, and influence have resulted in fundamental changes in the institution women are now making most progress in. Attributing causation is not possible, yet by tracing gender composition, material resourcing and funding, and symbolic status, (1) an erosion in the status of diplomacy and (2) the decline in the relative importance and funding of traditional diplomacy in favour of 'hard' defence and security-led Australian international affairs have specifically gendered ramifications.

Indeed, in the last three decades women have gone from representing a minority of diplomatic roles to now occupying an overall majority of DFAT and a majority of executive leadership (EL) roles. They also verge on equal representation in senior executive service (SES). Yet Conley Tyler[12] has argued that diplomacy's 'special' position in international affairs has lessened, and the Lowy Institute has consistently argued that DFAT's funding and footprint is shrinking or stagnating. Indeed, The Lowy Institute[13] noted that between 1995 and 2013, DFAT's allocation was reduced by more than a third (as a proportion of total government expenditure). To compare, Conley Tyler[14] notes that as of 2019–2020 the Department of Defence budget had increased by 291 per cent since 2011, while the allocation for the Australian Security Intelligence Organisation grew by 528 per cent and the Australian Secret

Intelligence Service by 578 per cent. In 2019 the Lowy Institute noted that despite being the premiere agency for foreign affairs, out of all the agencies studied, DFAT had the least funding. Their report states that 'since 2009, the Lowy Institute has consistently argued that Australia's Department of Foreign Affairs and Trade (DFAT) has been underresourced over a period of several decades. As a result, its overseas network has thinned out significantly'. In the most recent 2022 budget, the government will reduce spending on diplomacy and overseas aid by a further 19 per cent in the years to 2026.[15] From representing almost 9 per cent of the federal budget in 1949, Australia's diplomacy, trade and aid budget is now at one of its lowest points — at 1.3 per cent of the total federal budget.

I have separately deeply analysed these statistics and more in my article on the diplomatic glass cliff in *The Hague Journal of Diplomacy*. The conclusion is that just as women are beginning to gain traction in diplomacy, DFAT is losing strategic power to militaristic agencies and withdrawing from maintaining a presence in the world. The substantive nature of women's representation therefore remains constrained by the institution's wider status and resourcing. Indeed, at a time when women are gaining opportunities in international affairs, the locus of power has shifted away from diplomacy to other institutional arenas of foreign affairs, including the 'harder', more militaristic agencies of national security and intelligence. Women remain least represented in these portfolios, meaning that, as in Chappell and Waylen's[16] research, men's access to power has been reinforced over time. Building on devaluation and glass cliff theory, if found more widely, this indicates that women's newly made gains in representation are constrained by the shrinking functional power of the roles and institutions they occupy.

Women with Wives Fit the Heteronormative Diplomatic Institution

The fourth key finding is that women with wives were a better fit for the traditional roles of diplomat and spouse. Whilst there remained clear challenges reversing the roles of the 'traditional' heteronormative institution from male envoy with female trailing spouse, to female envoy with male trailing spouse, queer women with wives can do the work that straight male diplomats with wives can do. Queer women (specifically, those who currently have women partners) appeared to fare better than their straight female colleagues in terms of meeting the demands of international deployment and the extraordinary requirements of diplomacy. It was not that participants who had same-sex relationships were inherently more equal, sharing paid and unpaid labour. Rather, female spouses tended to be more engaged in managing diplomatic households and the informal functions that are a mainstay of international negotiation, than male spouses tended to be. Female spouses of the participants who were interviewed were also more likely to undertake the burden of unpaid domestic labour or primary child and eldercare responsibilities, to allow their spouses to dedicate more time for their paid deployed role. A considerable number of heterosexual women noted that the most successful deploying partnerships they witnessed were 'women with wives', a quip that highlighted a theme that if they could choose it, they would have a 'wife' to help them carry out the tasks required of international deployment.

Despite this, queer women's experiences demonstrated a deeply entrenched marginalisation and isolation from within the field and their agencies—demanding more whilst simultaneously subjecting them to greater forms of discrimination and harassment. The inability to be visible or 'out', or the requirement to be visible or 'out' only in certain circumstances, placed a heavy burden on those women who were perhaps most able to perform the duties required of a diplomatic couple. It also highlights a problematic reality of international affairs: that representation on the world stage is only possible by externalising costs onto spouses and families, and that much of this diplomatic housework is *still* done by women. The heteronormative structuring of diplomacy prevails but is not equal between heterosexual couples comprising a male envoy and female spouse, and couples comprising a female envoy and male spouse. The diplomatic double burden is both gendered and heteronormative, and ultimately relies on the unpaid labour and goodwill of both straight and queer women, that straight men do not appear as willing or able to undertake.

The analysis of queer women's experiences and roles in international affairs represents a significant addition to the literature, particularly given diplomacy's historic focus on men, and LGBTI + accounts' focus on gay men. While further research is needed to understand and substantiate some of these emerging findings, it holds merit for considering what is required to make international affairs possible.

Domestic Gendered Challenges Trump Those of International Representation

Fifthly, as highlighted throughout this book and the literature, international affairs work is understood as more complex, and therefore more difficult to negotiate, than domestically based work, simply by virtue of requirements to relocate internationally for work *and* represent the state internationally. The presumption that different cultures, gender norms and expectations would present more gendered challenges for women has underpinned historical justifications for excluding women from international affairs.[17] Yet surprisingly, the gendered challenges of international deployment did not stand out above what was already being experienced domestically. While women did have gendered experiences internationally and at times experienced sexual harassment and discrimination, participants were quick to shrug these experiences off as part of working with different cultures. The data indicated that women's worst experiences of gender-based discrimination, harassment or differential treatment was experienced within their agencies in Australia rather than internationally. Four salient explanations were found for this, including (1) the women's level of seniority, (2) diplomatic norms, (3) the women's representational status, and (4) women's expectations of gendered treatment at home versus abroad.

Firstly, participants were at a senior level of leadership when interviewed, and therefore had a stronger role in setting the agenda and workplace culture. Similarly, when they deployed, they were generally part of small cohorts at post, which seems to have been a benefit over larger workgroups, which may carry more entrenched gendered practices with them. Secondly, participants' colleagues internationally were often highly educated, worldly, and more progressive than the general population of either host or home country. The people and organisations participants were exposed to were often well-versed in diplomacy and had a high degree of intercultural understanding and awareness that minimised overt gender discrimination. This is particularly so, given that most significant international governmental organisations or forums which diplomats interact with, such as the UN, evidence formal policies and commitments around gender and representation. Thirdly, participants deployed internationally were often principally judged according to their rank and role. Participants noted that because they were chosen as the representative for Australia, their host countries and colleagues generally just accepted that the privilege of role or rank (or even uniform, in the case of militaries) was at times more important for distinguishing their treatment than their gender. One DFAT representative summed up the feeling of many, when she noted:

> I do find as a diplomat or as representative of your country, you don't have gender, because you're representing Australia. So even in places where they don't normally deal with or they don't have women in their own service, it's okay, you're a foreigner and you're representing your country.[18]

One representative from the Army further commented that no one questions why you are there, expressing that while women's voice may not be equal, they could dismiss this perspective as a cultural issue, rather than a personal issue. Lastly, as in Chapter 7, many participants noted that they expected to experience gendered difficulties in some postings overseas, and so were prepared for it. In Australia, participants relied more on the progressive formal policies mandating equality—which inevitably, did not deliver as intended. The result was that women reported greater sexism, discrimination, and harassment from within their own agencies, not from countries in which they were hosted, which has important ramifications globally on gaining and retaining women in international affairs leadership. It encourages institutions to turn inward and reflect on what can be controlled from an agency level.

Women's Experiences of International Affairs Are Consistent Across Agencies

While it might be assumed that the gendered experiences of police officers, Defence Attachés, ambassadors, immigration counsellors, border protection officers, and surveillance and intelligence envoys would vary, overall participants' experiences were broadly homogenous. All experienced similar challenges in preparing for posting, on posting, and on return. The most significant differences were based around career progression, where, generally speaking, women had better opportunities for progression in the more militaristic agencies. What explains the homogeneity?

As explored at the end of the last chapter, international affairs agencies are not so unique and exceptional that the challenges they face are radically different from each other. Norms associated with each of the lines of work, as well as with the international affairs sector more broadly, had a lot of duplication, similarities, and 'root causes'—in terms of historical male-domination. Further, the unique privileges, roles and responsibilities these agencies share in the international system has a homogenising effect. Regardless of participants' agency, overseas they represent Australia.

Given the varying nature of their work and requirements of their service, this is a surprising finding, indicating that gendered institutions in the field of international affairs are pervasive enough to infiltrate a range of difference portfolios and types of work. This suggests that the findings of this research may have broader application beyond just the four case agencies studied, adding weight to the theoretical framework as a key tool to understand women's representation and experiences in international affairs.

Implications of These Findings

These six novel empirical findings add nuance to what is known about women's representation in Australian international affairs and the field globally. All six findings reinforce a need to ensure that gendered issues within international representation are firmly dealt with domestically. They also provide a deeper understanding into why women may remain underrepresented. If women have the highest chance of reaching leadership (proportional to overall representation) in what many would consider our most militaristic, male-dominated agencies of Defence and the AFP, then it suggests that achieving true gender *equality* in international affairs is far more than just achieving gender *parity*, as in DFAT and Home Affairs. If gendered challenges are pushed underground or obscured by gentility and the diplomatic craft of the field, it suggests that even agencies that appear to be doing 'well' regarding women's representation are still affected by crushing inequalities hampering wider gender (and racial, and so on) process. If women only make it to leadership at the same time that institutions are shrinking or stagnating, it suggests that women's functional ability to use their leadership will be constrained by the status of the institution they occupy. If the most successful women who are deployed internationally are those with wives, then it suggests that the unpaid labour required by spouses and 'externalised costs' of international affairs are a key reason why many women experience burnout and fatigue and leave their agencies and the field. If women's worst experiences of gender discrimination and harassment occur at home, and not overseas, then domestic challenges remain the main impediment to women's equal representation overseas. Finally, if women's challenges are relatively homogenous across the four agencies studied, then it suggests a damning narrative for international affairs more broadly.

The Historical Gendered Legacies of Institutions

Over the course of this book, institutional change has been analysed to conclude that despite some pockets of progress, many gendered (and other) inequalities endure and evolution. Recent gendered changes across the agencies, including the introduction of formal gender policies, have begun to change participant experiences, with most participants expressing how much better represented women now were in their agencies, and that they thought that general experiences were improving. Statistics also show a general upwards trajectory, with a few exceptions. However, also in all cases, gendered institutional rules, behaviours, and norms remain, or have been reinstated across the agencies, often covertly and without planned intent.[19] This occurred even though all agencies were actively working to dismantle any formal gendered challenges that limited women's leadership and representation. This highlights the primacy of informal institutional rules and norms to maintaining gendered divisions across Australian international affairs agencies. Informal institutions reflect a historical status quo, often seen as 'natural' and 'immutable', reinforcing historical legacies that continue to shape women's contemporary experiences in leadership, despite their growing numbers and (in cases) improving experiences.[20] As Chappell and Waylen note: 'With the weight of history on their side, defenders of the gender status quo—those advantaged by existing power arrangements—have often defeated attempts to subvert the existing regime'.[21]

In DFAT, formal policies such as the *Women in Leadership Strategy* and *Gender Equality and Women's Empowerment Strategy* were successful at reaching initial targets for women's overall representation and representation in EL and SES roles. As noted in Chapter 4, the Women in Leadership Secretariat had power, as part of the executive, to enforce these formal institutions, resulting in women now verging on parity in international leadership for the first time in history. This can be seen as a formal institutional success, reliant on DFAT's will and power to enforce new gendered institutions, as well as the leadership of critical actors to advocate and reinforce gendered changes.

However, the enduring gap between overall representation and SES ranks, as well as women's reported experiences, does suggest 'nested' change—institutional change that is 'nested' within old institutional structures and norms.[22] Informal gendered norms of diplomacy remain important to the agency, giving primacy to men as the diplomats. These norms are also somewhat outside the realm of the agency's control—they are negotiated, enforced, and reinforced not only by individuals within DFAT, but also those in the diplomatic field, and home and host society. Because of the pervasiveness of these informal norms, there is therefore tension between the rules within DFAT and those in the wider field and society.

Given that women do form most of the agency now, it is particularly interesting that many of the expectations around 'trailing spouses' and unpaid labour continue to dominate agency behaviour internationally, especially since women remain more affected by this 'diplomatic double burden'. Yet perhaps this highlights the limits to the powers of critical actors, particularly while a woman remains as Departmental Secretary *and* there remains notions that you cannot be 'a woman who only cares about women'. Additionally, this continued reliance on women's unpaid labour internationally highlights the fact that much of the paid work of the wider economy relies on the unpaid work of predominantly women—it is simply too big of a reality to change these norms through one agency. Internalising these 'externalised costs' would seem prohibitive. Coupled with the diplomatic glass cliff and overarching funding and status shifts, it means that gendered institutional change within DFAT has been only partially successful.

In Defence, the low overall number of women in the agency and in leadership initially indicates an agency resistant to change. Despite the number of high-profile reviews on gender discrimination and harassment, and the substantial recommendations issued, institutional change does not necessarily follow formal policy intent. In fact, the deeply historical and live nature of past gendered norms and identities have resulted in an agency with perhaps the most engrained masculine norms. The agency remains deeply gendered, a 'man's world' that still relies on tropes about men's strength and physicality as being central to the ability to do the job and advance. These notions were particularly salient in informal conversations with senior leaders, who continually reinforced the *operational needs* of Defence above improving gender relations. In instances where critical actors did stand for institutional change, informal enforcement mechanisms sent the clear message that challenging the gender order in Defence amounted to sacrilege.

Within this context, the more proportional representation of women across the agency challenges the simplicity of McGlen and Sarkee's[23] (and others') arguments that military institutions remain the most masculine and male-dominated spheres of the state. The structure of Defence had an effect here—the ability to 'pull rank' in a heavily hierarchical system, plus partake in the highly developed paths to leadership, ensured that Defence did offer women considerable opportunities and credibility. However, the visibility of gendered institutions is also significant—and is one of Defence's main historical legacies. Defence has always been gendered. It has maintained gender-segregated units more consistently and publicly than any other agency of government. It has demonstrated the powerful and complete ways in which women remain marginalised throughout the agency. It has been public and exposed in the face of allegations of gender harassment, discrimination, and mistreatment. However, as a result, the agency and those in it *know* that it is gendered in a way in which many of the other agencies insist they are not. The visibility of challenges aid in navigating them.

The obvious point, of course, is that women can only get so far. No woman has occupied position of Chief of the Defence Force (CDF) or the service lines yet, which suggests that absolute limits to women's progression endure.

In Home Affairs, the historical predominance of women has resulted in a very different institutional context over the past few decades. Despite representing over two thirds of the agency in 1996, women have been declining in their representation, overall and in leadership, ever since. At no point did women represent a majority of the SES—the highest and most prestigious positions of power. The lack of formal policies in Home Affairs (until recently) can be easily seen as a positive—the fact that they were not there to institute positive gendered change is because they were not needed. Yet the reality was that without formal institutional support, gender equality was not instituted at the highest levels, particularly as each of merger had a progressively more male-dominated and paramilitaristic influence. Additionally, there was a tendency for Home Affairs (and DFAT) to adopt a 'lowest common denominator' approach to institutional structuring, resulting in gendered institutions that *regressed* with each successive merger. Not only is this shown by the falling representation of women in leadership, but also by women's reported experiences.

Finally, in the AFP, formal institutional change has made progress at transforming historical gendered enforcement cultures. The fact that women are most represented in the SES in AFP sworn roles (proportional to opportunity) is significant—in no other agency has this been so starkly achieved. Yet inconsistency, and therefore instability, in the new formal institutions has hampered their application, their credibility, and their ability to be enforced. This is evident in the stagnation of women's overall representation, and in EL and international posts, as well as in women's experiences, which highlighted enduring discrimination and harassment. Participants' expressed confusion as to what the new (often-unstable) rules were, and the application of new rules was often up to individual discretion of managers or dominant cultures, some of whom continued to perpetuate informal gender-exclusionary rules. The result was an institutional context that was unstable, fostering an environment that has reverted to, and become more reliant on, informal policing and paramilitaristic rules of engagement. Again, institutional change across the AFP appeared to be 'nested' within 'old' institutional structures and norms.[24]

Change is occurring in all the agencies studied. Women continue to make the most impressive gains in DFAT, AFP sworn SES roles, and Defence, which show consistent growth in women's representation in leadership. But representation is falling in Home Affairs and stagnating more generally in the AFP. Gaps between overall representation and leadership are particularly stubborn in DFAT, and the progress made in Defence seems inadequate given the depth of formal institutional interest in gender equality. Historical legacies of male domination and women's subordination across international affairs continue to influence the agencies, highlighting inequalities' evolution—changing from time to time in shape, but not overall in nature, ensuring that gender inequalities remain.

Layering and Duplication of Gendered Institutions

The institutionalisation of gender inequalities is particularly troubling in international affairs, which remains a complex sphere influenced by domestic, international and 'intermestic' factors.[25] There are few fields that are so amorphous in shape, rapidly changing, and inherently international by nature. Gendered scripts operate across many different institutional contexts and are reinforced on so many levels it is difficult to combat them in one institutional context, without addressing the rest. This research has focused more closely on agency context as a critical factor enabling or constraining women. Yet even with very progressive and gender equitable formal policies and rules, institutional contexts across other spheres continue to enforce often informal rules that restrict or are in direct opposition to gendered progress. This section therefore argues that institutional layering and duplication has strengthened gender equality moves in some spheres, and yet acted as a point of tension and inconsistency in others, enabling resistance to institutional change. Layering has almost exclusively been used in the literature to highlight the layering of new (progressive) gendered institutions on top of already existing ones.[26] In this section, layering refers to the layering of (regressive) gendered institutions, and is a perspective overlooked in explaining resistance to progressive gendered change.

The theoretical framework established Chapter 2 highlights these different sites of institutional resistance. In Chapter 2, Figure 2.1 highlights that asides from the agency context, the diplomatic field more generally is one of the primary sites of gendered institutions affecting women leaders, as is the host and home country contexts and individual context.

Characterising the diplomatic field is difficult: it is a unique point where international governmental norms, diplomatic charter norms, and local and national norms all meet. Power shifts between not only states and intergovernmental organisations, but also within states' agencies too—a theme occurring not just in Australia but globally. Interactions in the field include those with fellow diplomats or counterparts, plus their agencies and governments, and the complex sets of rules, protocols and orders of behaviour that fluctuate according to context. Often, these rules, protocols and behaviours worked to reinforce gendered divisions through language, silencing and behaviour, and often had little to no visible enforcement mechanisms or protocols for when things went wrong.

Gendered norms in the field occur outside of the realm where most agencies have significant influence, which leads to a 'norms clash' between the agency and the outside world. For instance, Grace from DFAT noted:

> Last year I worked on the Foreign Policy White Paper and we held consultations all over Australia including with all of the big international relations think tanks like the Lowy Institute or ASPI [Australian Strategic Policy Institute]. I was absolutely shocked [at] how male dominated the conversations were. Not only did men self-select in some of the more public forums—we invited an equal number of men and women—but the women didn't come, and the men were there in greater numbers. Also, the ones where we didn't control who was invited—those big policy think tanks—they are dominated by men. At the ASPI [Australian Strategic Policy Institute] roundtable we had 24 people and 22 of them were men.[27]

Particularly given that international affairs involves working with myriad different organisations and agencies all part of the field, this norms clash results in a context ultimately more resistant to change, than not—an outside environment still marked by high levels of gender imbalance, and often, misogyny.[28]

Home and host country dynamics, plus individual circumstances, were sites of further institutional layering and duplication. Each family and individual circumstance was different; however, there was a trend across participants that despite progress at work, participants often had to return to the same gendered institutions in the home that had not progressed at the same rate. In fact, one Defence woman commented that most of her female colleagues' husbands are also deployed in Defence, which can be extremely taxing on families, doubling the misogynistic effect of workplace and home. Further, women were often deployed in countries that reinforced traditional gender roles that affected their work.

Each case demonstrated this duplication of rules across individual, home and host society, agency, and diplomatic field contexts. Returning to the mixed methods approach to research canvased in Chapter 3, the deeply grounded analysis of women's experience and the triangulation of data across multiple forms allows us to better understand institutional layering and duplication and represents a significant contribution to FI methodological approaches. The layering and duplication of gendered institutions is best illustrated by an exemplar from each agency context, which brings depth to an intersectional feminist institutional (IFI) approach.

Leila's Story: Working in DFAT

> In the end, the diplomatic life is very old-fashioned.[29]

Leila was employed in DFAT during the introduction of gender equality and women in leadership strategies that had seen her able to take up more opportunities for senior leadership. As a CALD woman of colour however, it was overtly obvious how underrepresented other people like her were in the agency, and she expressed frustration at working double as hard as a woman, and double as hard again because of her ethnic background. For her, it was not just the issue of not being taken as seriously as her white, male (or female) colleagues. From her perspective, the CALD inclusion policies in her agency all came from a position of 'helping' those who are 'disadvantaged', rather than recognising the core advantages to the field that came from being from an ethnic background. For her, these included greater cultural understanding, language skills and connections.

Leila also operated within the diplomatic field in her work, where her gender and ethnic background were often a surprise to the counterparts she met in her line of her work. She felt that they were more surprised because she was an *ethnic* woman in leadership, and often her host country counterparts expected her to be more subservient because of her ethnicity. Many colleagues within the agency had experienced decades of discrimination and bias, and it has since driven her to lobby for change within the department.

On the home front, Leila had deployed both when she was married, and later, divorced, and single. Both experiences were occasions where she was expected to bear the entire paid and unpaid burden in her role as a diplomat, plus the hospitality and organisational duties of the diplomatic household that usually would have been shouldered by her spouse. She notes that even when she had a spouse, he would not perform these duties, and she wished she had a diplomatic 'wife' to help share the burden of externalised costs, which were not properly compensated for by her agency. Further, balancing diplomatic work and the demands of raising children required long periods at home in Australia, which meant that she progressed to leadership and senior international representation much later than her male colleagues. Since she became single, she dealt with fewer gendered challenges in her personal life; however, she was restricted from going out and socialising in some types of informal settings as many of her male colleagues do, as that was considered inappropriate in the diplomatic and country context.

When posted internationally, she worked predominantly with other diplomats or senior representatives that were generally quite educated and worldly. Often, she did not feel the full extent of gender inequality in the societies she was posted to, even though they generally scored lower than Australia in gender equality measures. However, she did get several surprised reactions from locals when they learn of her position, and locals often wanted to know where her husband was, and why she did not have one.

Danielle's Story: Working in Defence

> Work out whether you want to be one of the boys, or you don't want to be one of the boys.[30]

In Defence, Danielle was the first female DA of any country to be deployed to her host country. She was appointed as DA around the same time that Defence changed the role of DA from a 'golden handshake' opportunity for those nearing retirement, to a higher prestige and rewarding post only for those who can combine military expertise with political and diplomatic nous and can continue to work with Defence after completing the post. This meant that she was likely to get more future opportunities than previous DAs. Yet Danielle stood out as one of a few women in a sea of older white male DAs and was still very much in the gender minority in her work. She had developed an attitude to survive and thrive in the agency, and was not easily shaken, having progressed through the agency over decades of particularly well documented sexism and misogynistic behaviour. She was beginning to see much better opportunities for women, following agency reviews and an attitude from the Chief of the Defence Force (CDF) that seemed committed to progress for women.

When Danielle was deployed internationally, she was keenly aware of military norms and different chains of command. Her rank helped her to establish credibility and achieve the outcomes she needed. Mostly, she received the curiosity and surprise of her counterparts good-naturedly and did not let it bother her. Occasionally, she was subjected to lewd comments and behaviour about her gender, which she thought should not be happening even in the relatively conservative society where she was posted. She noted that while her host society were increasingly aware of international norms and standards for gender equality, differential treatment between herself and her male colleagues continued. Frequently she was the only woman in the room.

As Danielle was single, and until recently, did not have any children, she felt relatively protected from many of the extra responsibilities others' reported. However, since having a child of her own, she felt that she would need extra support going forwards. As a result, she thought that her DA post would be the last major deployment she undertook—the burden of being single with a young child whilst employed at a post that still centred on the ideal of a diplomatic DA *couple,* would be too much. The enormous flexibility and mobility required of her role also influenced this decision, particularly given that agency provisions for wider family support were not always there.

Talia's Story: Working in Home Affairs

> When you get there... meet all the ministers' mums and you'll be able to do what you need to for work.[31]

In Home Affairs, Talia was part of the ABF, after previously having an enforcement-based career in border patrol and detention centres. Her career path had been operational; however, since she reached a higher rank, her international roles had become increasingly diplomatic. She had been at the centre of several high-profile initiatives, which required her to juggle a high level of responsibility and a high level of media scrutiny. Being in the more masculine side of Home Affairs, Talia was used to the more enforcement, strength-based and 'blokey' culture of the agency, unlike some of her colleagues who came from the Immigration side of the department and for whom the merger to create Home Affairs was a more difficult transition.

As a CALD woman of colour, Talia felt less out of place in the agency than other CALD women of colour interviewed. She felt appreciated by her agency and useful for the greater cultural understanding she was able to bring to some of her particularly sensitive work in the Pacific. Her cultural background and understanding enabled her to confidently navigate the different gender expectations of the locations where she was posted. Whilst almost all the positions of power in her host countries were occupied by men, she knew that informally, the wives and mothers of these men were very important to their culture, and so was able to work with them to get the desired outcomes she required from her counterparts in-country.

At an international level, much of the work she engaged in involved negotiation around the settlement of refugees and asylum seekers—a humanitarian field more dominated by women than men. Unlike some of her counterparts in the other agencies, she did not speak about the gendered challenges of the field as much, perhaps because her offices were not predominantly based in embassies where diplomatic culture and norms predominate. However, for some of her colleagues who *were* posted in embassies, they reported gendered and racialised challenges—even if their agency was a culturally diverse workforce, often CALD staff who worked in the embassies felt that they were the 'token' or 'diversity hire', particularly for international postings.

At the home level, Talia's experiences of deployment were similar: deployments were very stressful, demanding long hours, and requiring much more negotiation and commitment than an ordinary nine-to-five job based in Australia. Even when she was not posted overseas, she was often posted to different locations around the country, which meant that mobility was a crucial part of her work. When she was on posting (both domestically and internationally), she returned home every now and then to visit her husband, who remained in the one location in Australia. They partly made this arrangement out of financial necessity, which required them both to be earning in their jobs, partly out of career fulfilment, where it was important that her husband remained gainfully employed and progressing in his career too, and partly out of the operational requirements of her roles, which were often not accompanied postings.

Meaghan's Story: Working in the AFP

> You can wave the flag of equality all you want . . . [but] it isn't play-fighting or anything, there's really deadly consequences.[32]

Meaghan had been an employee for close to 30 years and had deployed overseas multiple times. She had witnessed dramatic change in the AFP, having experienced firsthand the sexism and homophobia that for decades, together with a tough and sometimes bullying approach, was part of the ingrained culture of the agency. When she deployed overseas, as a queer woman, she was careful not to use the pronouns of her partner in conversation, if she mentioned her partner at all. In fact, she was able to get away with not revealing her partner for sometimes three or four years whilst on deployment. This was a mental burden, and affected her personal relationship with her partner, but she felt was a reality of posting to countries with varying levels of acceptance of homosexuality and was something she ultimately had to reconcile within herself. It was easier to keep this part of her life invisible. She was steadily progressing up the ranks; however, she has also witnessed many female colleagues leave over the years or remain stuck at the same level with little career progression.

Most of the police forces she worked with internationally were heavily male-dominated, and she was often the only woman in the room or on a case.

The teams she worked with were generally very cooperative, and people understood her skills and expertise because of her rank, which was formally represented through her title and uniform. Her rank often gave her the credibility she needed to operate successfully overseas, although not all ranks were universally shared. Between her female colleagues and their international counterparts, there was sometimes confusion as to whether they were senior or junior to those they were meeting—and being women, they were often assumed the junior. She learned to be confident in asserting herself. Even so, her colleagues sometimes sent junior male staff in their place to meetings because it was easier than fighting the status quo.

At home, she felt her relationship was equal, which made her job easier. It was difficult to keep her partner hidden, and she was angry about the unequal treatment she received compared to some of her straight and male counterparts. However, she learned to self-select out of appointments where she felt she would not have been able to bring her partner, as she felt it was important to have her spouse there for support. Having her partner supported and recognised at an agency level was a key factor in making her deployments possible.

Implications

These four short vignettes exemplify intersectional institutional layering of a regressive nature across the range of institutional contexts highlighted in the theoretical framework. Gendered (and racialised, heteronormative, etc.) challenges were evidenced on multiple levels across multiple sites, often at the same time, reinforcing international affairs as a place where women can only make it through careful negotiation. Interestingly, there was generally at least one sphere—the individual context, home and host society context, agency context, or diplomatic field context—where participants experienced less gendered institutions in each of these stories. This indicates that gendered institutions could be negotiated to a degree, depending on participants' personal circumstances, place of employment, and where they were posted.

Participant narratives highlighted that, perhaps more than any other field, the gendered institutions in international affairs are layered, duplicated, and complex. Institutional layering may strengthen institutions, such as in the case of introducing targets on top of equal opportunity policies, yet institutional layering across multiple contexts also highlighted tensions whereby there appeared no 'complete' set of institutions to ensure gender equality. These gaps and points of tension were powerful sites of institutional resistance and informal institutional dominance. The mixed methods approach, providing multiple points of analysis, has aided in the identification and characterisation of these layered regressive institutions, and provides a strong approach from which to conduct further IFI research.

Compounding Effect of Gendered Institutions

Flexibility and mobility underpin international affairs and are a core reason why gendered institutions have a compounding effect on women at different stages of their career. Gendered institutions intersected with personal challenges at any given point of participants' careers, posting cycles and lives, which, when combined, had a compounding effect on women's experiences. While the analysis of gendered institutions has often remained focused on one set of institutions or one institutional context, the reality for many women across international affairs is that the field is particularly complicated by gendered challenges that affect women at every turn and have a compounded effect on women over a lifetime of posting and progression cycles.

Enormous flexibility was required of participants, from flexible work hours that required participants to maintain communication with headquarters in Australia, to flexibility in cases of disasters or extreme emergencies, particularly where participants represented the most senior Australian on the ground. Flexibility was required in terms of determining their role, which on any given day may have involved administrative and logistical work at many scales below their level of employment, or key negotiations with international representatives and world leaders many leaps above their level of responsibility. Flexibility was also required in order to deal with different cultural norms; organisational norms; chains of command; political requirements; diplomatic protocol; gendered expectations of their colleagues; gendered expectations of their counterparts; gendered expectations of their family; education systems for children; workplaces for spouses; transport systems; safety requirements in countries with varying levels of social and political safety, especially for LGBTI + women and women with children; and the externalised costs of the whole system that continued to depend on the unpaid labour of women and institutionalised forms of feminised sacrifice.

Mobility was also a key part of women's experiences, determined by the logistical ability to deploy in the first place, as well as the need to travel in-country and across regions with little notice when emergencies broke out. Mobility placed extraordinary demands on individuals and their support systems.

These demands of flexibility and mobility are combined with the layering and duplication of rules and institutions across multiple contexts—individual, agency, field, home, and host contexts—which are combined *again* with individual timing. Gendered challenges are experienced differently for women on the pathway to posting, compared to being on posting, and returning from posting. Similarly, gendered challenges are experienced differently at each of the stages of women's careers—with women often at the mercy of gendered challenges *most* when their power is *least*. Early career postings typically occurred when children were younger, and the needs of families were likely to be greater. Senior postings tended to occur later in life when adult children were more likely to have left the home, but care for aged parents was more likely to be part of the picture.

This compounding effect of gendered challenges was evidently too much for some women, at some points. Key periods when women left their agencies, or were considering leaving their agencies, were after returning from posting (sometimes involving returning from post early to do so). This was both a good career move in terms of leaving after completing an international posting that added to their skills and experiences, and a pragmatic move indicative of women coming to the end of their ability to cope with the extraordinary demands that international representation placed on them.

Ultimately, the compounding effect of institutions on women is important to analyse in global contexts and other fields of work. The increasingly globalised workplace has ramifications for women, potentially increasing their exposure to gendered challenges to a greater degree than more domestic work might involve. Exploring these implications across other fields of international affairs and other fields of work could add tremendously to what is known about the nature and layering of gender inequality at work.

Evolving Inequalities

The legacy effect of historical gendered rules and norms continue to influence women's experiences of international representation today. The layering and duplication of gendered rules across multiple contexts highlights international affairs as a workplace particularly contextual, fluctuating, and complex for women to navigate. The compounding effect of rules at different stages of career, life, and posting cycles also helps to explain why women continue to be underrepresented in international affairs—the gendered challenges are often confronting, sometimes crushing, and remain to be constant.

There are considerable consistencies across the case agencies, in which all women studied were employed in organisations that should be the 'gold standard' in employment opportunities and conditions: an important part of forming a legitimate government service. Yet the agencies are evidently still not reaching this standard. Gender (and other) inequalities evolve as institutions change—remaining not only to explain women's enduring underrepresentation (and inequality) in international affairs, but also explaining women's considerable challenges despite more women overall in the field and a more feminist turn in Australian foreign policy and global politics.

Conclusion

How Inequality Evolves in International Institutions

> I am optimistic that with that degree of thoughtfulness we will continue to see more and more women in high level appointments in foreign affairs.
>
> —Julia Gillard, 21 May 2019[1]

This book has gone beyond a look at a single case or even single context, to deeply understand the lives, work and ways in which gender and other hierarchies impact on women on the global stage. Women may no longer be severely underrepresented across most of the international affairs agencies studied, and indeed considerable pockets of progress are witnessed. However, gendered norms continue to affect women's representation and experiences, sometimes with devastating consequences in terms of career and personal development. Intersectional feminist institutionalist (IFI) theory demonstrates the deep pervasiveness of gendered (and other) challenges across international affairs—a field teeming with complex and multifaceted formal and informal rules that challenge women at every turn. Despite recent shifts in Australian foreign policy and an overall rise in women's representation, gendered rules and norms continue to impact on women. This is a leading reason why women remain underrepresented and experience government differently. It is not simply that institutions, once made, are enduring and difficult to change.[2] Rather, drawing on Cornut's[3] notion of liquid institutions, gendered institutions endure through evolution and adaptation, at times proving to be infuriatingly adaptable in the context of international affairs.

In this book, comparison demonstrated how gendered, racialised, heteronormative institutions are experienced across national and international contexts. Comparison has demonstrated factors that may aid or hinder institutional change and demonstrated that international affairs agencies do not easily lend themselves to tried-and-true strategies of other industries because of the reality of posting cycles, operations, and international deployment.

Not only has this opened the door for future research on gender in increasingly globalised workplaces well beyond diplomacy, but it has also allowed analysis of institutions undergoing change, with diplomacy in decline in some states at the very moment women's representation is increasing. Are women only gaining traction in shrinking institutions? Does women's representation really equate to substantive change, or do gendered challenges continue? Does the level of visibility or invisibility of gendered challenges matter to women's representation?

Statistical analysis from multiple points of view has revealed that depending on *what* statistics are analysed, quantitative data can obscure women's real circumstances. This form of statistical structural inequality highlights the need for both multiple points of statistical analysis and analysis and observation of individual experiences. In fact, understanding the ways in which international institutions are gendered would have been impossible without the mixed methods approach to research and critical feminist friend methodology. This overarching approach enabled understanding of institutions from different perspectives, at different points in individuals' postings and lives, and from a grounded perspective in the field. Given the 'hidden' and often difficult nature of studying informal rules and norms in particular, this methodological approach provided important IFI insights and has wider applicability for other research, allowing analysis 'beyond just the inputs and outputs' of institutions.[4] This adds to the significant methodological, theoretical, and empirical contributions this book makes to the fields of international affairs, feminist institutionalist research, globalising workplaces, and shrinking institutions. This chapter concludes by summarising the key findings, exploring the research ramifications, and highlighting suggested areas for further research.

The Big Lessons Learned

The overarching question of this book sought to get to the heart of *why women remain underrepresented in international affairs*, exploring the many nuances of gender inequality and detailed questions such as:

- Why are women underrepresented across the four agencies? What accounts for the variation in their underrepresentation among the agencies?
- Why are women underrepresented in international deployment? What accounts for the variation in their deployment among agencies?

- What explains the ratio of women in leadership positions in each agency? Why is leadership proportionate in some of the agencies but not in others?
- Why do women still experience gendered (and racialised, heteronormative, and so on) challenges despite international affairs seismic changes over recent decades (from globalisation and increased internationalisation of domestic departments, to the rise in gender equality mandates, norms, commitments, and leadership rebalancing)? Why are the challenges so homogenous across the agencies?

This book started by interrogating who gets chosen to represent the nation internationally and understanding why *right now* matters. The international affairs context is in many ways increasingly feminist, from the explicit feminist foreign policy of Sweden to stealthy attempts at an Australian feminist foreign policy orientation. Women are verging on parity for the first time ever in international affairs. Whilst COVID-19 has led to some regressions for diverse women across the globe, it has also demonstrated convincingly the ways in which women's leadership is essential and valued at this level of international relations.

In the past, a focus on singular actors or institutions has proven interesting, if not entirely useful for understanding the breadth and depth of women's continued underrepresentation now. Therefore, not only is the focus on institutions an important lens for understanding women's underrepresentation, but so is comparison across multiple sites and pushing the feminist institutionalist literature a step further to incorporate intersectionality and the layering of inequality more holistically. This has allowed the book to address the lack of in-depth qualitative and quantitative research on gender in international affairs representation and leadership, and pioneer new frameworks for analysis beyond the narrow corridors of diplomacy.

Indeed, one of this book's original contributions is developed in Chapter 2 from FI theory and insights gained during an initial round of background interviews, informing development of (a) an intersectional feminist institutionalist (IFI) approach, (b) a framework for analysing *international* institutions, and (c) an approach to studying the evolution of inequalities and institutional change. The IFI approach has highlighted the salience of centring gender in analysis, but not at the expense of everything else (race, ethnicity, class, ability, rural or regional background, religion, and so on). The framework for studying *international* institutions has wider currency beyond international affairs, for all kinds of globalising workplaces. It highlights four main sites as salient to understanding gender and institutions: the field, home, and host society contexts, the agency or organisational context, and individual (and often familial) contexts. Finally, the prism through which to understand institutional change is considered, firstly in the context of 'shrinking' institutions (and rising women's representation), secondly in the context of general changes witnessed in any institution over time, and thirdly in the context of the evolution of inequalities. This theme of inequalities' evolution describes the notion that inequality itself is not static but can evolve as other things around it evolve. This perspective advocates for an understanding that eliminating or even reducing gender (and other) inequalities may not be possible. However, inequalities can, and do, change. The task is to recognise how, and account for it in the process of formal and informal policies, strategies, behaviours, and procedures.

The methodological considerations of this book have been equally important and explored in Chapter 3. The book has sought to do justice to both the women interviewed and their agencies, whilst provoking a critical appraisal and reflection around formal and informal challenges that persist. My desire to be a critical feminist friend to the agencies studied was at times a difficult line to walk yet proved effective in aligning the emancipatory goals of feminist research with agency aims, as well as gaining access, navigating 'elite' institutions, extending findings beyond a single case, and unpacking similarities and differences through four very different agencies. My methodological choices have produced substantive original findings that are both theoretically rigorous and empirically robust and allow space for further research.

By exploring historical forces in Chapter 4, institutional 'stickiness' and resistance to change was found across all the agencies studied, despite the increasing proportions of women in the agencies. As one of the first concerted efforts to map the evolution of continued inequalities, the chapter demonstrated that gendered challenges endured, shifting in shape, but not necessarily nature. Critical actors were highlighted as important for advocating for gendered change; however, several cases demonstrated that even critical actors met resistance from pre-existing 'old' gendered rules and norms. This highlighted a continuing predominance of informal rules that guided these agencies' cultures, and the weight that historical legacies still have over contemporary institutions.

By unpacking *who* was given the opportunity to represent the state internationally in Chapter 5, it became clear that gender, race, ethnicity, sexuality, class, and other core factors of individuals' lives and background intersect in a multiplicative and complex manner. Rules exist around who can represent Australia overseas, with women of colour and those from sexually diverse backgrounds least represented. Progress for women is being made; however, this chapter reinforced the importance that we ensure straight, white, male bodies are not simply replaced by straight, white, female bodies in international affairs.

This became more crucial to understand in the following chapter, Chapter 6, which identified the deceptive nature of measuring women's progress only by their representation in leadership. While hierarchy and militaristic structuring has resulted in the marginalisation of some women from international affairs positions, the (1) benefits of structured opportunities and (2) visibility of gendered rules acted as a positive for women in the more militaristic and paramilitaristic agencies. It was found that women in these agencies were most proportionally represented in leadership and internationally, as opposed to the more traditionally diplomatic agencies that demonstrated significant gaps between overall employment and leadership and international representation—gaps that endured over more than a 20–30 year period. It was not simply that all women, if employed by these more militaristic agencies, would be more likely to make it to leadership. However, they did have a proportionately higher chance of doing so than those in the other agencies studied. Women in more militaristic agencies demonstrated a kind of uniformity in that they were more likely to be single and these agencies attracted (or retained) women who more closely fit the masculine mould of representative. It was a significant finding that in Australia's premiere agency for international affairs, DFAT, women had both the lowest chance of gaining international leadership and the lowest chance of gaining SES representation (proportional to opportunity) out of all the agencies studied. Would these results repeat in other contexts? There is reason to suspect so, with Cassidy[5] highlighting that women's nominal representation has not necessarily substantively changed their seniority of representation. More research is encouraged.

In Chapter 7, the experiences of women in leadership and international representation highlighted how gendered institutions remained part of women's 'lived' experiences across multiple career stages, and also pre-, during and post- deployment. The return from posting was found to be a particularly challenging time for women, highlighting a gap in organisational support around the post-deployment phase and reinforcing the 'domestic' basis to many of the gendered challenges experienced. Overall, it was clear that international representation and leadership took more than a combination of skills and experiences; it also required a mental attitude and layered support systems that were foundational to women's success. The experience was described as 'isolating', 'lonely', 'exposed', a '24/7 job' that 'strains relationships' and 'at some point [just] becomes de-stabilising and absent'. Further, the opportunity to be able to represent Australia overseas remained subordinate to whether the opportunity was even possible, logistically, in the first place—with the field of international affairs remaining stubbornly reliant on externalising costs onto employees, their spouses, and their families.

From this deep perspective of women's experiences, it became increasingly clear that gendered 'rules of the game' are pervasively experienced in international affairs. Women's ability to be heard, valued, and seen was policed and enforced across the agencies, which had a flow on effect on the distribution of power and resources: not just their vertical segregation, but horizontal segregation internationally, across rank, position, and status. Through analysing these 'rules of the game' and what it meant to *be* an international representative, 'toxic' masculine norms and scripts came to the fore. Rather than the overt and easily recognisable forms of masculine dominance that were more predominant in Defence, the AFP and the enforcement branches of Home Affairs, more traditionally diplomatic agencies evidenced more 'genteel' types of gendered challenges or toxic masculinities and more covert forms of discrimination. The result is that the overall gendered nature of diplomacy or international affairs is not necessarily disappearing with women's increased representation, but rather changing.

Indeed, by tracing trend data and listening to, collecting, and analysing the narratives of the women participants, it was clear that the centres of power are shifting in international affairs. DFAT committed to the largest expansion of the diplomatic network in the past 40 years;[6] however, compared to the other three more enforcement- and security-based agencies, their funding and strategic importance were considerably diminished. Even though more women are reaching leadership, women remain a stubbornly marginalised majority, and further, women may be gaining representation in diplomacy just as the relative importance of 'soft' diplomacy undertaken by DFAT is decreasing in favour of security-led 'hard' forms of diplomacy. In fact, Defence, Home Affairs and the AFP all provided evidence that they were investing considerable time and energy into their own 'diplomatic' network, a reality of shifting political imperatives and policy decisions. This was demonstrated by the increased importance of Defence Attachés, expanded roles of the AFP internationally to SES roles and more jurisdictions, as well as more 'preventative' streams of work, and the amalgamation of most of Australia's top security and intelligence agencies under Home Affairs. There are several ramifications of this for other fields of research, including that a deeper analysis of shrinking institutions and gender representation is warranted. Are women making the most progress in institutions in decline? And is the feminisation of institutions behind their resourcing or strategic power declines, or is it that the decline in the institution has made it easier for women to gain purchase? These are just two questions that warrant further analysis.

The core answers to this book's research question of why women remain underrepresented (and unequal) in leadership are explored in Chapter 8. Six core novel and surprising findings were identified. These included findings mentioned earlier around the militaristic-diplomatic nature of agencies: that despite the impressive gains made by the more traditionally diplomatic, nonuniformed agencies, more militaristic and paramilitaristic agencies tended to represent women more proportionally, inverting conventional theory on gender and militaries. Further, covert forms of 'genteel' toxic masculinity and gendered norms were found to dominate diplomacy, with more traditionally diplomatic agencies more likely to evidence covert informal gendered challenges that were often obscured and rendered invisible by progress made. Combined with a diplomatic glass cliff that sees women's functional power in leadership constrained by the shrinking or stagnating state of diplomacy, there are wider, worrying trends at play for gender and diplomacy research. I argued that because of the overreliance on women's historical unpaid labour and the consistent devaluing of women's work, women were expected to produce what seemed to be double the output with half the resources. Whilst women with female partners may have been best equipped, logistically, to handle the double burden of diplomatic work, they were also most affected by institutionalised heteronormativity and homophobia in the field. I also argued that while informal and formal rules existed across multiple sites from home to host country and the diplomatic workplace, agencies themselves remain the core enforcers of gendered institutions, leading domestic factors to be the most significant to women's experiences internationally. Finally, I found that women's experiences were relatively homogenous across agencies due to overriding norms and the homogenising effect of representing 'Team Australia' abroad. This indicates that the gendered elements of international affairs have far broader implications than the literature has thus far acknowledged.

IFI theory was applied to the findings from the previous chapters to underline that women remain underrepresented in Australian international affairs due to (1) the historical legacy of gendered (raced, and so on) institutions, (2) the layering and duplication of challenges, and (3) the compounding effect of rules at different stages of individuals' careers, posting cycles and lives. The data finds a field teeming with gendered institutions that require depths of resilience and extra support structures for women to flourish—and despite challenges, some do.

Implications for Global Affairs

Ultimately, international affairs institutions shoulder a significant task in upholding states' values, maintaining sovereignty, and reinforcing national interest. They also shoulder the increased burden of fulfilling international agreements and commitments around the Women, Peace and Security (WPS) agenda, Convention on the Elimination of All Forms of Discrimination Against Women (CEDAW), and calls for gender and other forms of equality globally. And in contexts like Australia, the US, the UK, Canada, or Sweden, for instance, democratic ideals of equality, opportunity, and genuine representation in leadership further press states to do better—in cases as explicit parts of a feminist or First Nations foreign policy agenda.

In these nations, the underrepresentation of women in international affairs could be said to be problematised by both moral and strategic reasons. Morally, women's underrepresentation undermines the representative nature of these states' democracy and national interests overseas.[7] Strategically, states lose out on the benefits women's equal contribution to international relations decision-making.[8] Of the Australian case, Cass and Rubenstein state: 'In light of Australia's international obligations and the growing international focus on the under representation of women in public life, any deficiency in the Australian constitutional system of representative democracy is unsatisfactory'.[9]

Legitimacy is therefore particularly salient in international affairs,[10] where the key roles of actors are to represent the state and its interests authentically and without exception. While typically foreign policy has not been a major electoral issue, with ministers not traditionally expected to 'look like' their constituents, Conley Tyler[11] argues that citizens, perhaps increasingly, expect that public-facing agencies should reflect the community that they represent. This is as true for the US, with leaders like Alexandria Ocasio-Cortez pushing more authentic styles of representation, as it is for Australia or Canada or the UK or beyond, where the need for public sector agencies to better reflect the communities they serve has been highlighted by everyone from Royal Commissions to incumbent and opposition governments, major policy upheavals and more. As Byrne, Conley Tyler, and Harris Rimmer state: 'A diverse service is likely to be viewed more favourably by domestic constituencies, and more credibly in the eyes of regional and global stakeholders and interlocutors'.[12]

Indeed, Conley Tyler[13] argues that women and other marginalised groups' representation in diplomacy results in improved function and better representation. Peace processes that include women have a 20 per cent increase in the probability of the agreement lasting at least two years, and 35 per cent increase in an agreement lasting at least 15 years.[14] Women are instrumental to peace resolution in conflict situations and are often key in preventing international disputes escalating to armed conflict.[15] Women contribute to global gross domestic product and have a key role to play in international economic engagement and integration.[16] Women are vital to ensuring that issues of environmental degradation, climate change, bio-warfare, pandemics, and threats of terror are addressed, and solutions are found.[17] Because higher levels of domestic gender inequality are associated with higher levels of inter-state violence,[18] women's greater gender equality is imperative to outcomes on measures of national security and stability.[19]

As Secretary of State, Hillary Clinton made history by enshrining women as a cornerstone of foreign policy, concluding that 'the subjugation of women is a direct threat to the security of the United States'.[20] With global violence and conflict costing an estimated US$14.3 trillion, women's inclusion in international affairs leadership goes beyond moral imperatives to pragmatic and strategic decision-making.[21] Ultimately, since government makes the laws concerning employment standards, including affirmative action and gender equality, the government, as an employer, is under pressure to deliver on these policies and practices itself.

Where to From Here?

This book has considered the gendered, racialised, heteronormative, and other ways in which institutions operate in international affairs yet represents just the start of where future research could go. Placing this study within a predominantly Australian case context has helped to understand how little has changed even within some of our leading cases internationally. However, there is more scope to understand the generalisability of findings to wider international affairs, other case contexts or indeed other more globalising fields of work. While the sample size for the study represents the largest qualitative research on the topic in Australia to date, it is restricted to the agencies studied, and in some cases, the portfolios or divisions participants were drawn from. Given these limitations, a key area for further research includes extending the framework to a wider range of international affairs agencies, particularly in other security and intelligence fields. Such agencies would be expected to have a high degree of invisibility, and perhaps even lack of accountability, around gendered institutions due to the inherently 'secretive' and classified nature of their work. More research is needed around the achievement of targets, and what substantive affects this has on women in international affairs. Further research directions also include the experiences of LGBTI + and CALD diplomats and attachés, recognising the paucity of research globally on these topics.

The impact of women leaders in international affairs should also be considered—is the increase in women's leadership in Australian international affairs leading to more feminist policymaking, and how lasting is the effect of these moves for gender equality? How important is leadership, and politics, to the status of women in international affairs? Additionally, research is needed on the gendered impacts of the shift from 'soft' to 'hard' forms of diplomacy and international affairs, the securitisation of international affairs, and the ramifications of rising forms of police-led and military diplomacy particularly as they relate to gender.

Theoretical gaps are also identified. Further sites of research include analysis of the effect of the layering of regressive gendered institutions, as well as understanding how institutions may be racialised or explicitly racist, and heteronormative, as well as gendered—in essence, the testing, application, and extension of the IFI framework to other fields and forms of research. Exploring the wider prevalence of women's progress in shrinking institutions is also warranted, and understanding institutional change and inequalities evolution presents many fruitful future directions for research.

Final Thoughts

Thinking about the ways in which inequalities evolve may be a somewhat depressing undertaking, whether you are studying international affairs or anything else. Yet the concept creates a new standard for analysing inequalities, not just in tracing their increase or demise, but in tracking the 'hows' and 'whys' of their adaptation. Whilst the scorecard for Australian international affairs institutions is mixed, there are some pockets of progress that are worth supporting and further resourcing. Additionally, we remain at this crucial moment in international affairs: just *before* parity in leadership is achieved. Indeed, as has been reinforced through this book, women verge on parity in international leadership for the first time in history. And there is considerable cause for optimism because more is known—about these agencies and the way that gender affects experiences in international affairs—than ever before. Given that the visibility of challenges has been a key theme throughout this book, there is hope that the findings of this book and future research will help to change the narrative on women's experiences and the gendered institutions that remain.

From sitting perched in the Consul General's home on the hillside of Hong Kong, surveying a depressed landscape for women's leadership globally, to my research office across from Australia's diplomatic headquarters in Canberra, the world has already irrevocably shifted. Global challenges are rising, and it is no longer enough to continue with business as usual. International affairs, like other fields across the world, requires innovative solutions, real talent, and flexibility. The need for comprehensive, durable, and adaptable decision-making represents an enormous opportunity for our globe—and for women.

Yet as long as gendered challenges continue to impede women's inclusion in international affairs, this damages states' abilities to accurately determine and maintain state sovereignty, as well as represent and decide on matters of national interest. Institutions provide a way for transforming knowledge into action, and more intersectional approaches to international affairs have much to offer in the way of not just addressing gender inequalities, but racial and other axes of inequality too. Ultimately, decisions made at the national level about who represents the state affect the quality of international decision-making. This permeates international contexts where gender equality is increasingly seen to legitimate governments and their actions internationally.[22] Leaders at this level act as the filter through which all international decisions are communicated, assessed, implemented, and evaluated.

Who leads, matters.

Notes

Chapter 1

1. Interview: Grace, DFAT, 5 October, 2018.
2. United Nations Security Council (2020), Report of the Secretary-General on Women Peace and Security, para. 15.
3. A. Towns and B. Niklasson, 'Gender, International Status, and Ambassador Appointments', *Foreign Policy Analysis* 13, no. 3 (2017): 521–540.
4. C. Blanco, 'From Cairns to Madrid: The First Female Indigenous Ambassador Takes her Charm to Spain', *SBS Spanish*, 22 April 2020, https://www.sbs.com.au/language/english/from-cairns-to-madrid-the-first-female-indigenous-ambassador-takes-her-charm-to-spain.
5. V. Hudson and P. Leidl, *The Hillary Doctrine: Sex & American Foreign Policy* (New York: Columbia University Press, 2015).
6. D. Cass and K. Rubenstein, 'Representation/s of Women in the Australian Constitutional System', *Adelaide Law Review* 17, no. 1 (1995): 3–48.
7. UN Women 2021, *Facts and Figures: Women's Leadership and Political Participation*, last updated 7 March 2023, https://www.unwomen.org/en/what-we-do/leadership-and-political-participation/facts-and-figures.
8. A. Wittenberg-Cox, 'The Best Defense? How About More Women in the Military?', Forbes, 30 April 2020, https://www.forbes.com/sites/avivahwittenbergcox/2020/04/30/the-best-defense-how-about-more-women-in-the-military/?sh=44bd0dd87bdc.
9. C. Enloe, *Bananas, Beaches and Bases: Making Feminist Sense of International Politics*, updated edition (Berkeley: University of California Press, 2014).
10. Interview: Jenny, AFP, 1 February 2019.
11. R. Connell, *Short Introductions: Gender* (Cambridge: Polity Press, 2009).
12. See for instance Enloe, *Bananas, Beaches and Bases*.
13. See for instance N. McGlen and M. Sarkees, *Women in Foreign Policy: The Insiders* (New York: Routledge, 1993).
14. R. Tanter, 'Tightly Bound: The United States and Australia's Alliance-Dependent Militarization', *The Asia-Pacific Journal* 16, no. 11 (2018): 1–8; M. Vanderwerdt-Holman, 'The Fix: How to Rebuild Australia's Diplomatic Capacity', *Australian Foreign Affairs* (2021).
15. Australian Public Service Commission, Women, accessed 7 July 2017, https://catalogue.nla.gov.au/catalog/4740358.
16. Ethnic Communities' Council of Victoria, 'Fact, Australia is the most ethnically diverse country in the world', media release, 29 June 2017.
17. Towns and Niklasson, 'Gender, International Status, and Ambassador Appointments'.
18. Department of Foreign Affairs and Trade, Australian Ambassadors and Other Representatives, accessed 2 March 2018, http://dfat.gov.au/about-us/our-people/homs/Pages/australian-ambassadors-and-other-representatives.aspx.

19. Department of Defence, *Women in the ADF Report*, accessed 14 November 2021, https://www.defence.gov.au/AnnualReports/.
20. L. Chappell and F. Mackay, 'What's in a Name? Mapping the Terrain of Informal Institutions and Gender Politics,' in *Gender and Informal Institutions*, ed. G. Waylen (London: Rowman & Littlefield International, 2017); F. Mackay, M. Kenny, and L. Chappell, 'New Institutionalism Through a Gender Lens: Towards a Feminist Institutionalism?', *International Political Science Review*, 31, no. 5 (2010): 580.
21. L. Chappell, *The Politics of Gender Justice at the International Criminal Court: Legacies and Legitimacy* (New York: Oxford University Press, 2016), 3.
22. J. Cornut, 'Diplomacy in Liquid Modernity', paper presented at Diplomacy in liquid modernity: Disruption and transformation of diplomatic practices workshop, Asia-Pacific College of Diplomacy at ANU, Canberra, Australia, 20 February, 2019; J. Cornut and S. Harris Rimmer, 'The liquidification of international politics and Trump's (un)diplomacy on Twitter', *International Politics* 59, no. 2 (2022): 367–382.
23. Z. Bauman, *Liquid Modernity* (Cambridge: Polity Press, 2000).
24. Bauman, *Liquid Modernity*.
25. M. Angrosino, *Doing Ethnographic and Observational Research* (Thousand Oaks, CA: Sage Publishing, 2007), 1.
26. K. Aggestam and A. Towns, 'The Gender Turn in Diplomacy: A New Research Agenda', *International Feminist Journal of Politics* 21, no. 1 (2019): 9–28.
27. S. Rossetti, 'Changes for Diplomacy Under the Lens of Feminist Neo-Institutional Theory: The Case for Australia', *The Hague Journal of Diplomacy* 10, no. 3 (2015): 286.
28. N. Adler, 'Global Leadership: Women Leaders', *Management International Review* 37 (1997): 176.
29. M. Conley Tyler, E. Blizzard, and B. Crane, 'Is International Affairs Too 'Hard' for Women? Explaining the Missing Women in Australia's International Affairs', *Australian Journal of International Affairs* 68, no. 2 (2014): 156–176; Elizabeth Broderick & Co., *Cultural Change: Gender Diversity and Inclusion in the Australian Federal Police*, 2016, https://www.afp.gov.au/sites/default/files/PDF/Reports/Cultural-Change-Report-2016.pdf; J. Westendorf and R. Strating, 'Women in Australian International Affairs', *Australian Journal of International Affairs* 74, no. 4 (2020): 1–15.
30. Westendorf and Strating, 'Women in Australian International Affairs'; M. Dee and F. Volk, *Women with a Mission: Personal Perspectives* (Canberra: Commonwealth of Australia, 2007).
31. Department of Foreign Affairs and Trade, Australian Ambassadors and Other Representatives, accessed 2 March 2017, http://dfat.gov.au/about-us/our-people/homs/Pages/australian-ambassadors-and-other-representatives.aspx; Australian Public Service Commission, Women, accessed 7 July 2017, http://www.apsc.gov.au/about-the-apsc/parliamentary/state-of-the-service/sosr-2012-13/chapter-five/women.
32. See Australian Human Rights Commission 2014, Review into the Treatment of Women in the Australian Defence Force: Audit Report, accessed 19 March 2020, https://www.humanrights.gov.au/sites/default/files/document/publication/adf-audit-2014.pdf; Australian Human Rights Commission 2013, Review into the Treatment of Women at the Australian Defence Force Academy: Audit Report, accessed 19 March 2020, https://www.humanrights.gov.au/sites/default/files/document/publication/adf-audit-2014.pdf; Australian Human Rights Commission 2012, Review into the Treatment of Women in the Australian Defence Force: Phase 2 Report, accessed 11 July 2017, http://defencereview.humanrights.

gov.au/sites/default/files/adf-complete.pdf; Australian Human Rights Commission 2011, Review into the Treatment of Women at the Australian Defence Force Academy, accessed 19 March 2020, https://defence.humanrights.gov.au/sites/default/files/ADFA_2011.pdf.
33. Strategic Research and Communications Division, Women in Leadership in Department of Home Affairs as at 31 December 2018, unpublished raw data; Strategic Research and Communications Division 2018, Department of Immigration and Border Protection A-Based Positions at 12 December 2017, unpublished raw data.
34. Commonwealth of Australia, 2017 Foreign Policy White Paper, accessed 31 December 2017, https://www.fpwhitepaper.gov.au/foreign-policy-white-paper, 43.
35. Australian Public Service Commission, Gender Equality, accessed 16 March 2020, https://www.apsc.gov.au/gender-equality.
36. K. Lee-Koo, 'Pro-Gender Foreign Policy by Stealth: Navigating Global and Domestic Politics in Australian Foreign Policy Making', *Foreign Policy Analysis* 16, no. 2 (2020): 236–249, 236.
37. Lowy Institute, Foreign Territory: Women in International Relations, accessed 9 April 2020, https://www.lowyinstitute.org/sites/default/files/CAVE%20et%20al_Foreign%20territory_Women%20in%20international%20relations.pdf.
38. Embassy Magazine, Women Envoys on the Rise, accessed 9 September 2016, https://embassymagazine.com/women-envoys-on-the-rise/; Towns and Niklasson, 'Gender, International Status, and Ambassador Appointments'.
39. Australian Public Service Commission 2022, State of the Service Report 2021–2022, https://www.apsc.gov.au/working-aps/state-of-service-reports.
40. Westendorf and Strating, 'Women in Australian International Affairs'.
41. Conley Tyler, Blizzard, and Crane, 'Is International Affairs Too "Hard" for Women?'.
42. Public Service & Merit Protection Commission 2001, State of the Service Report, Commonwealth of Australia, https://catalogue.nla.gov.au/catalog/2202451; Australian Public Service Commission, Gender Equality, accessed 16 March 2020, https://www.apsc.gov.au/gender-equality.
43. M. Evans, M. Edwards, B. Burmester, and D. May, '"Not Yet 50/50"—Barriers to the Progress of Senior Women in the Australian Public Service', *Australian Journal of Public Administration* 73, no. 4 (2015): 501–510.
44. Pew Research Centre, 'Despite Global Concerns About Democracy, More Than Half of Countries are Democratic', 14 May 2019, https://www.pewresearch.org/fact-tank/2019/05/14/more-than-half-of-countries-are-democratic/.
45. The Legislative Assembly for the Australian Capital Territory, *The Westminster System*, accessed 14 November 2021, https://www.parliament.act.gov.au/visit-and-learn/resources/factsheets/the-westminster-system#:~:text=The%20Westminster%20system%20is%20a,based%20on%20the%20Westminster%20system.
46. J. Thomson, 'The Growth of Feminist (?) Foreign Policy', *E-International Relations*, 10 February 2020, https://www.e-ir.info/2020/02/10/the-growth-of-feminist-foreign-policy/.
47. M. Conley Tyler and R. Jheengun, 'Women in Diplomacy in Asia', *Australian Institute of International Affairs*, 8 March 2020.
48. C. Ramanazoglu and J. Holland, *Feminist Methodology: Challenges and Choices* (Thousand Oaks, CA: Sage Publishing, 2002), 155; L. Chappell and F. Mackay, 'Feminist Critical Friends: Dilemmas of Feminist Engagement with Governance and Gender Reform Agendas', *European Journal of Politics and Gender* 4, no. 3 (2020): 321–340.

49. Aggestam and Towns, 'The Gender Turn in Diplomacy'; S. Harris Rimmer, 'Women as Makers of International Law: Towards Feminist Diplomacy', in *Research Handbook on Feminist Engagement with International Law*, ed. S. Harris Rimmer and K. Ogg (Cheltenham: Edward Elgar, 2019), 26–43; E. Bjarnegård and M. Kenny, 'Who, Where and How? Informal Institutions in the Third Generation of Research on Gendered Dynamics of Political Recruitment', in *Gender and Informal Institutions*, ed. G. Waylen (London: Rowman & Littlefield International, 2017), 203–222; L. Chappell, 'Comparative Gender and Institutions: Directions for Research', *Symposium* 8, no. 1 (2010): 183–189.
50. Plassnik in General Assembly of the United Nations 2008, para 2.
51. Interview: Julia Gillard, 21 May 2019.
52. C. Byrne, M. Conley Tyler, and S. Harris Rimmer, 'Australian Diplomacy Today', *Australian Journal of International Affairs* 70, no. 6 (2016): 587.
53. B. Ackerly and J. True, 'Studying the Struggles and Wishes of the Age: Feminist Theoretical Methodology and Feminist Theoretical Methods', in *Feminist Methodologies for International Relations*, ed. B. Ackerly, M. Stern, and J. True (Cambridge: Cambridge University Press, 2006), 252.
54. Rossetti, 'Changes for Diplomacy Under the Lens of Feminist Neo-Institutional Theory'; McGlen and Sarkees, *Women in Foreign Policy*.
55. A. Wyse and T. Vilkinas, 'Executive Leadership Roles in the Australian Public Service', *Women in Management Review* 19, no. 4 (2004): 205–211; Harris Rimmer, 'Women as Makers of International Law'; J. Cassidy, *Gender and Diplomacy* (New York: Routledge, 2017); Towns and Niklasson, 'Gender, International Status, and Ambassador Appointments'.
56. G. Banks, 'Evidence-Based Policy Making: What Is It? How Do We Get It?', presented at ANU Public Lecture Series, Productivity Commission, 4 February 2009, https://www.pc.gov.au/__data/assets/pdf_file/0003/85836/cs20090204.pdf.
57. Chappell and Mackay, 'Feminist Critical Friends'.

Chapter 2

1. Interview: Julie Bishop, 3 April 2019.
2. J. A. Tickner, *Gender in International Relations: Feminist Perspectives on Achieving Global Security* (New York: Columbia University Press, 1992), 3.
3. E. Blanchard, 'Gender, International Relations, and the Development of Feminist Security Theory' *Signs* 28, no. 4 (2003): 1289–1312.
4. C. Enloe, *Bananas, Beaches and Bases: Making Feminist Sense of International Politics*, updated edition (Berkeley: University of California Press, 2014).
5. G. Waylen, 'What Can Historical Institutionalism Offer Feminist Institutionalists?', *Politics & Gender* 5, no. 2 (2009): 246.
6. J. G. March and J. P. Olsen, 'The New Institutionalism: Organisational Factors in Political Life', *The American Political Science Review* 78, no. 2 (1984): 734–749.
7. E. Ostrom, 'Institutional Rational Choice: An Assessment of the Institutional Analysis and Development Framework', in *Theories of the Public Policy Process*, ed. P. Sabatier (Oxford: Westview Press, 1999), 21–64.
8. V. Schmidt, 'Taking Ideas and Discourse Seriously: Explaining Change Through Discursive Institutionalism as the Fourth 'New Institutionalism'', *European Political Science Review* 2, no. 1 (2010): 1–25. V. Schmidt, 'Discursive Institutionalism: The Explanatory Power of Ideas and Discourse', *Annual Review of Political Science* 11 (2008): 303–326.

9. P. DiMaggio and W. Powell, *The New Institutionalism in Organisational Analysis* (Chicago: University of Chicago Press, 1991).
10. K. Thelen, 'Historical Institutionalism in Comparative Politics', *Annual Review of Political Science* 2 (1999): 386.
11. P. A. Hall and R. C. R. Taylor, 'Political Science and the Three New Institutionalisms', *Political Studies* 44, no. 5 (1996): 947.
12. J. G. March and J. P. Olsen, *Rediscovering Institutions: The Organisational Basis of Politics* (New York: The Free Press, 1989), 161.
13. S. Steinmo, K. Thelen and F. Longstreth (eds.), *Structuring Politics: Historical Institutionalism in Comparative Analysis* (New York: Cambridge University Press, 1992).
14. J. Thomson, 'Resisting Gendered Change: Feminist Institutionalism and Critical Actors', *International Political Science Review* 39, no. 2 (2018): 178–191.
15. F. Mackay, M. Kenny, and L. Chappell, 'New Institutionalism Through a Gender Lens: Towards a Feminist Institutionalism?', *International Political Science Review* 31, no. 5 (2010): 580.
16. L. Chappell, *Gendering Government: Feminist Engagement with the State in Australia and Canada* (Vancouver: University of British Colombia Press, 2002).
17. S. Leach and V. Lowndes, 'Of Roles and Rules: Analysing the Changing Relationship between Political Leaders and Chief Executives in Local Government', *Public Policy and Administration* 22, no. 2 (2007): 183–200.
18. V. Lowndes, 'How Are Things Done Around Here? Uncovering Institutional Rules and Their Gendered Effects', *Politics and Gender* 10, no. 4 (2014): 686.
19. L. Chappell and F. Mackay, 'What's in a Name? Mapping the Terrain of Informal Institutions and Gender Politics', in *Gender and Informal Institutions*, ed. G. Waylen (London: Rowman & Littlefield International, 2017), 23–45.
20. G. Helmke and S. Levitksy, 'Informal Institutions and Comparative Politics: A Research Agenda', *Perspectives on Politics* 2, no. 4 (2004): 725–740.
21. M. Andrew, 'Women's Movement Institutionalisation: The Need for New Approaches', *Politics and Gender* 6, no. 4 (2010): 609–616.
22. G. Waylen (ed.), *Gender and Informal Institutions* (London: Rowman & Littlefield International, 2017.
23. M. Kenny, *Gender and Political Recruitment: Theorising Institutional Change* (London: Palgrave Macmillan, 2013).
24. J. Piscopo, 'Leveraging Informality, Rewriting Formal Rules: The Implementation of Gender Parity in Mexico', in *Gender and Informal Institutions*, ed. G. Waylen (London: Rowman and Littlefield International, 2017), 137–160.
25. J. Thomson, 'Resisting Gendered Change: Feminist Institutionalism and Critical Actors', *International Political Science Review* 39, no. 2 (2018): 178–191; S. Nazneen, 'Negotiating Gender Equity in a Clientelist State: The Role of Informal Networks in Bangladesh', in *Gender and Informal Institutions*, ed. G. Waylen (London: Rowman and Littlefield International, 2017), 161–182; L. Chappell, 'Conflicting Institutions and the Search for Gender Justice at the International Criminal Court', *Political Research Quarterly* 67, no. 1 (2014): 183–196; F. Mackay, 'Nested Newness, Institutional Innovation, and the Gendered Limits of Change', *Politics & Gender* 10, no. 4 (2014): 549–571.
26. Kenny, *Gender and Political Recruitment*.
27. Kenny, *Gender and Political Recruitment*, 175.
28. Interview: 30 November 2019.

29. G. Waylen, 'Informal Institutions, Institutional Change, and Gender Equality', *Political Research Quarterly* 67, no. 1 (2014): 212–223.
30. Waylen, 'Informal Institutions, Institutional Change, and Gender Equality', 219.
31. J. Thomson, 'Resisting Gendered Change: Feminist Institutionalism and Critical Actors', *International Political Science Review* 39, no. 2 (2018): 178–191.
32. Australian Public Service Commission, *Capability Review: Department of Foreign Affairs and Trade* (Canberra: Australian Government Publishing Service, 2013).
33. L. Chappell, 'Conflicting Institutions and the Search for Gender Justice at the International Criminal Court', *Political Research Quarterly* 67, no. 1 (2014): 184.
34. Chappell, 'Conflicting Institutions and the Search for Gender Justice', 193.
35. L. Chappell and G. Waylen, 'Gender and the Hidden Life of Institutions', *Public Administration* 91, no. 3 (2013): 612.
36. V. Hudson and P. Leidl, *The Hillary Doctrine: Sex & American Foreign Policy* (New York: Columbia University Press, 2015), 62.
37. J. Halley, P. Kotiswaran, H. Shamir, and C. Thomas, 'From the International to the Local in Feminist Responses to Rape, Prostitution/Sex Work, and Sex Trafficking: Four Studies in Contemporary Governance Feminism', *Harvard Journal of Law and Gender* 29, no. 2 (2006): 335–423.
38. V. Hughes, 'Women, Gender and Canadian Foreign Policy, 1909–2009', *British Journal of Canadian Studies* 23, no. 2 (2010): 159–178; G. Wilson, 'Inuit Diplomacy in the Circumpolar North', *Canadian Foreign Policy Journal* 13, no. 3 (2007): 65–80; C. Sjolander, 'Canadian Foreign Policy: Does Gender Matter?', *Canadian Foreign Policy Journal* 12, no. 1 (2005): 19–31; D. Steinstra, *Women's Movements and International Organisations* (New York: St Martin's Press, 1994).
39. J. True, 'Normalising Gender in Global Governance', paper presented at Gender in International Governance Conference, Graduate Institute for International Development Studies, Geneva, October 2010, 2.
40. Halley et al., 'From the International to the Local'.
41. True, 'Normalising Gender in Global Governance'.
42. R. Keohane, 'Beyond Dichotomy: Conversations Between International Relations and Feminist Theory', *International Studies Quarterly* 42, no. 1 (1998): 197.
43. True, 'Normalising Gender in Global Governance'.
44. K. Crenshaw, 'Demarginalising the Intersection of Race and Sex: A Black Feminist Critique of Antidiscrimination Doctrine, Feminist Theory and Antiracist Politics', *University of Chicago Legal Forum* 1989, no. 1 (1989): 139–167.
45. J. Kantola and E. Lombardo, 'Feminist Political Analysis: Exploring Strengths, Hegemonies and Limitations', *Feminist Theory* 18, no. 3 (2017): 323–341. doi:https://doi.org/10.1177/1464700117721882
46. M. Hawkesworth, 'Congressional Enactments of Race-Gender: Toward a Theory of Raced-Gendered Institutions, *American Political Science Review* 97, no. 4 (2003): 529–550.
47. M. Verloo, P. Meier, S. Lauwers, and S. Martens, 'Putting Intersectionality into Practice in Different Configurations of Equality Architecture: Belgium and the Netherlands', *Social Politics: International Studies in Gender, State and Society* 19 (2012): 513–538.
48. M. Krook and M. Nugent, 'Intersectional Institutions: Representing Women and Ethnic Minorities in the British Labour Party', *Party Politics* 22, no. 5 (2016): 612.
49. Krook and Nugent, 'Intersectional Institutions', 612.

50. L. Downing, 'The Body Politic: Gender, The Right Wing, and 'Identity Category Violations", *French Cultural Studies* 29, no. 4 (2018): 367–377.
51. J. Acker, 'Gendered Organisations and Intersectionality: Problems and Possibilities', *Equality, Diversity and Inclusion: An International Journal* 31, no. 3 (2012): 214–224.
52. A. Krizsan, H. Sjeie, and J. Squires, *Institutionalising Intersectionality: The Changing Nature of European Equality Regimes* (London: Palgrave Macmillan, 2012), 238.
53. C. Hermanin and J. Squires, 'Institutionalising Intersectionality in the 'Big Three': The Changing Equality Framework in France, Germany and Britain', in *Institutionalising Intersectionality: The Changing Nature of European Equality Regimes*, ed. A. Krizsan, J. Sjeie, and J. Squires (London: Palgrave Macmillan, 2012), 89–118.
54. M. Conley Tyler, 'Diversity and Diplomacy', *Australian Journal of International Affairs* 70, no. 6 (2016): 695–709; E. Stephenson, 'Invisible While Visible: An Australian Perspective on Queer Women Leaders in International Affairs', *European Journal of Politics and Gender* 3, no. 3 (2020): 427–443.
55. I. B. Neumann, *At Home with the Diplomats: Inside a European Foreign Ministry* (Ithaca, NY: Cornell University Press, 2012); I. B. Neumann, 'The Body of the Diplomat', *European Journal of International Relations* 14, no. 4 (2008): 671–695.
56. M. Budig, M. Lim, and M. Hodges, 'Racial and Gender Pay Disparities: The Role of Education', *Social Science Research* 98 (August 2021). doi:https://doi.org/10.1016/j.ssresearch.2021.102580
57. J. Dammeyer and M. Chapman, 'A National Survey on Violence and Discrimination Among People with Disabilities', *BMC Public Health* 18, no. 1 (2018).
58. C. Douglas, 'Lesbians in Heterosexist Institutions', *Off Our Backs* 13, no. 8 (1983); 1.
59. A. Krizsan, H. Sjeie, and J. Squires, *Institutionalising Intersectionality: The Changing Nature of European Equality Regimes* (London: Palgrave Macmillan, 2012), 209.
60. Waylen, 'Informal Institutions, Institutional Change, and Gender Equality'.
61. C. Ragin, 'Comparative Methods', in *The SAGE Handbook of Social Science Methodology*, ed. W. Outhwaite and S. Turner (Thousand Oaks, CA: Sage Publishing, 2011), 67–81; C. Ragin, *The Comparative Method: Moving Beyond Qualitative and Quantitative Strategies* (Berkeley: University of California Press, 1987), 23–33.
62. E. Bjarnegård and M. Kenny, 'Who, Where and How? Informal Institutions in the Third Generation of Research on Gendered Dynamics of Political Recruitment', in *Gender and Informal Institutions*, ed. G. Waylen (London: Rowman & Littlefield International, 2017), 203–222.
63. Waylen, *Gender and Informal Institutions*.
64. Mackay, Kenny, and Chappell, 'New Institutionalism Through a Gender Lens'.
65. J. Cornut, 'Diplomacy in Liquid Modernity', paper presented at Diplomacy in Liquid Modernity: Disruption and Transformation of Diplomatic Practices workshop, Asia-Pacific College of Diplomacy at ANU, Canberra, Australia, 20 February 2019.
66. Z. Bauman, *Liquid Modernity* (Cambridge: Polity Press, 2000).
67. D. North, *Institutions, Institutional Change and Economic Performance* (Cambridge: Cambridge University Press, 1990), 94.
68. J. Pettman, 'Gendering International Relations', *Australian Journal of International Affairs* 47, no. 1 (1993): 47.
69. Pettman, 'Gendering International Relations', 47.
70. H. Charlesworth, C. Chinkin, and S. Wright, 'Feminist Approaches to International Law', *The American Journal of International Law* 85, no. 4 (1991): 613–645.

250 Notes

71. J. A. Tickner, *A Feminist Voyage Through International Relations* (New York: Oxford University Press, 2014); Tickner, *Gender in International Relations*.
72. Enloe, *Bananas, Beaches and Bases*.
73. C. Cohn, 'Sex and Death in the Rational World of Defense Intellectuals', *Signs* 12, no. 4 (1987): 687–718; D. Campbell, *Writing Security: United States Foreign Policy and the Politics of Identity* (Minneapolis: University of Minnesota Press, 1992).
74. L. Sjoberg, 'Gender, Structure and War: What Waltz Couldn't See', *International Theory* 4, no. 1 (2012): 1–38.
75. W. Danspeckgruber, 'Reflections on Women Leaders in International Relations', in *Women Leaders in International Relations and World Peace* (Princeton, NJ: Woodrow Wilson School of Public and International Affairs, 2010), 3–6.
76. B. Ackerly and J. True, 'Studying the Struggles and Wishes of the Age: Feminist Theoretical Methodology and Feminist Theoretical Methods', in *Feminist Methodologies for International Relations*, ed. B. Ackerly, M. Stern, and J. True (Cambridge: Cambridge University Press, 2006), 241–260.
77. A. M. Morin, 'Do Women Make Better Ambassadors? Study of 50 Years of Female Envoys Shows Gender Can Be an Advantage', *Foreign Service Journal* (December 1994): 26–30.
78. J. Shoemaker and M. L. Poire, 'Progress Report on Women in Peace and Security Careers: US Congressional Staffs', (Washington DC: Women in International Security, 2014).
79. J. Shoemaker and J. Park, 'Progress Report on Women in Peace & Security Careers: U.S. Executive Branch', (Washington DC: Women in International Security, 2010).
80. K. Aggestam and A. Towns, 'The Gender Turn in Diplomacy: A New Research Agenda', *International Feminist Journal of Politics* 21, no. 1 (2019): 9–28.
81. A. Towns and B. Niklasson, 'Gender, International Status, and Ambassador Appointments', *Foreign Policy Analysis* 13, no. 3 (2017): 521–540.
82. K. Niskanen and A. Nyberg (eds.), *Gender and Power in the Nordic Countries: Part II Summary Discussion and Analysis* (Oslo: Nordic Council of Ministers, 2010).
83. R. d. S. Farias and G. F. do Carmo, 'Brazilian Female Diplomats and the Struggle for Gender Equality', in *Gendering Diplomacy and International Negotiation. Studies in Diplomacy and International Relations*, ed. K. Aggestam and A. Towns (Cham: Palgrave Macmillan, 2018), 107–124.
84. M. A. Dewi and I. Rachmawati, 'Gender and Diplomacy: Practice and Challenge in Indonesia in the Covid-19 Pandemic Era', *Proceedings of the First International Conference on Democracy and Social Transformation*, 15 September 2021.
85. P. R. Flowers, 'Gender Representation in Japan's National and International Diplomacy', *The Hague Journal of Diplomacy*, 17, no. 3 (2022): 488–517.
86. B. Rumelili and R. Suleymanoglu-Kurum, 'Women and Gender in Turkish Diplomacy: Historical Legacies and Current Patterns', in *Gendering Diplomacy and International Negotiation*, ed. K. Aggestam and A. Towns (Cham: Palgrave Macmillan, 2017), 87–106.
87. S. Tolleson-Rinehart and S. Carroll, ' "Far From Ideal": The Gender Politics of Political Science', *American Political Science Review* 100, no. 4 (2006): 507–513; H. Smith and J. Cornut, 'The Status of Women in Canadian Foreign Policy Analysis', *Journal of Women, Politics & Policy* 37, no. 2 (2016): 217–233.
88. L. Chappell, *The Politics of Gender Justice at the International Criminal Court: Legacies and Legitimacy* (New York: Oxford University Press, 2016).

89. S. Rossetti, 'Changes for Diplomacy Under the Lens of Feminist Neo-Institutional Theory: The Case for Australia', *The Hague Journal of Diplomacy* 10, no. 3 (2015): 285–305.
90. E. Crapol, *Women and American Foreign Policy: Lobbyists, Critics and Insiders* (Westport, CT: Greenwood Press, 1987).
91. R. Jeffreys-Jones, *Changing Differences: Women and the Shaping of American Foreign Policy, 1917–1994* (New Brunswick, NJ: Rutgers University Press, 1995).
92. I. B. Neumann, *At Home with the Diplomats: Inside a European Foreign Ministry* (Ithaca, NY: Cornell University Press, 2012).
93. N. McGlen and M. Sarkees, *Women in Foreign Policy: The Insiders* (New York: Routledge, 1993).
94. Morin, 'Do Women Make Better Ambassadors?'
95. Towns and Niklasson, 'Gender, International Status, and Ambassador Appointments'.
96. B. Niklasson and A. Towns, 'Gender, Status and Ambassador Appointments to Militarised and Violent Countries', *Gender and Diplomacy*, ed. J. Cassidy (New York: Routledge, 2017), 100–119.
97. Niskanen and Nyberg, *Gender and Power in the Nordic Countries: Part II Summary Discussion and Analysis*.
98. S. Bashevkin, *Women as Foreign Policy Leaders: National Security and Gender Politics in Superpower America* (New York: Oxford University Press, 2018).
99. Towns and Niklasson, 'Gender, Status and Ambassador Appointments', 101.
100. McGlen and Sarkees, *Women in Foreign Policy*.
101. G. Duerst-Lahti, 'Gender, Power Relations in Public Bureaucracies', PhD diss., University of Wisconsin-Madison, 1987.
102. G. Powell, *Women and Men in Management* (Thousand Oaks, CA: Sage Publishing, 1988).
103. R. A. W. Rhodes and A. Tiernan, 'Executive Governance and its Puzzles', in *International Handbook of Public Administration and Governance*, ed. A. Massey and K. Miller (Cheltenham: Edward Elgar, 2014), 81–103.
104. Rossetti, 'Changes for Diplomacy Under the Lens of Feminist Neo-Institutional Theory', 285.
105. R. Connell, *Short Introductions: Gender* (Cambridge: Polity Press, 2009), 11.
106. F. Fukuyama, 'Women and the Evolution of World Politics', *Foreign Affairs* 77, no. 5 (1998): 27.
107. E. M. Edwards, 'Gender, International Relations, and the Development of Feminist Security Theory', *Signs* 28, no. 4 (2003): 1302.
108. Tickner, *Gender in International Relations*, 4, emphasis added.
109. Neumann, 'The Body of the Diplomat'.
110. Towns and Niklasson, 'Gender, International Status, and Ambassador Appointments'.
111. Enloe, *Bananas, Beaches and Bases*.
112. Tickner, *Gender in International Relations*, 2.
113. See, for instance H. McCarthy, *Women of the World: The Rise of the Female Diplomat* (London: Bloomsbury Publishing, 2015); Towns and Niklasson, 'Gender, International Status, and Ambassador Appointments'.
114. McCarthy, *Women of the World*.
115. Aggestam and Towns, 'The Gender Turn in Diplomacy', 6.
116. A. Eagly and Karau, 'Role Congruity Theory of Prejudice Toward Female Leaders', *Psychological Review* 109, no. 3 (2002): 573–398.
117. Tickner, *Gender in International Relations*, 2.

118. L. Boyce and A. Herd, 'The Relationship Between Gender Role Stereotypes and Requisite Military Leadership Characteristics', *Sex Roles* 49, nos. 7/8 (2003): 374.
119. Eagly and Karau, 'Role Congruity Theory of Prejudice Toward Female Leaders'.
120. Neumann, 'The Body of the Diplomat'.
121. Connell, *Short Introductions*.
122. M. L. Krook and F. Mackay, 'Introduction: Gender, Politics and Institutions', in *Gender, Politics and Institutions: Towards a Feminist Institutionalism*, ed. M. L. Krook and F. Mackay (Basingstoke: Palgrave Macmillan, 2011), 6.
123. Neumann, 'The Body of the Diplomat', 687.
124. Ibid., 688.
125. Ibid., 688.
126. Tickner, *A Feminist Voyage Through International Relations*.
127. M. Sawer, 'Housekeeping the State: Women and Parliamentary Politics in Australia', Papers on Parliament No. 17, accessed 15 January 2020, https://www.aph.gov.au/~/~/~/link.aspx?_id=4770FE53E2AC484480D2431A451B44C0&_z=z.
128. Ibid., 8.
129. Neumann, 'The Body of the Diplomat', 688.
130. M. Edwards, B. Burmester, M. Evans, M. Halupka, and D. May, 'Not Yet 50/50: Barriers to the Progress of Senior Women in the Australian Public Service', *ANZSOG Institute for Governance* (2013): 6.
131. See for instance Shoemaker and Park, 'Progress Report on Women in Peace & Security Careers'; Shoemaker and Poire, 'US Congressional Staffs'; J. Cassidy, *Gender and Diplomacy* (Routledge: New York, 2017).
132. Connell, *Short Introductions*; Cassidy, *Gender and Diplomacy*.
133. Neumann, 'The Body of the Diplomat'.
134. Shoemaker and Poire, 'US Congressional Staffs'.
135. Mackay, Kenny, and Chappell, 'New Institutionalism Through a Gender Lens'.
136. Morin, 'Do Women Make Better Ambassadors?'
137. S. Harris Rimmer, 'Women as Makers of International Law: Towards Feminist Diplomacy', in *Research Handbook on Feminist Engagement with International Law*, ed. S. Harris Rimmer and K. Ogg (Cheltenham: Edward Elgar, 2019), 26–43; S. Harris Rimmer, 'Women in Global Economic Governance: Scaling the Summits', in *Gender and Diplomacy*, ed. J. A. Cassidy (New York: Routledge, 2017), 140–169.
138. Morin 'Do Women Make Better Ambassadors?', 26.
139. Ibid., 27.
140. Ibid., 27.
141. J. Rost, *Leadership for the 21st Century* (New York: Praeger, 1991).
142. Morin 'Do Women Make Better Ambassadors?', 28.
143. Ibid., 28.
144. Cited in McGlen and Sarkees *Women in Foreign Policy*, 99–100.
145. Rossetti, 'Changes for Diplomacy Under the Lens of Feminist Neo-Institutional Theory'.
146. Cassidy, Gender and Diplomacy.
147. E. Broderick, C. Goldie, and E. Rosenman, '2010 Gender Equality Blueprint', The Australian Human Rights Commission, accessed 22 March 2017, https://www.humanrights.gov.au/our-work/sex-discrimination/publications/gender-equality-blueprint-2010; M. Conley Tyler, E. Blizzard, and B. Crane, 'Is International Affairs Too 'Hard' for

Women? Explaining the Missing Women in Australia's International Affairs', *Australian Journal of International Affairs* 68, no. 2 (2014): 156–176.
148. M. Dee and F. Volk, *Women with a Mission: Personal Perspectives* (Canberra: Commonwealth of Australia, 2007), 3.
149. Conley Tyler, 'Diversity and Diplomacy'; Dee and Volk, *Women with a Mission*.
150. Towns and Niklasson, 'Gender, Status and Ambassador Appointments', 538.
151. AIATSIS 2021, *Serving their Country*, accessed 13 November 2021, https://aiatsis.gov.au/explore/serving-their-country#:~:text=Despite%20discrimination%20and%20exclusion%2C%20thousands,in%20the%20Second%20World%20War.
152. Dee and Volk *Women with a Mission*.
153. Clunies Ross in Dee and Volk, *Women with a Mission*.
    A. Tange, 'Plans for the World Economy: Hopes and Reality in Wartime Canberra. A Personal Memoir', *Australian Journal of International Affairs* 50, no. 3 (1996): 259–267.
    P. Edwards, *Arthur Tange: Last of the Mandarins* (Sydney: Allen and Unwin, 2006).
154. Dee and Volk, *Women with a Mission*.
155. McGlen and Sarkees, *Women in Foreign Policy*, 99.
156. Australian Bureau of Statistics 2019, Media Release: Two Million Employed in the Public Sector in June 2019, accessed 28 April 2020, https://www.abs.gov.au/ausstats/abs@.nsf/lookup/6248.0.55.002Media%20Release12018-19.
157. Commonwealth of Australia 2017, 2017 Foreign Policy White Paper, accessed 31 December 2017, https://www.fpwhitepaper.gov.au/foreign-policy-white-paper.
158. E. Cech and M. Blair-Loy, 'Perceived Glass Ceilings? Meritocratic Versus Structural Explanations of Gender Inequality Among Women in Science and Technology', *Social Problems* 57, no. 3 (2010): 371.
159. 'In the Room' 2021, *Ms Represented*, Series 1, Episode 3, ABC TV.
160. C. Burton, *Redefining Merit* (Canberra: Australian Government Publishing Service, 1988), 2.
161. S. Williamson and M. Foley, Embedding Gender Equality in the Australian Public Service: Changing Practices, Changing Cultures, UNSW Public Service Research Group, accessed 17 March 2020, https://www.unsw.adfa.edu.au/school-of-business/sites/bus/files/uploads/172084%20Gender%20Equality%20Publication_171122.pdf.
162. R. Simpson, A. Ross-Smith, and P. Lewis, 'Merit, Special Contribution and Choice: How Women Negotiate Between Sameness and Difference in their Organisational Lives', *Gender in Management: An International Journal* 25, no. 3 (2010): 199.
163. J. Westendorf and R. Strating, 'Women in Australian International Affairs', *Australian Journal of International Affairs* 74, no. 3 (2020): 1–15.
164. Lowy Institute, Foreign Territory: Women in International Relations, accessed 9 April 2020, https://www.lowyinstitute.org/sites/default/files/CAVE%20et%20al_Foreign%20territory_Women%20in%20international%20relations.pdf.
165. Stephenson 'Invisible While Visible'; E. Stephenson, 'Domestic Challenges to International Leadership: A Case Study of Women in Australian International Affairs Agencies', *Australian Journal of International Affairs* 73, no. 3 (2019): 234–253.
166. Rossetti, 'Changes for Diplomacy Under the Lens of Feminist Neo-Institutional Theory'.
167. Conley Tyler, 'Diversity and Diplomacy'.
168. Conley Tyler, Blizzard, and Crane, 'Is International Affairs Too 'Hard' for Women?'
169. Harris Rimmer 2019.

254 Notes

170. S. Hewitt, 'Gender, Peace and Security in the Australian Defence Force: Sarah Hewitt in Conversation with Captain Jennifer Wittwer, CSM, RAN', *International Feminist Journal of Politics* 19, no. 1 (2017): 104–111.
171. L. Shepherd and J. True, 'The Women, Peace and Security Agenda and Australian Leadership in the World: From Rhetoric to Commitment?', *Australian Journal of International Affairs* 68, no. 3 (2014): 257–284.
172. S. Roggeveen, 'Reader Riposte: Where Are the Interpreter Women?', *The Interpreter*, 19 May 2008 .
173. R. Shanahan, 'Women and the Commentariat', *The Interpreter*, 30 August 2011, http://www.lowyinterpreter.org/?d=D%20-%20Women%20and%20the%20foreign%20policy%20commentariat.
174. Conley Tyler, Blizzard and Crane, 'Is International Affairs Too 'Hard' for Women?', 161.
175. Elizabeth Broderick & Co., 'Cultural Change: Gender Diversity and Inclusion in the Australian Federal Police', accessed 13 November 2021, https://www.afp.gov.au/sites/default/files/PDF/Reports/Cultural-Change-Report-2016.pdf.
176. Department of Foreign Affairs and Trade, Women in Leadership Strategy: Promoting Equality and Dismantling Barriers, accessed 9 June 2017, https://www.dfat.gov.au/sites/default/files/women-in-leadership-strategy.pdf, 4.
177. Embassy Magazine, Women Envoys on the Rise, accessed 9 September 2016, https://embassymagazine.com/women-envoys-on-the-rise/.
178. Elizabeth Broderick & Co., 'Cultural Change'.
179. Edwards et al., 'Not Yet 50/50'.
180. Conley Tyler, Blizzard and Crane, 'Is International Affairs Too 'Hard' for Women?'
181. Ibid., 163.
182. M. Cowden, K. McLaren, A. Plumb, and M. Sawer, 'Women's Advancement in Australian Political Science', report, Australian National University, accessed 24 January 2019, http://genderinstitute.anu.edu.au/sites/default/files/imce/WomensAdvancement_Report_0.pdf.
183. Edwards et al., 'Not Yet 50/50'.
184. Community and Public Sector Union, What Women Want Survey Report 2010–2011, accessed 24 January 2019, https://apo.org.au/node/20554.
185. Department of Education, Skills and Employment, A statistical snapshot of women in the Australian workforce, (Canberra).
186. K. Lee-Koo, 'Feminism', in *An Introduction to International Relations: Australian Perspectives*, ed. R. Devetak, A. Burke, and J. George (Cambridge: Cambridge University Press, 2007), xx–xx.
187. Commonwealth of Australia, The Review of Employment Pathways for APS Women in the Department of Defence, accessed 20 March 2020, https://www.defence.gov.au/PathwayToChange/_Master/docs/Review-of-Employment-Pathways-for-APS-Women-in-Defence-full-report.pdf, 8–9, emphasis added.
188. McGlen and Sarkees, *Women in Foreign Policy*.
189. Conley Tyler, 'Diversity and Diplomacy'.
190. N. Riseman, *In Defence of Country: Life Stories of Aboriginal and Torres Strait Islander Servicemen and Women* (Canberra: ANU Press, 2016).
191. D. Lomas, '#ForgetJamesBond: Diversity, Inclusion and the UK's Intelligence Agencies', *Intelligence and National Security* 36, no. 7 (2021): 1003.
192. Ibid., 1003.

193. Ibid., 1004.
194. Stephenson, 'Domestic Challenges to International Leadership'.
195. Crenshaw, 'Demarginalising the Intersection of Race and Sex'.
196. McGlen and Sarkees, *Women in Foreign Policy*.

Chapter 3

1. Interview: Jane, DFAT, 15 November 2015.
2. L. Chappell and F. Mackay, 'Feminist Critical Friends: Dilemmas of Feminist Engagement with Governance and Gender Reform Agendas', *European Journal of Politics and Gender* 4, no. 3 (2021): 2, 20; V. Lowndes, 'The Institutional Approach', in *Theory and Methods in Political Science*, 3rd ed., ed. D. Marsh and G. Stoker (Basingstoke: Palgrave Macmillan, 2010), 60–79.
3. A. Costa and B. Kallick, 'Through the Lens of a Critical Friend', *Educational Leadership* 51, no. 2 (1993): 49.
4. Ibid., 49.
5. A. Holvikivi, 'Gender Experts and Critical Friends: Research in Relations of Proximity', *European Journal of Politics and Gender* 2, no. 1 (2019): 131–147, 132.
6. L. Chappell and L. Hill, L. *The Politics of Women's Interests: New Comparative Perspectives* (London: Routledge, 2006), 158.
7. L. Chappell and F. Mackay, 'Critical Friends and De(con)structive Critics: Dilemmas of Feminist Engagement with Global Governance and Gender Reform Agendas', paper presented at the European Consortium for Political Research 4th European Conference on Politics and Gender, 11–13 June 2015, Uppsala, Sweden, p. 10.
8. Chappell and Mackay, 'Critical Friends and De(con)structive Critics', p. 18.
9. Holvikivi, 'Gender Experts and Critical Friends'.
10. B. Ackerly and J. True, 'Studying the Struggles and Wishes of the Age: Feminist Theoretical Methodology and Feminist Theoretical Methods', in *Feminist Methodologies for International Relations*, ed. B. Ackerly, M. Stern, and J. True (Cambridge: Cambridge University Press, 2006), 255.
11. L. Shepherd, *Gender Matters in Global Politics: A Feminist Introduction to International Relations* (New York: Routledge, 2010).
12. Shepherd, *Gender Matters*, p. 30.
13. S. Harris Rimmer, 'Women as Makers of International Law: Towards Feminist Diplomacy', in *Research Handbook on Feminist Engagement with International Law*, ed. S. Harris Rimmer and K. Ogg (Cheltenham: Edward Elgar, 2019), 26–43.
14. A. Towns and B. Niklasson, 'Gender, International Status, and Ambassador Appointments', *Foreign Policy Analysis* 13, no. 3 (2017): 521–540.
15. J. A. Tickner, *Gender in International Relations: Feminist Perspectives on Achieving Global Security* (New York: Columbia University Press), 9.
16. L. Chappell, 'Comparative Gender and Institutions: Directions for Research', *Symposium* 8, no. 1 (2010): 183–189.
17. J. Vickers, 'The Problem with Interests: Making Political Claims for "Women"', in *The Politics of Women's Interests: New Comparative Perspectives*, ed. L. Chappell and L. Hill (London: Routledge, 2006), 149–183.
18. Chappell, 'Comparative Gender', 184.

19. J. Ramji-Nogales, 'Revisiting the Category 'Women'', in *Research Handbook on Feminist Engagement with International Law*, ed. S. Harris Rimmer and K. Ogg (Cheltenham: Edward Elgar, 2019), 240–252.
20. R. McNae and K. Vali, 'Diverse Experiences of Women Leading in Higher Education: Locating Networks and Agency for Leadership Within a University Context in Papua New Guinea', *Gender and Education* 27, no. 3 (2015): 298.
21. J. Momsen, 'Women, Men, and Fieldwork: Gender Relations and Power Structures', in *Doing Development Research*, ed. V. Desai and R. B. Potter (Thousand Oaks, CA: Sage Publishing, 2011), 45.

    C. Madge, 'Boundary Disputes: Comments on Sidaway (1992)', *Area* 25, no. 3 (1993): 294–299.
22. C. Ramanazoglu and J. Holland, *Feminist Methodology: Challenges and Choices* (Thousand Oaks, CA: Sage Publishing, 2002).
23. B. Ackerly, M. Stern, and J. True, *Feminist Methodologies for International Relations* (Cambridge: Cambridge University Press, 2006).
24. W. Harvey, 'Strategies for Conducting Elite Interviews', *Qualitative Research* 11, no. 4 (2011): 431–441.
25. Ramanazoglu and Holland, *Feminist Methodology*, 155.
26. A. Bryman, *Social Research Methods*, 4th ed. (New York: Oxford University Press, 2012).
27. N. Adler, 'Global Leadership: Women Leaders', *Management International Review* 37 (1997): 174.
28. J. Rost, *Leadership for the 21st Century* (New York: Praeger, 1991).
29. H. Fenichel Pitkin, *The Concept of Representation* (Berkeley: University of California Press [1967] 1972).
30. C. Enloe, *Bananas, Beaches and Bases: Making Feminist Sense of International Politics* (Berkeley: University of California Press, [1989] 2014); Towns and Niklasson, 'Gender, International Status, and Ambassador Appointments'.
31. T. Jacoby, 'From the Trenches: Dilemmas of Feminist IR Fieldwork,' in *Feminist Methodologies for International Relations*, ed. B. Ackerly, M. Stern, and J. True (Cambridge: Cambridge University Press, 2006), 153–173.
32. Ibid., 161.
33. Chappell, L and Mackay, F 2017, 'What's in a Name? Mapping the Terrain of Informal Institutions and Gender Politics', in *Gender and Informal Institutions*, ed. G. Waylen (Rowman & Littlefield, London, p. 24.
34. C. Cohn, 'Motives and Methods: Using Multi-Sited Ethnography to Study National Security Discourses', in *Feminist Methodologies for International Relations*, ed. B. Ackerly, M. Stern, and J. True (Cambridge: Cambridge University Press, 2006), 94.
35. J. Corbett and A. Liki, 'Intersecting Identities, Divergent Views: Interpreting the Experiences of Women Politicians in the Pacific Islands', *Politics & Gender* 11, no. 2 (2015): 320–344.
36. C. Spark, J. Cox, and J. Corbett, 'Being the First: Women Leaders in the Pacific Islands', Development Leadership Program, Birmingham, UK, 2018.
37. N. Emmel, *Sampling and Choosing Cases in Qualitative Research: A Realist Approach* (Thousand Oaks, CA: Sage Publishing, 2014), 48.
38. Ibid., 47.
39. P. Fusch and L. Ness, 'Are We There Yet? Data Saturation in Qualitative Research', *The Qualitative Report* 20, no. 9, (2015): 1408–1416.

Notes 257

40. M. Marsden, D. Ibanez-Tirado, and D. Henig, 'Everyday Diplomacy', *Cambridge Anthropology* 34, no. 2 (2016): 2.
41. Bryman, *Social Research Methods*.
42. G. Fletcher, 'Of Baby Ducklings and Clay Pots: Method and Metaphor in HIV Prevention', *Qualitative Health Research* 23, no. 1 (2013): 1555.
43. K. Halvorsen, *To Research Society: An Introduction to Social Science Method* (Oslo: Bedriftsøkonomens Forlag, 1987).
44. Ramazanoglu and Holland, *Feminist* Methodology, 119.
45. Bryman, *Social Research Methods*.
46. M. Bevir and R. Rhodes, *Routledge Handbook of Interpretive Political Science* (New York: Routledge, 2016).
47. Department of Foreign Affairs and Trade 2018, Australian Ambassadors and Other Representatives, viewed 2 March 2018, http://dfat.gov.au/about-us/our-people/homs/Pages/australian-ambassadors-and-other-representatives.aspx. Department of Foreign Affairs and Trade 2017, Australian Ambassadors and Other Representatives, viewed 2 March 2017, http://dfat.gov.au/about-us/our-people/homs/Pages/australian-ambassadors-and-other-representatives.aspx; Department of Foreign Affairs and Trade 2019, *2018–2019 Annual Report*, viewed 14 November 2021, https://www.dfat.gov.au/sites/default/files/2020-01/dfat-annual-report-2018-19.pdf.
48. Australian Federal Police 2018, Statistics of AFP Staff in Overseas Posts, accessed 11 January 2018, https://www.afp.gov.au/news-media/facts-and-stats/afp-staff-statistics/statistics-afp-staff-overseas-posts. Australian Federal Police 2018, Statistics of AFP Staff in Overseas Posts, accessed 20 January 2019, https://www.afp.gov.au/news-media/facts-and-stats/afp-staff-statistics/statistics-afp-staff-overseas-posts.
49. S. Loeb, P. Morris, S. Dynarski, S. Reardon, D. McFarland, and S. Reber, *Descriptive Analysis in Education: A Guide for Researchers* (Washington, DC: US Department of Education, 2017).
50. M. Baumgartner and D. Schneider, 'Perceptions of Women in Management: A Thematic Analysis of Razing the Glass Ceiling', *Journal of Career Development* 37, no. 2 (2010): 559–576.
51. E. Guba, *Towards a Methodology of Naturalistic Inquiry in Educational Evaluation* (Los Angeles: CSE Monograph Series, 1978).
52. D. Collier, 'Understanding Process Tracing', *Political Science and Politics* 44, no. 4 (2011): 823–830.
53. R. Rhodes, P. 't Hart, and M. Noordegraaf, *Observing Government Elites: Up Close and Personal* (New York: Palgrave Macmillan, 2007), 206.
54. A. Podger and H. Chan, 'The Concept of 'Merit' in Australia, China and Taiwan', *Australian Journal of Public Administration* 74, no. 3 (2015): 259.
55. C. W. Mills, *The Power Elite*, New Edition (Oxford University Press, [1956] 2000), 3–4.
56. K. Lancaster, 'Confidentiality, Anonymity and Power Relations in Elite Interviewing: Conducting Qualitative Policy Research in a Politicised Domain', *International Journal of Social Research Methodology* 20, no. 1 (2017): 93–103.
57. Aldridge in A. Kezar, 'Transformational Elite Interviews: Principles and Problems', *Qualitative Inquiry* 9, no. 3 (2003): 407.
58. Ibid., 409.
59. Z. S. Morris, 'The Truth About Interviewing Elites', *Politics* 29, no. 3 (2009): 209–217.

60. L. Dexter, *Elite and Specialised Interviewing* (Evanston: Northwestern University Press, 1970).
61. Cohn, 'Motives and Methods'.
62. Ibid., 96–97.
63. Kezar, 'Transformational Elite Interviews', 406.
64. L. Martin, 'Julie Bishop Laments "Gender Deafness" During Her Time in Politics', *The Guardian*, 13 August 2019, https://www.theguardian.com/australia-news/2019/aug/13/julie-bishop-laments-gender-deafness-during-her-time-in-politics, para 1.

Chapter 4

1. Interview: Lucy, Home Affairs, 2 May 2018.
2. B. Hocking, *Foreign Ministries: Change and Adaptation* (London: Palgrave Macmillan, 1999), 1.
3. J. Dittmer, 'Distributed Agency: Foreign Policy Sans MFA', *The Hague Journal of Diplomacy* 15 (2019): 156.
4. B. Gülmez, 'The Impact of COVID-19 Pandemic on Diplomacy', *5th International EMI Entrepreneurship & Social Sciences Congress* (2020): 367–378.
5. A. Cooper and J. Cornut, *The Changing Nature of Diplomacy* (Oxford: Oxford Bibliographies, 2016). https://www.oxfordbibliographies.com/display/document/obo-9780199743292/obo-9780199743292-0180.xml#:~:text=The%20changing%20nature%20of%20diplomacy%20merits%20detailed%20attention.,to%2Dday%20activities%20of%20diplomats
6. R. P. Barston, *Modern Diplomacy* (London: Routledge, 2019).
7. R. Tanter, 'Tightly Bound: The United States and Australia's Alliance-Dependent Militarization', *The Asia-Pacific Journal* 16, no. 11 (2018): 1–8.
8. A. Colvin, 'Keeping Australia Safe Through Police-Led Diplomacy', *DFAT Blog*, 23 June 2017, https://blog.dfat.gov.au/2017/06/23/keeping-australia-safe-through-police-led-diplomacy/; R. Young and O. Meli, 'Trusted, Ethical, Fast-Moving and Effective: The AFP Investigative Team of 2030', *Future Insights Report, ANU National Security College*, 2019; B. Taylor, J. Blaxland, H. White, N. Bisley, P. Leahy and T. Seng, 'Defence Diplomacy: Is the Game Worth the Candle?' *The Centre of Gravity Series, Strategic and Defence Studies*, ANU College of Asia and the Pacific, 2014.
9. K. Aggestam and A. Towns, 'The Gender Turn in Diplomacy: A New Research Agenda', *International Feminist Journal of Politics* 21, no. 1 (2019): 9–28; S. Bashevkin, *Women as Foreign Policy Leaders: National Security and Gender Politics in Superpower America* (New York: Oxford University Press, 2018).
10. A. Towns, K. Jezierska, A. K. Kreft and B. Niklasson, 'COVID-19 and Gender: A Necessary Connection in Diplomatic Studies', *The Hague Journal of Diplomacy* 15, no. 4 (2020): 636–647.
11. J. Cassidy, *Gender and Diplomacy* (New York: Routledge, 2017).
12. C. Wright, *You Daughters of Freedom: The Australians Who Won the Vote and Inspired the World* (Melbourne: Text Publishing, 2018).
13. M. Sawer, 'Housekeeping the State: Women and Parliamentary Politics in Australia', Papers on Parliament No. 17, accessed 15 January 2020, https://www.aph.gov.au/~/~/~/link.aspx?_id=4770FE53E2AC484480D2431A451B44C0&_z=z.

14. C. Wright, 'How Australia Became a Nation, and Women Won the Vote', The Conversation, 6 June, accessed 2 May 2020, https://theconversation.com/how-australia-became-a-nation-and-women-won-the-vote-78406, para 18.
15. S. Harris Rimmer, 'Women in Global Economic Governance', in *Gender and Diplomacy*, ed. J. A. Cassidy (New York: Routledge, 2017), 140–169.
16. M. Conley Tyler, 'Diversity and Diplomacy', Australian Journal of International Affairs 70, no. 6 (2016): 696.
17. M. Clark and S. May, *Macassan History and Heritage: Journeys, Encounters, and Influences* (Canberra: ANU Press, 2013).
    R. Ganter, 'Turning the Map Upside Down', *Griffith Review* no. 9 (2005): 167–176.
18. Ethnic Communities' Council of Victoria, 'Fact, Australia Is the Most Ethnically Diverse Country in the World', media release, 29 June 2017.
19. Australian Public Service Commission, The APS Merit Principle, accessed 28 April 2020, https://www.apsc.gov.au/aps-merit-principle.
    F. Argy, 'Equal Opportunity in Australia: Myth and Reality', Discussion Paper 85, The Australia Institute, April 2006.
20. L. Chappell, 'Moving to a Comparative Politics of Gender?', Critical *Perspectives on Gender and Politics* 2 (2006): 226.
21. Ibid., 226.
22. Workplace Gender Equality Agency 2020, WGEA Data Explorer, accessed 18 March 2020, https://data.wgea.gov.au/.
23. B. Williams, 'It's Reigning Men: Media Portrayal and Betrayal of 2 Women PMs', BroadAgenda Blog, 30 March, http://www.broadagenda.com.au/home/httpwww-broadagenda-com-auhomeits-a-mans-world-gendered-representations-of-two-female-prime-ministers/; B. Williams, 'A Gendered Media Analysis of the Prime Ministerial Ascension of Gillard and Turnbull: He's "Taken Back the Reigns" and She's a "Backstabbing Murderer"', *Australian Journal of International Affairs* 52, no. 4 (2017): 550–564.
24. S. March, 'Australia's US Ambassador Joe Hockey Accepts Responsibility for 15 White Men 'Mateship Patrons'', ABC News, 7 July 2018, https://www.abc.net.au/news/2018-07-07/australia-us-mateship-patrons-all-white-men/9953102.
25. I. B. Neumann, 'The Body of the Diplomat', *European Journal of International Relations* 14, no. 4 (2008): 676.
26. G. Waylen, 'Informal Institutions, Institutional Change, and Gender Equality', *Political Research Quarterly* 67, no. 1 (2014): 212–223.
27. V. Lowndes, 'How Are Things Done Around Here? Uncovering Institutional Rules and Their Gendered Effects', *Politics and Gender* 10, no. 4 (2014): 685–691.
28. Hooper in L. Chappell and G. Waylen, 'Gender and the Hidden Life of Institutions', *Public Administration* 91, no. 3 (2013): 601.
29. Interview: Bel, Home Affairs, 4 February 2019.
30. T. Arklay, A. Tiernan and H. White, 'Advising Ministers—The Special Problem of Defence', *Australian Journal of Public Administration* 70, no. 4 (2011): 365–376.
31. B. Wadham and B. Connor, 'The Dark Side of Defence: Organisational Deviance and the Australian Defence Force', in *Proceedings of the Australian Sociological Conference* (2014): 269–287.
32. E. Lindquist, 'From Rhetoric to Blueprint: The Moran Review as a Concerted, Comprehensive and Emergent Strategy for Public Sector Reform', *Australian Journal of Public Administration* 69, no. 2 (2010): 115.

260 Notes

33. Lowy Institute, Foreign Territory: Women in International Relations, accessed 9 April 2020, https://www.lowyinstitute.org/publications/gender-australia-ir-sector.
34. S. Harris, 'The Merger of the Foreign Affairs and Trade Departments Revisited', *Australian Journal of International Affairs* 56, no. 2 (2002): 223–235.
35. C. Byrne, M. Conley Tyler, and S. Harris Rimmer, 'Australian Diplomacy Today', *Australian Journal of International Affairs* 70, no. 6 (2016): 581–589.
36. Harris, 'The Merger of the Foreign Affairs and Trade Departments Revisited'.
37. Ibid., 230.
38. T. Peacock, 'Australian Women in Diplomacy: Australian Diplomacy for Women', 7 March 2012, Eastern Mediterranean University, Cyprus, https://dfat.gov.au/news/speeches/Pages/australian-women-in-diplomacy-australian-diplomacy-for-women.aspx, para 8.
39. Ibid., para 9.
40. M. Dee and F. Volk, *Women with a Mission: Personal Perspectives* (Canberra: Commonwealth of Australia, 2007).
41. Peacock, 'Australian Women in Diplomacy', para 12.
42. Australian Public Service Employee Database Request for Information 763.
43. Harris 'The Merger of the Foreign Affairs and Trade Departments Revisited', 230.
44. Australian Public Service Commission, APS Employment Database internet interface (APSEDii), accessed 16 April 2019, https://www.apsc.gov.au/aps-employment-database-internet-interface-apsedii.
45. J. Corbett, *Australia's Foreign Aid Dilemma: Humanitarian Aspirations Confront Democratic Legitimacy* (Oxon: Routledge, 2017).
46. Interview: Esther, DFAT, 21 June 2018.
47. Interview: Selena, DFAT, 18 June 2018.
48. Ibid.
49. Ibid.
50. Ibid.
51. Lowy Institute, Global Diplomacy Index—Australia's Diplomatic Network, accessed 3 May 2019, https://www.lowyinstitute.org/global-diplomacy-index-australias-diplomatic-network.
52. Ibid., para 11.
53. Ibid., para 10.
54. Interview: Jane, DFAT, 15 November 2018.
55. M. Conley Tyler and M. Vandewerndt-Holman, 'Australia's Incredible Shrinking Department of Foreign Affairs and Trade', The Mandarin, 28 October 2019, https://www.themandarin.com.au/118942-australias-incredible-shrinking-department-of-foreign-affairs-and-trade/.
56. N. McGlen and M. Sarkees, *Women in Foreign Policy: The Insiders* (New York: Routledge, 1993), 12.
57. Ibid., 42.
58. K. Lee-Koo, 'Pro-Gender Foreign Policy by Stealth: Navigating Global and Domestic Politics in Australian Foreign Policy Making', *Foreign Policy Analysis* 16, no. 2 (2020): 237.
59. E. Stephenson, 'The Diplomatic Glass Cliff: Women's Representation and Diplomacy's Decline', *The Hague Journal of Diplomacy* 17 (July 2022): 577.
60. Lowy Institute, Global Diplomacy Index—Australia's Diplomatic Network.
61. A. Oliver, 'Diplomatic Disrepair: Rebuilding Australia International Policy Infrastructure', accessed 13 December 2022, https://archive.lowyinstitute.org/publications/diplomatic-disrepair-rebuilding-australia-international-policy-infrastructure.

62. Department of Foreign Affairs and Trade, Australian Ambassadors and Other Representatives, accessed 2 March 2017 and 2 March 2018, http://dfat.gov.au/about-us/our-people/homs/Pages/australian-ambassadors-and-other-representatives.aspx.
63. Interview: Rani, DFAT, 1 February 2019.
64. J. Webster, 'Resisting Change: Toxic Masculinity in the Post Modern United States Armed Forces (1980s—Present)', PhD diss., University of Central Oklahoma, 2019.
65. S. Barrington, 'From Marriage Bar Towards Gender Equality', in *Gender and Diplomacy*, ed. J. Cassidy (New York: Routledge, 2017), 48–64.
66. J. Cassidy, *Gender and Diplomacy* (New York: Routledge, 2017), 210.
67. McGlen and Sarkees, *Women in Foreign Policy*.
68. Ibid., 78.
69. Ibid., 78.
70. Quoted in ibid., 84.
71. Interview: Julie Bishop, 3 April 2019.
72. J. Acker, 'Inequality Regimes Gender, Class, and Race in Organisations', *Gender and Society* 20, no. 4 (2006): 441–464.
73. Interview: Julienne, DFAT, 18 October 2018, emphasis added.
74. Interview: Julienne, DFAT, 18 October 2018, emphasis added.
75. McGlen and Sarkees, *Women in Foreign Policy*, 36.
76. H. Smith, 'Women in the Australian Defence Force: In Line for the Front Line?', *The Australian Quarterly* 62, no. 2 (1990): 126.
77. Department of Defence, First Principles Review: Creating One Defence, accessed 4 May 2020, https://www.defence.gov.au/Publications/Reviews/Firstprinciples/Docs/FirstPrinciplesReviewB.pdf; Commonwealth of Australia, 2016 Defence White Paper, accessed 17 March 2020, https://www.defence.gov.au/WhitePaper/Docs/2016-Defence-White-Paper.pdf.
78. Australian Human Rights Commission, Review into the Treatment of Women in the Australian Defence Force: Phase 2 Report, accessed 11 July 2017, http://defencereview.humanrights.gov.au/sites/default/files/adf-complete.pdf, 15.
79. Smith, 'Women in the Australian Defence Force'; B. Wadham, D. Bridges, A. Mundkur and J. Connor, '"War-Fighting and Left-Wing Feminist Agendas": Gender and Change in the Australian Defence Force', *Critical Military Studies* 4, no. 3 (2018): 264–280.
80. Smith, 'Women in the Australian Defence Force'.
81. D. V. Bridges, 'The Gendered Battlefield: Women in the Australian Defence Force', PhD diss., Western Sydney University, 2005, 29.
82. M. Mackenzie, *Beyond the Band of Brothers* (Cambridge: Cambridge University Press, 2015).
83. Smith, 'Women in the Australian Defence Force', 127.
84. R. Connell, *Short Introductions: Gender* (Cambridge: Polity Press, 2009).
85. L. Sjoberg and C. Gentry, *Mothers, Monsters, Whores: Women's Violence in Global Politics* (New York: Zed Books, 2007), 2, emphasis in original.
86. Bridges, 'The Gendered Battlefield'.
87. J. Bomford, *Soldiers of the Queen: Women in the Australian Army* (South Melbourne: Oxford University Press, 2001), 1.
88. D. V. Bridges, 'Grounded? Female Pilots, Gender Identity and Integration into the Australian Defence Force', in *Absent Aviators: Gender Issues in Aviation*, ed. A. Mills, N. Neal-Smith, and D. Bridges (Farnham: Ashgate Publishing, 2014), 147.

Notes

89. Department of Defence, *Annual Report 2018–2019*, accessed 4 May 2020, https://www.defence.gov.au/AnnualReports/18-19/.
90. J. B. Elshtain, 'On Beautiful Souls, Just Warriors, and Feminist Consciousness', *Women's Studies International Forum* 5, no. 3–4 (1982): 341.
91. Smith, 'Women in the Australian Defence Force', 127, emphasis in original.
92. Bridges, 'Grounded?'.
93. C. Holbrook, *Anzac: The Unauthorised Biography* (Sydney: NewSouth Publishing, 2014); Australian Human Rights Commission, Understanding Anzac Day—What Were We Fighting For, accessed 8 May 2020, https://humanrights.gov.au/about/news/understanding-anzac-day-what-were-we-fighting.
94. B. Dwyer, 'Place and Masculinity in the Anzac Legend', *Journal of the Association for the Study of Australian Literature* 4 (1997): 226–231, 226.
95. Ibid., 226; S. Johnson, 'Theorising Language and Masculinity: A Feminist Perspective', in *Language and Masculinity*, ed. U. H. Meinhof and S. Johnson (Oxford: Blackwell, 1997).
96. A. McWatters, 'Australian Women and War', *Australian Defence Force Journal*, no. 166 (2005): 34–48.
97. N. Riseman, *Defending Whose Country? Indigenous Soldiers in the Pacific War* (Lincoln: University of Nebraska Press, [2012] 2016); McWatters, 'Australian Women and War', 37.
98. Bomford, *Soldiers of the Queen*.
99. Ibid., 27.
100. Ibid., 55.
101. Ibid., 27.
102. Ibid., 27.
103. O. Sasson-Levy, 'Feminism and Military Gender Practices: Israeli Women Soldiers in 'Masculine' Roles', *Sociological Inquiry* 73, no. 3 (2003): 440–465.
104. O. Sasson-Levy, 'Ethnicity and Gender in Militaries: An Intersectional Analysis', in *The Palgrave International Handbook of Gender and the Military*, ed. R. Woodward and C. Duncanson (London: Palgrave Macmillan, 2017), 125–143.
105. Bomford, *Soldiers of the Queen*, 124.
106. Deloitte, Long Term Economic and Demographic Projections: ADF Posture Review, accessed 8 May 2020, https://www.defence.gov.au/Publications/Reviews/ADFPosture/Docs/AttachD.pdf.
107. C. Enloe, 'Women in NATO Militaries—A Conference Report', *Women's Studies International Forum* (1982): 331.
108. Department of Defence, *Annual Report 2021–22*, accessed 14 December 2022, https://www.defence.gov.au/AnnualReports/.
109. Bomford, *Soldiers of the Queen*, 1.
110. Bridges, 'The Gendered Battlefield'; B. Wadham, D. Bridges, A. Mundkur, and J. Connor, '"War-Fighting and Left-Wing Feminist Agendas": Gender and Change in the Australian Defence Force', *Critical Military Studies* 4, no. 3 (2018): 264–280.
111. Department of Defence, *Annual Report 2021–22*.
112. E. Broderick, 'Reflections on the Review into the Women in the Australian Defence Force', accessed 9 May 2020, https://humanrights.gov.au/about/news/speeches/reflections-review-women-australian-defence-force.
113. N. Riseman, 'Escaping Assimilation's Grasp: Aboriginal Women in the Australian Women's Military Services', *Women's History Review* 24, no. 5 (2014): 757–775.

114. Bridges, 'The Gendered Battlefield'.
115. Department of Defence, *Annual Report 2021–22*.
116. Andrea Argirides, 'Women in the RAN: The Road to Command at Sea', accessed 8 May 2020, https://www.navy.gov.au/history/feature-histories/women-ran-road-comm and-sea.
117. A. Morral, T. Schell, M. Celafu, J. Hwang, and A. Gelman, 'Sexual Assault and Sexual Harassment in the US Military', Volume 5, Estimates for Installation- and Command-Level Risk of Sexual Assault and Sexual Harassment from the 2014 RAND Military Workplace Study, (Santa Monica, CA: Rand Corporation, 2018).
118. Department of Defence, *Annual Report 2017–2018*, accessed 19 March 2020, https://www.defence.gov.au/AnnualReports/17-18/.
119. Department of Defence, *Annual Report 2021–22*.
120. Australian Human Rights Commission, 'Review into the Treatment of Women in the Australian Defence Force'.
121. B. Wadham, D. Bridges, A. Mundkur and J. Connor, '"War-Fighting and Left-Wing Feminist Agendas": Gender and Change in the Australian Defence Force', Critical Military Studies 4, no. 3, (2018): 264–280.
122. M. Mackenzie, *Sexual Assault Still Plagues Australia's Defence Forces and 'Boys Will Be Boys' Doesn't Help*, accessed 14 October 2019, https://www.abc.net.au/news/2019-07-17/sexual-assault-military-adf/11310814?pfmredir=sm, para 14.
123. Australian Human Rights Commission, 'Review into the Treatment of Women in the Australian Defence Force', 17.
124. Ibid., 39.
125. Webster, 'Resisting Change', VI.
126. Department of Defence, *Annual Report 2017–2018*, 24.
127. Interview: Sarah, Defence, 19 February 2019.
128. Interview: Angela, Defence, 12 April 2019.
129. Interview: Danielle, Defence, 4 March 2019).
130. Department of Defence, *Annual Report 2018–2019*.
131. Interview: Danielle, Defence, 4 March 2019).
132. Mackenzie, *Sexual Assault Still Plagues Australia's Defence Forces*.
133. McGlen and Sarkees, *Women in Foreign Policy*, 104.
134. Interview: Rebecca, Defence, 19 February 2019.
135. Interview: Lee, Defence, 26 February 2019.
136. D. Morrison, 'Australian Chief to Sexist Soldiers: Respect Women or GET OUT', accessed 19 March 2020, https://www.youtube.com/watch?v=dRQBtDtZTGA; ABC News Online, Chief of Army David Morrison Tells Troops to Respect Women or 'Get Out', 14 June, accessed 9 May 2020, https://www.abc.net.au/news/2013-06-14/chief-of-army-fires-broadside-at-army-over-email-allegations/4753208.
137. See A. Greene, 'David Morrison: War Veteran's Attach 'Sickening' Australian of the Year Choice', ABC News, 29 January 2016, https://www.abc.net.au/news/2016-01-29/david-morrison-war-veterans-upset-with-australian-of-the-year/7125952; M. Devine, 'It's Not Too Late to Say Sorry, David Morrison. Many Are Still Waiting to Hear a Few Simple Words', *The Daily Telegraph*, 23 October 2016, https://www.dailytelegraph.com.au/rendezview/its-not-too-late-to-say-sorry-david-morrison-many-are-still-waiting-to-hear-a-few-simple-words/news-story/fa861060b1187f75598c0dbcff4288e9; K. Aubusson, 'David Morrison Defends Australian of the Year Honour on Q&A', *Sydney Morning*

Herald, 2 February 2016, https://www.smh.com.au/politics/federal/david-morrison-defends-australian-of-the-year-honour-on-qa-20160201-gmj4dn.html.
138. B. Wadham, D. Bridges, A. Mundkur, and J. Connor, '"War-Fighting and Left-Wing Feminist Agendas": Gender and Change in the Australian Defence Force', *Critical Military Studies* 4, no. 3 (2018): 264–280.
139. Waylen, *Gender and Informal Institutions*, 5.
140. Interview: Rebecca, Defence, 19 February 2019.
141. Interview: Danielle, Defence, 4 March 2019.
142. Interview: Gabrielle, Defence, 20 March 2019.
143. McGlen and Sarkees, *Women in Foreign Policy*, 78.
144. Australian Public Service Commission, Table 4: All Employees: Agency by Base Classification and Employment Category, 31 December 2016, http://www.apsc.gov.au/about-the-apsc/parliamentary/aps-statistical-bulletin/december-2016/table4total.
145. Department of Immigration and Border Protection, *A History of the Department of Immigration: Managing Migration to Australia* (Canberra: Commonwealth of Australia Publishing Service, 2015).
146. Ibid.
147. G. Powell and S. Macintyre, *Land of Opportunity: Australia's Post-War Reconstruction* (Canberra: National Archives of Australia, 2015).
148. Department of Immigration and Border Protection, *A History of the Department of Immigration*, 27.
149. A. M. Jordens, Alien to Citizen: Settling Migrants in Australia, 1945–75 (Sydney: Allen & Unwin, 1997).
150. Jordens in Department of Immigration and Border Protection *A History of the Department of Immigration*, 31.
151. Ibid., 31.
152. Ibid., 52.
153. G. Strachan, 'Still Working for the Man?: Women's Employment Experiences in Australia Since 1950', *Australian Journal of Social Issues* 45, no. 1 (2010): 120.
154. Interview: Lucy, Home Affairs, 2 May 2018.
155. Department of Immigration and Border Protection, *A History of the Department of Immigration*.
156. Ibid., 53.
157. S. Herbert, '"Hard Charger" or "Station Queen": Policing and the Masculinist State', *Gender, Place and Culture* 8, no. 1 (2001): 55–74; T. Prenzler, J. Fleming, and A. King, 'Gender Equity in Australian and New Zealand Policing: A Five-Year Review', *International Journal of Police Science and Management* 12, no. 4 (2010): 584–595.
158. Interview: Lucy, Home Affairs, 2 May 2018.
159. D. Dingwell, 'Newly-Honoured APS Trailblazer Helen Williams Defied Stereotypes', *Sydney Morning Herald*, 25 January 2019, https://www.smh.com.au/politics/federal/newly-honoured-aps-trailblazer-helen-williams-defied-stereotypes-20190124-p50tfg.html.
160. D. Marr and M. Wilkinson, *Dark Victory: How a Government Lied its Way to Political Triumph* (Sydney: Allen & Unwin, 2004).
161. B. Doherty, 'Australia's Offshore Detention is Unlawful, Says International Criminal Court Prosecutor', *The Guardian*, 15 February 2020, https://www.theguardian.com/austra

lia-news/2020/feb/15/australias-offshore-detention-is-unlawful-says-international-criminal-court-prosecutor, para 1.
162. Australian Public Service Commission, *Capability Review: Department of Immigration and Citizenship* (Canberra: Australian Government Publishing Service, 2012).
163. Personal communication, Strategic Research & Communications Division 2018, 2019.
164. Interview: Lucy, Home Affairs, 2 May 2018.
165. Australian Public Service Commission, Australian Public Service Employee Census 2019: Highlight Report: Home Affairs, accessed 9 May 2020, https://www.homeaffairs.gov.au/reports-and-pubs/files/aps-census-home-affairs-highlights.pdf; M. Doran, 'Bleak Outlook for Home Affairs Morale, as Staff Report Dissatisfaction with Work and Leadership', ABC News Online, 29 August 2019, https://www.abc.net.au/news/2019-08-29/bleak-outlook-for-home-affairs-staff-morale/11461442.
166. J. Massola and D. Wroe, 'Peter Dutton the Big Winner as Malcolm Turnbull Creates Home Affairs Office', *Sydney Morning Herald*, 18 July 2017, https://www.smh.com.au/politics/federal/peter-dutton-the-big-winner-as-malcolm-turnbull-creates-home-affairs-office-20170718-gxdbou.html.
167. M. Pezzullo, 'Immigration and Nation Building in Australia: Looking Back, Looking Forward', Australian National University Public Lecture, 21 April 2015, https://newsroom.abf.gov.au/releases/immigration-and-nation-building-in-australia-looking-back-looking-forward, para 29.
168. Interview: Lauren, Home Affairs, 9 May 2019.
169. Interview: Tess, Home Affairs, 1 February 2019.
170. J. Button, 'Dutton's Dark Victory', *The Monthly*, February 2018, https://www.themonthly.com.au/issue/2018/february/1517403600/james-button/dutton-s-dark-victory, para 121.
171. Interview: Lorelle, Home Affairs, 11 December 2018.
172. N. Hasham, '"Pure, Torturous Hell": The Harrowing Story of a Broken Border Force Officer and His Desperate Wife', *Sydney Morning Herald*, 21 July 2019, https://www.smh.com.au/politics/federal/pure-torturous-hell-the-harrowing-story-of-a-broken-border-force-officer-and-his-desperate-wife-20190719-p528nd.html, para 4–5; N. Hasham, 'Leaked Border Force Report Shows One in Five Staff Bullied or Harassed', *Sydney Morning Herald*, 4 December 2018, https://www.smh.com.au/politics/federal/leaked-border-force-report-shows-one-in-five-staff-bullied-or-harassed-20181203-p50juw.html; N. Hasham, '"Blood on Their Hands": Border Force Slammed After Second Employee Suicide', *Sydney Morning Herald*, 23 December 2018, https://www.smh.com.au/politics/federal/blood-on-their-hands-border-force-slammed-after-second-employee-suicide-20181218-p50mym.html.
173. Button, 'Dutton's Dark Victory'.
174. H. Belot, 'Immigration Boss Michael Pezzullo Calls for 'Insurgency and Revolution' for Women Leaders', accessed 7 May 2019, https://www.smh.com.au/public-service/immigration-boss-michael-pezzullo-calls-for-insurgency-and-revolution-for-women-leaders-20160621-gpobf6.html, para 1.
175. Pezzullo in Belot, 'Immigration Boss Michael Pezzullo Calls for 'Insurgency and Revolution', para 3, 5.
176. Interview: Penny, Home Affairs, 14 December 2018.
177. Button, 'Dutton's Dark Victory', para 7.
178. Interview: Tess, Home Affairs, 1 February 2019.
179. Pezzullo, 'Immigration and Nation Building in Australia', para 38.

180. M. Head, 'Lessons for the 'War on Terror'? 30 Years Since Sydney's Hilton Hotel Bombing', *Alternative Law Journal* 33, no. 2 (2008): 97.
181. M. Hess, 'UN Security Council Resolution 2185—AFP and International Policing', *AFP Platypus Magazine*, Jan.–Jun. 2015, http://www.austlii.edu.au/au/journals/AUFPPlatypus/2015/4.pdf, 17.
182. Interview: Meaghan, AFP, 26 June 2018.
183. Commonwealth of Australia, 'Australian Federal Police: The First Thirty Years', accessed 19 March 2020, https://www.afp.gov.au/sites/default/files/PDF/afp-the-first-thirty-years.pdf.
184. C. Niland and Associates 1995, Niland Report: Executive Summary (Canberra, ACT).
185. Commonwealth of Australia, 'Australian Federal Police', 41.
186. Interview: Billy, AFP, 4 October 2019.
187. Australian Federal Police, *International Engagement 2020 and Beyond* (Canberra: Commonwealth of Australia, 2017).
188. Commonwealth of Australia, 'Australian Federal Police', 6.
189. Ibid.
190. Elizabeth Broderick & Co, *Cultural Change: Gender Diversity and Inclusion in the Australian Federal Police*, (2016) viewed 19 March 2020, https://www.afp.gov.au/sites/default/files/PDF/Reports/Cultural-Change-Report-2016.pdf.
191. Australian Federal Police, Statistics of AFP Staff in Overseas Posts, accessed 11 January 2018, https://www.afp.gov.au/news-media/facts-and-stats/afp-staff-statistics/statistics-afp-staff-overseas-posts.
192. M. Palin, 'AFP Suicides: Former AFP Staffer Julie Woodward Found Dead', news.com.au, 27 November 2019, https://www.news.com.au/national/afp-suicides-longserving-afp-staffer-julie-woodward-found-dead/news-story/475a6a7564a330962d15f891441bcde0.
193. S. Herbert, '"Hard Charger" or "Station Queen": Policing and the Masculinist State', *Gender, Place and Culture* 8, no. 1 (2001): 55–74; Prenzler, Fleming, and King, 'Gender Equity in Australian and New Zealand Policing'.
194. Australian Human Rights Commission, The Gender Gap in Retirement Savings, accessed 29 January 2020, https://www.humanrights.gov.au/our-work/gender-gap-retirement-savings.
195. McGlen and Sarkees, *Women in Foreign Policy*, 78.
196. Elizabeth Broderick & Co. *Cultural Change: Gender Diversity and Inclusion in the Australian Federal Police* (2016), 5.
197. Interview: Meaghan, AFP, 26 June 2018.
198. Elizabeth Broderick & Co. *Cultural Change: Gender Diversity and Inclusion in the Australian Federal Police* (2016).
199. Interview: Delilah, AFP, 17 January 2019.
200. Interview: Jacqueline, AFP, 31 January 2019.
201. Stephenson, 'The Diplomatic Glass Cliff', 580.

Chapter 5

1. Interview: Sunny, DFAT, 15 October 2018.
2. S. Peterson, 'Transgressing Boundaries: Theories of Knowledge, Gender and International Relations', *Millennium: Journal of International Studies* 21, no. 2: 1992): 45.

3. Ibid.; N. Smith and D. Lee, 'What's Queer About Political Science?', *British Journal of Politics and International Relations* 17, no. 1 (2014): 49–63; D. Altman, *Global Sex* (Chicago: University of Chicago Press, 2001).
4. C. Enloe, *Bananas, Beaches and Bases: Making Feminist Sense of International Politics*, updated edition (Berkeley: University of California Press, 2014).
5. I. B. Neumann, *At Home with the Diplomats: Inside a European Foreign Ministry* (Ithaca, NY: Cornell University Press, 2012).
6. C. Lequesne, G. Castillo, M. Holm, W. J. B. Abdullah, and H. Leira, 'Ethnic Diversity in the Recruitment of Diplomats: Why MFAs Take the Issue Seriously', *Hague Journal of Diplomacy*, 15, no. 1 (2019): 1–23, 7.
7. Ibid., 7.
8. Federal Foreign Office, 'Inclusion: Diplomats with Disabilities', accessed 16 December 2022, https://www.auswaertiges-amt.de/en/about-us/inklusion/2499570.
9. D. Janoff, 'The Emergence of Queer Diplomacy: Navigating Homophobia and LGBT Human Rights in International Relations', PhD diss., Carleton University, 2021.
10. E. Rainer, 'Global Norm Diffusion of LGBTI Diplomacy', *The Hague Journal of Diplomacy*, 17, no. 3 (2022): 588–610.
11. E. Stephenson, 'Invisible While Visible: An Australian Perspective on Queer Women Leaders in International Affairs', *European Journal of Politics and Gender*, 3, no. 3 (2020): 427–443.
12. C. Standfield, 'Who Gets to Be a Virtuoso? Diplomatic Competence Through an Intersectional Lens', *The Hague Journal of Diplomacy*, 17, no. 3 (2022): 1–32.
13. I. B. Neumann, *At Home with the Diplomats: Inside a European Foreign Ministry* (Ithaca, New York: Cornell University Press, 2012).
14. B. Ackerly and J. True, J 2006, 'Studying the Struggles and Wishes of the Age: Feminist Theoretical Methodology and Feminist Theoretical Methods', in *Feminist Methodologies for International Relations*, ed. B. Ackerly, M. Stern, and J. True (Cambridge University Press, 2006), 241–261; J. Acker, 'From Glass Ceiling to Inequality Regimes', *Sociologie du Travail* 51, no. 2 (2009): 199–217.
15. O. Sasson-Levy, 'Ethnicity and Gender in Militaries: An Intersectional Analysis', in *The Palgrave International Handbook of Gender and the Military*, ed. R. Woodward and C. Duncanson (London: Palgrave Macmillan, 2017), 125–143.
16. B. Wadham, 'The Minister, The Commandant, and the Cadets: Sex Scandal and Military Modernisation', *Journal of Sociology* 52, no. 3 (2016): 272.
17. M. Clark and S. May, *Macassan History and Heritage: Journeys, Encounters, and Influences* (Canberra: ANU Press, 2013).
18. Mercer, D 2003, '"Citizen Minus"? Indigenous Australians and the Citizenship Question', *Citizenship Studies* 7, no. 4, 426.
19. Ibid., 422; N. Peterson and W. Sanders, *Citizenship and Indigenous Australians* (Cambridge: Cambridge University Press, 1998), 14.
20. J. Blackwell, 'The Future of Foreign Policy is First Nations. Where Then Are Our Voices?', *Australian Institute of International Affairs*, 5 August 2022, https://www.internationalaffairs.org.au/australianoutlook/the-future-of-foreign-policy-is-first-nations-where-then-are-our-voices/.
21. From the Heart, 'What is Constitutional Recognition Through a Voice to Parliament?', accessed 16 December 2022, https://www.yes23.com.au/

22. M. Conley Tyler, 'Diversity and Diplomacy', *Australian Journal of International Affairs* 70, no. 6 (2016): 696.
23. Australian Human Rights Commission, *Leading for Change: A Blueprint for Cultural Diversity and Inclusive Leadership Revisited*, accessed 19 March 2020, https://www.humanrights.gov.au/our-work/race-discrimination/publications/leading-change-blueprint-cultural-diversity-and-0.
24. Ibid.
25. R. Van Der Veen, 'Are Policies Sufficient to Foster Change in Diversity and Inclusion in the Australian and New Zealand Intelligence Sectors?, *International Journal of Intelligence and Counter-Intelligence* 35, no. 4 (2002): 674–693.
26. M. C. Parent, C. DeBlaere, and B. Moradi, 'Approaches to Research on Intersectionality: Perspectives on Gender, LGBT, and Racial/Ethnic Identities', *Sex Roles: A Journal of Research* 68, no. 11–12 (2013): 640.
27. V. Colic-Peisker and J. Hlavac, 'Anglo-Australian and Non-Anglophone Middle Classes: "Foreign Accent" and Social Inclusion', *Australian Journal of Social Issues* 49, no. 3 (2014): 366.
28. Interview: Sonia, Home Affairs, 22 February 2019.
29. Interview: Andrea, DFAT, 2 November 2018.
30. Interview: Talia, Home Affairs, 18 February 2019.
31. Interview: Rebecca, Defence, 19 February 2019.
32. S. Larkin, 'Race Matters: Indigenous Employment in the Australian Public Service', PhD diss., Queensland University of Technology, 2014.
33. Interview: Andrea, DFAT, 2 November 2018.
34. Interview: Lyn, DFAT, 5 March 2019.
35. Interview: Bel, DFAT, 4 February 2019.
36. J. Y. Chua, 'Eurovision and the Making of Queer (Counter-)Cultural Diplomacy', *The Yale Review of International Studies* (February 2016) http://yris.yira.org/essays/1650#:~:text=Although%20queers%20initially%20exploited%20Eurovision,influence%20attitudes%20towards%20a%20country.
37. G. Chauncey, *Why Marriage? The History Shaping Today's Debate on Gay Equality* (New York: Basic Books, 2005); C. Crawford, 'The Love That Dared not Speak its Name in the Foreign Office', *The Independent*, 30 March 2010, https://www.independent.co.uk/news/uk/this-britain/the-love-that-dared-not-speak-its-name-in-the-foreign-office-1931127.html.
38. D. Lomas, '#ForgetJamesBond: Diversity, Inclusion and the UK's Intelligence Agencies', *Intelligence and National Security* 36, no. 7 (2021): 12.
39. R. Callum, 'The Case for Cultural Diversity in the Intelligence Community', *International Journal of Intelligence and Counter Intelligence* 14, no. 1 (2001): 28.
40. Smith and Lee, 'What's Queer About Political Science?'
41. M. Marinucci, *Feminism is Queer: The Intimate Connection Between Queer and Feminist Theory* (London: Zed Books, 2010), 106.
42. Interview: Felicity, AFP, 26 June 2018.
43. Interview: Esther, DFAT, 18 June 2018.
44. S. Robinson, 'Witch-Hunts and Surveillance: The Hidden Lives of LGBTI People in the Military', *ABC News*, 25 April 2017, https://www.abc.net.au/news/2017-04-25/anzac-day-hidden-lives-of-lgbti-people-in-the-military/8467806, para 17.
45. Interview: Aria, Defence, 20 March 2019.
46. J. Cassidy and A. Althari, 'Introduction: Analyzing the Dynamics of Modern Diplomacy through a Gender Lens', in *Gender and Diplomacy* (New York: Routledge, 2017), 1–12.

47. Marinucci, *Feminism is Queer*, 107.
48. T. Christo, 'The Perceptions of Self-Identified Lesbian and Gay Senior Higher-Education Administrators Regarding their Leadership Effectiveness', PhD diss., Colorado State University, 2015.
49. I. B. Neumann, 'The Body of the Diplomat', *European Journal of International Relations* 14, no. 4 (2008): 687.
50. D. Altman and J. Symons, *Queer Wars: The New Global Polarisation Over Gay Rights* (Cambridge: Polity Press, 2016).
51. J. Southern, *A Class of its Own? Social Class and the Foreign Office, 1782–2020* (London: Foreign & Commonwealth Office, 2020), 5.
52. Interview: Bel, DFAT, 4 February 2019.
53. Parliament of Australia, *Chronology of Changes in the Australian Public Service 1975–2010*, accessed 5 May 2020, https://library.bsl.org.au/jspui/bitstream/1/2161/1/Chronology_of_changes_AustPS.pdf.
54. C. Matheson, 'Staff Selection in the Australian Public Service: A History of Social Closure', *Australian Journal of Public Administration* 60, no. 1 (2001): 43.
55. H. McCarthy, *Women of the World: The Rise of the Female Diplomat* (London: Bloomsbury Publishing, 2015).
56. Interview: Bel, DFAT, 4 February 2019.
57. Interview: Jacqueline, AFP, 31 January 2019.
58. S. Webb, A. M. Bathmaker, T. Gale, S. Hodge, S. Parker, and S. Rawolle, 'Higher Vocational Education and Social Mobility: Educational Participation in Australia and England', *Journal of Vocational Education and Training* 69, no. 1 (2017): 147–167.
59. Interview: Odette, AFP, 21 June 2018.
60. Ibid.
61. Interview: Laura, AFP, 13 June 2018, emphasis added.
62. Interview: Tess, Home Affairs, 1 February 2019.
63. E. Stephenson and S. Harris Rimmer, 'A Slap in the Face for Diverse Diplomacy', accessed 5 May 2020, https://www.lowyinstitute.org/the-interpreter/slap-face-diverse-diplomacy.
64. E. Stephenson, 'Domestic Challenges to International Leadership: A Case Study of Women in Australian International Affairs Agencies', *Australian Journal of International Affairs* 73, no. 3 (2019): 234–253; E. Stephenson, 'Invisible While Visible: An Australian Perspective on Queer Women Leaders in International Affairs', *European Journal of Politics and Gender* 3, no. 3 (2020): 427–443.
65. Interview: Lauren, Home Affairs, 9 May 2019.
66. C. Enloe, *Maneuvers: The International Politics of Militarising Women's Lives* (Berkeley: University of California Press, 2002).

Chapter 6

1. Interview: Grace, DFAT, October 5 2018.
2. J. Westendorf and R. Strating, 'Women in Australian International Affairs', *Australian Journal of International Affairs* 74, no. 4 (2020): 1–15.
3. Lowy Institute, *Foreign Territory: Women in International Relations*, accessed 9 April 2020, accessed 9 April 2020, https://www.lowyinstitute.org/sites/default/files/CAVE%20et%20al_Foreign%20territory_Women%20in%20international%20relations.pdf.
4. C. Enloe, *Bananas, Beaches and Bases: Making Feminist Sense of International Politics*, updated edition (Berkeley: University of California Press, 2014); C. Enloe, *Bananas, Beaches*

and Bases: Making Feminist Sense of International Politics (Berkeley: University of California Press, 1989); C. Duncanson and R. Woodward, 'Regendering the Military: Theorising Women's Military Participation', Security Dialogue 47, no. 1 (2016): 3–21.
5. Since all data in this section comes from a range of dates, dates have been clearly labelled in each graph or table, and each data source. Even within the same year, there are variations in the data depending on which source is used—agency annual reports, or APSED statistics. For ease of comparison, I have chosen to rely on agency annual reports for the most recent data. Agency annual reports generally contain more detailed data on gender and rank/role. For older data that was not available in agency annual reports, I have relied on the APSED statistics—this data has more consistent gender reporting, but less detailed data as far as rank and role is concerned. International deployment data for Defence and Home Affairs was previously unpublished, and therefore this data was requested directly from the agencies. Where data was sourced directly, I have compared it to data on overall representation and leadership in the same year (rather than more recent data), in order to gather the most accurate reflection on women's opportunities within the same year. Due to delays in the release of annual reports, the data gained was the most recently available data at the time. Finally, it should be noted that most data was almost exclusively reported in the gender binary—male and female. Where data beyond this binary was found, the breakdown was male, female and 'indeterminate'—with 'indeterminate' frequently blank. Only Defence included male, female, and 'not disclosed'—however this was because they were in the midst of replacing the person in the role, and did not yet have the gender of the replacement. While the call to collect data beyond the gender binary has been made (Churchill 2019; AIDS Action Council 2017), this was not yet reflected data reporting.
6. Interview: Penny, Home Affairs, 14 December 2018.
7. Australian Human Rights Commission, Review into the Treatment of Women in the Australian Defence Force: Audit Report, accessed 19 March 2020, https://www.humanrights.gov.au/sites/default/files/document/publication/adf-audit-2014.pdf, 2.
8. F. Mackay, 'Nested Newness, Institutional Innovation, and the Gendered Limits of Change', Politics & Gender 10, no. 4 (2014): 549–571.
9. E. Stephenson, 'Domestic Challenges and International Leadership: A Case Study of Women in Australian International Affairs', Australian Journal of International Affairs 73, no. 3 (2019): 234–253.
10. A. Towns and B. Niklasson, 'Gender, International Status, and Ambassador Appointments', Foreign Policy Analysis 13, no. 3 (2017): 521–540.
11. The gap remains relatively consistent between the overall proportion of women within the department and proportion of women in SES and Head of Mission (HOM) or Head of Post (HOP) roles particularly.
12. In 2018, women represented 58.5 per cent of positions, yet were represented in HOM/HOP roles at 24.7 percentage points lower, at 33.8 per cent of positions
13. Department of Foreign Affairs and Trade, Women in Leadership Strategy: Promoting Equality and Dismantling Barriers, accessed 9 June 2017, https://www.dfat.gov.au/sites/default/files/women-in-leadership-strategy.pdf.
14. Department of Defence, Women in the ADF Report 2020–2021.
15. Department of Defence, Women in the ADF Report 2018–2019, accessed 5 May 2020, https://www.defence.gov.au/annualreports/18-19/downloads/WomenintheADFreport2018-19.pdf.
16. International Policy Division, Defence Attaché Staff, unpublished raw data, Canberra 2017.

17. N. McGlen and M. Sarkees, *Women in Foreign Policy: The Insiders* (New York: Routledge, 1993), 77.
18. Ibid., 93.
19. Towns and Niklasson, 'Gender, International Status, and Ambassador Appointments'.
20. Ibid.
21. Elizabeth Broderick & Co., *Cultural Change: Gender Diversity and Inclusion in the Australian Federal Police*, accessed 19 March 2020, https://www.afp.gov.au/sites/default/files/PDF/Reports/Cultural-Change-Report-2016.pdf.
22. E. Ostrom, 'Institutional Rational Choice: An Assessment of the Institutional Analysis and Development Framework', in *Theories of the Public Policy Process*, ed. P. Sabatier (Oxford: Westview Press, 1999), 38.
23. V. Lowndes, 'How Are Things Done Around Here? Uncovering Institutional Rules and Their Gendered Effects', *Politics and Gender* 10, no. 4 (2014): 685–691.
24. Lowy Institute, *Foreign Territory: Women in International Relations*, accessed 9 April 2020, https://www.lowyinstitute.org/sites/default/files/CAVE%20et%20al_Foreign%20territory_Women%20in%20international%20relations.pdf.
25. Department of Defence, *Women in the ADF Report 2018–2019*, accessed 5 May 2020, https://www.defence.gov.au/annualreports/18-19/downloads/WomenintheADFreport2018-19.pdf; https://www.defence.gov.au/annualreports/18-19/downloads/WomenintheADFreport2018-19.pdf.
26. T. Mohr, 'Why Women Don't Apply for Jobs Unless They're 100% Qualified', *Harvard Business Review*, 25 August 2014, https://hbr.org/2014/08/why-women-dont-apply-for-jobs-unless-theyre-100-qualified.
27. Interview: Meaghan, AFP, 26 June 2018.
28. Interview: Esther, DFAT, 4 May 2018.
29. Towns and Niklasson, 'Gender, International Status, and Ambassador Appointments'.
30. B. Niklasson and A. Towns, 'Gender, Status and Ambassador Appointments to Militarised and Violent Countries', *Gender and Diplomacy*, ed. J. Cassidy (New York: Routledge, 2017), 538.
31. Lowy Institute, *Global Diplomacy Index—Australia's Diplomatic Network*, accessed 3 May 2019, https://globaldiplomacyindex.lowyinstitute.org/.
32. Department of Foreign Affairs and Trade, *Australian Ambassadors and Other Representatives*, accessed 20 March 2020, https://www.dfat.gov.au/about-us/our-people/homs/Pages/australian-ambassadors-and-other-representatives.
33. M. Sabharwal, 'From Glass Ceiling to Glass Cliff: Women in Senior Executive Service,' *Journal of Public Administration Research & Theory* 25, no. 2 (2015): 399–426; M. Ryan and S. Haslam, 'The Glass Cliff: Exploring the Dynamics Surrounding the Appointment of Women to Precarious Leadership Positions', *The Academy of Management Review* 32, no. 2 (2007): 549–572.
34. Department of Foreign Affairs and Trade, *Women in Leadership Strategy: Promoting Equality and Dismantling Barriers*, accessed 9 June 2017, https://www.dfat.gov.au/sites/default/files/women-in-leadership-strategy.pdf.
35. J. Cassidy, *Gender and Diplomacy* (New York: Routledge, 2017), 211.
36. McGlen and Sarkees, *Women in Foreign Policy*.
37. Department of Defence, *Women in the ADF Report 2018–2019*, accessed 5 May 2020, https://www.defence.gov.au/annualreports/18-19/downloads/WomenintheADFreport2018-19.pdf.

38. Cassidy, *Gender and Diplomacy*.
39. Ibid.

Chapter 7

1. Interview: Rani, DFAT, 1 February 2019.
2. Australian Public Service Commission 2020, *Sect 8 Working Overseas*, accessed 20 March 2020, https://www.apsc.gov.au/publication/aps-values-and-code-conduct-practice/section-8-working-overseas, para 6, emphasis added.
3. I. Goffman, and W. Helmreich, 'On the Characteristics of Total Institutions', in *Asylums* ed. I. Goffman (New York: Routledge 1961), 13–137.
4. E. Stephenson, 'Domestic Challenges to International Leadership: A Case Study of Women in Australian International Affairs Agencies', *Australian Journal of International Affairs* 73, no. 3 (2019): 234–253.
5. Interview: Grace, DFAT, 5 October 2018.
6. Interview: Andy, Defence, 19 February 2019.
7. Australian Human Rights Commission, *Set the Standard: Report on the Independent Review into Commonwealth Parliamentary Workplaces*, accessed 16 December 2022, https://humanrights.gov.au/sites/default/files/document/publication/ahrc_set_the_standard_2021.pdf.
8. Australian Human Rights Commission, *Review into the Treatment of Women in the Australian Defence Force: Phase 2 Report*, accessed 11 July 2017, http://defencereview.humanrights.gov.au/sites/default/files/adf-complete.pdf, 26.
9. Interview: Andy, Defence, 19 February 2019.
10. A. Towns and B. Niklasson, 'Gender, International Status, and Ambassador Appointments', *Foreign Policy Analysis* 13, no. 3 (2017): 521–540.
11. Interview: Jane, DFAT, 15 November 2019.
12. M. Conley Tyler, E. Blizzard, and B. Crane, 'Is International Affairs Too 'Hard' for Women? Explaining the Missing Women in Australia's International Affairs', *Australian Journal of International Affairs* 68, no. 2 (2014): 156–176.
13. J. Westendorf and R. Strating, 'Women in Australian International Affairs', *Australian Journal of International Affairs* 74, no. 4 (2020): 1–15.
14. Lowy Institute, *Australia, It's Time to Put Our Political Diplomats to the Test*, accessed 3 February 2019, https://www.lowyinstitute.org/the-interpreter/australia-it-s-time-put-our-political-diplomats-test.
15. Interview: Laura, AFP, 13 June 2018.
16. Interview: Jacqueline, AFP, 31 January 2019.
17. M. Kenny, *Gender and Political Recruitment: Theorising Institutional Change* (London: Palgrave Macmillan, 2013).
18. L. Chappell and Mackay, 'What's in a Name? Mapping the Terrain of Informal Institutions and Gender Politics', in *Gender and Informal Institutions*, ed. G. Waylen (London: Rowman & Littlefield International, 2017), 32.
19. Stephenson 'Domestic Challenges to International Leadership'.
20. Interview: Laura, AFP, 13 June 2018.
21. Interview: Jacqueline, AFP, 31 January 2019.
22. C. Enloe, *Bananas, Beaches and Bases: Making Feminist Sense of International Politics*, updated edition (Berkeley: University of California Press, 2014).

23. H. McCarthy, *Women of the World: The Rise of the Female Diplomat* (London: Bloomsbury Publishing, 2015).
24. F. Cangia, 'Precarity, Imagination, and the Mobile Life of the "Trailing Spouse"', *Ethos* 46, no. 1 (2018): 9.
25. Workplace Gender Equality Agency, *WGEA Data Explorer*, accessed 18 March 2020, https://data.wgea.gov.au/.
26. Interview: Selena, DFAT, 18 June 2018.
27. Interview: Ellie, AFP, 18 January 2019.
28. Interview: Lorelle, Home Affairs, 11 December 2018.
29. Interview: Lorelle, Home Affairs, 11 December 2018.
30. L. Chappell, 'Moving to a Comparative Politics of Gender?', *Critical Perspectives on Gender and Politics* 2 (March 2006): 223.
31. Interview: Jeanne, AFP, 21 June 2018.
32. Department of Home Affairs, *Plans, Policies and Charters*, accessed 19 March 2020, https://www.homeaffairs.gov.au/commitments/Pages/Plans-policies-charters/gender-equality-action-plan.aspx, 16.
33. Ibid., 30.
34. Ibid., 66.
35. Commonwealth of Australia, *Independent Review of the APS: Priorities for Change*, accessed 11 May 2020, https://www.apsreview.gov.au/sites/default/files/resources/aps-review-priorities-change.pdf.
36. Australian Human Rights Commission, *Review into the Treatment of Women in the Australian Defence Force: Phase 2 Report*, accessed 11 July 2017, http://defencereview.humanrights.gov.au/sites/default/files/adf-complete.pdf, 35.
37. Interview: Jade, DFAT, 2 August 2018.
38. Interview: Sarah, Defence, 19 February 2019.
39. Australian Human Rights Commission, *Review into the Treatment of Women in the Australian Defence Force*.
40. Interview: Lauren, Home Affairs, 9 May 2019.
41. Interview: Jane, DFAT, 15 November 2015.
42. Interview: Selena, DFAT, 18 June 2018.
43. Australian Federal Police, *Australian Federal Police Enterprise Agreement 2017–2020*, accessed 4 July 2019, https://www.afp.gov.au/sites/default/files/2023-07/afp-enterprise-agreement-2017-2020.pdf.
44. Interview: Rani, DFAT, February 1 2019.
45. J. Marriott, 'Women in Foreign Lands: Women Diplomats and Host-Country Cultures', in *Gender and Diplomacy* (New York: Routledge, New 2017), 115–135.
46. Interview: Lee, Defence, 26 February 2019.
47. McCarthy, *Women of the World*; Marriot, 'Women in Foreign Lands'.
48. Interview: Jane, DFAT, 15 November 2018.
49. Interview: Jane, DFAT, 15 November 2018.
50. Harris Rimmer, 'Women as Makers of International Law: Towards Feminist Diplomacy', in *Research Handbook on Feminist Engagement with International Law*, ed. S. Harris Rimmer and K. Ogg (Cheltenham: Edward Elgar, 2019), 26–43.
51. Interview: Selena, DFAT, 18 June 2018.
52. Interview: Jane, DFAT, 15 November 2018.
53. Interview: Rani, DFAT, 1 February 2019.

54. Interview: Bel, DFAT, 4 February 2019.
55. Interview: Bel, DFAT, 4 February 2019.
56. Interview: Bel, DFAT, 4 February 2019.
57. Interview: Grace, DFAT, 5 October 2018.
58. Interview: Bel, DFAT, 4 February 2019.
59. Interview: Sally, DFAT, 19 June 2018.
60. Interview: Rani, DFAT, 1 February 2019.
61. Interview: Rani, DFAT, 1 February 2019.
62. Interview: Leila, DFAT, 2 November 2018.
63. N. McGlen and M. Sarkees, *Women in Foreign Policy: The Insiders* (New York: Routledge, 1993), 106.
64. Interview: Lee, Defence, 26 February 2019.
65. Interview: Lee, Defence, 26 February 2019.
66. A. M. Morin, 'Do Women Make Better Ambassadors? Study of 50 Years of Female Envoys Shows Gender Can Be An Advantage', *Foreign Service Journal* December 1994): 26–30.
67. J. Fliegel, 'Unprecedented: Women's Leadership in Twenty-First Century Multilateral Diplomacy', in *Gender and Diplomacy*, ed. J. Cassidy Routledge, 2017), 184–207.
68. Interview: Meaghan, AFP, 26 June 2018.
69. Interview: Meaghan, AFP, 26 June 2018.
70. Interview: Meaghan, AFP, 26 June 2018.
71. Interview: Jeanne, AFP, 21 June 2018, emphasis added.
72. Interview: Zara, Home Affairs, 15 January 2019.
73. Interview: Ellie, AFP, 18 January 2019.
74. Interview: Zara, Home Affairs, 15 January 2019.
75. Interview: Cindy, Home Affairs, 14 January 2019.
76. Interview: Lauren, Home Affairs, 9 May 2019.
77. Interview: Rani, DFAT, 1 February 2019.
78. A. Vinokur, P. Pierce, and C. Buck, 'Work-Family Conflicts of Women in the Air Force: Their Influence on Mental Health and Functioning', *Journal of Organisational Behaviour* 20, no. 6 (1999): para 5.
79. Department of Defence, *Annual Report 2017–2018*, accessed 19 March 2020, https://www.defence.gov.au/AnnualReports/17-18/.
80. Interview: Julia Gillard, 21 May 2019.
81. O. Sasson-Levy, 'Feminism and Military Gender Practices: Israeli Women Soldiers in 'Masculine' Roles', *Sociological Inquiry* 73, no. 3 (2003): 459.
82. J. Rost, Leadership for the 21st Century (New York: Praeger, 1991).
83. S. Harris Rimmer, E. Stephenson, and T. Verhelst, 'New Dimensions of Gender and Political Leadership During COVID-19: Linking Feminist Stewardship and Electoral Success in Queensland, Australia', *SAIS Review of International Affairs* 41, no. 1 (2021): 49–59.
84. Interview: Rani, DFAT, 1 February 2019.
85. Interview: Jane, DFAT, 15 November 2019.
86. McGlen and Sarkees, *Women in Foreign Policy*.
87. McCarthy, *Women of the World*, 345.
88. Interview: Esther, DFAT, 21 June 2018.
89. Interview: Julie Bishop, 3 April 2019.
90. Interview: Penny, Home Affairs, 14 December 2018.
91. Interview: Cindy, Home Affairs, 14 January 2019.

Chapter 8

1. Interview: Julie Bishop, 3 April 2019.
2. J. Thomson, 'Resisting Gendered Change: Feminist Institutionalism and Critical Actors', *International Political Science Review* 39, no. 2 (2018): 178–191; F. Mackay, M. Kenny, and L. Chappell, 'New Institutionalism Through a Gender Lens: Towards a Feminist Institutionalism?', *International Political Science Review* 31, no. 5 (2010): 573–588.
3. L. Chappell and G. Waylen, 'Gender and the Hidden Life of Institutions', *Public Administration* 91, no. 3 (2013): 599–615.
4. S. Acker, 'New Perspectives on an Old Problem: The Position of Women Academics in British Higher Education', *Higher Education* 24, no. 1 (1992): 567.
5. Mackay, Kenny, and Chappell, 'New Institutionalism Through a Gender Lens'.
6. C. Duncanson and R. Woodward, 'Regendering the Military: Theorising Women's Military Participation', *Security Dialogue* 47, no. 1 (2016): 4.
7. C. Enloe, 'Women in NATO Militaries—A Conference Report', *Women's Studies International Forum* 5, no. 3–4 (1982): 331.
8. A. Towns and B. Niklasson, 'Gender, International Status, and Ambassador Appointments', *Foreign Policy Analysis* 13, no. 3 (2017): 521–540; J. A. Tickner, *Gender in International Relations: Feminist Perspectives on Achieving Global Security* (New York: Columbia University Press, 1992); C. Enloe, *Bananas, Beaches and Bases: Making Feminist Sense of International Politics* (Berkeley: University of California Press, 1989); C. Enloe, *Bananas, Beaches and Bases: Making Feminist Sense of International Politics*, updated edition (Berkeley: University of California Press, 2014); B. Wadham, 'The Minister, The Commandant, and the Cadets: Sex Scandal and Military Modernisation', *Journal of Sociology* 52, no. 3 (2016): 551–568.
9. J. Webster, 'Resisting Change: Toxic Masculinity in the Post Modern United States Armed Forces (1980s—Present)', PhD diss., University of Central Oklahoma, 2019.
10. M. Sabharwal, 'From Glass Ceiling to Glass Cliff: Women in Senior Executive Service,' *Journal of Public Administration Research & Theory* 25, no. 2 (2015): 399–426; M. Ryan and S. Haslam, 'The Glass Cliff: Exploring the Dynamics Surrounding the Appointment of Women to Precarious Leadership Positions', *The Academy of Management Review* 32, no. 2 (2007): 549–572.
11. B. Hocking, *Foreign Ministries: Change and Adaptation* (London: Palgrave Macmillan, 1999), 1
12. M. Conley Tyler, 'Australia Has Not Just Had a "Diplomacy Fail"— It Has Been Devaluing the Profession for Decades', *The Conversation*, accessed 15 November 2022, https://theconversation.com/australia-has-not-just-had-a-diplomacy-fail-it-has-been-devaluing-the-profession-for-decades-171498.
13. Lowy Institute, 'Global Diplomacy Index — Australia's Diplomatic Network', accessed 17 December 2022, https://globaldiplomacyindex.lowyinstitute.org/.
14. Conley Tyler, 'Australia Has Not Just Had a "Diplomacy Fail"'.
15. M. Page, 'A Silver Lining to DFAT's Budgetary Woes', *Lowy Institute*, accessed 17 December 2022, https://www.lowyinstitute.org/the-interpreter/silver-lining-dfat-s-budgetary-woes.
16. Chappell and Waylen, 'Gender and the Hidden Life of Institutions'.
17. H. McCarthy, *Women of the World: The Rise of the Female Diplomat* (London: Bloomsbury Publishing, 2015); E. Stephenson, 'Domestic Challenges to International Leadership: A Case Study of Women in Australian International Affairs Agencies', *Australian Journal of International Affairs* 73, no. 3 (2019): 234–253.

18. Interview: Sunny, DFAT, 18 October 2018.
19. Mackay, Kenny, and Chappell, 'New Institutionalism Through a Gender Lens'; R. Goodin, *The Theory of Institutional Design* (Cambridge: Cambridge University Press, 1996).
20. Chappell and Waylen, 'Gender and the Hidden Life of Institutions'; Waylen, *Gender and Informal Institutions*.
21. Chappell and Waylen, 'Gender and the Hidden Life of Institutions'.
22. M. Kenny, *Gender and Political Recruitment: Theorising Institutional Change* (London: Palgrave Macmillan, 2013).
23. N. McGlen and M. Sarkees, *Women in Foreign Policy: The Insiders* (New York: Routledge, 1993).
24. Kenny, *Gender and Political Recruitment*.
25. C. Byrne, M. Conley Tyler, and S. Harris Rimmer, 'Australian Diplomacy Today', *Australian Journal of International Affairs* 70, no. 6 (2016): 581–589.
26. G. Waylen, 'Informal Institutions, Institutional Change, and Gender Equality', *Political Research Quarterly* 67, no. 1 (2014): 212–223; S. Nazneen, 'Negotiating Gender Equity in a Clientelist State: The Role of Informal Networks in Bangladesh', in *Gender and Informal Institutions*, ed. G. Waylen (London: Rowman and Littlefield International, 2017), 212–223.
27. Interview: Grace, DFAT, 5 October 2018.
28. J. Westendorf and R. Strating, 'Women in Australian International Affairs', *Australian Journal of International Affairs* 74, no. 4 (2020): 1–15.
29. Interview: Leila, DFAT, 2 November 2018.
30. Interview: Danielle, Defence, 4 March 2019.
31. Interview: Talia, Home Affairs, 18 February 2019.
32. Interview: Meaghan, AFP, 26 June 2018.

Conclusion

1. Interview: Julia Gillard, 21 May 2019.
2. F. Mackay, M. Kenny, and L. Chappell, 'New Institutionalism Through a Gender Lens: Towards a Feminist Institutionalism?', *International Political Science Review* 31, no. 5 (2010): 573–588.
3. J. Cornut, 'Diplomacy in Liquid Modernity', paper presented at Diplomacy in Liquid Modernity: Disruption and Transformation of Diplomatic Practices workshop, Asia-Pacific College of Diplomacy at ANU, Canberra, Australia, 20 February 2019.
4. G. Waylen, (ed.), *Gender and Informal Institutions* (London: Rowman & Littlefield International, 2017), 3.
5. J. Cassidy, *Gender and Diplomacy* (New York: Routledge, 2017).
6. Department of Foreign Affairs and Trade 2019, *2018–2019 Annual Report*, accessed 14 November 2021, https://www.dfat.gov.au/sites/default/files/2020-01/dfat-annual-report-2018-19.pdf.
7. D. Cass and K. Rubenstein, 'Representation/s of Women in the Australian Constitutional System', *Adelaide Law Review* 17, no. 1 (1995): 3–48.
8. C. Gilligan, *In a Different Voice: Psychological Theory and Women's Development* (Cambridge, MA: Harvard University Press, 1982).
9. D. Cass and K. Rubenstein, 'Representation/s of Women in the Australian Constitutional System', *Adelaide Law Review* 17, no. 1 (1995): 6.

10. S. Farhang and G. Wawro, 'Institutional Dynamics on the US Court of Appeals: Minority Representation Under Panel Decision Making', *Journal of Law, Economics and Organisation* 20, no. 2 (2004): 299–330.
11. M. Conley Tyler, 'Diversity and Diplomacy', *Australian Journal of International Affairs* 70, no. 6 (2016): 695–709.
12. C. Byrne, M. Conley Tyler, and S. Harris Rimmer, 'Australian Diplomacy Today', *Australian Journal of International Affairs* 70, no. 6 (2016): 586.
13. M. Conley Tyler, 'Diversity and Diplomacy', *Australian Journal of International Affairs* 70, no. 6 (2016): 695–709.
14. UN Women 2017, *Facts and Figures: Peace and Security*, accessed 13 June 2017, http://www.unwomen.org/en/what-we-do/peace-and-security/facts-and-figures.
15. V. Asal, R. Legault, O. Szekely, and J. Wilkenfeld, 'Gender Ideologies and Forms of Contentious Mobilisation in the Middle East', *Journal of Peace Research* 50, no. 3 (2013): 305–318.
16. Department of Foreign Affairs and Trade, *Gender Equality and Women's Empowerment Strategy*, accessed 16 March 2020, https://www.dfat.gov.au/about-us/publications/gender-equality-and-womens-empowerment-strategy; M. Verveer, 'FP: Why Women Are a Foreign Policy Issue', *Council on Foreign Relations*, accessed 16 September 2016, http://www.cfr.org/women/fp-why-women-foreign-policy-issue/p28023.
17. UN Women, *Facts and Figures: Leadership and Political Participation*, accessed 27 April 2016, http://www.unwomen.org/en/what-we-do/leadership-and-political-participation/facts-and-figures#notes; UN Women 2019, *Facts and Figures: Peace and Security*, accessed 3 July 2019, http://www.unwomen.org/en/what-we-do/peace-and-security/facts-and-figures.
18. M. Caprioli and P. F. Trumbore 2003, 'Ethno-Inequality and International Violence: Testing the International Impact of Domestic Behaviour', *Journal of Peace Research* 40, no. 1 (2003): 5–23; M. Caprioli and M. Boyer, 'Gender, Violence, and International Crisis', *Journal of Conflict Resolution* 45, no. 4 (2001): 503–518; M. Caprioli, 'Gendered Conflict', *Journal of Peace Research* 37, no. 1 (2000): 51–68.
19. H. Charlesworth, 'Are Women Peaceful? Reflections on the Role of Women in Peace-Building', *Feminist Legal Studies* 16, no. 3 (2008): 347–361; V. Hudson and P. Leidl, *The Hillary Doctrine: Sex & American Foreign Policy* (New York: Columbia University Press, 2015).
20. Clinton in Hudson and Leidl, *The Hillary Doctrine*.
21. World Economic Forum, *Conflict Costs the Global Economy $14 Trillion a Year*, accessed 16 March 2020, https://www.weforum.org/agenda/2018/01/conflict-costs-global-economy-14-trillion-a-year/.
22. K. Haack, 'Breaking Barriers? Women's Representation and Leadership at the United Nations', *Global Governance* 20, no. 1 (2014): 37–54.

Index

For the benefit of digital users, indexed terms that span two pages (e.g., 52–53) may, on occasion, appear on only one of those pages.

Tables and figures are indicated by *t* and *f* following the page number

ABF. *See* Australian Border Force
AFP. *See* Australian Federal Police
Air Force, 72, 75, 93–94, 157
APS. *See* Australian Public Service
APSC. *See* Australian Public Service Commission
APSED. *See* Australian Public Service Employee Database
AusAID. *See* Australian Agency for International Development
Australian Border Force
 hierarchical structure of, 105–8, 120
 merger of, 111–12, 145–46, 158
 organisational culture of, 109–73, 148*f*
 reintegration policy, 196
 women, representation, challenges faced by, in, 118–19, 149–50, 149*f*, 150*f*, 167
 women's leadership in, 151, 151*t*, 158, 166
 workforce training, 170–71
Australian Federal Police
 Culture Change: Gender Diversity and Inclusion, 43, 118, 159–60
 hierarchical structure of, 116
 historical forces, 115–16, 117
 organisational culture of, 43, 44, 110, 116–17, 118
 women's leadership in, 108, 160–61
 women's representation and roles in, 14, 116, 117–18, 159–60, 160*f*
Australian Public Service
 Gendered challenges, 38, 43
 gender equality and diversity strategy, frameworks, within, 14, 73
 Gender Equality Strategy 2016-2019 75
 Not Yet 50/50: Barriers to the Progress to the Progress of Senior Women in the Australian Public Service, 43

 organisational culture of, 77
 preferential treatment in, 137
 principles and values of, 41–42, 72
 racial discrimination and experiences in, 131
 The Review of Employment Pathways for APS Women in the Department of Defence, 44
 Thodey Independent Review of, 182
 women's career progression in, 43–44, 161–62
 women's representation in, 41–42, 147
Australian Public Service Act 1999 87–88
Australian Public Service Commission, 113, 171
Australian Public Service Employee Database, 18, 55
AusAID. *See* Australian Agency for International Development
Australian Agency for International Development, 79, 80–81
army, 93–94, 97–98, 157

birth, giving, miscarriage, 168, 180, 185
Bishop, Julie, 1, 13, 23, 67, 83, 85–86, 172–73, 202, 206
border protection, 104–5, 108–9
 officers, 17, 216
bullying
 Australian Border Force, in, 111–12
 Australian Federal Police, in, 116–17, 118–19, 122, 226
 Department of Foreign Affairs and Trade, in, 113, 188–89
 Queer diplomats, of, 133–34

CALD. *See* culturally and linguistically diverse

Index

chain of command, 98–99, 103, 120. *See also* hierarchy
Chappell, L., 25, 27–28, 33–34, 53, 72. *See also* Chappell, L and Mackay, F
Chappell, L and Mackay, F., 50–51, 57, 175, 217–18
children, 39, 96, 135, 139, 140–34, 172–73, 186–87. *See also* family
deployment, 175–76, 178–79, 180 (*see also* posting)
classism, 6–7, 12, 80
Colvin, Andrew, 115, 117–18, 120–21
Commonwealth Marriage Bar, 40, 77, 78, 136, 139, 147
comparative case study methodology, 18
COVID-19 50, 69, 72, 233
critical actors, 27, 87–88, 100–1, 120–73, 184–85
critical feminist friend, 20, 50–52, 64
critical juncture, 6, 117
culturally and linguistically diverse, 31, 128–31, 223, 225–26
customs, 109–12. *See also* Home Affairs, Department of

DA. *See* Defence attaché
defence. *See* Department of Defence
Defence Australian Public Service Gender Equality Strategy Action Plan 2016-2019 13
DoD. *See* Department of Defence
Department of Defence
Cultural and Linguistic Diversity in, 130–31
Defence Australian Public Service Gender Equality Strategy Action Plan 2016-2019 13
family, children, in, 139, 172–73, 178, 222
gendered challenges, 140, 172–73, 181, 199, 219
gendered experiences of deployment in, 181–97, 224–25
hierarchy, leadership, structure, in, 44, 98–104
historical forces, 72–98
organisational culture, 44, 123, 201
reviews and inquiries, 75
women's leadership in, 141–42, 156–58, 165–66, 219
women's representation in, 2, 14, 145–48, 147f, 164

defence-led diplomacy, 35, 69, 181–82
DFAT. *See* Department of Foreign Affairs and Trade
Department of External Affairs, 77
Department of Foreign Affairs and Trade
career progression, 170–71, 179–80, 199–200
classism in, 137–38
deployment and postings, 125, 152, 174
devaluation of diplomacy in, 16, 123–24, 212–13
elitism in, 137
flexible work arrangements, 183
formal policies, 43, 75, 154, 165, 218
gendered experiences, issues, norms, 123–24, 163, 187–95, 218, 223–24
hierarchy, leadership, structure, in, 84–88, 173–74
historical forces, 76–84
women's leadership, 12, 142, 150–51, 154–56
women's representation, 145, 152–53, 212–13
Department of Home Affairs
cultural and linguistic diversity, 129–31, 225–26
deployment, 140, 141–26, 179–80, 182, 195–97, 226
family, 139
gendered policies and strategies, 75, 185
hierarchy, leadership, structure, in, 112–14
historical forces, 76, 104–12, 220
women's leadership, 14, 148
women's representation, 145–46, 158–59
Department of Immigration, 105–9, 111–14
Department of Trade and Customs, 77
Defence attaché, 14, 96–98, 139, 164
deployment, 16, 93, 139–42, 151–52, 158, 160–61, 164
geographic reach and patterns of, 140–42
queer experiences of, 175–76, 213–14
women's experiences of, 120, 139–40, 181–97, 204, 223–27
women's pathways to, 169–81
diplomatic glass cliff, 9, 16–17, 164, 212–13
diplomacy, 5–6, 7–8
changes, trends in, 5–6, 7–8, 20, 69, 78–79
decline of, 212–13
definitions, understandings of, 10, 181–82
gendered nature of, 35–40, 43, 84, 190

indigenous, Cultural and Linguistic
  Diversity, 71, 130
LGBTIQ+, heteronormativity in, 126,
  132–36, 214
studies of, 33–34, 35, 240

EEO. *See* equal employment opportunity
EL. *See* executive level
elites, eliteness. *See also* classism
  access, interview, strategies, 57, 65–66
  defence, in, 90
  DFAT, in, 76–84, 137
  power in relation to, 64–65
Enloe, C. 4, 36, 93, 143, 176–77, 209
equal employment opportunity, 14–15, 78–79, 85–86, 116, 118–19
evolution of inequality, 9, 48, 212, 217–19, 229, 233–34
executive level, 14–15, 64, 83, 94–95, 141–42, 147f, 147, 149–50, 151, 154–57, 158–61, 159f, 160f, 166–67, 182, 218–21

family, 43–44, 139–40, 175–77
feminist foreign policy, 13–14, 15, 233
feminist institutionalism, 7–8, 24–26, 29–32, 206–7, 233–34. *See also* intersectional feminist institutionalism
feminist turn, 13–14, 81
Foreign Minister, 13–14, 127–28, 172–73
Foreign Policy White Paper 2017 13–14, 222

Gender Equality and Women's Empowerment Strategy, Department of Foreign Affairs and Trade, 13, 76–77, 83
gender inequality, 8–9, 13–14, 72, 135, 172, 207
gender parity, 14, 71–72, 149–50, 154, 217
Gender Strategy, Australian Federal Police, 13, 75, 118
genteel toxic masculinity, 9, 16, 83–84, 153, 210–12
Gillard, Julia, 19, 67, 72, 172–73, 199, 231
glass ceiling, 12, 40, 78, 145–46, 149–50
glass cliff, 9, 16–17, 82–83, 164, 212–13

heads of mission, 12, 59, 78, 155–56, 177–78
heads of post, 59, 155–56, 173–74
heterosexism, 133–35
heteronormative, 11, 15–16, 31, 46–49, 135–36, 176–77, 208–9, 213–14

hierarchy, 37, 85–87, 98–100, 119–20, 165–66, 235
Hilton Hotel bombing, 115
historical legacies, 70, 217–21, 234
HOM. *See* heads of mission
Home Affairs. *See* Department of Home Affairs
homophobia, 45–46, 132–35, 188–89, 226, 237
HOP. *See* heads of post
horizontal segregation, 17, 41, 44, 96, 106, 161–62, 202, 236. *See also* vertical segregation
Hudson, V and Leidl, H., 28

IDG. *See* International Deployment Group
IFI. *See* intersectional feminist institutionalism
Immigration Restriction Act 1901 71–72, 78, 105–6, 127
Indigenous, 1–2, 41, 45, 71–72, 73, 74, 127, 131
Inequality regimes, 29
informal institutions, 27–28, 29, 32, 116–17, 165, 206–7, 217–18, 227–28
institutional change, 28–29, 49, 218
  diplomatic agencies, within, 92–93, 101–2, 218–19, 220
  layering, 27, 221–22
  unintended effects, 28, 29–30
intermestic, 19–20, 221
International Deployment Group, Australian Federal Police, 13, 117–18
international relations
  intersectionality in, 52–55, 133
  leaders, leadership, 56
  theory, 23, 33–37, 52
International Policy Division, 59, 95, 102, 192
international affairs agencies
  diversity, intersectionality, 45–46, 128–29
  gendered challenges, 16, 42–44, 73, 124
  history, context, 71–76
  women's representation and leadership, 7, 14, 40–42
International representation
  Australia, comparison, trends, 12–15, 34, 129, 144, 165, 166–67
  dynamics, history, norms, 126–27, 132–33, 137, 205
  women, 15–17, 71, 139, 150–54, 156–58, 159–61, 163, 194–95, 203–4

Index

intersectional feminist institutionalism, 19, 29, 31–32, 46–47, 52–55, 231
intersectionality, 29, 30–31, 45, 53–54, 143
invisibility, visibility, 124, 133–34, 188–89, 210–11, 238, 239–40
IPD. *See* International Policy Division
IR. *See* international relations

JOC. *See* Joint Operations Command
Joint Operations Command, 95

leave, 41, 86, 173, 176, 182, 184–86, 198
Lee-Koo, K., 44, 82
lesbian, 45–46, 92, 132–36
LGBTIQ+ 45–46, 126, 141, 142–43
liquid institutions, 7–8, 231
Lowy Institute, 76, 81, 82–83, 144, 161, 163, 212–13

Mackay, F, Kenny, M and Chappell, L., 25
marginalised majority, 152–53, 156, 165, 210, 236–37
Marriage Bar. *See* Commonwealth Marriage Bar
mateship campaign, 72, 174
McGlen, N and Sarkees, M., 4, 34, 39–40, 41, 44, 47, 82, 84–85, 88, 99, 103–4, 120, 156–57, 165–66, 191–92, 219
merit, 41–42, 43, 72, 93, 109, 174
MFAs. *See* Ministries of Foreign Affairs
militarism, 112–13, 144, 209, 212
militaristic agencies, 9, 73, 148–53, 165, 166–67, 208, 209–11, 235
militaristic-diplomatic continuum, 148*f*, 148, 149*f*, 150*f*, 165–66
Ministries of Foreign Affairs, 5–6, 34–35, 69, 84, 125–26, 212
Morrison, David, 73, 100–1

Navy, 94, 97, 157, 171
neutrality, 72, 87

organisational culture, 43, 76, 79, 108, 175
othering, 80–81, 135, 136
overseas conditions of service, 182, 185–86

paramilitaristic agencies. *See* militaristic agencies
parental leave. *See* leave
path dependent, path dependence, 17, 25, 124

patriarchy, 6–7, 36, 89–90, 124, 142–43, 209–10
Pezzullo, Michael, 110–11, 112–14
political appointments, appointees, 12, 39, 56, 78, 174
positionality, 53, 126
posting
  gendered experiences, 15–16, 39, 41, 81, 153, 169–205, 225–26
  geographic reach, patters of, 140–42
  institutional barriers, challenges, 78, 80, 139, 228–29
  prestige, 96–97, 174
prestige. *See also* elites, eliteness
  gendered patterns, 17, 97–98, 123–24, 125, 158, 211
  MFAs, 5–6, 77, 78–83, 96–97
promotions, 3, 15–16, 40, 78, 89, 97, 116–17, 121–22, 172–73, 179–80, 196–97, 199
  understandings, dynamics, evolution of, 173–74, 179–80, 197, 212

qualitative interviews, 17–18, 56–62
quantitative trend data, 62–64
queer theory, queering, 132–36. *See also* intersectional feminist institutionalism
queer women, 4, 9, 31, 126, 133–35, 188–89, 213–14. *See also* lesbian, LGBTIQ+

racialised institutions, 2–3, 49, 128, 136
rank, 64, 65–66, 85, 97–98, 99–102, 112–13, 119–20, 142, 156–57, 165–66, 173–74, 226–27. *See also* hierarchy
recruitment, 38, 41–42, 45, 109, 131–32, 166–67
reporting, 62, 113, 123, 124, 145, 156
retention, 45, 116, 119–20, 134, 197

senior executive service, 12, 64, 83, 94–95, 141–42, 147*f*, 147, 149–50, 151, 154–57, 158–61, 159*f*, 160*f*, 166–67, 182, 218–21
September 11 69, 110–11, 115, 117, 170–71
SES. *See* senior executive service
sexism, 2–3, 11–12, 108, 146, 192–95, 199, 208, 210
sexuality, 16, 24, 35–36, 45–46, 53–54, 132–36
shrinking institutions, 9, 16, 123–24, 212–13, 217. *See also* diplomatic glass cliff
single, 135, 139, 184, 189, 190–91, 223, 224–25. *See also* spouses, family

skype sex scandal, 95–96
spouses, 9, 19, 38–39, 79, 134–35, 139–40, 177–79, 187–92, 195–96, 208–9, 213–14, 223
status, 9, 16, 33–34, 36–37, 64–65, 80, 99, 123–24, 158, 173–74, 208, 212. *See also* prestige
suicide, 111–12, 118

trailing spouse. *See* spouses
Towns, A., 10, 33–34. *See also* Towns, A and Niklasson, B
Towns, A and Niklasson, B., 33–34, 40, 158, 163, 173–74

Varghese, Peter, 13, 76–77, 83, 86–87, 113
vertical segregation, 17, 44, 106, 165, 167, 202, 236

violence, 31, 95–96, 101–2, 133–34, 141, 143, 238–39
visas, 134

Waylen, G., 26–27, 32, 101–2
White Australia Policy. *See* Immigration Restriction Act
Women in Leadership Strategy, Department of Foreign Affairs and Trade, 12–13, 43, 73, 76–77, 83, 86–87, 155–56, 165, 218
Women's Royal Australian Air Force, 93–94
Women's Royal Australian Army Corps, 93
Women's Royal Naval Service, 41, 94
Wong, Penny, 75, 127–28, 168
WRAAC. *See* Women's Royal Australian Army Corps
WRAAF. *See* Women's Royal Naval Service
WRANS. *See* Women's Royal Naval Service